BETTER THAN
WE FOUND IT

BETTER THAN WE FOUND IT

Conversations to Help Save the World

Frederick Joseph and **Porsche Joseph**

CANDLEWICK PRESS

First edition 2022

Library of Congress Catalog Card Number pending
ISBN 978-1-5362-2452-8

22 23 24 25 26 27 LBM 10 9 8 7 6 5 4 3 2 1

Printed in Melrose Park, IL, USA

This book was typeset in Chaparral Pro.

Candlewick Press
99 Dover Street
Somerville, Massachusetts 02144

www.candlewick.com

To anyone who has ever seen a problem
and wanted to do something about it
FJ

To Paris and Preston, my first and most loyal friends.
Your companionship and love were the highlight of my
childhood, and I am so thankful to have your continued
support as we make our way through every stage of life.
PJ

CONTENTS

BETTER
THAN
WE FOUND IT

FOREWORD

by **Taylor Denise Richardson**

Advocate, activist, speaker, student, and philanthropist

A person's character is shaped largely by their experiences, and my generation, Gen Z, is astutely conscious that our experiences not only shape our identities but are also the reason we recognize the true, deep similarities in others—similarities that extend beyond race, ethnicity, gender, sexuality, and socioeconomic status. Gen Z has come of age in a time of tremendous upheaval. Whether it's dealing with the effects of COVID-19, mass school shootings, or police brutality (either directly or through the media), we have experienced these events as a generation and have recognized the change that needs to occur in our society. Part of that change has meant unlearning many of our parents' traditional views and redefining life for ourselves.

The common ground of shared experiences has given root to an empathy that allows our generation to feel and understand the inequalities perpetrated against one another in ways that were not common in previous generations. The internet and social media have been integrated into our lives since birth, which has facilitated this understanding, making it easy to find someone who has been down a similar path and wants to know that they are not alone. Digital communities and the ability of real-time information to spread widely is the reason our generation has the capability to learn, grow, and apply what we have learned. But with so much access to information about vital issues vying for our attention and resources, it can feel impossible to know where to turn, whom to trust, or how to help.

Better Than We Found It shines a spotlight on sixteen of the most pressing issues in today's society. Each chapter breaks down a long-standing problem that is ripe for change by shining a light on the gray areas so that the black-and-white issues are there for all to see. This is vital if the goal of progress is going to be met, because ignorance and plausible deniability are two of the biggest roadblocks in the way of progression. Progress begins with accountability and the desire to fix the issues that appear in society without an immediate response of defensiveness. It is impossible to work toward a solution if we aren't aware of the core issues and where they originated.

Through heart-moving stories and conversations with experts and activists, *Better Than We Found It* looks at problems from multiple angles and asks questions like: Whom does this problem affect? Why is the issue still prevalent? and What are people doing to ameliorate the situation? Each chapter taught me something new and aided me in better understanding who I am and who I want to be—as an activist, advocate and, most importantly, as a young Black woman.

One chapter that strongly resonated with me was chapter 3: "Sledgehammers and Glass Ceilings," which is about being a feminist and womanist accomplice. It discusses how when sexism and the patriarchy work together in our society, a disservice is done to humankind because women are not celebrated for being their unapologetic selves due to stereotypical beliefs, misogynistic standards, and contrived barriers. For K Torch, it was gaslighting men telling her how she should look and act based on their limited vision of what successful female rappers looked like. For me, it was men telling me that I could never be an astronaut because it was a "boys' game" and that engineering and the medical fields were "too difficult" for me to partake in. This is something I've heard since I was a nine-year-old girl at Space Camp. That's why it is crucial for people, specifically men, to understand that gender roles and sexist beliefs were created to feed into the patriarchy and prohibit women from being in power and reaching their full potential. We have to remind girls and women that it's not enough to break barriers, but that we must do everything in our power to eliminate them completely for the betterment of humankind. And to do so, we need men who fight alongside us, not against us.

This book is a great reminder for young readers to stay true to themselves, no matter what. But being true to yourself also means being truthful with yourself. We all need to recognize the pivotal roles our words and our ignorance play in the lives of those around us. Each chapter has not only widened my lens on issues I didn't know all that much about, but has also touched my heart personally and reminded me why it's paramount to continue to listen, learn, and grow. More than anything, this book made me want to do even more to make this world a better place for myself and others by aiding my generation of future leaders to listen and digest the stories of those impacted by these issues and by putting together tailored plans of actionable steps that lead to realistic solutions.

To my friends who are working on themselves and trying to grow: I hope that this book will help you learn from the mistakes of others so you can make better decisions and take away the excuse of being ignorant to the issues. I know it will provide you with comfort to know that there are people out there fighting for the issues we care about. I can say that I am now confident enough to go out into the world, be aware of the things I am experiencing, and correctly label them so that I can help others better understand me—and so that I can better understand others. This is something that I know our generation struggles with. Communication is hard, and clearly expressing one's point of view can prove difficult when it's wrapped in emotions. *Better Than We Found It* is a sophisticated GPS that will help readers be efficient on their world-saving journey and aid them in avoiding the dangers and pitfalls of being complacent. With that being said, I hope everyone who opens this book gains a new level of assurance in themselves and feels empowered to join in the fight to make our world one that is truly respectful, open-minded, and kind to all—to make the world indeed better.

Signed with love,
Taylor

INTRODUCTION
TOGETHER, WE CAN . . .

Dear one,

Progress isn't the longest word in the dictionary, but in many ways it's the largest. Housed within its definition are words such as *courage*, *hope*, *learning*, and *effort*. But progress is more than just a word; it's an ideal and a direction toward who and what we may become.

Progress by its very definition requires change, and unfortunately the concept of change is something deeply opposed by many people. There are those who find change intimidating or frightening, and there are also those who actively try to stop change because they benefit from things remaining the same.

But the truth is that change is necessary. The scourge of destructive forces such as racism, sexism, climate change, and gun violence have left the fabric of our society in tatters. Communities, families, cultures, individuals, and entire races have been devastated and even destroyed because of these forces.

And the devastation continues. Too many people are still suffering and far too much will be lost if we do not act.

Growing up, neither of us had the tools or resources necessary to combat or even understand many of the issues we discuss throughout the book. Which is why we wanted to give others what we wish we would have had sooner. What would Porsche's life as a young biracial woman have been like if she hadn't had to worry about her family being houseless when her apartment burned down or about how horribly her brother was treated by the justice system because he is half Black? How would Fred's life as a young Black man have been different if he hadn't constantly been afraid someone might bring a gun to school or if he hadn't felt ashamed about his interests because people around him said a young boy should enjoy football more than musicals?

While we each faced these traumas and hardships as individuals, we are part of a community of billions around the world who have faced similar experiences of poverty, violence, and prejudice. Understanding that the various challenges that exist in our society are all connected is the first step to eradicating these challenges.

We called upon this community when putting together this book. Like everyone, the two of us come from very specific backgrounds and have experiences that shaped who we are and what we say in this book. But we are aware that our perspectives can't speak for everyone. There are communities we don't belong to and experiences we don't share—but at the center of progress is the ability to make space to learn from and be better for those unlike ourselves. Which is why we've made space for others to offer their knowledge and perspectives. The book features conversations with numerous thought leaders, activists, and experts to help create a deeper and more **intersectional** lens through which to view these vital topics.

SIDE NOTE: In the back of the book, we've added definitions for the words that are bolded throughout. We've also created an online toolkit focused on the topics discussed throughout the book, which includes additional resources and actionable steps to make change. Be sure to check out BetterThanWeFoundItBook.com.

When we began writing, we didn't want to simply tell stories about the ways the world might have wronged us; we also wanted to provide an opportunity to see how all of us might be unknowingly wronging the world. No one is perfect, and there are many ways that the two of us have had to listen and learn. As much as this book is an opportunity to take action, it's also an opportunity for growth. Because we're all still learning.

In forging a path to a better world, stumbling is inevitable. Many of the struggles, missteps, and mistakes you will make, we have made as well—and we will all continue to make mistakes. But there should be grace for those who are willing to be held accountable when they stumble. A person is remembered for how they got up, not how they fell. What did they learn? How did they grow? Did they have the courage to be better the next time? Progress is a journey filled with imperfection; the important part is that you take the journey.

Our imperfections give us the opportunity to constantly strive for better. This book offers all of us that opportunity.

These pages are both a labor of love and a leap of faith. In them we offer our truths, our failures, and the ways in which we've grown, in hope that readers will feel not only inspired—but loved.

Love for others is fundamental to the work we're doing. In so many ways, we are all family, connected by our pain and our joy. In the stories and conversations throughout this book, we have tried to help people understand these connections and the importance of considering why even a stranger should be dear to you.

We hope that even if some, many, or most of the experiences relayed in this book do not resonate for you firsthand, the stories and interviews still serve to create the building blocks of empathy that will inspire you to take action. Our greatest desire is that you will choose to use whatever privilege you may have to understand and protect others, and that others will do the same for you in spaces where you lack privilege.

For the sake of the dear ones in our lives and for the sake of the children we hope to have one day and the people they will consider dear ones, we've challenged ourselves to give more to this world than we take, and we are challenging you to do the same. More thoughtfulness, more acceptance, more respect—and more love.

Progress *is* possible—if we lean into the bravery and leadership it will take to create it. This book is our attempt to do that. With it, we hope to shed light on some of the most critical issues we face as a society and inspire you to create necessary change—inspire you to be brave along with us and to lead alongside us, and alongside the millions of others already growing and taking action.

Better Than We Found It isn't just a title; it's the manifestation of our wildest dream: that future generations won't have to face the challenges we are facing. The world is changing quickly, no matter how much some may try to avoid or even prevent it, and together we will decide in what direction it goes. All of us are the youth of yesterday and the ancestors of tomorrow. As such, let us be remembered for progress, let us be remembered for saying "enough is enough," and let us be remembered as leaders who saw the greatest issues and challenges of our time and chose to boldly overcome them.

Because having a vision for what the world should be means nothing if you won't do what's necessary to create a world in that image.

With love,
The Josephs

A NOTE ON THE ANECDOTES: While we strove to make these scenes as accurate to reality as possible, the dialogue has been re-created from memory, which means it's a representation of what happened and not a literal transcript of what was said. Names, too, have largely been fictionalized.

1
NOT ALL INFORMATION IS CREATED EQUAL

Frederick Joseph on the Dangers of Disinformation

Featuring **Chelsea Clinton** and **David Villalpando**

Have you ever known someone who believed something that was factually, *provably* incorrect, yet they refused to accept that they were wrong because their information came from a trusted source? I'm sure many of us have experienced this particular frustrating scenario at one point or another. What we might not have realized is that those people may have been victims of someone's plan to purposely spread false information.

Throughout history there have been people with a vested interest in ensuring that others believe things that are untrue. From political rivals spreading lies about one another in order to sway voters to a classmate taking credit for someone else's work, lying has been around for a long time. While lying might not be new, many of the tools, strategies, and goals are.

As I was working on this chapter, I read an article about a

company based in London that was attempting to pay social media influencers from around the world to post false information about one of the COVID-19 vaccines. While many of those influencers didn't post the false information, a few from Brazil and India apparently did. When attempts were made to research the company, it was found that there was no company existing at the London address given and that the content on the company's social media accounts had been completely deleted.

What this company was asking those influencers to spread is called **disinformation**, which is false information that is deliberately spread to deceive people. (This is different from **misinformation**, which is false information as well, but not deliberately so.) There could be many reasons why they were purposely trying to spread lies—for example, perhaps they were attempting to undermine one company's vaccine in favor of another's—but what matters is that during a global pandemic, they were attempting to make people afraid of a vaccine that is saving lives. One person spreading lies about a vaccine could become millions of people believing those lies and refusing to get that particular vaccination.

Understanding the importance of combating false information with the truth is essential to the fight for progress. It's why we chose to make this the first chapter of the book—and in many ways it's the reason we needed to write the book in the first place. There are people invested in spreading lies that are damaging the world, and so there must also be people invested in spreading the truths that will help save it.

When I was growing up, I often heard the saying "Truth is in the eye of the beholder," which I felt essentially meant that as individuals we decide what is true and what is not based on our own opinions and experiences. I was much older when I realized how problematic that idea could potentially be.

While it's important to understand that people may have different perspectives, there are certain things that are simply true and others that are untrue. For example, there are millions of people who believe that **climate change** is a **hoax**—something purposefully made up to look like the truth—and others who think the impact of it is exaggerated, even though countless scientists and governments around the world have said otherwise and the effects of climate change are devastating the world as you read this. These people are often referred to as "climate deniers" (something Porsche delves further into within the next chapter). Though they are endangering others and holding back needed progress, if we want to change their actions or the results their actions have on others, it's important to understand how and why people such as climate deniers believe what they do.

There are millions of social media posts, YouTube videos, and books that reaffirm the idea that climate change is a lie. For many, it can be difficult to discern what's true and what isn't, which sources to trust and which not to. Heck, we had a recent president of the United States who often publicly denied that climate change existed, even as experts in his own government said he was wrong. When lies and false information come from sources that we believe we should trust, it becomes difficult to know when we should *not* trust them.

One of the worst parts of disinformation is that it's typically spread among teenagers or people who belong to a **marginalized group**—people who are socially, economically, educationally, and/or culturally discriminated against or excluded from mainstream groups. These are all people seen as susceptible to believing false information. Essentially, because of their status or struggles in society, people think they can take advantage and use them as the foot soldiers of false information.

For example, on the anniversary of one of the largest school shootings in US history, I posted a few words in remembrance on social media. A young man sent me a message in response to my post telling me that the shooting never happened and was invented to "take away people's guns." I asked where he had heard this lie, and he shared a website where I found countless false claims about how school shootings and other disasters were hoaxes.

Similar to that website, there is a ton of disinformation spread through online forums, video games, and social media groups, all of which are often frequented by teenagers. People who spread disinformation want to take advantage of the fact that many teens are still open to learning new things. This is no different from how they attempt to take advantage of other groups mentioned who may be more vulnerable to both learning and spreading lies—and who likely believe they are doing something positive when they do so.

You know who preys on vulnerable people? Oppressors.

Even though I'd long known that disinformation was a huge problem, it wasn't until I witnessed its damage firsthand that I understood just how vital it is that we all learn how to better assess and combat it.

In 2020, the Democratic **primaries** had so many people running for president that I can barely remember some of their names. But what I do remember is the fact that the group of candidates was easily the most diverse assortment of people running for president in America's history. The number of people from marginalized communities who had a chance to become leader of the United States was stunning. Candidates included people of color, women, people in the **LGBTQ+** community, and people of widely varying ages. But beyond their varied identities, many of them also had differing **political ideologies**, though they belonged to the same **political party**. Whatever your beliefs might have been, there was likely a person running for president whom you could agree with and feel represented by.

When I'm deciding which politicians I will support, I have a list of questions I ask myself about each candidate. Whichever candidate gets the most yeses ultimately becomes the person I decide to support.

MY LIST OF QUESTIONS:

▶ Will this person understand or listen to my personal experiences?

▶ Does this person have similar personal experiences?

▶ Will this person help create change so that people don't have to live in poverty?

▶ Will this person help create change for women?

▶ Will this person help create change for the LGBTQ+ community?

▶ Does this person have plans to create more access to education?

▶ Does this person have plans to create more access to health care?

▶ Does this person have plans to stop gun violence?

▶ Does this person have plans to help fight climate change?

▶ Is this person going to help people of color?

▶ Is this person honest about how white supremacy, capitalism, and the patriarchy have hurt our country?

▶ Does this person have a chance to win?

I know; it's a pretty long list. But personally, I think all of our lists should be long when it comes to deciding who is going to represent us in the ways and places that most of us will never be given the chance to represent ourselves. Voters not thinking deeply or critically about whom they support and why is actually how some of the most dangerous people in history have gained power—people who espouse hatred for women, Black people, immigrants, and many other communities. People such as the forty-fifth president of the United States.

After tallying up the results, Senator Elizabeth Warren was my top choice—though former secretary of housing and urban development Julián Castro and Senator Bernie Sanders were extremely close seconds.

I publicly announced my endorsement for Senator Warren and eventually became a national surrogate for her campaign, which is kind of like being a super-volunteer who is asked to travel, meet people, and share their support online with their fans or followers. Basically, you're a spokesperson for the campaign, shaking hands and kissing babies on behalf of the candidate while they are busy elsewhere shaking other hands and kissing other babies. I was more than happy to do it, as I deeply believed in what Senator Warren wanted to do for the country.

Sadly, agreeing to the awesome opportunity of becoming a national surrogate for the Elizabeth Warren presidential campaign is how I ended up on the wrong end of a disinformation campaign.

Being a surrogate for a political campaign isn't just about meeting people; it's specifically about meeting people who might listen to you, and oftentimes the people most likely to listen to you are people who you share similarities with. People you relate to and who might also relate to you. These are the people who you hope will allow you to explain your reasons for supporting the candidate you do, and potentially become supporters of that candidate as well. Which is why I asked that much of my time as a surrogate be spent traveling to places where I could meet people from Black and **Latinx** communities, especially Black men. It wasn't just a matter of feeling like I would have the most in common with those groups, but also that I felt Senator Warren's plans showed a great deal of support for those communities, which have been historically ignored.

I spent months flying to Texas, South Carolina, and elsewhere, speaking to people in nail salons, beauty salons, churches, and barbershops. All of these are spaces where people are used to having all sorts of debate and discourse about differing opinions, but none more so than barbershops, where I had the opportunity to reach many Black men in spaces that often welcome authentic and honest conversations—especially about politics. The discussions I had while traveling for the campaign were some of the best I've had in my life. People talked with and debated me on everything from education to criminal justice. I heard about people's fears of bigotry and hopes for their children's futures. Not every conversation ended with people agreeing to support Senator Warren, as big decisions often take time (and long lists). But there was never an instance when people didn't agree to consider learning more about her or how her plans may have been best positioned to support their wants and needs.

As I mentioned earlier, I wasn't just talking with people when I traveled; I was also posting on social media and talking about the campaign with anyone I encountered who would listen. Most of my friends, family, followers, and even the people who work at my local deli knew that I was supporting Senator Warren. One of the people I spoke most often to about the campaign was my own barber back home in New York City. He's someone who has always been interested in politics and social issues, and he wanted the other barbers in his shop to learn more. So every week when I went to get my hair cut (yes, I get my hair cut every week, at least when I'm not writing—right now I look like a wolf), we would discuss the election and who people were supporting and why.

One week, I went to get my hair cut the night after an important presidential debate in which Elizabeth Warren performed extremely well and called out presidential candidate and former New York City mayor Michael Bloomberg for his support of a racist policy called stop-and-frisk during his time as mayor.

SIDE NOTE: Stop-and-frisk essentially allowed cops to stop and search anyone in the street they thought seemed "suspicious." This gave them the ability to legally harass people in the street, which they disproportionately did to Black and brown people.

I had been a victim of stop-and-frisk when I was in college; I'd talked about it with Senator Warren, and before the debate, her campaign had posted a video on social media of me speaking about my experience and how harmful Mayor Bloomberg's policy was. I'd shared the video on social media as well. By the time I came for my haircut, my barbers had watched both the video and the debate, and all of them were beyond excited about what they saw Senator Warren do. Especially because some of them had also been victims of the stop-and-frisk policy.

As soon as I walked into the barbershop, I was flooded with praise for the candidate and campaign I had been trying to get these people to support for months: "Warren was great last night, can't lie!" "She's got my vote." "She was out there killing—she really did her thing!" I decided to post on Twitter about the excitement for Senator Warren during my barbershop visit.

This was the beginning of everything spiraling into the lies I'm still dealing with as I write this.

A few hours after posting on Twitter, I started receiving notifications on my phone of responses from people claiming the conversations in the barbershop were staged. "This never happened." "The Warren campaign has to lie about its support, I guess." "People don't speak like this in barbershops.

Who talks about politics while getting a haircut?" Most of these comments were from people either working for or supporting other campaigns, which didn't surprise me. Because there were so many people running for president, there were a ton of people who tried to find anything they could to lessen support for other candidates, especially those who were seen as having a great deal of popularity—such as Senator Warren.

The comments and shares saying I was lying about the experience lasted for a few days, and while it was aggravating, in the grand scheme of things it wasn't that bad. Well, at least it wasn't as bad as what was about to happen.

After the debate, there was even more energy and interest in the Warren campaign, so I headed back out on the road. While traveling, I always had a team of brilliant people with me who would take photos and videos to create content I could post on social media. On a trip in South Carolina, I went to a barbershop and spoke with a few people waiting to get a haircut and with the owner of the shop, who happened to be the only person still cutting, because they were about to close. Per usual, we had a great conversation and the team took photos, which I posted on Twitter.

The day after that trip, I had to fly to Miami for a wedding. While I was there, I left my phone on silent in my pocket and decided not to check it so I could focus on the event. When the wedding was over and I went back to my hotel, I had more notifications than I had ever seen in my life. There were thousands of people commenting on the photos of me in the last barbershop I visited, saying that the barbershop was fake. As in, the barbershop had been created by the Warren campaign so that I could take pictures in it. The people online saying this argued that the barber in the photo wasn't a real barber, the person getting his hair cut wasn't actually getting his hair cut, and the entire thing was staged. What did they believe was proof of this, you ask? Well, they said that barbers didn't wear button-down shirts as the barber had worn, that the jerseys and movie posters on the walls didn't make sense, oh, and let's not forget the fact that I "lied" about my experience in the *other* barbershop when people praised Senator Warren's debate performance.

The lies caught like wildfire—and spread well beyond Twitter.

People posted about the "fake barbershop scandal" on Reddit, Facebook, Instagram, and YouTube. Thousands of people who supported other campaigns went through my social media posts about the Warren campaign and commented with things such as "fake" and "liar" on nearly all of them.

Over the next few weeks, I spent most of my time online arguing the legitimacy of the work and conversations I had dedicated months of my life to. I was exhausted from traveling, challenging myself mentally and emotionally, missing holidays and events with my loved ones, all so I could do my part to help our country become better, especially for the most marginalized of us. I was exhausted from being told primarily by white people not only that I was a liar, but also that there was no way that the Black and Latinx people I was visiting with were having conversations about the things I said they were. People too often believe that their experiences and assumptions are a reflection of the entire world—especially when it comes to people who they perceive as being different from themselves.

A few weeks after what I've coined #BarberShopGate began, Senator Warren dropped out of the race for president. While the lies spreading about the barbershop had nothing to do with her ending her campaign—it may have blown up on social media, but thankfully it never reached the mainstream media, where it would've done much more widespread damage—it was symbolic of the false information and dishonesty about her campaign and the campaigns of other candidates that were purposely being spread by people to discredit, delegitimize, and ultimately end those campaigns. It wasn't just unfair; it was oftentimes a strategy rooted in racism, sexism, and other hatred—even if the people doing it didn't realize it. But it is undeniably racist to insinuate that it was impossible for Black men to be actively discussing politics in barbershops or other places, and it is racist to imply that Black men aren't engaged enough to have their excitement grow for a candidate other people may have not supported.

After Senator Warren's campaign ended, I endorsed Senator Bernie Sanders, whose campaign ended a few weeks after my endorsement. (I suppose my endorsements are bad luck politically.) While #BarberShopGate may not have had a negative impact on the campaigns I worked for, it certainly had a negative impact on my personal and professional lives. Months after Democrats had settled on which candidate would be the party's nominee for president, people were still commenting on my social media posts and saying that I was a liar and a fraud—even on posts that had nothing to do with the campaigns or with politics at all.

For example, at the height of the COVID-19 pandemic I was raising money online to help people who had been impacted pay for their rent, food, and other needs. Though I had a history of raising millions of dollars for various causes before the presidential election, people went to my posts about the fundraiser and said things such as, "He lied about barbershops during the election. He's probably going to steal the money." Which didn't derail the fundraiser but may have stopped some people from donating, which ultimately stopped many people from being helped. While I was still able to send money to more than ten thousand families, I'll never know how many more could've been helped if not for those comments questioning my integrity.

The character smears continued when I announced the publication of my debut book, *The Black Friend*. People posted things such as "No one should support him or his book. He's the guy who lied about the barbershops during the election to help Elizabeth Warren." It's one thing if you don't want to buy my book because you're not interested in the topic (though you should be!), but it's another thing if you decide not to buy my book because you believe a lie someone on the internet told about me. My livelihood was being impacted by this disinformation.

But by far the worst instance was when a friend of mine passed from complications from COVID-19 and I posted about his death on Twitter. So many people responded saying that I was making his death up, the way I supposedly had with the barbershops, that I broke down. I stood in the shower, turned on some Donny Hathaway (always good when you're feeling emotional), and cried not just for my friend who was gone, but also for how an act of love and hope in trying to better my country had been mutated into a gross attack that was now disrespecting the life of someone I knew.

There are people who understand how much power a lie may contain, and because of that they invest in making sure as many people believe their lies instead of the truth as possible. They tell their lies so thoughtfully and strategically that people who believe them often will refuse to hear anything else. To them, that lie *is* the truth. And anyone upholding the *actual* truth—anyone disagreeing with the liar or pushing back against the lies—is seen as a liar themselves. This is when a lie isn't just a lie, but rather misinformation or disinformation—as was the case with the fake London company hiring influencers to smear a vaccine and with the barbershop accusations.

What happened to me with #BarberShopGate was likely not just misinformation; the speed at which it spread and the specific people who spread it (many of whom worked for rival campaigns) indicates that it was likely disinformation—a deliberate effort to destroy the Warren campaign by delegitimizing the work that I was doing for it. It was never really about *me*. I was the collateral damage of a disinformation campaign that was created to help ensure that Elizabeth Warren did not become president. As the (il)logic went, if I was a liar who had staged the barbershop visit, then Elizabeth Warren either supported my lies or was a poor judge of surrogates for her campaign. But as I've explained, what started out as an effort targeted at a political campaign ended up impacting my future work and my ability to help people.

As was the case then, disinformation works most efficiently and effectively when the people who believe it help amplify it and attack the victim of it, even without realizing what they are doing. Great power exists in controlling the narratives people believe, because if you do that, you can also control what they do and don't do.

This strategy isn't new. It has been used for decades by individuals and governments around the world to win—or begin—wars, sway elections, and spark violence. In fact, the first disinformation department existed in Russia as far back as 1923. That's nearly a century of organized efforts to manipulate people through lies. But it's not just Russia; other countries have invested in disinformation, including the United States. In 2002, the Pentagon shut down its disinformation department, which was open for less than two years, due to unfavorable responses to its creation from American citizens. The US government says it is no longer engaged in creating disinformation, and President Joe Biden has spoken about the dangers of disinformation and the negative impact it can have on national security.

But disinformation is not just about who creates it— it's also about who allows it to have life. For example, social media companies make money based on how many people are using their platforms. The more engagements and users a platform has, the more money they can charge companies to advertise their products and ideas to the people using the platform. Disinformation on these platforms keeps people engaged and active through the conversations they are having, even if those conversations are actually arguments based on hatred, anger, and lies. I was on Twitter way more often than usual while I was arguing with people that I wasn't lying, and the engagement on my posts was more than I had ever seen, even if it was negative. My harm benefited the platform.

An engaged user is a user, regardless of how they are using the platform, right?

As the world becomes more digitally connected by the day and new forms of communicating and information sharing are invented, I believe it's more crucial than ever to understand how disinformation may impact us and how to identify it. Disinformation poses real dangers to the most essential parts of our society. Elections have been swayed by it, health crises have been prolonged by it, and lives have been devastated by it.

To better understand how disinformation works and the impact it can have and has had, I spoke with my friends Chelsea Clinton and David Villalpando about their experiences and expertise related to disinformation.

An Interview with CHELSEA CLINTON

Best-selling author, global health advocate, and vice-chair of the Clinton Foundation

Chelsea Clinton is a force in her own right, but long before she was the accomplished woman she is today, she was the young daughter of Bill and Hillary Clinton. Chelsea grew up in the public eye. The media has not always been honest about Chelsea and her family, and a great deal of that has been on purpose.

SIDE NOTE: In case you didn't know, Bill Clinton was the forty-second president of the United States; Hillary Clinton was the 2016 Democratic nominee for president and is a former senator for New York State, and a former United States secretary of state.

CHELSEA: You know, when I was a little girl, the first thing I learned how to read was the newspaper, because my parents wanted me to know what was happening in our hometown of Little Rock, Arkansas, and in our state and our country, and the world, to some extent. They also wanted me to understand the difference between facts that were being reported and opinions that were being offered. And they wanted me to have my own opinions and to understand the difference between my opinion and facts. And we would talk about what was really on my mind, which admittedly, when I was a kid, were a lot of things like, "Why do we have sloppy joes for lunch? I wish we had more chicken."

So we would have mock debates where my mom, my dad, and I would play different people to make the process less intimidating, to make me feel very much like I was part of my father's life and my parents' work. But I think also that I really was understanding how to marshal facts to help make an argument, but to always know the difference between an opinion and a fact. And so I think these parenting decisions that my parents made because of the circumstances of our lives actually were hugely important to me becoming a media-literate person.

When my father ran for president in 1992, I came to one of the debates with a cast on my leg. I had fallen in ballet class and hurt my foot and then gone home and I thought that it was fine. And then I was cleaning my room and I fell again. I was like, "Oh gosh, my foot really hurts. I need to go to the doctor." I had fractured my foot; I had to get a cast. So I go to the debate. Don't really think anything of it. And then—I don't remember if it was the next week or soon thereafter—one of the tabloids ran the story about how I'd thrown myself off the

roof of the governor's mansion, because I just was so despon-
dent that my parents had abandoned me while my father was
running for president. I remember just being so gobsmacked.

I actually think that was weirdly also a really helpful experience to prepare me to live in this moment where there are so
many stories that have no grounding in reality, that are so sen-
sationalist and so often absurd, because I grew up having to
navigate that, as my parents' daughter. It's just that the veloc-
ity and the amount has changed so much. Whereas it was an
errant tabloid story in 1992, if that story would have been written
about me this year, almost thirty years later, it would have gotten turned into memes and people would have either been sharing it saying, "Oh my gosh, look, she threw herself off the roof." Or
even sharing it saying, "Oh my gosh, of course she didn't throw
herself off the roof." But all of that would give it oxygen. And
it would spin into other stories and TikTok product videos and
Instagram posts and Facebook posts and Twitter threads and
Discord chats. And there would maybe even be a Reddit sub-
forum on other famous people who threw themselves off roofs.

Chelsea is right—many things have changed in the past
thirty years. Gone are the days of hearing false information
solely in tabloids or on less-respected news channels. From
TikTok to Reddit, now everyone has the ability to create
media, tell stories, and share information that may not even
be true. Not only are lies moving faster; they are also moving
in more places and reaching more people. They are also
moving past the political realm and into daily life. Nothing is
stopping me from going online right now and sharing a lie

about you on my Twitter or Instagram. I can say anything I like, and far too often it's then up to you to spend your time disproving the lie I told about you.

So the question is whether the companies that allow these lies to exist on their platforms are in part to blame. Should they have a role in making sure this kind of thing doesn't happen?

CHELSEA: I do think they very much have a responsibility that they have never acknowledged. And while I'm talking about Facebook—and clearly then its platforms Instagram and WhatsApp—I think the same is true of any of the platforms. And yet they've never faced any consequences. Facebook hasn't even followed its own dictates; I don't have confidence that they will do more in other areas where I desperately think it is needed. I wish they would limit the reach, if not actually remove the miasma of misinformation, on the January 6 white nationalist insurrection. They still have permitted a number of pages that claim that it was antifa or Black Lives Matter who attacked the Capitol or that it was all just fabricated and not real.

I'm not confident that they will impose any consequences on themselves, and I'm not confident that they will make internal changes to their policies to limit or remove misinformation—things that we know are factually untrue about history, whether long ago or more recent, or public health, science. And so I do think we need our **regulatory bodies** all over the world, ideally, to have more scrutiny and oversight of these major companies that have huge influence over how people understand and experience and then help create reality.

The world has changed, and the dissemination and access to information has changed with it. The groups who seem to truly understand the power of information and controlling narratives have been nimble and evolved as necessary to best use the new tools at their disposal. Sadly, it seems that every day brings another moment in which the people who need to be protected from those who are attempting to make them believe false narratives and blatant lies are left defenseless. This ultimately helps grow an often unassuming and unconscious army of misinformation spreaders, which can have a deeply dangerous impact.

CHELSEA: I think we have to recognize that digital technology, especially social media platforms, have changed the way we consume information, the way we share information, the way we communicate, the way we build relationships, the way we experience the world. And, again, the way we truly are creating reality today and into the future. Because these really are huge threats to our public health, our security, our democracy. I think those are really important questions for countries all over the world to really reckon with—how to assert real scrutiny and regulation in a way that isn't limiting important fact-based information. Fair questions to be asked. Relationships to be built.

It won't solve the entire issue, but it does limit the spread of racist, misogynistic, anti-science, Islamophobic, anti-Semitic, homophobic, transphobic speech and narratives—all of these vectors of hate that have been so empowered and emboldened by the social media companies. I think there have to be different strategies, solutions, and different regulatory frameworks going forward. Because clearly the posture of not having really any regulation, I think, hasn't worked and we see that quite painfully in the explosion of the anti-vaccine movement and the explosion of the big lie about the 2020 election and in so many other very real-world ways all over the world.

Chelsea's experience with disinformation speaks not only to how nuanced and insidious it can be on a personal level, but to how dangerous and life-altering it can be as well. Where information was once created and spread by small groups of people who controlled media such as printed news, now essentially anyone has the power to spread and create true or false stories through social media and other tools. Which makes understanding the systemic and personal implications of disinformation that much more important.

An Interview with DAVID VILLALPANDO
Digital safety expert in the technology industry

David Villalpando works for an online crowdfunding company, which allows people to raise money online to help themselves or others in need. His job is to work to keep the site safe and ensure people are being truthful on the company's platform. David has taken a great deal of interest in the digital landscape since he was a child, giving him both a professional and personal lens of experience that are unmatched by most people I know. I wanted to speak to David in large part because of the perspective he offers on the responsibility that social media, and digital information companies in general, have to protect the public from the spread of false information.

DAVID: As you can imagine, crowdfunding needs to be safe and trusted. I've always had a penchant for activism, ethics, and morality, especially in online spaces but mostly in my own community. Finding ways where I can impact how things are done so that more vulnerable communities aren't harmed has always been kind of a magnet for me. In my role, ultimately the goal is to assert morals and ethics, trying to protect users and individuals. Basically, my job is to act as a shield for vulnerable people who may be taken advantage of online.

Whether it is arguing with a bot, falling for a scam, or being victimized by a lie, many people don't even realize what's happening to them or how to stop it—until it's too late. So what can platforms do to prevent such things from happening?

DAVID: At the most basic level, it's content moderation. You're looking at vulgarity, violence, illegal activity, regulated activity. Users harassing one another, targeted harassment—even when you get into more explicit and inappropriate content, that's still the very surface level. As you get deeper into it, you're looking at the more serious threat, which is fraud on the platform. So, making sure that people aren't lying about what they're saying they're raising money for, that the money gets to where it needs to go, to who the money is ultimately for. Then even further than that responsibility is the types of people who are using your platform. So, understanding that it isn't simply a free-for-all, wild-wild-west, anybody-gets-to-use-this platform. You want to make sure that your platform reflects the community you're trying to keep and the space you're trying to keep safe and equitable for everyone.

These points about the responsibility of keeping people safe speak to my point about some social media companies being complicit. If these companies are allowing harmful acts to happen and can stop them, they are at fault for not doing so. People often forget that regardless of who might have a large following or a well-known voice on these platforms, the ultimate power and responsibility still lies with the company controlling the platform. For example, I have a fairly large social media following, but my engagement (likes, shares, saves) on posts depends not only on the interests of my followers but also on the algorithms created and controlled by the platform. There have been many instances in which I've posted about things such as social justice and the algorithms have suspended my account or content because it was perceived as "divisive." If the algorithms can do this, they can certainly hold users responsible for causing harm.

DAVID: The goal for many users on sites like Reddit, YouTube, 4Chan, and others has been to influence propaganda; what we are seeing at times is not accidental. These are intentional disinformation campaigns to make people believe things. You look at the **alt-right** pipeline online and you look at how they very intentionally target impressionable sixteen- to nineteen-year-olds who are googling things or reading discourse online. They're targeted with the goal of being brought over to certain ideologies. I think by the 2016 election it was impossible to ignore the effects that this pipeline had on individuals and who they supported.

Whether it be very maliciously photoshopped images, posts on Twitter lying about events, or conspiracy theories about where viruses and diseases originated, there was a turning point around 2010, when we saw an uptick in these things online. If you look back even to the 2005-era internet and then early 2007-era internet, the sort of discourse that was happening online was really juvenile. The kind of images photoshopped were a silly caricature of a president, very basic images and jokes. But by 2016, this was fully fake online profiles putting out fake information and we're all corralled and enlisted to spread the information of political groups.

Consider that many of the people who were eligible to vote for the first time in the 2016 election would have been about twelve or thirteen years old in 2010, when this shift toward more sophisticated online disinformation began. What impact might this unprecedented level of propaganda and outright lies have had on these future voters? How might these disinformation campaigns have shaped these impressionable minds—and how might they be shaping minds to this very day?

There are many dangers that can come to pass if a person believes all of the negative things they are doing are actually positive because they've been conditioned to believe so since they were a child.

In order to arm ourselves against these disinformation campaigns, it's important to try to determine who is behind the lies being spread and what they stand to gain from spreading them. But just as important is understanding who is enabling the lies to spread—that is, who controls the platforms and online spaces.

DAVID: When you look at the internet historically, who are the first adopters of the internet, who had access to computers, who had access to the internet? Also, by the time the infrastructure was built up, who was running these sites? Who were the loudest voices on these sites? Who kind of got to decide what was front-paged on these sites? Just based on demographics, global demographics and global access, inherently it's going to mirror other forms of media.

So you look at social media compared to print media. You look at magazines. Who had access to run a magazine company? And then, depending on who's running that company, the front page of that magazine? And then also who's going to be able to speak within that magazine? The voices in that magazine are going to reflect the leadership and their goals. So, I think, inherently social media and online spaces almost exactly reflect our real-world spaces or alternative media in terms of who holds the power.

The goal of most companies (online or otherwise) is to make money, and when capital is the center of it—when your primary purpose or goal is to make more money or make your platform larger so that you can make more money—inherently you're going to try to appease people who already have power and voices. Whether it's intentional or not, if you're in the business of making money, which most digital platforms are, then you're going to make decisions that are the most profitable and not always the best for users. Which is why even when safety and trust teams do exist, they don't always do the best job they can of protecting users. Some teams are actually not even people, but algorithms and bots themselves, which are often designed with whatever bias the creator had.

Anything created and managed by humans will always have both the beauty and the ugliness that comes along with those humans. Biased views of racism, sexism, homophobia, ableism, and so much more—including capitalism itself—influence what we see online. One example of this can be found in the bots David mentioned, which many people don't even know how to identify, making them very dangerous.

Some people use bots to distract and traumatize people online who can't differentiate them from a real person behind an account. This is something I've often faced myself, where I've posted things about racism, for instance, and had numerous bots attack and even threaten me under the post. Before understanding how to identify them as bots, I would spend a great amount of time arguing back and forth with them—not realizing I was arguing with something someone had created to waste my time and/or to traumatize me.

SIDE NOTE: For tips on how you can identify bots, check out our online toolkit.

Another example of how creator or company biases can manifest in digital spaces is through algorithms that decide what content and voices are platformed, or that decide who is deemed to be saying negative things on a given platform. Imagine if these algorithms were designed by a person who has oppressive views of people who are immigrants in their country. Those algorithms may take on the bias of their creator. Next thing you know, content based on helping and supporting immigrants is deemed negative or not given the opportunity to be seen by as many people because of those algorithms. Instead, the algorithms allow content that says negative things about immigrants to be seen by many people.

From algorithms that control how and when you see what you see to the lies that are allowed to flourish online, all of it is underscored by the desires of companies and individuals to make money and attain or keep power. The sad reality is that hatred and oppression are often lucrative because they create engagement and interest, which are often avenues for revenue.

Capitalism, biased algorithms, and a lack of understanding the manifestations and widespread impact of lies have allowed disinformation to flourish. It's vital that we learn how to identify disinformation and equip ourselves with the tools and knowledge to overcome it.

The truth is that the first step to creating change on the issues discussed in this book—issues such as climate change, homelessness, gun violence, racism, homophobia, and sexism—is understanding and shining a light on how people have been lied to and kept in the dark about these issues. Because until those lies are exposed, we'll all continue wasting precious time arguing with bots—literally and metaphorically—instead of making real progress.

To find out more about how you can help put a stop to disinformation, visit: BetterThanWeFoundItBook.com.

2
WE'RE THE PLANETEERS; YOU CAN BE ONE, TOO

Porsche Joseph on the Threat of the Climate Crisis
and Environmental Racism

Featuring **Willy** and **Jo Lorenz** and **Mari Copeny**, aka **"Little Miss Flint"**

I grew up in the Pacific Northwest—in Seattle, Washington—but most of my family lives in the South. My grandparents hail from Alabama, and as Black people from the South, they've faced their fair share of adversity. Though many of their struggles have been caused by other people, there are those that came from something greater—Mother Nature. As they will tell you, there is nothing quite like a natural disaster. I remember visiting them during my summer breaks when I was young and having to plan my trips around the hurricane season and the *two* tornado seasons (yes—two), which all run consecutively from spring through fall. As terrifying as that always was, the weather scares were not as frequent or intense as they are today.

My grandparents are older now, and it isn't rare for me

and my husband to call them and find that they're huddled in their closet, waiting for a tornado to pass, a torrential downpour to let up, or the howling winds sweeping through the area to subside. They are in their late eighties and don't know much about climate science, but they know that they find themselves in that closet more often than ever before and that something has changed.

In recent decades we've seen an influx of devastating wildfires, droughts, floods, hurricanes, tornadoes, and blizzards throughout the country and all over the world. There's no denying that climate change is real and that it is having a major impact on weather patterns and natural disasters. And yet despite the evidence before us and despite mountains of scientific evidence, some people *do* deny it. Some of these individuals, called **climate deniers**, believe that climate change is a hoax—a scheme to get their tax dollars or a nefarious plot being carried out by a foreign government in order to destroy the US economy. Many more people are influenced by the corporations and government officials who have worked hard to downplay or invalidate climate change in order to avoid shaming the industries that profit from environmental destruction, such as oil, agriculture, transportation, and manufacturing, to name a few. Then there are the people who may admit that the Earth is warmer but write it off as not that serious, a natural cycle, or something that the Earth will heal itself from. (These people might more accurately be called climate downplayers.)

I personally believe that all of these people are driven by fear. Fear of the monumental implications of climate change (major destruction), fear of the accountability that acknowledging climate change may entail, or fear of the inconvenience it would cause to have to evaluate the human role in the current predicament.

But for those of us who are willing to acknowledge the scientific facts and expert opinions, it doesn't take much to realize that the planet we depend on for survival isn't doing so well and that it's beginning to affect the way we live.

I was seventeen years old when the seriousness of the effects of climate change fully hit me. It was in 2005, when Hurricane Katrina, one of the deadliest hurricanes in US history, touched down in New Orleans. A storm that ripped the veil off for many on climate change, anti-Blackness, and poverty.

It was the summer before my senior year of high school, and I had been coordinating my trip to New Orleans since the beginning of the year. As I mentioned, I was raised in Seattle, but my father and his family aren't from there, so none of his family lived in Washington State. For that reason, I always looked forward to summers—when I would go spend extended amounts of time with my cousins, who primarily lived in the South like my grandparents. I suppose I saw myself as something of a southern belle lost in the Pacific Northwest.

So many of my best childhood memories are wrapped up in those summers spent sitting on the porch under the hot southern sun with a giant cup of sweet tea while my older cousins did my hair or we put fake tattoos from vending machines on each other. We rode bikes around the neighborhood and chalked hopscotch patterns in the church parking lot, which would keep us busy for hours, until it was time to play double Dutch or go to the mall. We did things cousins probably do all over the country, all the time, but it was special to me because I was only able to see my cousins during the summer. I really didn't have much family at all in Seattle; even from my mother's side, I only had one cousin, who is a boy, and being that I only had brothers, having my girl cousins around during those summers was my only opportunity for lip gloss tutorials or to have someone dress me up in their clothes and apply a fresh set of press-on nails as the finishing touch.

I admit, I may romanticize those summers now that I'm older. These days my summers come and go much quicker and are a lot less carefree, but as a child, there was just something magical about those southern summers. To this very day, humid weather that others would face with disgust brings me a feeling of contentment and nostalgia for my childhood.

But as I got older, I began wanting to stay in Seattle and spend summers with friends or working, so it had been years since I had visited my family. When my cousin Tanisha invited me to come visit her in New Orleans, where she was attending Xavier University, I worked tirelessly to save up my money so I could make the trip. She was a couple of years older than me, and I had always looked up to her. It wasn't typical for people in my family to go to college, so Tanisha was the first and only person I knew who had made it that far in their schooling, which meant a lot to me, because while she was the first, I had no intention of her being the last.

Tanisha always seemed to have her stuff together—she got good grades, was sweet and kind, and always wore the flyest outfits. Now she was at college in a cool city that matched her cool personality, and she was making it look effortless and fun. Her social media showcased her with friends in the French Quarter, or in pictures that looked straight out of a student brochure—studying with a large group or lounging in a common area on campus. I wanted to be just like her. Tanisha and her friends were in sororities and fraternities, and I would see her pictures from Homecoming, step shows, parades and parties, weekend crawfish boils, and crowded festivals. Though I had never experienced this place in person, from the looks of Tanisha's MySpace pictures (yes, I am "myspace.com" years old), I knew that I would enjoy spending four years there. I couldn't wait to join her!

Xavier University sits right in the heart of New Orleans. I had spent a lot of time in the South, but that was a place I had never been. The city is unique. It is iconic and has some of the best music and food in America. It also has a strong culture and deep history that is very different from what I knew growing up in Seattle. The history of slavery, Indigenous people, and French colonization creates a distinct blend of influences, reflected in the cuisine, religions, and traditions of the region.

Xavier is a historically Black college (**HBCU**). I had just started to learn more about HBCUs and was set on attending one. So many important Black figures have gone to Black colleges: Toni Morrison, Langston Hughes, Oprah Winfrey, Spike Lee—even Two Chainz and Diddy went to HBCUs. Plus, the movie *Drumline* had come out a few years before, and if that was any indicator of life at an HBCU, it looked like a lot more fun than the predominantly white colleges my classmates wanted to go to, which seemed bland and were often in the middle of Nowhereville, USA.

Truth be told, a lot of HBCUs are also in the middle of nowhere, and sadly, some are also deeply underfunded and unable to give out scholarships, despite often having lower tuition than predominantly white schools. But none of that mattered. I knew I wanted to be at an HBCU. Come to think of it, Xavier didn't even have a marching band, but my rose-colored glasses were extra thick from seeing how much my cousin loved her school.

Another cousin, Stephanie, who was graduating from high school the next year as well, had recently told me that she was also planning on going to Xavier. Suddenly, it seemed like this could turn out to be some sort of grand sequel to all the fond summers I'd spent with my cousins growing up.

Stephanie had always been the funny cousin. You know the kind of person who always does the best impersonations and finds something hilarious in every situation? That's Stephanie. She is extremely outgoing and can always make me smile. I haven't always been the best at making new friends, but if my cousins and I were at college together, it would be as if I had built-in friends. I was the studious one, Stephanie was the funny one, and Tanisha was the social one; together we'd make the perfect team.

Stephanie and I planned to go visit Tanisha and Xavier in August, before our senior years of high school started. It had been years since I had seen them, and we had been texting back and forth and talking on the phone about our plans. Excited is an understatement. The plan was to visit New Orleans and see the campus for a few days, then Tanisha would drive us up to Montgomery to spend time with our grandparents. We decided that August would be best because classes at Xavier resumed that month and I would have the opportunity to sit in on some college courses, so I booked my flight to arrive on August 26, the day after Stephanie.

Stephanie and Tanisha called me once she got into New Orleans that Thursday and I made them promise not to do anything fun without me. Everything seemed fine; they didn't mention a thing about the tropical storm in the Atlantic that was escalating into a hurricane. The next day, I was set to go when my mother put a damper on my plans.

"Porsche, have you seen the forecast for New Orleans? I've been talking to your aunt, and I don't want you flying during the storm. Why don't you let it pass, then head down in a few days? Your aunt is telling Steph and Tanisha they have to drive up to Montgomery to wait it out at your grandparents'."

I was upset and thought my mom was being overbearing. There had already been at least five hurricanes in New Orleans that year, and who knew how many storms. Besides, Tanisha lived there and she wasn't even worried about it. The fact that I even thought that seems delusional now, but most people really didn't expect that Katrina would turn into what it did. New Orleans experiences some of the strongest hurricanes in the country, but the aftermath of this one was something no one could have imagined.

I contacted my cousins, and they still didn't seem bothered at all. "It will just end up being a regular storm," Tanisha predicted. "These happen all the time, and they always pass. But my mom is insisting that we go visit Granny and Granddaddy, so we're just going to make our way up there a few days early." She sounded frustrated that the storm was derailing our plans. I was disappointed as well, but sometimes (oftentimes) a mother's intuition is unmatched. My mom and aunt turned out to be right.

By the next day, Saturday, August 27, Katrina had escalated to a Category 4 hurricane and evacuation orders were given. By Sunday morning, it became a Category 5 storm, with winds at about 160 miles per hour. By the end of the day, up to thirty thousand New Orleans residents had sought shelter in the Superdome, a sports arena that normally hosted rowdy football games but was now being used to shelter refugees. My family and I watched the news as the storm made landfall in New Orleans on Monday, August 29. The destruction was devastating. Some people who didn't leave their homes were left stranded on their rooftops in the hot, humid weather or were forced to wade through murky floodwater. We saw images of a completely tattered city and of people hanging on for dear life, floating in floodwater on everything from mattresses to doors. Almost no one had expected this; the word that kept being used on the news was "unprecedented."

My mother and I were trembling as we sat in front of the TV, which had been showing the CNN *Storm Watch* for hours. This could have so easily been me or my cousins. And it *was* somebody's cousins and children and parents and loved ones. "Those are families!" my mother said through tears when we saw a crowd of men wading through water with children on their backs and women holding suitcases of their belongings above their heads to keep them dry.

"Why is no one coming to help them? What is wrong?" I asked, distraught. The federal government was nowhere to be seen, but the media was, and as we watched aerial views of cars flipped over from winds, makeshift boats floating through the floodwaters crowded with families, and seemingly endless groups of people gathered on rooftops, many of which were marked with pleas for help, I couldn't imagine how people in power could see the reporting on the devastation and not be doing everything they could to help. We saw one group of about fifteen people waving their shirts in the air from a roof that displayed handmade signs reading, in all caps, TWO DEAD BODIES INSIDE PLEASE HELP.

My heart ached. These images went on for days. Images of floating bodies, sick and elderly people sitting helplessly, and children outside the Superdome chanting "We want help" were forever etched in my mind. Also burned into my brain was the fact that these people were disproportionately Black.

I had seen this kind of stuff in other countries, but never imagined that this could have happened in America. If my mom hadn't forced me to delay my trip, that could have been me. If Tanisha didn't have a car with which to drive herself and Stephanie out of the city . . . Even with a car, if she had tried to flee even one day later, she could have been trapped in the gridlock traffic and forced into the Superdome. We could so easily have been among the tens of thousands of people who were locked inside the stadium with backed-up sewage, a leaking roof, no medical aid, and violent uproars.

President Bush and many of the local politicians pretended to have everything under control, while the footage that was captured said otherwise. "To listen to politicians thanking each other and complimenting each other, I've got to tell you, there are a lot of people here who are very upset," said one CNN host.

What really shook me up was when I saw thousands of people trying to evacuate via the Crescent Bridge, which connects to the high-ground suburb of Gretna and is the primary route out of New Orleans. These people were faced with the entire Gretna police force pointing guns at them and firing above the heads of anyone that attempted to pass through. Gretna, which is primarily white, with a very white police department, trapped people trying to leave, saying that they didn't want thugs and looters coming through their town, an action the chief of police continued to defend for years afterward. The "thugs and looters" were nearly all Black, including parents with babies in their arms and elderly people hunched over canes.

"Why aren't they letting that woman with the stroller cross the bridge? Or those people in wheelchairs? They are going to let them all die!" my mom exclaimed in disgust. At that point, we had to step away from the news; even watching it was too hard. The thought that I could have been there gave me chills. The knowledge that nearly a hundred thousand people *were* there broke my heart.

The results of the hurricane were devastating. Eighty percent of New Orleans ended up underwater, up to twenty feet high. More than 1,800 people died during the storm, and many more went missing. People were without food and water supplies for weeks on end. Families were torn apart, the homeless population increased dramatically, and the destruction took years to even attempt to repair. To this day, rebuilding continues to be a work in progress; while most of the tourist areas and expensive neighborhoods have recovered, much of the surrounding neighborhoods have not been restored and many people never returned.

The communities that were affected the worst were the Black neighborhoods, particularly poor Black neighborhoods like the Lower Ninth Ward, where the residents were living on an average income of $16,000 before Katrina. Black home-owners were more than three times as likely to have experi-enced flooding than white homeowners. Because of housing discrimination, white people have historically lived on high ground while the lower land that is more susceptible to weather damage was all that was left available for Black people. After Hurricane Katrina, the government moved slowly to pump the water out of this part of town, even though it suffered the most damage, and it is still not fully recovered to this day.

Louisiana and the Gulf Coast have always experienced hurricanes but, as forecasters have anticipated for a long time, they've been getting worse. In fact, the 2020 Atlantic hurricane season was the most active recorded to date. One of the major reasons is how warm the ocean water has become. High-temperature ocean water can be catastrophic, causing rapid intensification of storm systems that leaves forecasters little to no time to warn people of the danger to come—as was the case with Hurricane Katrina when we watched it quickly escalate from a Category 3 to a Category 5 within a matter of a few days. Officials might decide against evacuation for a Category 2 storm one day and wake up the next to a Category 4, and by then it's difficult to move quickly.

In the case of Hurricane Katrina, there is much discus-sion about the failure of the levees—structures built to hold back floodwater during storms—which were built and funded by the US government. Due to budget issues, the levees had been left incomplete for years and contained weaknesses that were discovered in prior storms. Most of the weak spots in the levees threatened Black neighborhoods, which many argue is why they were ignored.

SIDE NOTE: There's a strong mistrust of government and power among the disenfranchised, particularly in Louisiana. During the Great Mississippi Flood in 1927, which was the worst natural disaster in US history until Hurricane Katrina, the government used dynamite to blow up a levee in a poor Black neighborhood outside of New Orleans's city center in order to relieve the tensions on other levees and avert the floodwaters away from more affluent parts of the city.

During Hurricane Betsy in 1965, the majority-Black Lower Ninth Ward withstood the worst of the storm damage, with an estimated 164,000 homes flooded, mainly in that area. There was little impact to other parts of the city. Many people accused the government of deliberately breaching the levees once again, though that was never proven. But the accusation was made again during Katrina.

Though racism may well have been a factor in the failures of the levees, the fact is that we cannot depend on any levee system, no matter how equitable or perfectly built, to sufficiently protect us from the effects of climate change and the rise in sea levels. New Orleans, which is mostly below sea level and surrounded by bodies of water, will continue to be difficult to protect as sea levels continue to rise and storm surges become worse—as the "unprecedented" becomes the new normal. Regardless of the structures we build, we cannot disregard the realities of climate change forever. As the oceans grow warmer and storms become worse, these types of experiences will become not only more common but also more extreme. If major changes are not made, coastal cities will disappear under floodwaters while drought and wildfires decimate inland areas. Climate change is now, and we cannot keep ignoring it.

Tanisha never did return to Xavier University. Although the school eventually reopened about five months later, by that time she was resettled in another city. I never had the chance to see the Xavier campus, and at the age of only seventeen, I had to begin seriously considering what areas of the country were safe places to live in terms of climate change. But my cousins and I were some of the lucky ones. Because while our own Katrina stories didn't end in tragedy, many people's did.

The truth is, most places are vulnerable to climate change, whether it's hurricanes, ice storms, tornadoes, wildfires, blizzards, droughts, or something else. And if they're not impacted now, they will be soon. The climate crisis is one of the most critical and pressing issues we need to address as global citizens. But we can't do it alone. No single person's efforts, no matter how heroic, will be enough to address the problem. It's going to take all of us.

Full disclosure: I have always hated group projects—all too often, a few dedicated people end up carrying the whole team, or a few jerks end up dragging the entire group down. But every once in a while, the right group comes together at the right time, and extraordinary things can happen. Addressing global warming is the ultimate group project—and we can't afford to have any slackers. We need everyone to pitch in to reduce the collective impact that we are having on the environment. But in order to achieve our goal, we need to understand what changes need to be made and what we can do to help. Basically, we need to be sure we understand the assignment. To help us with that, I turned to some good friends who are experts in the environmentalism space to find out what actions they suggest in order to do our part.

Interview with WILLY and JO LORENZ
Environmental activists and influencers

Because climate change is a global crisis, I felt it was important to get the perspective of someone—or *someones*—living abroad. Willy and Jo Lorenz lived in Australia during the 2019–2020 bushfire season, which was one of the worst on record. It destroyed countless animals' habitats and created thick smoke similar to that emitted by a volcano. The fires were so large and intense, they burned 27 million acres, an area larger than Portugal. And yet people around the world seem to have quickly moved on and forgotten about what happened.

WILLY: There's this term, "the bystander effect," where you can be on a train in New York City, a subway, and someone falls over, and people go, "Oh, not my problem." They step over the person. That's what's happening with climate change. Everyone goes, "Someone else will manage that. I'm a good person. I'll recycle. Everything will be fine. I don't need to worry about that." The fact is, we all need to worry about it. Everyone thinks there's some magic technology in the future that's going to save us all.

JO: Which I was completely guilty of when I was younger. But as Willy and I have seen the effects of climate change, we've become very passionate about it. There's no magical tool that sucks the CO_2 out of the sky, so we have to figure out how we're going to do this. We have to start looking at the fact that if the sea levels continue to rise, certain countries will be underwater while others will be on fire.

So often we disregard extreme weather, considering it normal, and when the impact is unusually destructive, we claim it is a rare disaster. But the truth is, these extreme weather trends are predictable and scientists say they are getting worse. As Jo mentioned, we can put off thinking about it—sure, 2050 isn't for years—but by then hundreds of millions of people will be permanently displaced by the rising sea levels.

A study shows that most parts of densely populated Shanghai, China, are expected to be covered in water in the next thirty years. *Thirty years!* Mumbai and other parts of India are in the same situation. By the next century, many island nations and even some of the world's most famous cities will be covered in water or will experience near-unlivable flooding regularly. And rising sea levels are far from the only threat. Many parts of the world are at risk of being decimated by droughts, typhoons, hurricanes, wildfires, mudslides, and other natural disasters. Continuing to ignore the problem of climate change or putting off addressing it will not change the reality.

WILLY: There's a lot of false narrative about how we're going to destroy the world. The world's going to be just fine. We're destroying the habitat for *us*. There's so many of these things that we've tipped off but will only happen a long way down the road. That in itself makes it really hard to tell people that we need to do something, because they don't see it . . . It's so far down the road that it doesn't affect them. We're not going to see the world destroyed. We're going to see some bad things happen like we're already seeing bad things happen.

Bad things are happening. Russia's on fire. The boreal forest in Canada and Russia is on fire in the summer. That's not even touched upon in the international news. Those forest fires are contributing CO_2, but not many people live there, so people don't care. That's just one of the many different areas of destruction that's happening today and we're not paying attention.

Many people are aware of the effects of climate change but feel like it isn't impacting them directly—at least not on a daily basis—and so they're not motivated to act, particularly if the actions required are significant. But not everyone is insulated from the effects of climate change. People in poverty are among the first to experience the results of climate change, and they often bear the brunt of it, while wealthy people can afford to live in less-impacted areas, as we saw in New Orleans. Low-income communities of color also tend to bear the brunt of pollution and harm from fossil-fuel infrastructure, such as fracking and pipelines. The system of such infrastructure is based on the idea of sacrifice zones, or areas that are considered inconsequential if destroyed. Unfortunately, people in poverty, especially people of color, have less power, and the concerns of their communities are regularly ignored.

JO: The harsh reality is that as we've known it, if you have a whole bunch of money, you can buy your way out of climate change. You can move to a country where it's not going to affect you. You can get a good job and continue to make more money and provide for your future and your children's future and all the rest of it. If you have this privilege and these opportunities, you can get out of it. If a natural disaster is coming, you can take off. So people aspire to just buy their way out of climate change rather than confronting it.

WILLY: Climate change is only seen as an inconvenience for the rich, and it's literal death and destruction for the poor and marginalized communities around the world. If you want an example of this, Ted Cruz fled Texas when they had a deadly ice storm in 2021 to go on vacation with his family in Cancún. Rich people who are inconvenienced can use their money to escape climate change.

JO: Australia's prime minister did the same thing in 2020 during the bushfires. Our prime minister, Scott Morrison, jumped on a plane to Hawaii when it was happening. All of Australia just went, "What? Are you actually going to just flee and not do anything?"

WILLY: This is when Sydney was covered by smoke for the first time ever and all of the rich white people were aghast, like, "Why is this happening to us, oh my God, when we're in Sydney?"

Meanwhile this happens in other parts of the world all the time; it just doesn't affect the wealthy.

JO: These aren't bad people. They're just people who thought it was someone else's problem, or a problem for a long way away, and suddenly they realized it was their problem.

Many people might care more about the future of our planet and global warming, but they don't feel as if it is truly urgent or that they can meaningfully contribute to solving the problem. Much of the reason they feel that way is because of the media. Media has not only normalized these natural disasters, but they often provide platforms for climate change deniers and treat global warming as a casual political topic up for debate rather than a call to action.

WILLY: The media has a lot to do with why people don't care and don't have the correct information. Rupert Murdoch, the Fox News founder, is from Australia, and he owns 71 percent of the newspapers in Australia. So 71 percent of what people read in Australia reflects his views, which are anti–climate change and pro-industry.

Many people have been conditioned for decades through news media and other sources to deny or ignore climate change. All of a sudden, they're like, "Wait a sec . . . Maybe this is real." Meanwhile, there're a lot of people who live in poverty in the world who are not going to be okay. It's not even an emerging-country problem. Look at what happened in Texas. While Ted Cruz took off for a vacation, people literally died because of climate change, because they lived in poverty and could not escape. In America, the richest country in the world, they died because the government failed them on climate change.

> **SIDE NOTE:** Because he had the money and privilege to do so, Texas senator Ted Cruz left Texas during a deadly winter storm in 2021 that left millions without power or safe drinking water—even though he was supposed to be on the ground performing the duties of his leadership position and solving problems.

Before the topic of climate change was a common discussion, scientists who studied the effects of global warming warned world leaders (including American presidents), oil companies, and other industries about the dangers ahead. So many people knew about global warming and the potential harm but intentionally kept the information from society so that they could continue doing business as usual without pushbacks. Many of the powerful politicians and business owners that own media programming had investments in the industries that were contributing to climate change, so they went above and beyond to make sure that the information wasn't provided to the people. Because of this, for a long time many people didn't even realize that driving cars, eating meat and dairy for every meal, or building big factories that billowed smoke were affecting the environment. That may sound unbelievable, but this was during the same time that cigarette companies went out of their way to hide the fact that cigarette smoke causes cancer. Money is a powerful thing, especially in capitalist societies.

So now that many people, even those with ties to the industries responsible, acknowledge that global warming is real and is having a negative effect on the world, what can we do to confront it?

WILLY: There're two things that we can do: mitigation and adaptation. Mitigation means we create less pollution. We don't put out as much CO_2. But the number-two thing in our arsenal to deal with climate change is adaptation. That is what we saw a severe lack of in Texas, because they did not adapt their energy infrastructure to severe cold spells.

JO: And it shouldn't be just up to the individual to make these personal changes in their day to day. No matter how much recycling we do, no matter how many bamboo forks we use, nothing will happen unless the people at the top, the government, make significant change.

WILLY: Government and corporations have tricked us into thinking, as individuals, that we can solve this on our own.

SIDE NOTE: Too young to cast a ballot? You can still make your voice heard by politicians. As Willy advises: "In addition to voting the right politicians in, **lobbying** can be extremely powerful. It's effective to send a letter to your local government officials if you have time."

There shouldn't be any onus on people who have day-to-day problems to be thinking that they have a responsibility to manage all of climate change themselves.

JO: To Willy's point, it shouldn't be up to the younger generation to fix this, yet the reality is, they've been left with this big honking burden to shoulder. I think if they think about things in small areas and what they can do—their little area that they can focus on and how they can sustain a better livelihood for themselves and those around them—that would be a comfort for them. And they can prepare themselves now to be informed voters, as well as participating in the discussions that can inform others.

In a democracy, politicians win elections based on their proposal of ideas and policies that appeal to a majority of the public. The more of us that insist upon action by sending a lobby letter or email, the more attention the subject will receive. So let's force our politicians' hands by being the majority that gives a damn about climate and humanity's collective future!

This is important! We have to understand that although we all need to pitch in and live more sustainably, it is essential that policy makers work on all fronts to move industry and transportation systems away from burning fossil fuels to more climate-friendly, sustainable energy sources. And we can all play a role in advocating for these things.

Recently, the world has seen many prominent young environmental activists come to the forefront of the movement. Although the burden of climate change shouldn't be left to the younger generations, there is no denying that they will inherit the impact of hundreds of years of general disregard for the environment.

One thing we are seeing young people fight for is the right to clean water. As we watch our fresh water sources shrink—drying up in the unnatural heat—I cannot help but think of how access to clean water has increasingly become an indicator of privilege. When I went to graduate school in San Diego, California, I was shocked to learn that almost 90 percent of the drinking water was imported from Northern California and the Colorado River. Although we may not realize it, many places in America are water insecure, and without water transportation technology, many would be unlivable.

Limited access to clean water has often been portrayed as an issue of emerging countries, but recently a light has been shone on the limited access to clean water here in the United States. I wanted to speak with someone who is experiencing the effects of years of pollution and water insecurity, because unfortunately, it is one of the most difficult issues we will face as climate change intensifies.

Interview with AMARIYANNA (MARI) COPENY

Clean water and environmental activist and high-school student

When Mari Copeny was just eight years old, she wrote a letter to the president at the time, Barack Obama, begging him to pay attention to what was going on in her hometown of Flint, Michigan. After local politicians decided to change their water source, high levels of lead were detected in the drinking water and it was discovered that residents were becoming ill from the toxic water. In 2016, President Obama traveled to Flint and declared a federal state of emergency. Mari's efforts to raise awareness of the crisis in Flint earned her the nickname "Little Miss Flint." Today, Mari is in high school and is still working hard to raise awareness of the water crisis and to bring clean water to communities around the United States.

When she is not fighting for clean water, she likes to skateboard, draw, watch anime, and, of course, sleep.

MARI: The water crisis in Flint, Michigan, began in 2014 when the city government switched our drinking water supply from Detroit's system to the Flint River, which was polluted and corrupted the pipes with lead and other bacteria. It was making people extremely sick and causing them to die.

The choice to switch from using Detroit's water supply to the Flint River was purely due to a desire for the city government to cut costs. But the Flint River has been heavily polluted and poisoned for over a century, first as an unofficial waste dumping site for the many industrial factories in the area and then as a dumping site for the city's raw sewage waste treatment plant. As Mari said, the corrosive water ate through the pipes and the pipes began seeping lead into the already toxic water. Right after the switch in 2014, residents were complaining of smelly, poor-tasting, and discolored water, which they suspected was causing skin rashes and hair loss.

SIDE NOTE: According to the Centers for Disease Control and Prevention, "Exposure to lead can seriously harm a child's health, including damage to the brain and nervous system, slowed growth and development, learning and behavior problems, and hearing and speech problems. No safe blood lead level in children has been identified."

MARI: What inspired me to become an activist was seeing that my little sister was getting a really bad rash from the water and it made me upset. So I thought, *Maybe people will listen to me if I can spread more info about the type of stuff that's happening, so that people like my sister won't have to suffer.* I enjoyed talking to people about it, so then I began doing bigger things like water drives and events. And now I am making my very own water filter. Because seven years later and the water in Flint is still not fixed. They switched back the water supply, but the chemicals they're dumping in it to try to fix the lead problem it caused are also very irritating to our skin. And since my family is close to the water plant, we get a majority of the chemicals. We do have our filter, but it only works so well.

Water is essential, which is why clean water is proclaimed a human right under international law. However, more than thirty million Americans drink water that is in violation of safety rules.

MARI: I want the government to fix the water in Flint and everywhere else that has bad water—because it's not just Flint that has a water crisis. There are other states that have a water crisis. It's not talked about enough, but America has a water crisis. People think that the water crisis here inside Flint was unique to Flint. No! There are other states and cities that have really bad water. For instance, Newark, New Jersey. They have way worse lead levels than Flint. There's so many different cities and states.

The one thing that most of these places have in common is the residents are poor and often disproportionately people of color. The Michigan Civil Rights Commission did a study in 2017 that found that the negligent governmental response to the Flint water contamination was a "result of systemic racism." The same report detailed the long history of **segregation** and corrupt practices that denied non-whites access to household utilities such as water and sewage.

MARI: I think because Flint is predominantly Black—66 percent Black—they didn't think it was important to help us quickly, or give us basic human necessities like clean water.

During the height of the water crisis, those who could afford to fled. But many people there did not have the financial means to relocate, and many people who wanted to walk away were unable to sell their homes because it is illegal to sell a home with health hazards—hazards such as toxic water and eroded pipes. Because of this, the values of homes in Flint have dropped drastically.

Today, the pipes are still not fixed and the problem remains unresolved. There are filters that can be used, but most of these become corroded after just a few weeks of use. Many people in Flint do not trust the tap water at all and will not touch it.

Every day, I take a shower, put fridge-made ice in my huge cup of tap water, wash my produce and food in running water, and don't think twice about if doing so is safe. Yet for more than two million Americans—and for hundreds of millions of people around the world—these simple acts are unimaginable luxuries. This problem is not as far removed from us as many of us may think as we go about our day. This is real.

So what can young people do to bring awareness to this issue?

MARI: They can spread awareness about the topic. They can use social media. We have the whole world at our fingertips through cell phones and the internet. We can so easily just make a Twitter post about it and, boom, that info's getting spread so that we can get more people to know about it and continue to spread awareness about the topic. They can also support efforts to help.

Mari knows all about creating and supporting efforts to help. She is currently partnering with Hydroviv to create her own filter! During her preliminary testing, the product has outperformed all other major filter brands that are currently on the market.

Despite all the adversity she faces in her effort to secure clean water for her city, Mari clearly loves Flint.

MARI: I just want people to know that even though you may think that Flint is a bad place because we have bad water, it's not. It's my home. We have unique things here—for instance, we have all these really cool murals and artwork around the city—and there's just generally nice people here. Please don't assume that Flint's a bad place because we have really bad water. If you were to ever come visit Flint, I would take you to my favorite bookstore that's filled with a whole bunch of books by Black authors. I'd take you to see the giant Flint sign we have and we would probably go to the farmers' market. There's a really good farmers' market here.

I really love where I live. I just want clean water.

SIDE NOTE: If you're ever in Flint, be sure to stop by the Comma Bookstore. You can also order books from them online!

Hearing a fourteen-year-old have to explain this almost brought me to tears. Whereas Mari should be busy skateboarding or watching anime with her friends after school, she instead works on water filter designs in her free time or is discussing environmental racism with people like me and making a plea for support in her mission to help others avoid being poisoned by the water the government provides to them. While most of this pollution is at the hands of large corporations or the failure of government regulations, it is those that contribute the least to the problem that suffer the most. And although it's not fair, it's up to the people to demand change.

Whether you're one of the two million Americans without access to clean drinking water, whether you know someone who lived in New Orleans when Hurricane Katrina hit—or whether you're someone like me, who hasn't yet experienced these things directly but knows that's due to luck and privilege, and not because we're immune—the time has come to take action. There is finite space on this planet, and after destroying so much of our natural resources, it is only logical to assume that anyone's backyard could be next.

It's long past time we *all* fully committed to the biggest group project of our lifetimes.

To find out more about how you can help put a stop to climate change and environmental racism, visit: BetterThanWeFoundItBook.com.

3
SLEDGEHAMMERS AND GLASS CEILINGS

Frederick Joseph on Being a Feminist and Womanist Accomplice
Featuring **Brittany Packnett Cunningham** and **Mehcad Brooks**

A NOTE FROM PORSCHE

Patriarchy, by definition, is a social system that places **cisgender** men at the forefront of power, leadership, decision making, and the roles that encompass those things. Historically, not all societies have been patriarchal, but it is a system that has long been practiced by the colonial powers that have led us to the patriarchal society that we live in today.

When any one group is favored, other groups are inherently *disfavored*. Which is why in patriarchal systems, things such as homophobia, **transphobia**, sexism, and **misogyny** are incredibly common. Where sexism is the belief that women are unequal to men, misogyny enforces these beliefs by showing up as nuanced hate and punishment toward anyone who does not conform to the social expectations of what women should be. For instance, sexism is the assumption that women are just better nurturers and because of that it is more natural for a mother to stay home and take care of the children while the father goes to work, whereas misogyny is when family and friends ridicule the couple that makes the decision to reverse these roles (the mother working full-time while the father stays home with the children), claiming that he is "less of a man" or she is "not a good mother." Another example of sexism is the belief that women are simply not natural-born leaders the way that men supposedly are. Misogyny, then, is refusing to vote for a female presidential candidate or undermining and working against her candidacy.

While it is vital to listen to women's perspectives on feminism and womanism, I personally feel we also need more men to be having discussions about sexism and misogyny and analyzing not only the power they wield but also what they can do with that power. If we want patriarchal beliefs and practices to come to an end, we must ask men to dissect and cease certain behaviors. These behaviors may show up in different ways cross-culturally, but it is important that men understand the power they have and how they can be allies.

With that in mind, I asked my husband—a feminist and womanist who is an incredibly thoughtful and self-reflective ally—to write this chapter. I can think of no better opportunity for him to practice that allyship than for him to speak to you about feminism and womanism and what we need from people to break away from sexist expectations that are hurting us all.

　　—Porsche

As a Black man, I often speak about the importance of white people not just being allies of non-white communities, hoping to see **white supremacy** come to an end, but rather **accomplices** or co-conspirators—people who are actively engaged and taking action to help dismantle white supremacy. I feel the same is also necessary for those of us who benefit from the patriarchy. My personal belief is that if someone feels that the oppression of someone else is wrong, they should help make a change—and those who are benefiting from that oppression are often best positioned to dismantle the oppressive systems. For me, a cisgender **heterosexual** man who benefits from the patriarchy, helping to dismantle the patriarchy means listening to and supporting the women in my life, and supporting women's rights to **equity** and equality. It means stepping up and writing this chapter so that Porsche didn't have to.

Supporting women's rights to equity and equality doesn't just benefit women; it benefits everyone. How many scientific breakthroughs, artistic achievements, brilliant inventions, and vital perspectives have we have missed out on because of the patriarchy, because women either weren't given access or opportunities to live up to their potential or weren't acknowledged when they did? Everyone should have the ability to be whomever they want to be and do whatever they want to do, so long as doing so doesn't harm anyone else. By limiting who some people can be or who they can become, we limit the potential of our entire society.

I have many people to thank for helping me go from being a passive feminist ally to an active feminist accomplice, but one specific person comes to mind when I reflect on how I realized I needed to grow and actively do something: my friend

Keisha Randolph, a young Black woman once also known to many by her stage name, "K Torch."

Keisha was a rapper who earned the name K Torch (short for Keisha the Human Torch) because when it came to rapping, everything she said and wrote was fire. But long before Keisha was setting instrumentals and opponents in rap battles ablaze, she was just the ten-year-old girl whom I met when her family moved into the **housing project** building next to the one my grandmother lived in.

Growing up, I spent a great deal of time at my grandmother's apartment. She was from an era when neighbors were in many ways like family, so when Keisha's family moved in, my grandmother not only befriended them; she also made me become friends with the two children in their family, Patrick (Pat) and Keisha, who were twins the same age as me. Though my grandmother would have forced us to be close whether we wanted to be or not, becoming friends with them was fairly easy, as we shared many common interests—including a deep love for music.

All of us grew up in musically gifted families. My mom, their father, one of my uncles, and their grandparents had all been singers at some point in their lives, and both of Pat and Keisha's grandparents also played multiple instruments. Needless to say, music wasn't just constantly around us; it had been in the blood of our two families for generations. But while we grew up with a love for the music our families grew up with, such as soul, gospel, jazz, and R&B, we had something different as well. Something that contained a piece of all those genres and was born around the same time we were. That thing was hip-hop.

Growing up in New York in the 1990s and early 2000s, almost every Black and Latinx person I knew was a hip-hop fan, and the culture was booming. What had started in the South Bronx and West Bronx with a boom box and break dancing on cardboard was now suddenly in films, sports, and fashion and had spread to countries around the world. Many Black and Latinx communities around America were filled with people who cherished hip-hop because it showed love to our urban culture, and in return, the culture showed that love right back. But there was no one more proud and more dedicated to hip-hop than New Yorkers. It was our child.

One of the things that made hip-hop special was that anyone could be a part of it, and more importantly, anyone could create it—even three poor Black kids from Yonkers, New York. But as much as Pat loved hip-hop, he couldn't rap or write rhymes to save his life. I still cringe at the number of times I watched him try to find clever words to rhyme with *Yonkers*: *honkers, conkers, bonkers*—ugh. I was much better than Pat—though that wasn't saying much—but I was never one of the greats. Keisha, though—well, Keisha was something different.

There are people who love things so much that they eat, breathe, and sleep them. That was Keisha and hip-hop. From the moment she heard Jay-Z's *The Blueprint* album, everything changed. It only takes a moment for someone to fall in love, and she fell hard. "But did you hear what he said? Do you hear that beat? I have to do THIS!" From that day on, Keisha didn't just dabble in hip-hop for fun like we did; she wanted to become one of the people we idolized.

Keisha filled stacks of rhyme books, stayed up until the

wee hours of the morning to hear her favorite rappers inter-viewed on Hot 97 (the top hip-hop and R&B station in New York), spent every penny of her allowance on CDs, and had this huge radio she would carry everywhere. I mean *every-where*! Laundromat—Keisha has her radio. School—Keisha has her radio (until the teacher confiscates it). Basketball court—Keisha has her radio.

A few people used to joke and call her "Radio Raheem," like the character from Spike Lee's film *Do the Right Thing*. She despised being called that. "Raheem dies; I'm trying to live forever."

"Nobody lives forever, Keisha," I remember saying.

"Legends do. Raheem never had time to become a legend; he was a statistic," she responded.

We were thirteen when she said that, and I don't know that I fully grasped it until I was much older. In a country where Black beings are often relegated to becoming known for how they were taken from this world, Keisha was deter-mined to be known for more. Not just as a Black person, but specifically as a young Black woman who found an outlet that offered her a freedom so rare within an anti-Black patri-archal world.

By the time we were about fourteen, Keisha had battled Pat and me enough that he and I both knew our talents lay outside of hip-hop, and Keisha knew that she needed actual competition. There were always guys rapping outside in the neighborhood, and everyone around knew who was good and who wasn't. We even had rap battles that became so large that there were occasional rap-offs, sort of like sports playoffs but for rapping. But Keisha never dared to display her talents in those public spaces, as there were rarely, if ever, any women allowed to take part. Which is why in the eyes of most people around the neighborhood, Keisha was simply the young woman walking around with the radio. To them she wasn't a part of hip-hop; she was a spectator. But the three of us knew she was more.

It wasn't just the hip-hop community itself that excluded Keisha. Her own mother didn't want her to display her gifts. "Rapping and all of that is for boys. Don't you want to do something else? What about dance?" "What kind of boys are going to like you walking around with that big ol' radio?" Keisha received these affirmations of the patriarchy from her mother almost daily. Like many women, her mother had grown up being conditioned by messaging about what women were and weren't supposed to do. When you are taught limiting and oppressive ideas frequently enough, it's nearly impossible not to internalize them and then start teaching them to other people. Everyone who was rapping in our neighborhood, and just about every rapper on television and on the radio, was a man. Was it any wonder, then, that Keisha's mother—and so many others—believed that "rapping is for boys"?

So how did Keisha become "K Torch"? Well, ironically, it was because of a moment where she faced two trademarks of the patriarchy: misogyny and sexism.

There are some memories that stay with you with perfect clarity, the types of memories you will probably be able to describe every aspect of until the day you pass on. Keisha's first four public rap battles are some of those memories for me. It was a hot day in June, and our freshman year of high school had just ended earlier that week. To celebrate, we decided to do two of our favorite things: pick up some Jamaican food from a part of town that was about a twenty-five-minute walk away and watch old episodes of the television show *Martin*. That day, Keisha had decided to wear a sundress that her mother bought for her to celebrate the end of freshman year. She hated dresses, but figured if she gave her mother that one thing, maybe her mother would stop bothering her about all the other things she wanted her to do, such as wearing makeup and going to the nail salon with her.

Keisha had made a new mix CD the night before and put it in her radio so we could listen as we walked to get food. Whenever we went places and Keisha was playing music there was always a lot of attention on us—which I suppose is to be expected of a group of kids walking around blasting '90s hip-hop from a radio the size of a refrigerator. But as we walked that day, the attention might have been drawn in by the music, but it soon centered firmly on Keisha and the sundress she didn't want to wear.

At one point we encountered a group of about ten guys, all of them at least four or five years older than us, standing on the sidewalk we were walking on. As we got closer, I recognized a few of their faces from around the way. I was specifically familiar with two named Funk and Mellow, who were pretty widely known for rapping and producing music. In fact, there were rumors that Funk was going to sign a record deal.

As we walked through the group, one of the guys loudly said, "You wearin' that dress, ma. Why don't you leave them and come over here so we could listen to something with you?" Sadly, I had heard plenty of women catcalled before, including my own mother when I was a young child. But in all the years I had been hanging out with Keisha, this was the first time I saw it happen to her.

SIDE NOTE: Being an accomplice isn't always easy—and it's not always obvious what it should look like. Take the catcalling, for example. Even as I grew up, I always felt powerless to do anything when I witnessed catcalling, as it was often large groups of men taking part in the act while I was either with far fewer people or simply smaller and younger than them. Standing up against those men also meant potential violence—which could quickly escalate into a dangerous situation.

Still, I often think back on those moments from my youth and wonder if there was anything I could have done to be the accomplice or even ally I'm trying to be today. Could I have tried to speak up or defuse situations that weren't as dangerous? (Part of being an ally is reflecting on past actions and choices and asking yourself why you did what you did. Unpacking our behaviors and thoughts is one of the first steps to being better for those around us—and ourselves.)

I didn't know how to respond at first, and I suppose Pat didn't, either. But since Keisha hadn't given the guy the attention he wanted, he grabbed her arm. "You hear me talking to you?"

"Get your hands off me!" Keisha pulled her arm from the guy's grasp, dropping her radio in the process. Pat shoved the guy who had assaulted his sister. Though the guy was much

older and bigger than Pat, he fell to the ground. I followed
Pat's lead by shoving the person closest to me. He didn't fall
and immediately swung at me. (Thankfully he missed.)

SIDE NOTE: Sometimes it *is* obvious what you should do as
an accomplice, though—or what you *shouldn't* do. While
participating in a fight seemed like the right thing to do at
the time, I now know that it would've been much better to
confront the group of men without violence—and to check
on Keisha.

Before we ended up in an all-out brawl we had no chance
of winning, Mellow spoke up. "Yo, relax! I know them. Let
them rock."

"You know them?" asked the guy who had grabbed Keisha,
picking himself up from the ground.

"Yeah, that's what I said. I know them," Mellow responded.
"That's Radio Raheem from the block. Always walking around
with that big-ass radio listening to rap. She a superfan or
something. Let them rock." The scuffle ended almost instan-
taneously, and a moment later, one of the guys handed Keisha
her radio.

Keisha snatched her radio away from the guy in frustration. "My name isn't Raheem, and I'm not some superfan
groupie chick. I'm a rapper. I have bars." As soon as the words
left her mouth, all the guys began laughing.

"Oooooh, you a rapper, huh?" Mellow chuckled.

"Yeah, that's what I said, right?" Keisha responded.

Pat looked at the group and then at Keisha, obviously
angry at how his sister had been disrespected physically and

now was being disrespected over her talent. "Forget them, Keisha. Let's go."

"You should listen to him and leave, sweetheart," the guy who had grabbed her said.

She stared at him for a moment, and there was something in her eyes I hadn't seen before. It wasn't rage as much as the desire to destroy what was in her way. She began to nod and smile slightly, as if she had just assured herself of something. "I know one of y'all raps. What's up? Somebody battle me."

The group began to laugh harder until Mellow spoke up again: "You're killing me. I'm trying to help you. Get out of here."

Keisha didn't flinch. She stared at the guy who had grabbed her arm. "What's up? Y'all scared to get beat by a girl?"

If you ever want to convince toxic men or boys to do something, question their perceived dominance over a woman. The ego and entitlement that mediocre people develop because of the unearned power and privilege they hold is often their biggest downfall.

The guy I had shoved walked over to Keisha. "I got a couple of bars. I'll battle you. I'm fine with whatever. Ladies first."

She looked at him and said, "No ladies here. Just rappers. Go ahead."

The guy who had grabbed her said to his friend, "Yo, Kev, body her so we can get back to what we were doing. Get her and that ugly sundress out of here." As is often the case, when misogynistic men don't get what they want, they resort to belittling the women who won't give it to them. This is the danger of men not being taught that "no" is a valid answer from women. A danger that can quickly evolve from verbal assaults to life-or-death situations.

The guy I had shoved—Kev, apparently—began rapping. I don't remember what he said, but I do remember that it was terrible. (Obviously I'm biased, but I would be honest if he said something decent. He didn't.) Keisha responded by absolutely destroying him. I had never seen her battle anyone other than me and Pat—clearly, she had been holding back with us.

I don't remember Keisha's entire rap, but I do remember how she finished it:

I'm a girl so you tried to put me in a box,
but all y'all got was your boy put in a box.

Her whole rap was really good, but that last line was perfect. But as is always the case with sexists and misogynists, the guys were quick to diminish her. They all acknowledged that she surprised them, but they weren't impressed because Kev "couldn't rap, anyway." So she obliged them by battling two other people who they claimed could rap. Though they were much better than Kev, Keisha demolished them both. She probably could've gone easier on them and still soundly defeated them, but Keisha had something to prove. Maybe more to herself than anyone else.

"So who's the best?" Keisha asked, in a tone that reminded

me of when Maximus says "Are you not entertained?" in the film *Gladiator*. Funk calmly walked up to her and responded, "I am." Keisha looked at him; I could tell based on her slight shift in disposition that just like me, she had heard that Funk was good—though none of us knew how good.

"I'll go first or second, it's whatever to me," Funk said, cool and confident. "We stop when everyone around us says it's a wrap."

For those not familiar with battle rap, the rules are basically that the rappers go back and forth until the audience becomes loud and excited enough about a rap to deem that person the winner. This might not seem like the soundest way to choose a winner, but trust me, it's been working for generations.

"Cool. I'll go first," Keisha responded, before delivering some of the best punchlines I'd ever heard from her, taking sharp verbal jabs at Funk and his friends. But Funk's rebuttal was simply better, and it was easy to tell that he was the more polished rapper. He finished with something to the effect of:

> *You and your boy toys should have went another way*
> *I'm a real man, you not playing with Ken*
> *Oh you thought I was one them*
> *Nah, I'm a predator looking at prey*
> *This ain't a battle, this is the lion's den*
> *Matter fact I'm more exotic, call me a leviathan*
> *Get a Ouija board, your ancestors will ask why you*
> *   tryin' him.*

He was clever, poised, and confident, all the things you need to win a rap battle. But just as everyone was praising his response (even Pat and I, because fair is fair) and preparing to declare him the winner, Keisha started rapping again. This is the moment that changed everything. (I recall this word for word because we've talked about it so much over the years, ha):

A lion's den?
Y'all on the block looking like you auditioning for
    Boyz II Men
Concerned with me being a female, your priorities
    are wrong
I'm focused on who, what, where, why,
And when do you want to get eaten alive
I'll be your demise, I'm a lioness talking to a feast
The rumble in the jungle and you're in the ring with a beast
If your boy touches me again he'll find out this heart
    not sweet
I'm ready to eat, he's lanky, not even worth it for me
    to devour
Maybe instead I'll rain fire and brimstone on his head
    like meteor shower
Y'all just a bunch of sheep rollin' with creeps, but I'ma
    get y'all together
Keisha's that thing you heard go bump in the night
But y'all too worried about a dress, you should have
    prepared better for the quest
A bunch of Frodos, look how I'm baggin' 'em up,
Your ears are ringin', but I'm not even giving you little
    guys my best
Next time I'm here, refer to me as Ms. Randolph

A wizard with the bars, something like Gandalf
This supposed to be battle rap, but I'm dancing on 'em
Got his own friends bop their heads and saying mmm
*   after every line*
On the block like they're mobsters, but y'all just a boy
*   band*
Y'all went Hanson on 'em.

It felt like the world stood frozen for an eternity. No one was saying anything, but everyone was looking back and forth at one another. Then suddenly Mellow jumped in the air and exclaimed, "It's over! It's over! That's enough! That's enough!"

All the guys started jumping and huddled around Funk, berating him for the loss he had just taken. Meanwhile, Pat and I huddled around Keisha yelling, "Queen Keisha!" Keisha just stood there smiling, reveling in what had just happened. She didn't simply beat Funk; she beat him and three other rappers, and it was her first time battling anyone other than me or Pat.

A few moments later, Funk cut through everyone and stood in front of Keisha. "You got bars. Like real bars. You a flamethrower. What they call you?"

"My name is Keisha."

"Nah. Not your name—what they call you? What's your rap name?" Funk asked.

"Oh, I don't have one," Keisha said frankly.

"All that fire and no name to go with it?" Mellow chimed in.

"Right. Gotta have a name," Funk said. "All that fire . . . fire . . . like the Human Torch. Yeah, that's it. K Torch."

Keisha just stared at him for a moment as if she couldn't

comprehend the magnitude of what was happening. She looked over at Pat, who smiled, and then she looked back at Funk and said simply, "Let's get it."

K Torch was born.

Though they never apologized for how their friend had disrespected her, Funk and Mellow took Keisha under their wing. She let what they did go because she understood how being around them could help her rap career, especially once Funk had signed his record deal and was using Mellow as his primary producer.

> **SIDE NOTE:** This story is an example of how women are often forced to choose between standing up for themselves and/or other women and accepting disrespect or trauma to receive a seat at the tables that are often controlled by men.

K Torch began to battle anyone and everyone who was willing—and never lost. By the time we were seventeen, thanks in part to being around Funk and Mellow, Keisha learned how to turn her ability to write and deliver lines into a talent for making actual songs. Keisha started making mixes with her songs, which were becoming more popular in the neighborhood and around our city. It got to the point where people were lauding her talent so much, they began to compare her to many of the rappers we idolized, and her getting a record deal seemed like more of a question of when rather than if. Eventually, she made a demo of songs she had not only written and rapped herself but also produced. The demo was amazing. I mean, like, one of the best hip-hop projects I've ever heard in my life.

We all knew she was going to be a world-renowned artist. Not just because she had talent; a lot of people have talent. But because she was hungry and loved what she was eating. When you combine talent, passion, and determination—the sky's the limit.

At least that's what we thought before she started bringing the demo to record labels.

As I mentioned before, Keisha didn't enjoy wearing dresses, getting her nails done, or many other things that are often considered stereotypical interests of women. She wore what she felt comfortable in, which often meant a pair of Jordan sneakers and sweatpants, and she kept her hair in a high messy bun. This didn't go over well with many of the people—primarily white men—at the record labels, who would tell her that she looked too much like a "tomboy" and needed to dress sexier.

One of the symptoms of the patriarchy is how women, especially Black women, are often hypersexualized and viewed first and foremost as objects for the gaze of men. Those male record label execs weren't interested in what Keisha wanted; they were interested in what they and others like them wanted. Consider, too, that Keisha was only seventeen when she was being told by adult men to "dress sexier." Too often young Black women are adultified—seen and treated as older than they are because Black people are often not perceived as having innocence.

None of us could understand why Keisha needed to be "sexy" to rap. Jay-Z didn't need to dress sexy. Nas didn't need to dress sexy. Common didn't need to dress sexy. Eventually, Keisha pushed back on the idea when she heard it yet again during a meeting Funk had gotten her with his label to discuss her demo. She told the execs that they were wrong about her needing to be sexy to be a rapper, but they didn't listen. Instead, they became defensive and told her that that might be true if her songs were actually as good as she thought they were, but they weren't—which was why she needed a gimmick. Keisha was devastated. But in reality, they weren't just wrong; they were lying to her—though she didn't realize it until years later.

Instead of giving up or conforming to the appearance that labels wanted her to have, Keisha worked to make her music better. But as years passed and men at record labels continued to **gaslight** her about the quality of her music because she refused to dress or look how they wanted, her love for hip-hop eventually turned into resentment, and her music suffered for it. When we were juniors in college, I remember calling her to check on how she was, and she told me that she was switching her major from music theory to education. "What happened to learning more instruments for the songs you're planning to produce? Plus, how are you going to rap and teach at the same time?" I asked her.

"I was never that good at music. I think I'll be a much better teacher. You know I really like science," she responded.

I don't recall exactly what I said to her after that; I think I spent a few minutes trying to convince her that she was a great artist, but I didn't give it the effort that I should have. Maybe I never did. All of those men gatekeeping and telling her that she wasn't enough, simply because what she was didn't fit into their patriarchal worldview . . . I should have been a man who was just as adamantly telling her that they were wrong, doing whatever I could to support her. I could have been an active accomplice and tried to help figure out ways to promote her music, find opportunities, or simply help reaffirm her confidence that so many other men were working to tear down. Instead, I allowed misogyny to retire K Torch.

Because she had a bunch of music and rhymes she didn't need anymore, she sold them to Funk, who told her that he doubted there was anything he could do with them but took them off her hands to help her pay for school.

A year later, Keisha Randolph graduated from college with a degree in education. She was also accepted into a master's program to become a science teacher. This was the same year that one of Funk's songs was played on the radio for the first time. When we found out that the song was going to be played, everyone from our neighborhood decided to tune in. I was in my car driving home from work when the song first aired—and I had to pull over because I was so angry, shocked, and disappointed.

Funk's first song on the radio was one of the songs he had bought from Keisha—one of the songs that the men at his record label and countless others had said wasn't as good as she thought. Wasn't good enough for radio.

I called Keisha later that night and apologized for not having done more to help her keep going. The conversation was brief; she could barely speak because she was so devastated, and I didn't want to burden her with my guilt, as she was already navigating her own grief. As we hung up the phone, I felt the full weight of my complicity within a system that benefits people like me over people like Keisha. I knew it wasn't enough to be an ally and to disagree with the injustices of the patriarchy. I had to start actively doing my part to support women and to try to change the system to eradicate those injustices.

An Interview with BRITTANY PACKNETT CUNNINGHAM
Award-winning activist, educator, writer, and media host

Most of what I've learned about showing up for women and others oppressed by the patriarchy has been from Black women, who because of the intersections they've existed at, have oftentimes been at the forefront of and been the backbone of many movements for progress and change in our country's history. One of those women is my friend Brittany Packnett Cunningham, a brilliant thinker who has dedicated her life to helping build a better world for everyone who faces oppression, especially Black people.

BRITTANY: I would describe myself as a womanist and an intersectional feminist. I think I use both for two reasons, and both of them unsurprisingly have to do with Black women. I recognize the inherent necessity that Black women found in naming ourselves womanists, when feminism did not include us intentionally, and so I honor the folks on whose shoulders I stand by using the word that they gave us. And I also use the word *intersectional* with a great deal of intention because a Black woman gave that to us too.

I'm constantly thinking about how we live into the idea that nobody is free until everybody is free and how essential the work is to freeing everybody else.

When I really think about it, I think specifically about queer and trans Black women. There are unique experiences of violence and silencing that occur in those spaces because of the ways in which the patriarchy is deeply connected to power. Racism, homophobia, transphobia, sexism, Islamophobia, anti-Semitism—all of it comes down to a power struggle. All of it comes down to the idea that certain people believe that the power belongs inherently to them, and if you're one of these people, then over generations, all of the people who've had traditional forms of power have looked like you, they've spoken like you, they've spoken your language, they've had sex like you, they love who you love, they appear how you appear, they take things by force like you take things by force.

So you have now come to believe that this is the way that things should be because it's the way that things have always been. That it has always been straight, cisgender, Judeo-Christian, white men who've been in charge. And when you come to believe that you therefore inherently are divined the right of power, you will hoard whatever power you have. Which means that the idea that any group of people that is not you and yours could become more powerful is a threat to your power, because we treat power like it is this finite resource, like it will run out, like it is oil or something. But ultimately, power is not a finite resource. It's much more like air, and redefining power means understanding that if all of us are powerful in our own spaces, that is a material benefit to everyone.

While those in power oppress multiple groups—essentially anyone who is not like them—the truth is that some groups are more oppressed than others. This can be hard for some people to understand, particularly if you are yourself being actively oppressed. But acknowledging the oppression of others—and acknowledging how this oppression might even benefit you—is critical to ending not only *their* oppression, but your own as well.

BRITTANY: Queer and trans Black women in particular experience racism, they experience the particularities of anti-Blackness, which is global, they experience homophobia and transphobia—all of those things exist in their lives and all of them intersect in unique ways. So it's not just about the sum of those things; it's about the fact that when you put all of that stuff in a bowl and you mix it up, there are multiple systems and structures that are violent toward them. It is difficult to find safe employment, it is difficult to find safe housing, it is difficult to trust that the relationship you're in is going to be one of safety for you and not one that could potentially end in your death. The health care system is violent to you. People are literally arguing in **state legislatures** right now about whether or not people should have health care that is affirming of their gender, as if it's anybody else's business or should be up to anybody else's discretion.

All of these systems conspire at once in the lives of queer and trans Black women uniquely, and if we pay close attention to how they're being treated, we can predict how the rest of us will be treated. So as a cisgender Black woman, I can predict how I'm going to be treated based on how trans Black women are being treated. And if I'm trying to separate myself from what's happening with them, I will be sadly and sorely mistaken when my time comes. And so, yeah, if we're positioning ourselves to understand the trials, tribulations, and triumphs of queer and trans Black women, then I think we can be better positioned to understand ourselves and what our collective fight has to look like.

The intersections of identity have led oppressed groups to create identifiers to speak specifically to the complexities and nuances of how they are oppressed—as was the case with "womanism," which was created because white feminism wasn't inclusive of Black women.

BRITTANY: There is a pattern of exclusion that has occurred throughout social movements in history, and we always have to reckon with the difficult truth of when our freedom work is not actually intended to free everybody. You've got the suffrage movement in which white women in the UK and America are fighting for their right to the ballot. You've got the influence of a number of Black women, people like Nannie Helen Burroughs and others in the States, who are helping set the course and set the strategy for what that can look like. But when push came to shove, the Black women were shoved out because we were deemed inconvenient and inefficient. If Black women were going to be included, then they have to include all Black people and that could actually, in some people's minds—folks like Susan B. Anthony—slow down the rate of progress. So instead of treating us as part and parcel with their freedom, we got treated like we were a hindrance, like we were holding things up.

You go further ahead and you look at this feminist movement over the next few decades: you witness a cognitive dissonance between a lot of white women who are fighting for equality in the workplace and then returning to their homes and treating their Black domestic workers unfairly and not paying them a living wage. You have white women speaking about finally being able to enter the workplace; meanwhile, Black women and women of color have always been in the workplace because the only way we could keep roofs over our families' heads was if we were adding to the family income—if we were taking in boarders or we were doing domestic work, or we were taking in people's laundry, or we were working in supposedly male-dominated areas, especially during wartime, like factories and other places.

So there's this cognitive dissonance where white women are fighting for something and not even realizing how hypocritical their fight is based on how they're treating the Black women in their lives and often the Black women in their employ.

Black women have spent centuries raising other people's children, for example, and if you look at how we treat childcare in America, we treat it poorly, not just because we treat it like women's work, but we treat it poorly because we treat it like Black women's work. So therefore, we are all excused to not pay that much or to create systems where it is impossible for those very women who are working for us to even access the childcare and elder care that they need and deserve, or for them to access the living wages that they need to be able to pay for said childcare.

The truth of the matter is, there is not a social movement, certainly not in American history, that has not been a direct beneficiary of the sacrifice and the brilliance and the strategic thinking of Black women. We were either leading your movements from the back or, more recently, leading your movements from the front, designing your movements when you didn't give us any credit, or raising your families while you were out there thinking that you were moving without us but it was impossible for you to do so.

People who have been historically oppressed often work tirelessly to hold on to what power they may have, hoping to not lose that as well. As they're holding on to their individual group's power, they often fail to realize that if they were to combine forces with another group that is oppressed as well, they could accomplish much more and would subsequently have more power. White women, who are oppressed by the patriarchy but hold the privileges of whiteness, would do better to work with Black women and women of color to achieve gender equity. Cis women should align themselves with trans women, understanding that ending the oppression for trans women means ending the oppression for *all* women. And men of color would have a far better chance of dismantling white supremacy if they worked with women of color, rather than helping keep women of color oppressed.

As with any oppressive system, it's much easier for the patriarchy to be upheld if the people it's oppressing are fighting among themselves. If all the hungry mice are fighting over a slice of pizza, then the mouse who has the rest of the pie can hoard it in peace. Which is why we must see how all of our oppressions are interconnected—and why people who benefit from some oppressive institutions but are made powerless within others are actually better off for helping dismantle them all.

An Interview with MEHCAD BROOKS

Actor, producer, and entrepreneur

Mehcad Brooks is someone who sees the importance and merit of men helping end the patriarchy and is working actively to help make it happen. He is practicing feminism as opposed to just passively supporting it, which is what we hope all beneficiaries of the patriarchy will eventually do.

MEHCAD: I can't imagine what my mother went through. I can't imagine. I mean, I know what I've gone through as a six-foot-four, 250-pound tattooed Black male in 2021. And I couldn't imagine being the first African-American woman in a capitol bureau, in the newsroom in Austin, Texas, in the 1990s. Couldn't imagine it. I couldn't imagine what she had to go through. I've heard some of the horror stories even though she doesn't want to talk about them. Just seeing the strength and the perseverance, the transcending endurance that Black women have had to have in this country has been unbelievable. To watch someone deal with what Black women deal with and not want to do your part in making it better—I can't imagine that. Especially because I benefit from many of the things that have oppressed them. Meaning I have power to help stop it.

Unless you have a feminist liberation journey, you are having a wholly insufficient journey as it relates to any other liberation. No different to the fact that you're having a wholly insufficient feminist journey if it's not also an anti-racist journey. It's all so connected.

My journey started about five years ago, and then I started taking a look at all the minutiae around me—the patterns, the things that I would just sort of chalk up to, *Well, that's how it is.* Right? I'd be watching a boxing match and I'd see the only woman who was hired during that whole encounter is the one who's holding up the cards in between the two guys pushing each other, and everybody's whistling at her. But somehow that's okay. Somehow that's the way it is. And that's because we've been putting women in positions where that might have been the only opportunity she had to be a part of the event. It's been so rare that they've been able to produce the show or able to be the manager of the fighter.

The things we see on a daily basis that we just sort of accept as normal—you have to question those things. I saw firsthand even how really, really, really successful women, including women of color, had to struggle in so many ways and had to navigate situations. I watched my mom struggle, knowing she is just as qualified as, if not more qualified than, the men who were making her life difficult—these men who have power simply because they are men. And I watched my colleagues struggle, particularly on shows like *Supergirl* and *Desperate Housewives*. Regardless how much power or money a woman has within these systems that oppress them, they will always have to navigate these systems, and that's why we must destroy the systems.

Every form of oppression is a social limiter. Where would we be if we allowed everybody to reach their full potential? Where would we be if we hadn't forced philosophers to be cotton pickers? Where would we be if we hadn't forced an astronaut to be a stay-at-home wife who isn't allowed to do anything but cook and clean? When you start thinking about the generational effects of subjugation and oppression, you realize how much we've already lost. All of that potential lost to keep mediocre bigoted people in power.

This entire nation is traumatized. We have generational trauma, ancestral trauma. And I think one day most men are going to come to terms with the fact that much of what they are doing and have is based on generational ignorance. But frankly, none of it is sustainable. Look around—the world is falling apart in large part because you can't sustain a world on hate and oppression. I think that in this new world that many are building, we have to take the people who have processed the most trauma, who experienced the most trauma, and we have to focus on lifting them up and closing the gaps. For instance, if a Black woman is as lifted as I am as a Black man, that doesn't close the gap of how I have benefited from the patriarchy and she has been oppressed by it. The intersectionality of trauma, gender, and racial bias are so important to understand in order to undo or combat any of it.

That's why my focus is on protecting Black women and listening to Black women, because they are the most powerful teachers that we have in this country. They have been and still are the leaders of progress, even when others didn't want that to be known or seen. They're still everything that people tried to make them not be. Through the trauma, through the pain, through the patriarchy, through racist class structure—the north star of progress has to be Black women because they have such a unique perspective as it pertains to where we're going and the health of this country, sociologically, economically, and emotionally. If I want Black men to progress, I need to invest in Black women's progress, and if we as a people want all women to progress, then the most oppressed women need to progress.

But what does investing in another group's progress actually mean? How do we disrupt and challenge oppression?

MEHCAD: Human conversations and the dissemination of information changed forever with the invention of the printing press. Now we have Twitter. We have Instagram. We have social media. We have this external proof, this external manifestation of our collective consciousness and how we're intertwined. I can look on my phone right now and check out what's happening anywhere in the world. I can get the word. I can even spread that word out. Meanwhile, my grandmother had a rotary phone. In other words, anything is possible. We just have to want it bad enough—including progress.

We're at the precipice of change in this new pulse of consciousness, I believe. And it sounds like science fiction, but it's not. It's a science fact. We're right here. We're right here with this book, with people reading about how they can do more and do better. What we are becoming doesn't require white supremacy, capitalism, or the patriarchy. This land has only been occupied in this oppressive way for a few hundred years, and the patriarchy itself globally hasn't existed forever. And if you're telling me that we don't have the tools to change the next four hundred years, and can't change it more quickly than we thought, than we anticipated, then you're speaking science fiction.

I feel we are in the middle of this incredibly pivotal moment in human history. Not just our country, but human history. It's the oppressors who are also being oppressed realizing the depth of our interconnectedness, and with the internet, this book, and all these things, we can spread truth. And if we spread truth, and if we spread new ideas, the possibilities are endless. And I think that we can get there. I think that within our lifetimes, our children don't have to have the conversation about whether or not their lives matter, and specifically our daughters don't have to worry about whether our sons are going to be given more opportunities than them.

Because here's what I don't want. I don't want to have to explain to my granddaughter why fifteenth-century European ideologies and politics are still oppressing her on Mars. Because we're going to be on Mars sooner than later. So, are we going to export sexism, patriarchal racism, racial animus? Are we going to export these things to Mars? Are we going to be interstellar oppressors? I'm not talking about science fiction; I'm talking about liberation.

As I said before, limiting who a person is or can be through oppression limits the possibilities of society as a whole. It's the young hip-hop–loving Black woman who could have been the greatest rapper of all time, but we will never know because of misogyny, sexism, and toxic masculinity—the tentacles of the monster known as the patriarchy.

But it's not just about missed opportunities or society needing to do better; it's also about the fact that what we have been doing hasn't been working. The people who have long held power are failing us. Under their rule, we are being destroyed by wars, climate change, poverty, and bigotry. Creating thrones that only men have had the chance to sit on has nearly destroyed the kingdom. And so being an intersectional feminist isn't an argument that others are just as equipped to have power. The argument is actually that others may be *better* equipped to have power.

If something isn't working, common sense says to try something else. It's time to dethrone the king—and distribute power equitably to us all.

MORE REASONS TO BECOME AN INTERSECTIONAL FEMINIST

▶ In the United States, women earn an average of 82 cents for every dollar a man makes—with women of color earning even less than that.

▶ Globally, sixty-two million girls are denied education.

▶ Though there are statistically more women in the world than men, in 2021, only twenty-four countries around the world had a woman as the country's leader.

▶ Only ten countries in the world (Belgium, Canada, Denmark, France, Iceland, Ireland, Latvia, Luxembourg, Portugal, and Sweden) give equal legal rights to men and women.

▶ A study done between 2010 and 2013 showed that for every female character in films, there were 2.24 male characters.

▶ Of forty-one studied countries, the United States is the only one that does not provide any form of paid maternity leave by federal law.

To find out more about reasons and ways to become an intersectional feminist, visit: BetterThanWeFoundItBook.com.

4
LET THEM EAT CAKE

Porsche Joseph on the Damage Caused by the Wealth Gap

Featuring **Robert Reich**

Growing up, I always knew my family was poor. We didn't have money to take vacations, or for me and my brothers to do extracurricular activities that had fees, like sports or art classes. As a single parent, my mother did a phenomenal job of making sure we survived and worked hard to ensure we had the opportunity to live a bit when and where we could. By "living a bit," I mean doing things that might seem simple to most, such as going to the movies on occasion or celebrating birthdays with a store-bought cake. But anything beyond that often meant she had to apply for financial assistance for us to be able to do it.

This was true of things like attending summer camp, but it was also true of things that may have seemed basic to my middle-class classmates, like getting a school yearbook. In fact, I highly doubt that most of my classmates even knew assistance for something like that existed. But where a thirty- or forty-dollar yearbook might not mean much to most middle-class families, for many who live in poverty it could mean having to forgo paying a bill or buying groceries.

When I was a very young child, the fact that we were poor didn't mean much to me because most of the people around us were poor, too. But as I became school age and began meeting kids from families with different income levels, my awareness began to develop and I started to gather that not having money was something to be ashamed of. There are two moments where I recall feeling this keenly, and those moments are forever seared into my memory.

The first took place when I was around seven years old. One night we went to McDonald's, a rare occurrence for us because it was expensive, but my mom had had to work late that night and there was nothing in the house to make for dinner. My face grew red with embarrassment as the cashier drummed her fingers on the counter impatiently while my mother dug through her coin purse looking for the exact change for our three value menu items. (This was back before the Dollar Menu, but the idea was basically the same: these items were the cheapest ones on the menu.) "Why don't you just use dollar bills?" I asked, sounding annoyed. I wasn't annoyed, though. I was ashamed that my mother had to count change to pay for our four dollars' worth of fast food.

My older brother grabbed my arm and got close to my ear. "Be quiet, Porsche. She can pay for it however she wants. You should be grateful and instead you're acting like a brat." I sealed my lips and immediately felt ashamed for feeling ashamed.

"Three dollars and seventy-five cents, three eighty-five, three ninety, four fifteen, and three pennies makes four dollars and eighteen cents . . . There!" my mother announced with an accomplished smile on her face.

This is my first distinct memory of knowing that we were poor. It's when I realized that there are people who don't have to count change to pay for things or have strict guidelines on what menu options are available to them. Though it's been nearly thirty years, I still think of that moment from time to time and become disappointed in myself for ever feeling that way.

Being poor can be embarrassing and confusing for a kid. Growing up, I would see the commercials that featured happy families pulling up to the drive-through in their new cars, ordering the latest marketing push—the Happy Meals with the popular toys—and casually deciding to toss in a couple extra dollars to supersize their meals. That was unfathomable to me at the time. Those people's normal seemed like luxury.

I knew my mom worked hard, but it wasn't until she came to speak at career day when I was in the fourth grade that I realized that hard work has almost nothing to do with how financially well-off a person is. (If that were the case, my mom would've been raking it in!)

Career day was kind of a big deal in my school. We didn't have to do any classwork that day, simply listen to the parents' presentations about their jobs and take some notes. Some of the parents brought in souvenirs from work; I'd heard that the year before somebody's parents owned a pet shop and brought in all sorts of animals like puppies, kittens, and even a snake. I knew that the father of one of my classmates worked for Nestlé, so maybe we would all be watching his presentation while eating Butterfingers and drinking Nesquik. A girl could dream.

My mom was the oldest of seven children and had grown up poor as well. In fact, she had to drop out of school when she was eleven years old so that she could stay home and watch her younger siblings in order for her parents to work. My mother didn't have it easy growing up, and consequently she brought three children into the world with no more than a sixth-grade education. Although I didn't have to drop out of school to stay home and look after my siblings, our circumstances didn't allow for a lot of parental support when it came to school. Because my mom didn't have much formal education, she rarely had the capability to help me with homework, and because she was a single parent making **minimum wage**, she didn't have the time or resources to do things like join the PTA or volunteer in our classrooms. That's why I was so excited that she agreed to come speak to my fourth-grade class for career day.

My mom was hesitant when I asked her to come, but I wrote it off, assuming that it was because she rarely had days off and had other obligations. At this point, she had been working at a department store as a retail associate for a few months. I imagined that she got to work with shoppers to pick out outfits—maybe a dress for a special occasion, or a wardrobe for a new job. Going to the mall was a rare treat for me and my brothers, so I thought it was pretty cool that she got to go there for work, and I was impressed that she got to be around fashion every day and see all the latest styles.

My mom had spent a long time on the job hunt before she finally landed this position. She always looked so nice for her interviews and was well prepared, but consistently struck out when it came to getting hired. So when she secured the job at the mall, my brothers and I were so happy. The pay was minimum wage, but my mom expected that; she had never been paid anything more.

I knew she worked hard and complained a lot about her terrible manager and awful schedule, but I suppose I thought that was something all jobs entailed. (I actually still believe that's what all jobs entail to some extent, but we can talk about toxic work environments in another book.) I knew she was underpaid, as it was no secret to me and my brothers that we were barely scraping by each month, but that was normal to me.

Career day arrived and I couldn't wait to see my mom at school. We had just finished hearing from a classmate's father, a subdued middle-aged man who was an accountant. It's safe to say that we were all thoroughly bored after listening to him drone on in a monotone voice about taxes, but luckily we were about to be dismissed for lunch and recess and my mom would be up when we got back! (No shade to accountants; taxes are much more interesting to me now that I have to pay them, but my nine-year-old self felt differently.)

I sat down at a lunch table, and Cindy Shildon and her cronies made their way over a few minutes later and sat at my table. Cindy and I had been in the same class since kindergarten, and she had always been the same. She would brag about all of the cool places her family would go during the summer break and never hesitated to make a rude comment about someone for any shallow reason. Simply put, she was stuck-up. Toward the end of lunch, I overheard the group laughing hysterically. Cindy noticed I was looking at them and addressed me. "Hey, Porsche, isn't that funny that Malik's mom works at McDonald's? That's why she didn't come to speak at career day. Nobody wants to learn about how to make French fries!" she said through a belly laugh.

Before I could ask her why that was funny, the bell rang, so I rolled my eyes and got up to head to recess. But her comment was still bothering me. Malik was my neighbor; his mom was nice. Why was she laughing at them? Making fries wasn't any more boring than doing taxes. Then I realized the joke was that they were poor. I was poor, too. Would my classmates laugh at my mom as well?

When I returned to the classroom, my mom was there smiling and waving at me as I walked in. My excitement had transformed into nervous dread. *Maybe my mom's job isn't cool after all. Maybe people will laugh at me like Malik once they know my mom doesn't make a lot of money,* I thought as a rush of anxiousness consumed me.

My mom went up in front of the class and gave a brief talk about her job, affirming the basic things I knew about her work: she kept the clothes organized for the customers and made sure people were happy with the store's service, and she got to operate a cash register. I watched my mom and thought that she was indisputably the nicest and coolest parent in that classroom, and I began to relax a little bit. After her explanation of the job, students were encouraged to ask questions. We had been given some examples of "good questions" beforehand, which had resulted in those same questions being regurgitated throughout the day: "What do you like the most about your job?" "What's the hardest part of your job?" And so on.

After a few such questions from other students, Cindy

raised her hand. "What kind of stuff did you have to study in school to do your job?" she asked.

"Well, you don't really have to study anything special to be a retail associate. You just have to like people and be courteous," answered my mother.

"So you didn't go to college?" Cindy followed up.

"No, I didn't go to college," said my mother, who looked ready for the next question. But Cindy wasn't done. "My parents say you have to go to college to get a good job," she said matter-of-factly.

The teacher interrupted: "Okay, Cindy, that's enough questions from you."

My mother made eye contact with the teacher before acknowledging Cindy. "You don't have to go to college to do the job I have, but if you want a really good job, you should go to college," she replied somewhat haphazardly, unaware of the confusion that statement may cause among fourth graders. What exactly was a "good" job, anyway?

The next day, I noticed Cindy looking at me, not so indiscreetly, whispering and snickering with her friends. I was fed up with her bullying. Who did she think she was? And after the way she had tried to embarrass my mom the day before! I decided it was time to confront her.

"Why are you looking at me and laughing?" I asked assertively.

"I'm not laughing at you; we were just laughing at your mom. My sixteen-year-old sister works at the mall, too, you know," she said with a nasty tone. "That's not a job for a parent; that's a job for a teenager."

I struggled for a good comeback. (I've never been as good

at confrontation as I build myself up to be.) "So what if your sister works at the mall? My mom can work there, too. You're just jealous." (See what I mean?)

"Jealous?" Cindy scoffed. "My sister barely makes enough money to buy CDs and makeup. You guys must be *super* poor." She said this without an ounce of sympathy, as though being poor was something contemptible.

One of her friends jumped in before I could reply. "My mom said you have to go to college if you don't want to be poor. Your mom didn't go to college and that's why you have to live in apartments owned by the government. My mom said that everyone who lives in those apartments is lazy and that there are criminals and drug addicts living there."

Ouch. My heart sank. I knew we lived in **public housing**, and that it was nothing like those big houses in the neighborhoods I passed on the way to school that were probably full of families that supersized their Happy Meals, but I didn't know my classmates' parents talked about it. Was it *that* bad?

"What are you talking about?" I said. "My mom's not lazy . . . or a criminal! My mom works hard. And not everyone goes to college. Your mom doesn't even have a job, Cindy, unless tolerating you *is* her job." (*That* was more like it!) I was fired up and ready to go at this point. My older brother had given me a long list of one-liners to keep in my back pocket, and I was ready for verbal warfare. Unfortunately, the teacher came over when she heard me raising my voice and told us to go back to our seats immediately.

I went home that day and couldn't bear to tell my mom about the encounter, but I stayed up all night thinking about it. I ran through the different things I should have said to

Cindy and her friend over and over again. I was embarrassed and I was angry. My self-esteem was hit hard, and for the rest of my childhood, I concerned myself with trying to hide the fact that my family was poor and prove that I was not lazy or inferior. I became obsessed with having the right clothes and getting the best grades. It was as if the small moment of shame that I felt when my mother was counting change at McDonald's now permanently lived in my subconscious.

In retrospect, that interaction probably influenced most of my goals and career decisions. There was a chip on my shoulder since that day, and a drive to outperform all the Cindy Shildons I've met since. If I'd never had that experience, maybe I would have wanted to be an artist, or a nanny, or even work in the mall. But that moment always remained in the back of my head, telling me those careers weren't good enough because they didn't pay as much as other jobs. A "good job" paid well—and led to a person living in the kind of grand homes Cindy and her friends lived in.

Today I hold multiple college degrees and have a long résumé of what Cindy and her friends would consider "good jobs," but I will never enjoy the kind of **wealth** that Cindy Shildon's family enjoyed through generations and generations of inheritance. That's because a person's income—that is, how much they're paid—has nothing to do with how *wealthy* they are. Wealth doesn't just account for income or money; it's a measure of financial worth that includes the things a family or person owns, such as land, homes, businesses, stocks, cars, or other **assets** you could sell for cash.

The unfortunate truth is that people who are born into

poverty are extremely unlikely to become wealthy, no matter how hard they work. Even if someone works hard and goes on to make a considerably good salary, they will still, based on their family's historical poverty, most likely struggle to acquire wealth.

To demonstrate this point, let's look at two people, whom we'll call Joe and Jill.

Joe and Jill live in the same city, which means their **cost of living** is the same. Joe earns $45,000 per year at his job, while Jill earns $70,000 at hers—significantly more than Joe. But Joe has inherited a home that is paid-off and is worth $300,000. He also has no student debt because his parents paid for his college. Jill, on the other hand, rents her home and has student debt of $85,000.

If you only consider income, Jill is much better off than Joe. However, when the two situations are seen through the lens of wealth, Joe has a higher **net worth**. This results in him having more flexibility in how he spends his income, without having to worry about rent or education debt. Because his **debt-to-income ratio** is lower than Jill's, he's likelier than Jill to be approved for loans to purchase a car or another house—and to pay lower interest rates on those loans than Jill would pay if she were approved. Joe even has property that will most likely increase in value without his having to do anything, and he can give this property to his own children one day, setting the next generation of his family up to be financially secure or even wealthy.

The issue is that wealth is often inaccessible. Simply earning a better salary than one's peers will not give someone automatic access to wealth. Wealth is typically acquired in two ways: inheritance and entrepreneurship. Inheritance ensures generational wealth by passing down assets—a family business, money, or a home—from one generation to the next. If your wealth isn't inherited, the other primary path to wealth is being an entrepreneur. People who own businesses have an uncapped salary potential—the ability to earn so much money that they can afford the sorts of assets that lead to wealth—but the catch here is that most businesses have a lot of start-up costs and don't see a profit in the first few years.

In fact, about 45 percent of businesses fail altogether in the first five years. If an entrepreneur doesn't have enough **financial capital** to keep a business running when it's not profitable (while also covering their personal cost of living), the business will never get off the ground and they will end up worse off than they were before because all of their money was spent on the failed business. Oftentimes, the money invested in the business has been borrowed from a bank or other lender, meaning the entrepreneur has a debt they must repay regardless of whether the business is bringing in any profit. If they fail to pay the debt, they won't qualify for future loans and their opportunities will be limited.

While the two main paths to wealth—inheritance and entrepreneurship—are often inaccessible to people who come from poverty, these are far from the only opportunities those who grew up poor miss out on. Other examples include investments in professional growth, such as education or internships, that require a certain amount of financial privilege. A great example of this is my mother, who had to give up the opportunity to go to school in order to help with childcare that her parents could otherwise not afford. In doing so, she gave up her opportunity to earn more in the future. Many of the paths to higher salaries require a baseline of financial stability often not enjoyed by those who come from poverty.

Yet another reason it is difficult for people who come from poverty to save any sort of significant capital—with which to start a business, invest in their education or careers, or purchase assets—is because they may have to financially assist family members and help provide basic needs to those around them. The luxury of being able to save money or make investments is a privilege of those who don't bear the responsibility of others' survival.

Thus, a poverty trap is created, in which generation to generation cannot escape poverty because they cannot afford to take an investment risk or do anything other than survive. The same way that wealth can be inherited, poverty, too, is often inherited.

Although we know that gaining wealth on par with the country's wealthiest people cannot be done by simply working a good-paying job, as seen in the example of Jill, millions of people don't even have access to good-paying jobs. For these people, it is extremely difficult to even earn enough for their families to afford basics like food and housing. In fact, there is no place anywhere in America where a full-time minimum-wage worker can afford to rent a two-bedroom home, and in only 7 *percent* of counties in this country can they afford to rent a one-bedroom home.

In the two decades since Cindy made fun of my mom for working retail, federal minimum wage has increased by only about two dollars per hour (from $5.15 in 1997 to a whopping

$7.25 in 2021) and we have not seen an increase since it was last raised in 2009.

SIDE NOTE: While the federal minimum wage hasn't increased in twelve years, inflation has. The costs of goods— from food to rent to gasoline—have risen over time, which means that the $7.25 wage is worth less today than it was back in 2009. When adjusted for inflation, being paid $7.25 an hour in 2021 is like being paid $5.70 per hour in 2009. If the minimum wage were tied to inflation—as many politicians, economists, and activists argue it should be—today's minimum wage would be $9.23. Still appallingly low, but at least comparable to the increase passed in 2009.

The problematic assumption that minimum wage is reserved for teenagers or part-time workers who are on their way to better is hurting American families who depend on this minimum wage to live. Not only are the majority of minimum-wage workers adults who work full-time, but nearly 30 percent are parents and, contrary to my classmates' beliefs, over 40 percent have at least some college experience. So why do so many people believe this when we know it's not actually true? By creating stereotypes about people in poverty and the working class, the financially privileged can convince themselves that they've earned their financial security and avoid taking accountability for the inequity of wealth in America.

The **wealth gap** in America has been developing for hundreds of years—and it's only getting wider. A small fraction of the population hoards most of the country's wealth, while half of all people in the entire country share less than 2 *percent* of the nation's wealth. Many people actually have a negative worth (meaning they have no wealth, just debt), while some have more money than they could spend in a lifetime.

Race also plays a large role in the wealth gap. Today, on average, white families have *ten times* the wealth of their Black counterparts and *six times* as much as Latinx families. The racial wealth gap reveals the effects of the discrimination that this country was built on. There is a clear through line from **Jim Crow laws**, which prohibited Black people from attending certain schools and from working in certain careers and industries, to the present-day discriminatory practices that ensure that Black people and other people of color are paid less, hired less, and face barriers to accessing wealth.

SIDE NOTE: Racial covenants are laws that restricted non-white people from living in specific areas. Some cities that had well-known covenants are Chicago, Baltimore, Detroit, Milwaukee, Minneapolis, Los Angeles, Seattle, and St. Louis, among many others. These laws targeted specific groups, depending on racial relations in the area. For instance, Seattle had harsh laws prohibiting African-American, Jewish, and Asian people from living in certain parts of the city during a time when there was a fast-growing population of Filipino, Chinese, and Japanese Americans. These covenants were a pillar of **redlining**—which pushed different races to whatever part of town white lawmakers and city planners wanted them to be living in.

One such barrier is the racist policies and practice of redlining, which has forced families of color to lose out on the opportunity to accumulate hundreds of thousands of dollars of wealth that is associated with home ownership. To put it in perspective, according to the Federal Reserve, in 2016 the average homeowner had a household wealth of $231,400, compared to the average renter, whose household wealth was only $5,200. Although redlining is no longer backed by the government, as it once was, it still continues today. People of color find that their loan applications are denied at an exponentially higher rate than white people with similar (or worse) qualifications. Black applicants are denied by mortgage lenders at a rate 80 percent higher than white applicants. When they *are* approved, the lending terms for Black borrowers are more likely to be harmful—featuring high loan rates and stipulations that leave those purchasing the home vulnerable to being taken advantage of. (It's no surprise, then, that the majority of predatory mortgage loans in the years right before the **Great Recession** of 2008 were given to Black and Latinx borrowers.)

Another way that we continue to see redlining carried out today is in home values. Homes in neighborhoods that are non-white are valued much lower than what they would be if the same exact house were in a white neighborhood. This means that even if someone invested in maintaining a home or renovating it, they could not sell it for the amount it would be worth in a white neighborhood, despite it having all of the same—if not more—features and updates. Between how difficult it's been made to purchase a home and the difficulty of selling a home at a competitive price, people of color are still experiencing major setbacks when it comes to investing in and profiting from home ownership.

Due to redlining and other factors of systemic racism, including disparities in access to quality education and high-paying jobs, people of color have been pushed into living in **low-income housing** at higher rates than white people. It is not because they are lazy or drug addicts or didn't go to college—it is hundreds of years of prejudice and discrimination forcing the people deemed undesirable by white people into neighborhoods with the worst infrastructure, schools, and employment opportunities and seeing if they sink or swim.

SIDE NOTE: And race is not the only factor. Women have experienced oppression when it comes to wealth and the workforce as well. Despite great accomplishments in the fight for women's rights, a woman in the United States makes only 82 cents for every dollar a man makes. In Korea, it's even worse—women there make only 63 cents for every dollar earned by a man. This is a global issue, affecting women in every part of the world.

The relationship between wealth and poverty is far from simple. Society often likes to encourage people to "pull themselves up by their bootstraps," which essentially means to make something of themselves all on their own. I've really only heard the phrase used by old white men who claim they have done it and imply that therefore anyone can, but anyone who claims to have succeeded entirely on their own is either knowingly lying or is unaware of the many privileges that made their success possible—privileges that not everyone has.

We also need to understand that many people are not even able to strive to "pull themselves up by their bootstraps" or *succeed*, necessarily—those are lofty and fanciful dreams for the many people who are just trying to feed their families and *survive*.

So what can we do to tackle the pains of wealth disparities in America? We can look to models around the world that strive to provide a strong **social safety net** that ensures that all residents will have access to basic needs such as health care, affordable housing, higher education, food, and clean water, among other things.

In many countries, such as Canada and countries all over Europe, major expenses such as health care and education are covered by the government. Providing these services frees up people's finances to be spent on other things, and, even more importantly, it ensures that people have access to the means of staying healthy and pursuing their career goals without the added barrier of doctors' bills and education costs. This is not a perfect solution by any means, but it does begin to attempt to solve aspects of the oppressions of poverty. Although people are quick to attack the possibility of this approach leading to an increase in taxes, given that the United States actually spends more **per capita** on health care than any other industrialized country in the world—including all the countries that provide **universal health care**—it may actually just be a matter of the government restructuring taxes and spending to prioritize health care and education and divesting from systems that cost too much and don't work efficiently. In many cases an individual's take-home pay may actually *increase* if the costs of private health care were removed, even if their taxes were higher.

Reducing or forgiving student loan debt would also be meaningful for people who are struggling to make ends meet, and the tax increase plan put forth by some politicians would not affect or would be inconsequential to those of us who aren't super rich. (And when I say rich, I am talking about multi-millionaire rich.) Making both health care and higher education free would have a monumental impact on the standard of living for millions of Americans.

Another example of a social safety net that is being heavily experimented with all over the globe is **universal basic income (UBI)**, which is when the government gives citizens a set amount of money on a regular schedule, with no strings attached. (Think about it like an allowance.) We saw an increase in governments using these types of payments in response to the COVID-19 pandemic, such as in the Netherlands and France, where the governments paid for workers' salaries when the country was on lockdown and sent lump sums of money monthly to self-employed workers. The United States gave some people one-time direct payments of up to $1,200, followed by another one-time payment of up to $600, in addition to increasing unemployment pay during part of the pandemic. Such direct payments have proven to be successful in maintaining economies through a turbulent time, but some experts think it would be helpful to have direct payments in place permanently.

Although it is happening at a larger scale in places like Iran, Spain, and Kenya, one experiment that has gained notable attention is right here in Stockton, California. The mayor of Stockton led an initiative to give some residents $500 per month for two years and monitor the effects. Members of the group who received the payments found more full-time work than those who didn't, and suffered from less depression.

> **SIDE NOTE:** I highly encourage you to research some of the countries experimenting with UBI and read about their results. You might be surprised by some of the findings!

There are options as to how we address this issue, but what we cannot afford to do is allow the gap between wealth and poverty to continue to grow. While the historic structure that we currently have in place serves the people who designed it, we must look forward to the future and get creative on how to level the playing fields so that all people can do more *living*. While the number of billionaires continues to grow, no child should have to worry about not being able to afford a yearbook or miss a cake on their birthday because it's simply unaffordable. No child should have to stop going to school so that they can earn a paycheck, and no parent should be made to feel bad about working at a mall.

To learn more about wealth and poverty, and gain some perspective on creative solutions, I went to one of the world's leading experts, Robert Reich, with some questions.

An Interview with ROBERT REICH

Economist, professor, author, and former US secretary of labor

I began following Robert Reich a while ago on Instagram and found myself constantly reposting what he had to say. It was no surprise to me to learn that the course he teaches at the University of California, Berkeley—called "Wealth and Poverty"—has a wait-list of four hundred to five hundred students every semester, after already accommodating the 850 lucky students who are able to register. Clearly, Robert is someone we can all learn from.

ROBERT: The course is not a course just on economics. You can't talk about economics without understanding history and politics and ethics and much else. So it really is a course about the system. And increasingly, over the years, what I tend to teach—because of what I've tended to understand—is that there is, in fact, a system that is not just economics or politics or sociology; it is all of these things and more. Well, there are several systems, really. One is systemic racism, which is not new. It goes back to before the founding of this country; it goes back to the Constitution in which a Black person was considered to be less than a white person for the purposes of counting votes and counting people. They were not even permitted to vote.

It goes back to housing discrimination, redlining. And that itself, that history of housing discrimination, explains a lot of the wealth gap that is still with us. Because a house is the biggest single asset that people own. And if there's discrimination in the housing market, if it's very hard for Black people to get loans to buy homes—because there is a tremendous restriction, politically and culturally and sociologically, on where and how they can live—then that's going to affect what they end up with in terms of their wealth.

White wealth is about ten times greater than Black wealth in America today. And it's not all that different from what it was twenty or forty years ago. Twenty or forty years ago, white wealth was also about ten times greater than Black wealth. And one of the keys to it is the housing market.

The long history of housing discrimination affects people enormously. I mean, for example, most people who are poor—and a disproportionate number of poor people are Black and Latinx—can't even get into the housing market. You've got to have a certain amount of savings and money to get in to begin with. If you're not in the housing market, you're renting. Well, there are huge tax benefits to people who own homes, but if you're a renter, you get nothing. So the tax rules give a huge advantage just logically to people who tend to be white and tend to be affluent or at least middle-class. But wherever you look, you see aspects of discrimination and the kind of discrimination that leads to this widening gap.

Earlier I talked about some of the barriers that stop someone from being able to save up enough money to make the initial down payment that's required to get a home in the first place. Robert has thought extensively about those barriers and ways to help reduce them.

ROBERT: Well, there are a number of areas we can improve. One, we've got to raise wages. The minimum wage is very important. One thing we know is that when the minimum-wage laws changed in the 1960s, it included, for the first time, a lot of people who had been historically excluded from the minimum-wage law. I'm talking about people who are farmworkers and domestic workers and others who were purposely excluded. Because a lot of the members of Congress who voted on the creation of these laws in the 1930s were white southerners who did not want to include Black people. It wasn't until the 1967 amendments to Social Security and the minimum wage that, in fact, Black people were included in getting that minimum wage. That had a very dramatic impact on increasing the wages of Black workers and women.

People cannot live a healthy life at the current minimum wage. If a person works full-time (forty hours per week) every week of the year, taking no holidays or vacation time, they would make just over $13,000. The average annual rent in America is $9,477—meaning that they would have about $293 left over to survive on each month to pay for groceries, childcare, utilities and other bills, and any debt. In my mother's case, she was expected to support three children with minimum wage. Perhaps now you can understand why it was so difficult for her to afford our $30 yearbooks!

Recently, there has been a push from some politicians calling for a $15-per-hour federal minimum wage, which would more than double the current minimum wage. While many people will still struggle to make ends meet even with such an increase in pay—and others might use the additional money to offer more assistance to loved ones—millions of people will no doubt spend some of this money to purchase goods, which benefits the economy.

ROBERT: Another thing we have got to do is root out systemic discrimination with regard to employment. Because that also hurts people who are Black and Latinx and other people of color. We know that employers discriminate, and that discrimination makes it harder for people to get good jobs, to get promotions, to get better wages.

The system creates barriers of race, class, and gender in every aspect of people trying to accumulate wealth. For instance, while a woman in the United States makes only 82 cents for every one dollar a man makes, as referenced earlier, for Black women, that number drops to 63 cents, and for Latinx women it is only 55 cents—meaning that over a forty-year career, a Latinx woman is paid over $1 million less than a white man. The gap is even wider for transgender women.

However, even if someone has access to fair pay and a higher minimum wage, this will not allow people the leg up that some others have when it comes to accessing wealth.

ROBERT: I think we could go even much further. We could provide every child born in this country with a baby **bond** of a certain amount of money that, if it's invested in the stock market, would grow and could be a considerable amount of money by the time somebody is ready to buy a house, by the time somebody is twenty-two years old.

We could and should make it much easier for people to afford college and get the education they need. As we move toward the middle of the twenty-first century, a college education, sadly, is a prerequisite to getting into the middle class and getting the kind of jobs that a lot of people need in order to have the money to buy a home. Here, again, it is very difficult for a lot of poor kids, disproportionately Black and Latinx, to get into college, to afford a college education, to get a college loan, and to be able to pay off that college loan. I mean, we have a huge problem in this country: $1.6 trillion worth of college loans that a lot of people are having difficulty repaying.

My point is that "How can we help people afford to buy a house?" sounds like a simple question, but actually, it is connected to almost every other aspect of the system, and unless you deal with almost all of those aspects that we've been talking about, you're really not responding appropriately to the question you asked about reducing barriers to getting money.

Robert has been working on solving these kinds of problems for a very long time now. His ideas are based on a good understanding of what America can afford to do, and what would actually benefit not just individuals but the country.

ROBERT: I think that, inevitably, we've got to move toward a universal basic income (UBI). As more and more jobs are going to be automated because of artificial intelligence, the jobs we get left with—and this is particularly true of people who are at the bottom rungs of education and opportunity—the jobs that we get left with are jobs that are attention jobs or caring jobs: childcare, elder care. Those are important jobs, but they don't pay very much. And so as automation replaces middle-class and lower-middle-class jobs, we're going to need a basic survival income. It's not that this basic income is going to be enough to survive on, necessarily—people are still going to want to work and have to work—but it at least prevents people from falling into dire poverty.

If this sounds wild, and you don't know where we would ever get the money to pay all these people with, one place we can draw some resources from is the mega-rich. While Americans struggled to meet the most basic of needs during the early stages of the COVID-19 pandemic, billionaires made an unprecedented increase in money during the same time period.

ROBERT: We haven't seen this much wealth at the top since the 1890s. Just over the course of the pandemic, from February 2020 to April 2021, you have 667 billionaires in the United States who increased their combined wealth by $1.3 *trillion*. Now, that's an impossible sum to get your arms around. But one way of understanding that would be that they could give everybody in America—every man, woman, and child in America—$3,800 *and still be as wealthy as they were before the pandemic started.* We have not seen this degree of concentrated wealth for over a hundred years. So is there an argument for a wealth tax? Of course.

Even if we have more funds, another issue is where these funds will be directed. Should we be allocating the budget differently?

ROBERT: You have a vicious cycle setting in so that people who are privileged and who are wealthy have much better odds of increasing their wealth and increasing their privilege and also increasing the wealth and privilege of their children than people who are poor. It shows up in laws; it shows up in politics. The big banks got bailed out in 2008 when we had a **financial crisis,** but millions of people lost their homes, jobs, and savings while not a single Wall Street executive went to jail for all of the fraud that was committed leading up to the financial crisis. Meanwhile we have a judicial system and a legal system in which many young people, particularly young Black men, go to jail for dealing drugs, even small amounts of drugs.

I mean, that shows you, again, how power and systemic racism are worsening a situation rather than improving it. The federal budget does allocate some money for public assistance, but the public assistance budget is very tiny relative to what we spend for, let's say, national defense. We're spending over $700 billion a year for national defense. That's more than the ten next biggest nations put together spend on national defense, but what are we spending on our people, in terms of their education, their training, their opportunities and needs? In terms of even basic food and housing, we're spending really remarkably little.

It is interesting that so many Americans stigmatize and look down upon people using welfare, living in **subsidized housing**, or receiving other types of government assistance, rather than looking down on the rich CEOs or other leaders of large companies who hoard money and don't pay adequate taxes—or the government that tells us that we don't have the money to help people pay for things like education or health care but continuously pours taxpayer dollars into bombing other countries or expanding the prison system.

ROBERT: I think that much of the demonization of the poor we've seen started in the late 1970s when Ronald Reagan was the first politician to talk about welfare queens—which is this scary image of women who commit fraud to collect excessive welfare payments and don't take care of their children—and he exploited a certain current of racism and **fearmongering** among the white middle class. It was there already, but when wages began to stagnate for the middle class, many middle-class and working-class people became more vulnerable to racist rhetoric coming from politicians. Sadly, both parties have been guilty.

I think that if wages had continued to rise and the median wage in the United States had continued to rise, perhaps the middle-class and working-class whites would have been more generous, to some extent, but when the pie is not growing, when you are afraid that you are not going to live as well as your parents and that your children are not going to live as well as you live, then appeals to racism become easier for politicians to make and the public becomes more vulnerable to that.

Meanwhile, people at the very top, who might be called the **oligarchs** of America, who are gaining more and more wealth and power, and as the median wage has stagnated—I think they understand implicitly that they are in better shape and more protected politically if everybody else is fighting among themselves. If they can split the white working class from the Black working class and the white poor from the Black poor, then everybody else is fighting over the crumbs while they run off with the pie.

When Robert refers to oligarchs, he is talking about the richest of the rich billionaires who have power and influence due to their wealth. Many people consider the rich elite in the United States oligarchs because of the impact they have on US government policy and the protections we see them get when committing corporate crimes such as violating labor laws or stashing money in accounts that aren't reported in order to avoid taxes.

However, there is a long history of fearmongering in America that leads people to think that if the oligarchies are broken up, we will suddenly be moving toward **communism** or some radical **socialism** where the government will control everything and no one will be able to manage their own money or have financial success. Essentially, there is a lot of misinformation, and even disinformation, about threats to break up oligarchies also being a threat to capitalism. But this simply isn't true.

ROBERT: What are real alternatives to capitalism? Even China, which describes itself as a communist country, is quite capitalistic in terms of a lot of private property and a lot of dependence on the free exchange of goods and services. The question really is, What kind of capitalism? I think that in the Nordic countries—in Sweden, Norway, Denmark, and a few other places around the world—you have a very gentle kind of capitalism that is quite equitable, where there are a lot of public investments, in terms of making sure that everybody has access to good education, good job training, and good health care, which is critically important. You also have countries that provide very strong safety nets for anybody who might fall or who can't gain a footing in the economy. So they're very forgiving capitalist societies.

At the other extreme, you have the United States, which has socialism for the rich in terms of all sorts of benefits that they get. If you're the CEO of a company, even if you screw up, you get a **golden parachute**—meaning when you leave, you get treated extraordinarily well. However, if you are an average person or a poor person in American capitalism, you're treated to the harshest kind of capitalism in the world.

SIDE NOTE: An example of a golden parachute is the payment made to WeWork cofounder and former CEO Adam Neumann, who mismanaged the company's finances and operations and falsely reported to investors. Neumann was offered $1.7 *billion* to step down from his position. Meanwhile, the company had to lay off a large percentage of its employees (who received no payout or compensation) due to his missteps.

Everybody has their own view of what capitalism means or communism or socialism or **fascism**. I think that the important point is that you need a system in which everybody, regardless of the circumstances into which they are born, has an equal chance to get ahead and also has equal political rights, equal political voice, and you have to have strong safety nets and major public investments. If you don't have this, it's a system that is prone to going off the rails, a system in which wealth starts accumulating because power starts accumulating because wealth starts accumulating.

When politicians debate the merits of the current economic system here in the United States, there is often a false choice presented: you can have capitalism as we know it, with all its inherent inequalities, or you can have socialism—which in these discussions is often conflated with communism and is clearly meant to be the worse choice, implying that no one will ever be able to be rich because the government will control all of the resources in the country and distribute them evenly to everyone, regardless of how much (or little) someone works. But as Robert discussed, China—a communist country—has far more billionaires than the US, and they take up over one hundred seats on the Chinese parliament, meaning they have major influence in government and policy decisions. Clearly, capitalism can find a way.

Countries can have a free-market economy and still provide strong safety nets for people who struggle financially. In socialist countries such as the Netherlands or Norway, you can open businesses, accumulate wealth, and participate in a competitive market, but when the government collects taxes or makes regulations, they do so mainly in order to give back to the people. In America, however, the safety net is strongest for the super-rich. So when a large corporation or industry faces financial hardship, regardless of why, the government more often than not will give them a **bailout** so that the company won't collapse. Contrarily, if an individual is facing hardship, the government does very little damage control.

If we stay on the current path, the projection is that the wealth gap will continue to grow. What will that mean for the country?

ROBERT: The wealth gap is so closely tied to the racial wealth gap, and I really think that one of the mythologies that white middle-class and white working-class people—too many of them—have bought into is that somehow, Black people and brown people are different from white people. And if they're poor, they exist in a different space, a different place. The reality is that there are many more white poor people than Black and brown poor people. The reality is that, if you provide a good, strong safety net or good schools and good public investments, white people and Black people and brown people all benefit together, and if you fail to do that, the situation becomes worse for everybody.

And when I say "the situation becomes worse," I mean you're toying with political instability; you're toying with the demise of democracy. You're playing with the possibility that we could fall into—and I hate to use the word, but there is the possibility that we could fall into fascism or something equally bad. We did have four years of Donald Trump, after all. If we learned anything from Donald Trump, I think we should have learned that we are all in this together and that our democracy is precious and it is closely related to our economy and the opportunities that people feel either are or are not available to them.

And I look at what is happening under the Biden administration—it's very early on, but I'm encouraged in the sense that I think that, when you look at the initiatives that Joe Biden has taken and the public opinion about those initiatives, and the stance on things like minimum wage, health care, Medicare for All, the Green New Deal, the public is much more liberal and progressive than most of our politicians are.

I have spent the last forty years teaching young people. I have never taught a generation of young people as diverse or as committed to equal opportunity and improving the possibilities for everyone, regardless of race or ethnicity or gender, as the current generation of young people I'm teaching. So whenever I start feeling a little bit down or a little bit discouraged, I go back into the classroom. I am privileged, most of all, by being able to teach and see and feel that energy and that dedication and that commitment.

Whatever your political leanings, whatever your feelings about capitalism or even socialism, one thing is clear: the wealth gap in this country needs to close. America is the richest country in the world, yet *forty million* Americans live in poverty. Forty million Americans don't have enough to eat or are struggling to pay rent or are houseless. Countless children go to school in the cold with no jacket because their families cannot afford one, and far too many drop out of school because they can't afford to attend. There are young children growing up in poverty who face tremendous obstacles to escaping that poverty. We need to acknowledge that it is not as simple as being ambitious or "pulling yourself up by your bootstraps." Sometimes, there are people who simply have no boots.

It is time to start learning from other countries and listening to advice from economists like Robert Reich and many of the politicians who have strategic plans laid out that prioritize examining how we are working as a country to help close the wealth gap. Because in the richest country in the world, there's no excuse for millions of people to have to worry about where their next meal is going to come from or being able to afford a roof over their head.

To find out more about how you can help put a stop to the wealth gap, visit: BetterThanWeFoundItBook.com.

5
WE SHOULDN'T BE AFRAID TO LEAVE HOME

Frederick Joseph on the Devastation of Gun Violence

Featuring **Shannon Watts** and **Brandon Wolf**

Trigger Warning

There aren't many things in this world that I hate. The word is so strong and unforgiving that I try not to use it. In fact, growing up, my mother would tell me I should never use the word *hate*: "You shouldn't say that you hate things," she explained to me. "Say that you tastefully dislike them." (I'm still not sure what it means to *tastefully dislike* something, but I'll work on it, Mom.)

Nonetheless, I can say quite honestly that I hate bullies. I hate anyone who uses their power and privilege to harm, oppress, or belittle others. Especially those who may already be suffering in some way.

Up until high school, I was bullied mercilessly, which is partially why I'm so sensitive about people bullying others. I grew up in a neighborhood in Yonkers, New York, that was rough. It was filled with people who not only lived in poverty but were also navigating the violence, **over-policing**, drugs, and trauma that often come along with poverty. The last thing any of us needed was to be bullied by our peers, yet for many of us, that was our reality. I was made fun of so badly in middle school that sometimes I would cut school just to avoid the trauma of being around people who made me feel as if I was worthless. I can still remember what jokes my classmates would tell about me—about my dated clothes, thick eyebrows, short stature, acne, and anything else they could find to pick me apart about—as if they are whispering in my ear as I sit here and write this.

By the time I was in high school, most of the things I had been bullied for were no longer relevant. I had a part-time job and my mother was making more money, so my clothes were the latest style, my acne had cleared, I had shot up five inches over the summer, and I had started tweezing my eyebrows (though I didn't learn how to do this well until long after high school). Though I was no longer a victim of bullying, dealing with that trauma had a profound impact on me and made me hyper-aware of the importance of protecting others. (Which is not to say that I've always been perfect at protecting those around me—but we'll get to that in a moment.)

Not only was I no longer bullied, but the changes in my appearance actually made me popular—in school and also in my neighborhood. (I think it's important to take a second and acknowledge how foolish it is that someone is popular or viciously bullied because of appearance. Especially because we generally have no control over what we look like. Having acne, for example, shouldn't be the difference maker as to whether someone has friends or not.) Another reason I became more popular in my neighborhood was because I was constantly in the park playing basketball and hanging out. Before there was social media, people had to actually go out to engage with other people. The park was kind of like a mixture of Instagram and Twitter. You have a thought you think is important? Go tell people at the park. You just bought a new pair of sneakers? Make sure you wear them to the park so everyone can see. Want people to see the results of all that exercise you've been doing? Go show off at the park.

The park was where I met countless people, some of whom I'm still friends with to this day—others, not so much. But I gravitated toward anyone who enjoyed playing basketball, which we would do from sunup to sundown. There was a group of four guys who were a bit older than me—they were maybe sixteen or seventeen, and I was fourteen—that I would play with often: Dante, Marco, Anthony, and Felix. I only actually liked Marco and Dante; the other two were jerks. But they were jerks who were some of the best basketball players I had ever played with.

Not only did Anthony and Felix know how good they were at basketball; they also knew that most people in the neighborhood were afraid of them because they had a reputation for beating up people they didn't like. There were also rumors that Felix had a gun, and no one wanted to find out if that was true.

There was one summer day in the park that I'll never forget. The park was packed as if the entire neighborhood was there that day. Children were jumping rope, drawing with chalk on the sidewalk, and running through the water pouring from open fire hydrants. It was one of those days when the air was filled with laughter and music from the ice cream truck parked at the entrance of the park. Most importantly, there was no shortage of games or eager players on the courts.

As was typically the case, Anthony and Felix were team captains because they were the two best players at the park, and, as such, they had the chance to choose who they picked for their teams. Anthony had beaten Felix in a quick three-point shoot-out to see who would choose first. He chose Dante. Felix then chose Marco, Anthony chose me, and then they took turns choosing enough people to fill out our teams for a five-on-five game. When the teams were filled, almost no one complained about not being chosen, knowing that it might anger Dante, Marco, Anthony, or Felix.

One guy *did* complain about not being chosen to play, though. His name was Cory. I didn't know him well but had seen him around and heard a bit about him. He was maybe seventeen and lived in a local shelter. I wasn't sure what had happened to his parents, but people said he had dropped out of school and had been houseless since they had died some years before. "What's up? Why didn't one of you pick me for a team? My jumper is water," Cory asked in frustration as we were getting ready to begin the game.

Felix looked him up and down. "Look at your bum ass. Why would one of us choose you to play on a team?"

"Listen, man, I'm just tryin' to ball. It doesn't have to be all of that," Cory replied calmly.

Anthony laughed and pointed. "Look at his shoes! How you tryin' to play ball with a hole in your shoes? And you stink! Wasn't no way I was putting your homeless ass on my team!" Nearly everyone who was near the court started laughing at Cory's expense. I'm not sure whether they laughed because they were heartless or because if they didn't laugh, they knew they could face Felix or Anthony's wrath. But I didn't laugh—there's nothing funny about a person who is struggling in any way.

Cory didn't respond. He simply walked off and sat on a bench away from everyone as we started the game. I was so frustrated by how they had treated him that I no longer wanted to play, so a few minutes into the game I faked an injury.

"What are you doing?!" Anthony yelled as I walked off the court.

"I hurt my ankle, we 'bout to take an L if I play like this. Let me sit for a second," I responded.

"Whatever. You weren't doing anything, anyway. Just hurry up and choose somebody," Anthony said. This was just what I wanted to hear. I walked over to Cory and asked him to take my spot on the team, which he quickly agreed to do.

"You're buggin'. That hobo isn't playing on my team!" Anthony yelled from across the court.

"Nah! That's who Fred chose, so that's who is on your team!" Felix interjected hastily, clearly assuming that Cory wouldn't be a good player.

Cory ran onto the court, and the game continued. Within a few seconds, it was obvious that Cory wasn't only good; he was as good as, if not better than, everyone else on the court—including Anthony and Felix. Anthony's team easily won their game thanks in large part to Cory. But instead of commending him on playing well, both Anthony and Felix decided to make fun of him more.

"You're lucky I was taking it easy," Felix said to Cory. "I didn't want to cross you and make you tear up the rest of your worn-down sneakers." Anthony and the others laughed.

Cory stared at him for a moment, then looked around and said, "So why don't you and your friends play on one team against a team I choose?" Anthony and Felix agreed and chose Dante, Marco, and another guy they knew, since I was supposedly hurt. However, I made a miraculous recovery in time to play on Cory's team. I couldn't wait to help Cory beat them, and beat them we did—badly. The final score was something like 21–9. Though that was much more of a reflection of Cory than any of the rest of us; all that time none of us had known we had our very own LeBron James in the neighborhood.

People had come from all over the park to watch the game, including Felix's girlfriend, Rochelle, and her friends—all of whom had seen Cory destroy Felix and Anthony. There are few things more dangerous than angry young men who feel like they have a reputation or respect to keep.

To make matters worse, apparently Cory knew one of Rochelle's friends, so the group had walked over to congratulate him on the win and praise how he had played. When Felix saw this, he became enraged. He ran over to Cory and shoved him to the ground. "You think your bum ass can speak to my girl?!"

Rochelle tried to intervene. "Baby, we were just telling him that he played well—"

"Shut up!" Felix yelled at Rochelle with the rage of a thousand misogynists.

Felix was about to punch Cory when Dante walked over. "You buggin'—let's go. It's not that serious."

"Fine. Whatever." Felix let Dante lead him out of the park, followed closely by Anthony and Marco. As they reached the entrance of the park, though, Felix noticed that Rochelle and her friends had helped Cory up and were checking to see if he was okay. Felix ran back to the court and punched Cory in the eye. The blow sent him tumbling back to the ground.

Rochelle yelled in horror, "Felix, what are you doing?! Stop!"

As Cory attempted to get up, Anthony ran over and punched him in the face as well. Felix followed by kicking Cory, and then the two began taking turns beating on him. I looked over at Dante and Marco and yelled for them to stop their friends, but they just stood there. Like everyone else—myself included—they probably believed that if they helped Cory, they would become targets themselves.

The attack probably only lasted a minute or so, but it seemed like a lifetime. The sounds of joy that had filled the park earlier had been replaced by a morbid silence as we all looked on in fear as Cory was viciously attacked. Suddenly, that silence was pierced by the sounds of sirens from cop cars speeding down the street toward the park. As soon as they heard the sound, Anthony and Felix stopped hitting Cory and darted out of the park.

Once they were gone, everyone quickly ran over to tend to Cory, who was badly injured. Seeing Cory lying there unconscious made me feel as if I was frozen in a nightmare that I couldn't wake up from. A nightmare that I felt was partially my fault. Why hadn't I done anything to stop them? Why had I asked him to play, knowing how much Felix and Anthony disliked him? Why hadn't I spoken up earlier when they were bullying him, as I would have wanted someone to speak up for me?

When the cops got a good look at Cory, they immediately called for an ambulance. The paramedics arrived within a few minutes, and in that time, Cory hadn't moved once, except for his chest ever-so-slightly expanding and contracting, which let us know he was still breathing. The paramedics placed Cory on a stretcher and drove him to the hospital in an ambulance. I walked home in tears—crying not just out of worry for Cory but out of guilt and shame for not having done anything to help him.

I stopped going to the park after what happened. A few months later, I was walking home and bumped into Marco and Dante, who said they had heard Cory was at the park for the first time since the beating. Apparently, his injuries were so bad that he had spent more than a week in the hospital. Marco and Dante told me they had stopped spending time with Anthony and Felix after what happened and wanted to apologize to Cory. I decided to go with them so I could apologize as well for not helping him as I felt I should have.

When we arrived at the park, it was late in the day, so most people were leaving the court. Cory was sitting on a bench with a large garbage bag and a small backpack. Marco and Dante stayed behind to speak with a few people they knew who were leaving the park. As I sat next to Cory on the bench, he sprang to his feet and grabbed his backpack, but relaxed and sat back down when he saw it was me.

"What's good, Cory? I wanted to say I'm sorry about what happened to you. I should have done something," I said remorsefully.

Cory looked at me for a second and shook his head. "Nah, that wasn't your fault. I know those aren't your people; you just be playing ball like everybody else. You're a kid, anyway. My beef is with Felix and them. They think they run the hood, they think they can do whatever they want." As Cory finished speaking, the last few people who were on the court left the park and Marco and Dante walked toward the bench where we were sitting.

"Yo, Cory!" Marco yelled as he and Dante came within a few feet of us.

Cory grabbed his backpack again and stood up. "I'm not gonna let y'all do that again!" Cory said as he reached inside his backpack. "Fred, go home," he said to me.

"We just came to apologize to you. Relax," Dante responded.

"Don't tell me to relax! The four of you think you own the hood! Nah, not no more." Then Cory pulled a gun from his backpack and pointed it at the two of them. My heart stopped; I had never seen a gun until then.

Marco and Dante looked as if they had seen a ghost, their dark-brown faces gone pale. "It's not that serious!" Marco yelled. "You're buggin' right now!"

"Don't tell me it's not that serious! You're not the one who was in the hospital for more than a week! You're not the one who lost his place in the shelter while he was in the hospital!" A tear rolled down his face, and the gun he was holding rattled uncontrollably in his shaking hand as he waved it back and forth between them.

"That wasn't our fault! That was them! It was just jokes!" Marco pleaded.

Cory wiped the tears from his cheek as his face seemed to harden with confidence and his hand became steady. He aimed at Marco when suddenly a woman's voice came from outside the park: "Don't do it! Don't throw your life away!"

We turned to see an older Black woman walking outside the park with two small children. For a moment, it felt as though her looking at us and us looking at her had brought peace to the chaos. But before I knew it, she was screaming in a way that still echoes in my mind. "Nooo! Nooo!"

Her voice was the last thing I heard before some of the worst sounds I had ever heard in my life: *Bang. Thud.* Silence. Heavy breathing.

While the rest of us were turned toward the woman and children outside of the park, Dante had pulled a gun—later I'd learn that he kept it under his shirt and tucked in the back of his jeans—and shot Cory in the back. "Where did you get that?! Why did you do that?!" Marco yelled in disbelief.

"It was him or us! He was gonna shoot us!" Dante exclaimed desperately. The more seconds that passed without a response, the heavier Dante began to breathe, until he ran out of the park, up the street, and out of sight.

I don't remember much about the next few minutes except what Cory looked like lying there motionless and the faint sound of people yelling for help and running over. The next thing I knew, the paramedics once again had Cory on a stretcher heading toward an ambulance. All I remember is sounds and words after that. The sounds of people who were terrified, and words such as "animals" and "typical" leaving the mouths of the cops who had been aiming their guns at us since the moment they entered the park. Those same cops forced me and Marco into the back of their car and drove us to the local precinct, where they questioned us as we both cried for our parents.

After hours of questioning and being told I was going to prison, the police released me because the woman who had been outside the park came and vouched for me. Over the next months, I was forced to give my testimony of the events multiple times. The trial was the first time I saw Anthony and Felix since their attack, and the last time I'd see them. Thankfully, Cory didn't die, but he was sentenced to nearly a decade in prison for a myriad of charges such as possession of a loaded firearm, illegally purchasing a weapon, the threats of death he made, and more.

Dante received a sentence of twenty years to life for various charges, including attempted murder. While I don't recall how much time Marco received, he was found guilty of being an accessory (a person who knowingly and willingly participates in a crime) in what was deemed an attempted murder of Cory. Marco argued that he had no prior knowledge of the gun and did nothing wrong. I went to court to testify on his behalf, but my testimony couldn't save him from a prison sentence. (The treatment of Cory, Marco, and Dante is a prime example of the overly harsh ways the justice system treats Black and brown people, which Porsche discusses further in chapter 14: "America's Modern Slavery," which is about the prison-industrial complex.)

The judge, jury, and media covering the case all seemed to view everyone involved similarly to the ways the cops that had brought us in for questioning saw us. We were simply animals from the south side of town doing the typical things that animals do to each other. I remember watching the local news during the trial and wondering why no one was talking about how a bunch of teenagers were able to get guns in the first place.

No one was talking about the fact that the guns these teenagers had were bought illegally from people who looked nothing like us. They weren't talking about the fact that a teenager who was living on the street was able to buy a gun for fifty dollars. That the price of a deadly weapon was less than the cost of buying a pair of sneakers he wouldn't have been bullied for. What about the fact that this all started because someone was being bullied? No one was talking about the how and why of the events that took place. All they cared about was what the people involved looked like and who they were: poor Black and brown kids who were now inmates because of bad decisions, trauma, and having access to the tools to destroy one another.

At the time, I couldn't understand how kids like me having guns was so normalized. Why no one seemed to care that these tools for chaos were so easily attainable. But I quickly found out that it wasn't just an issue in my neighborhood. The event that changed our lives forever was part of a much larger epidemic of gun violence in America.

SIDE NOTE: As of 2018, there were over 393 *million* guns in civilian hands in America. For context, there are roughly 330 million people in America, so there are more guns in America than people. The number of guns in America accounts for more than 40 percent of guns in the entire world. Yes, almost half the entire planet's guns are here in America. No wonder Dante, Cory, and other young people who aren't even able to vote are able to attain guns so easily. They're everywhere.

So, what happens when so many people have guns? You get an unfathomable number of lives destroyed because of violence.

SIDE NOTE: More than 300 people are shot in America every single day, causing more than 40,000 deaths per year. The rate of gun deaths in the US is thirteen times that of other **high-income countries**.

But it's not just about acts of violence committed against single individuals. America also leads the world in mass shootings.

SIDE NOTE: There have been mass shootings in the following supposedly **gun-free zones**: offices, airports, newsrooms, synagogues, temples, political events, middle schools, elementary schools, high schools, churches, bars, mosques, preschools, colleges, concerts, hospitals, nightclubs, yoga studios, city buildings, military bases, bowling alleys, movie theaters, and many more places. While gun-free-zone laws don't stop everything, they do bring accountability—which ultimately helps people from bringing guns into places they shouldn't. But we still have to do much more.

Then there is the disproportionate impact of gun violence on Black communities such as the one I grew up in. Black

Americans experience ten times the gun homicides, eighteen times the gun assaults, and three times the fatal police shootings as white Americans.

So, if gun violence is causing such harm in America, why aren't people doing something to stop it? Well, many people are. The problem is that there are also many individuals, companies, and organizations trying to stop *them*. I spoke with two good friends who are on the front lines of the fight against gun violence, to hear their perspectives on the issue and find out what they think we can do to help.

An Interview with SHANNON WATTS

Activist, advocate, writer, and founder of Moms Demand Action

At the moment, Shannon Watts's bio on Twitter says the location she lives in is the "NRA's head, rent free," which makes sense to anyone who knows how much work Shannon has done to try to stop gun violence in America. Thus, she is a thorn in the side of groups who are inherently helping sustain gun violence—groups like the **National Rifle Association** (NRA).

SHANNON: When I started out, I didn't know anything about organizing; I didn't know anything about gun violence or this issue politically. I just knew the nation was broken. And so I went online and looked for something like **Mothers Against Drunk Driving**. That was very pivotal to me in the '80s, as a teenager. It very much changed the culture around drinking and driving and the law. I couldn't find anything except these sort of think tanks run by men in DC. I also found one-off organizations and activist groups, but it wasn't what I was thinking of.

So I just started a Facebook page. I had seventy-five Facebook friends and I thought, "Okay, let's have an online conversation about the fact that this is needed. Gun violence is happening constantly." And then it was very much like you hear about social media when it is like lightning in a bottle. What I thought was going to be an online conversation became an offline grassroots movement.

Shannon's story is inspiring for me because it's an example of every great thing being born from someone simply deciding to take action. It demonstrates the fact that if you care about something, if you see something wrong, you can help do something about it regardless of who you are. In Shannon's case, what started as a Facebook group has become one of the largest anti–gun violence organizations in the world.

SHANNON: There's sort of these three buckets that we focus on. The first is legislative. Early on, we thought the first thing we would do is help pass a **bill**. Like, "Let's get this federal legislation passed and go back to our normal life." That bill failed in the spring of 2013, a few months after **Sandy Hook**, by a handful of votes in the Senate. That included some Democratic senators who voted against it. I kind of thought, *Okay, we tried. We should pack it up.* But, in fact, it was just beginning. If that bill had passed, I don't know if we would still exist. It failing was really the impetus for us pivoting to doing the work in statehouses and in boardrooms.

We very quickly realized that gun agendas had been just sailing through statehouses for years and that we would, first and foremost, have to play defense and stop it. We have a 90 percent track record of stopping the NRA, every year, for the last five years. Unfortunately, I think this year will look different because of the 2020 elections in states, but we've had a lot of success in stopping things like arming teachers, guns on college campuses, **"stand your ground" laws**, and permitless carry—stuff that comes up over and over again every year in the same states. We've also had a lot of success passing good proactive legislation. We've passed background checks now in twenty-two states. We've passed laws that disarm domestic abusers in twenty-nine states. We've passed **red-flag laws** in nineteen states.

Even though we haven't had that cathartic moment we're all waiting for in Congress, it's important to remember that even though the NRA gave tens of millions of dollars to Donald Trump in 2016, and they had a Republican president and a Republican Congress, they did not pass a single piece of their priority legislation in the two years that that was the case. That's one bucket; it's legislation.

The second bucket is electoral work. Immediately, when Moms Demand Action started, we wanted to get involved in electoral politics. For the first few years, it was really just state and federal elections. We've gotten very sophisticated inserting ourselves in these campaigns. One way we do so is by supporting what we call a **gun sense candidate**. There's a questionnaire that goes out. We give away thousands of these. Now, every election cycle, you have to have our gun sense candidate distinction in order to get an endorsement. Right in the primaries, we'll give you a distinction. Maybe three or four people in a primary have the same distinction, but then we will also give an endorsement. We give money through a **PAC**.

And then the third bucket is the cultural work we do. The reason we do cultural work is that MDA is led by women. We're mothers—and others now, as there are lots of men and non-moms, too, who are part of the organization—but it's led by women, and women only have certain levers of power because we only make up about 20 percent of the five hundred thousand elected positions in this country. We're only about 5 to 10 percent of Fortune 1000 CEOs. We're not making the policies that impact this issue. But we're the majority of the voting public, and we're the majority of the public period. So we work to change those numbers and put women in positions of power to make decisions.

We also teach people about secure gun storage through a program called Be SMART. About five million kids in this country live in homes with guns that aren't secured. Most school shooters are students with easy access to guns in their homes.

Not only does Shannon's work seems so common-sense; much of it is also supported by the majority of Americans, including gun owners. So why has the NRA been such an obstacle?

SHANNON: I was sort of shocked to learn that this underbelly of America even existed. I was in many ways living in a bubble. I was a white, suburban mom. I got involved in this issue because I was afraid my kids weren't safe in their schools. I never imagined—again, sort of sitting in my bubble—that I would immediately be attacked. I guess I just didn't realize it was that polarizing. I sort of thought after twenty first graders and six educators were murdered, that this was something we could all agree was egregious and must be stopped. I was wrong because the NRA has created this very vocal minority that has had, essentially, gun **lobbyists** writing our gun laws for decades.

More than 90 percent of Americans, including gun owners, including Republicans, support a background check on every gun sale. But that vocal minority is so loud, and so radicalized, and so rabid, that they would stop at nothing to marginalize people who want to make change on this issue. And so immediately, I started getting threats of death, sexual violence to me, to my daughters. (I have five kids; four of them are girls.)

People were—because all my public information was available—they were calling me, they were texting me, they were emailing me, they were sending me letters in the mail, they were coming to my house. I sort of had to make a decision in those early days. I can remember I called the local police. An officer came to the house, and I just kind of wanted to give them a heads-up. His response was, "Well, that's what you get when you mess with the Second Amendment, ma'am." That's the power of the NRA. And so I really realized quickly that I had to make a decision: Was I going to back down, or was I going to double down? When you work with survivors and you realize your own family and your own community are in jeopardy every single day in this country because of easy access to guns, and if you lose your kids, you have nothing left to lose, there's really no choice but to double down.

I think it's important that Americans know that the NRA is not sort of a sportsman defender of gun rights. It's toxic masculinity personified and armed. They are a lobbyist organization that serves only to seek profitability, and to serve the profitability of gun manufacturers, and they are bad actors. They are the people lobbying for people to continue to be able to buy guns online, for fewer background checks, and for young people to be armed. They are a major part of the reason that we as a society have decided that it's okay that we're going to teach kindergartners to run and hide or fight. It is a real sickness in our society that we've accepted this, or that some people have accepted this, or normalized this. We can't let them normalize this.

Hearing someone like Shannon speak with such passion and conviction about the need to end gun violence in America gives me hope that the end is truly possible. But if anyone out there still isn't sure the end is necessary, I hope they'll read my interview with Brandon Wolf. [Warning: This interview may be triggering for some readers.]

An Interview with BRANDON WOLF

*Media relations expert, nonprofit executive, and survivor of the
Pulse nightclub shooting*

I met Brandon while campaigning for Elizabeth Warren, and I consider him a dear friend, someone who is out there fighting the fights to help make the world better. But because of gun violence, Brandon and I almost never had a chance to know each other. I've sat with Brandon's story for quite some time, thinking about how too many people have similar stories. I hope you sit with it as well and let it wash over you to help you further understand just how brutal gun violence is and why we need to do everything in our power to stop it.

BRANDON: June 11 in our community is referred to as the last normal day. And it's important, I think, to underscore not just the importance of safe spaces and the places where queer people and specifically queer people of color congregate in order to be ourselves, but it's also important to underscore just how ordinary those actions are. That we for our entire lives have been afraid of people reacting to us in a violent fashion, to the point where it becomes normal for us to hide. It becomes normal for us to retreat to our spaces, to avoid certain alleyways, not walk on certain streets at night—that becomes normal behavior. And I know that as people of color yourselves, Fred and Porsche, you understand what that is to learn, to adapt, your own way of existing to fit in and blend in and go unnoticed.

So when I say that June 11, 2016, was ordinary, I mean it, from beginning to end. It was ordinary when I woke up and there was a pile of laundry on the couch. It was ordinary when my best friends, Drew and Juan, my chosen family, were on a date at SeaWorld. It was ordinary when I went to visit a friend for dinner and we sat by the pool outside. It was ordinary when the evening was coming to a close and I texted Drew and Juan and asked them if, after a really long week, they wanted to go and get a drink. Drew lived two doors down from me. That was actually by design. He got really tired of me being late to everything. And so he moved me in next door so he could keep an eye on me. And he was at first reluctant to go out. But I had just been through a really rough breakup and I told him, "I'm pulling the best-friend card. I really need your support."

And so of course, like any good friend, he agreed to be there for me. He walked the two doors down the sidewalk, got into my apartment, and it was ordinary. We listened to the same

soundtrack we always listened to. We watched the same horrible music videos that Drew put on repeat every weekend. We
laughed. We told jokes. We looked at pictures from the week. It
was in every way the same kind of ordinary chosen-family community safe space that we'd created with each other.

When we decided where to go, we essentially just flipped
a coin. We called a ride share and picked the club that was
closest. Pulse had become a part of who we were. I'd been
there almost a hundred times or over a hundred times at that
point. And so we knew it like the backs of our hands. We knew
the drive. It was almost exactly seven minutes from my apartment. I remember pulling up and the line being as ordinarily
long as it always was, the same drag queen at the front door
waiting to take my money. I remember walking inside and it
being just as busy as it always was. And there was this sense
that although it was Latin night and I am not Latino, that I
belonged there more than any other space in our community.
I remember making our way to the same bartender we always
ordered from, ordering the same drinks we always had.

And I also remember that Drew had a master's degree
in clinical psychology, had this way about him, that when he
would have a drink or two and maybe half of one of the ones
that I would have made, he would give you these free therapy
sessions. He would opine on life. And I remember us going to our
usual spot on the patio outside and him talking about life and
talking about spaces like Pulse and how frequently in marginalized communities, we allow the little things to get in the way.
We allow the outside oppressive systems and structures to tell
us that we have to belittle those who are in the same marginalized population as us in order to get a leg up. And he said, "You

know what I wish we did more often is tell each other that we love each other." I remember he had these long gangly arms and he would drape one over your shoulder, sort of like half holding himself up and also leaning in to make his point.

And I remember him draping his arm over my shoulder and making us go around in a circle and tell each other that we love each other. I also remember that in ordinary fashion, it usually got to be about 1:50 a.m. when we realized that we were far too old to be closing the club with eighteen- and nineteen-year-old kids. And so the same thing happened that night. We had our realization that we needed to go home. I just needed to wash my hands. I stepped into a bathroom that I'd been in dozens of times. And for some reason those next few moments are the most vivid memory I have of the early hours of June 12, 2016. I remember the posters. There were promo posters above the urinal of upcoming drag performances, faces that I was familiar with. I remember how cold the water was, coming from the faucet.

I remember this half-empty drink sitting on the edge of the sink, looking like it might fall off. I remember the first sound of gunshots and the confusion that followed. I remember about a dozen people rushing into the bathroom, looking like they had seen the purest form of hell. I remember this debate about whether to run or hide and the realization that we were in a men's-only restroom with only urinals, no stalls, no doors, no walls. All that was protecting us from whatever was happening in the club was a dark hallway. I remember when a second round of gunfire started, there was this smell of blood and gun smoke. And I remember locking arms with those twelve people and just making a run for it. I'd never seen them before. I didn't know their names, but they were my only hope for making it out of the club.

I remember making it down the hallway and across the bar and willing myself not to look left into the club because I knew that whatever I saw in there, I would never be able to forget. I remember this sliver of light in the back of the club from a door that I had never seen opened before. And I remember telling myself to just keep running one foot in front of the other. I remember somewhere halfway through the room, telling myself, I wish I'd gotten a chance to say goodbye to my parents, because I was sure that I was going to die there. And then I remember all of a sudden, the doors swinging open and being on the sidewalk. I remember the rush of night air. I remember this relentless *bang, bang, bang* in the background and people's screams. I remember them jumping over each other and climbing walls and scaling concrete structures outside, splashing through a broken fountain, just desperately trying to get away from the scene.

And I distinctly remember, although I wouldn't find out for sure until much later what heartbreak felt like, when I made it half a block away from Pulse and had the realization that my best friends, my brothers, my chosen family, Drew and Juan, had in ordinary fashion been standing underneath a disco ball, wrapped in each other's arms when that man walked in and opened fire. I learned a couple of days later that Juan made it out of the club on a stretcher, in an ambulance. He was rushed into surgery and ultimately died from his nine gunshot wounds. I learned not long after that, that Drew, his partner—they had both been talking about proposing to each other, although they didn't know it—his partner, Drew, had never made it off the dance floor. He sustained ten gunshot wounds.

Brandon's story isn't just heartbreaking; it's real. There were forty-nine people killed during that shooting and fifty-three others wounded. That was in 2016, and since then, there have been countless more mass shootings. Countless more stories like Brandon's. Countless more lives lost, like Juan's and Drew's. These are the implications of gun violence, and the result of us not doing enough is this continuing to happen.

BRANDON: The truth is that after Pulse, I wanted to run away and hide. At the time I was a store manager for Starbucks. I didn't know anything about politics. I didn't know anything about advocacy. I didn't know anything about showing up for my community because I had been fighting for so long just to belong in a community. I thought that's all that life was, was finding this little sliver of the world where people didn't judge you for who you were and holding on to it until the end of time. And all of a sudden, I was thrust into my worst nightmare. The thing that every queer person, the thing that every marginalized person is afraid of, that someone will walk into the safest of places and rip away everything you know and love.

A basketball court where you go to lose yourself in the game or a nightclub where you go to feel safe with the people you love—gun violence can happen anywhere. Which is why we have to have the courage to make sure that it happens *nowhere.*

BRANDON: I thought about running away. I thought about moving to New York City. I thought about moving away even farther. But I watched what the world did in the aftermath of Pulse. I watched panels of mostly white cisgender heterosexual people on cable news networks everywhere talking about us like we were some caged animals in a zoo. I watched them talking about whether or not to call it a terrorist attack. I watched them talking about whether gay people and Muslims could ever get along after this. I watched them talking about the trauma that Orlando was experiencing without ever acknowledging who we were or how we lived.

A few days after the shooting, we held a funeral service for Drew. He had been the first person in my life who taught me that it was okay to love myself. He had been the first person in my life who had been out and proud and queer and a person of color. And when his mom asked me to be a pallbearer that day, I said "Of course," and as I carried his casket down the aisle, I found myself holding on to the side so tightly that I thought my fingers might fall off. And it's because I didn't want to let go of him until I had found the right words to say goodbye, because he had done so much for me in my life.

So when I got to the front of the church, I looked down at the casket and I made a promise to him. I promised him that I would never stop fighting for a world that he would be proud of. And a part of that fight has meant resisting the epidemic of gun violence in America.

Brandon took his passion for creating change and combating the gun violence epidemic and has become one of the faces of that battle to save lives in this country. Brandon has even testified before Congress on this important matter. But advocating for change isn't easy, especially against forces that are extremely powerful.

BRANDON: I think what's sometimes hard for people to understand if they're in the advocacy space or in the legislative space entirely is the important balance and dance that happens between outside/inside game. And the truth is that both are necessary. It's not enough to elect politicians who go into their positions of power and introduce legislation and bring it to a floor vote. It's never going to bring about the kind of monumental shifts in policy and society that we need to make real, tangible change. I have the distinct honor and privilege of being able to do both at the same time. I think it's important to understand the inside game in order to be effective at the outside game. Sometimes what I see and what I fear is that there isn't an understanding of the legislative process, that there isn't a total understanding of the sort of dealmaking that happens behind closed doors.

And I think that can allow some advocates to be blindsided or deflated by what happens. They shoot for 100 percent of what they're looking for, it comes back at 80 percent, we settle somewhere around 65 percent of what we asked for and it feels like a failure. And in some cases, that means that we didn't go about advocating the right way. We should have started at 110 percent and then backed off toward one hundred, right?

And in other ways, it's also understanding that progress is designed to be incremental in our system as it is designed today. Our system is not designed to be overturned in a day. It is really difficult to move things forward, and it becomes even more challenging depending on the level of policy making you're talking about. It's a little easier to make changes in a rural city commission than it is to make changes in the state legislature. And both of those are significantly easier to tackle than making changes on a federal level in Congress. So I think number one is I want young people to be able to know the inside strategy of the legislative process so that they can learn how to work it in their favor instead of being stymied by it.

Gun violence is a firestorm of bullets and destruction that has engulfed our siblings, our parents, our friends, our chosen family, and our safety. The selfish and powerful have prioritized bullets over people. We are in the midst of an epidemic that only worsens by the day and threatens to steal our chance at seeing tomorrow whenever we leave the safety of our homes. But it doesn't have to be this way. We can find a cure for how gun violence has infected our lives.

Both Shannon's and Brandon's stories speak to the fact that it isn't about where you start, but rather that you just start somewhere. We shouldn't have to be brave when we go see a movie with our friends, shop in a store with our family, or when we're sitting in class. These shouldn't be dangerous places; it's guns that have turned them into that. If we stand together and use our voices and actions to say *"Enough,"* we can finally end the epidemic of gun violence.

To find out more about how you can help put a stop to gun violence, visit: BetterThanWeFoundItBook.com.

YOU CAN'T DISCOVER A PLACE IF PEOPLE ARE ALREADY THERE

Porsche Joseph on the Importance of Addressing
Indigenous Land Theft
Featuring **Anton Treuer** and **Andrea Tulee**

Growing up in Washington State, where there are more **federally recognized tribal nations** than in most states, I may have had more proximity to Native Americans than many people in the country, but I really didn't know much about them. Sure, I was exposed to the colonialist-absolving and historically inaccurate Thanksgiving curriculum in school and even had a few classmates with Native American lineage, but most of the things we learned about Native Americans were purely from a historical perspective, not acknowledging much about their existence today.

Historian David Chang (Native Hawaiian) wrote that "Nation, race, and class converged in land," but it wasn't until I met my friend Andrea in middle school that I realized how important the land we occupy truly is to Indigenous peoples and why that should be important to everyone.

Andrea was a petite kid with a big smile. She loved basketball and would beat almost any boy in the school in a game of one-on-one, despite her stature. Her jump shot was hard to stop. Our school had a basketball hoop in the courtyard, and during lunch you could find her there, playing a game of pickup. It wasn't uncommon for kids to bet a dollar or two that she would win, and they almost always made some money if they did.

Andrea's sense of style was unusual compared to most of the girls in our grade. Her outfits generally consisted of basketball shorts and a T-shirt, but she had a large collection of retro Jordan sneakers, which may be one of the only fashion staples that has withstood the test of time; even way back then they were the cool, expensive sneakers. For people who love sneakers, the right shoes can make the whole outfit, and Andrea always had the best pairs. She also styled her hair in different ways every day, often in styles I had never seen, typically with some kind of braid component. Her nails were always painted with some unique design and in colors that matched her shoes that day. She had a vibe of her own.

Back in middle school, it was relatively easy to get a sense of someone's personality even if you didn't know them because you could see who they sat with at lunch, what kind of electives they signed up for, or what activities or sports they did. But I struggled to put a finger on Andrea's personality. She came off as outgoing yet collected, which is a hard balance for a twelve-year-old to strike, and she only had one or two friends. Everything about her was a mystery to me, even her race.

"What ethnicity is Andrea?" I asked my closest friend, Aysha.

"I don't know. I think she's Cambodian," Aysha answered.

I had never met a Cambodian person at that point in my life, so I accepted it without question.

It wasn't until the last quarter of the school year that I actually got to know Andrea. We were two of the only girls in first-period wood shop class, which was an elective that most kids didn't go out of their way to choose. (It probably had something to do with the time our school quarterback accidentally cut part of his finger off with a table saw.)

On the first day of the new quarter, I was happy to look around and see Andrea in the room full of boys. I would have probably been too shy to say something to her first, but I didn't have to because she almost immediately walked over to me and asked, "Do you want to sit next to each other and be partners for stuff?" with her characteristic big smile.

That was the beginning of a quick-growing friendship. Every morning, we would sit together and sand our wood projects and swap CDs to listen to on our portable CD players. She had a computer at home, which I didn't, so she would regularly burn CDs for me. (If you've never experienced the love language that is receiving burned CDs from friends, then I truly do feel bad for you. You could liken it to someone making you a playlist, but there's something very special about someone being willing to destroy their entire computer with viruses and wait the many hours it would take just to download one song for you.)

We would hang out after school and make what we agreed was the best peanut butter and jelly sandwich ever: crunchy peanut butter and strawberry jam on potato bread. We would have sleepovers and watch the movie *Love & Basketball* on repeat, and every other word out of our mouths was our own personal inside joke. She even tried hard to help coach me into being a better basketball player so that we could play on the same team and spend even more time together. That was a failure, but we had fun playing together, anyway. We were inseparable.

Of course, I learned very fast that she was not Cambodian; rather she was Native American.

"People always think I'm Asian or Latina, because they don't know Native Americans even exist," she said after I told her about Aysha's and my conversation earlier in the school year. "My parents told me to expect that a lot of people have never met Natives before, but I didn't realize it would be this bad," she continued. "Where my family's from, it's mostly Native Americans."

Andrea's father is from the Yakama Nation Reservation a few hours' drive inland from Seattle, and her mother is **enrolled** in the Makah Tribe, which has a reservation about four hours from Seattle in the opposite direction, on the Pacific Ocean. After attending the University of Washington, her parents chose to raise their children in Seattle, but most of their extended family and friends were still on the reservations.

SIDE NOTE: An Indian reservation is an area of land designated for a Native American tribal nation to live on and govern independently. Reservations were usually created under **treaties**, or legal agreements, that the US government made with nations to define land rights, among other things. Not all federally recognized tribal lands are called reservations—some are referred to as pueblos, rancherias, missions, villages, communities, settlements—but they are all tribal homelands. Today, the majority of Native Americans live outside of tribal lands—per the US government census, though the accuracy of that data is debatable—but tribal lands are still significant places for tribal members.

Andrea's cultures are very important to her. When I would spend time at her house after school, I couldn't help but notice the beautiful coastal Native art all over her home: bold black-and-red paintings; carvings depicting distinguished birds, fish, and whales; intricately carved masks; and canoe oars hung on the walls.

One of Andrea's hobbies is beading and making jewelry, and I realized that she frequently uses these same colors and patterns in her work. Albeit modernized, Native practices are still very present and important in Andrea's home. Her parents would cook us smoked salmon hash on Saturday mornings with salmon that her uncles had caught, and make fresh frybread. For celebrations such as graduation parties or baby showers, they would sing customary Makah and Yakama songs, with drumming and sometimes dancing. There was a whole world that Andrea belonged to that her classmates knew nothing about. A world she was deeply connected to.

SIDE NOTE: Frybread is deep-fried dough that is a popular dish among Native Americans across the United States. The food dates back generations but was invented out of necessity after the United States government forcibly moved Native Americans to distant lands and disrupted customary Indigenous food systems, giving the tribal nations supplemental foods regularly found in the European colonizers' diet such as flour, sugar, salt, and lard (the ingredients for frybread). Although it is commonly served in Indigenous nations all over the country now, it is not a traditional pre-colonization food.

One day Andrea didn't show up for wood shop class, so I swung by her house on my way home from school unannounced. This was back in the days when a kid having a cell phone was still pretty rare and there was no such thing as Facebook or Instagram.

Her mom greeted me and told me I could head back to her room. I gave a few light knocks on her bedroom door, but when she didn't say anything, I decided to let myself in. I found Andrea lying on her bed shooting socks from her clean-laundry pile into a small hoop she had attached to the door. I could tell she was sad; she didn't even say anything when I walked in. We sat in silence for a moment before I picked up a sock and took my shot, which I completely missed, causing us to burst into laughter.

"Why weren't you at school today?" I asked.

"I had a bad day yesterday, so my parents let me stay home. I don't know why I even allow myself to get upset. Every year my parents have to come in and talk to the teachers about how they're teaching Native American history. They're so ignorant and racist.

"My history teacher is so horrible," she continued in a rush of anger. "She wanted to do some grading, and we're learning about Native Americans right now, so she thought it was a good idea to put on *Pocahontas* for us to watch during class. I told her that that movie is offensive, and that we should learn the real story of how Pocahontas was kidnapped, torn away from her child and husband, and held hostage. They literally murdered her real husband. The cartoon is so disrespectful; they make it out to be some grand love story, but in reality they forced her to marry an old English guy and convert to Christianity and she was treated terribly. She died by the time she was twenty-one and her father hadn't seen her since she was kidnapped. Did you know that they buried her in England and to this day her tribe can't get the government to send her remains back so that she can have a proper burial? It's a traumatic story and the story that Disney tells is a complete lie.

"I shouldn't be surprised that I was sent to the principal's office for trying to talk to the teacher about it. So I just didn't want to go back to school today, and my parents said I didn't have to. I am just so uncomfortable here sometimes. If it weren't for you and basketball, I probably wouldn't even go to school. This summer I just want to be on the rez as much as possible."

I didn't doubt what she was telling me for a moment. In our education system, the history of Indigenous peoples and colonizers is often painted as an encounter of cultural exchange, where Native Americans offered food and knowledge of the land to the friendly, empty-handed Europeans. This narrative is taught in order to avoid accountability for the brutal theft and murder committed by the colonizers who still rule the country to this day. Because Native Americans only make up about 2 percent of the US population, curriculum on Native Americans is rarely challenged, but it is often full of misinformation that can be hurtful and harmful.

"Well, luckily we only have one more week until summer vacation starts," I said, trying to be optimistic. "But I will be really sad if you leave for the entire summer."

She looked sad, too, but then her face lit up. "I have an idea!" she said. "My whole family is going to Canoe Journeys this summer; you should come for a few days."

SIDE NOTE: Intertribal Canoe Journey is a revitalized practice of the Indigenous peoples of the Pacific Northwest coast, in which nations all the way from Alaska, Washington, Oregon, and British Columbia use traditional-style canoes to travel routes that were once used by their ancestors. Along the journey, they cover up to three hundred miles—sometimes traveling as much as twenty-five miles each day. While en route to the final host destination, they stop to rest and visit other nations and tribal lands, where people welcome the canoes with celebrations and protocols stretching back generations. When they reach the final destination, there is a huge welcoming party that lasts for days.

The purpose is to revive and commemorate the practice of traveling by canoe along historical trade routes to bring together and strengthen relations among nations. The contemporary Canoe Journeys began in 1989, when Emmett Oliver (Quinault) organized the Paddle to Seattle as part of Washington State's centennial celebration. The entire journey can last for more than a month, depending on the endpoint, which changes every year.

While Canoe Journeys are open to the public, not all Native gatherings or celebrations are. If you are a non-Native person, it is important to only be in cultural spaces that are appropriate for you to attend and that you are invited into.

We made it through the last week of school, and some weeks later, I was looking forward to heading to Neah Bay with Andrea and meeting her family and experiencing more of her culture. I was anticipating being an outsider. I felt a bit nervous that my introversion would get the best of me or that I might say something ignorant or offensive. But at the same time, I was confident that my best friend knew what she was doing when she invited me.

After a ferry ride and a long drive, we finally approached the reservation. We wound down a steep, narrow road that revealed the most stunning place I had ever seen. Large cliffs peeked through the ocean as waves crashed peacefully into them, and a heavy fog sat on the top of the lush green trees that bordered the long, sprawling beach. I'm not sure what I had expected, but I certainly hadn't expected *this*. I hadn't even known there were places in Washington that looked like this. (Google "Shi Shi Beach" if you need a visual.)

Andrea's aunt's house was small, but at least ten people came out to help us with our bags. As soon as they greeted us, I could see how happy Andrea was to be surrounded by family and friends. Everyone was laughing and joking, and they all teased each other *heavily*. They had a good time cracking jokes about Andrea being an **urban Indian** because she lived in the city. They used a lot of words I didn't know, though I had heard some of them from Andrea. Like any other community, they had their own ways of speaking and interacting among themselves.

I was noticeably out of my element, but nobody seemed to pay that any mind. "Go ahead and put your stuff in the guest suite," her aunt said, gesturing to the other side of the living room. I looked over at the couch she was nodding to, apparently not responding quick enough, as everyone in the room began to laugh. "I'm joking with you. Is the couch good enough for the kids from the city?" I laughed politely and assured her I had no problem with sleeping on the pull-out couch.

Andrea had four cousins who all appeared to be around our age. At one point they suggested we go outside and shoot some baskets. There was a hoop at the end of the driveway, so we played a game of HORSE from the street. As I looked around, I saw that there were basketball hoops up and down the street and in more than half the yards and realized in that moment that Andrea wasn't just randomly obsessed with basketball; it was a huge part of where she was from. Then I realized almost all her cousins and other kids our age, boys and girls, wore basketball clothes and Jordan sneakers. I knew that her love for basketball was an important part of her personality, but I hadn't understood the cultural relevance of basketball to Native Americans.

Toward the end of the nineteenth century, many Native children in the United States and Canada were forced to leave their families and communities and enter government- and missionary-operated boarding schools, otherwise known as "Indian boarding schools." The mission was to erase Native identities and force **assimilation**. Their hair was cut short, and they were forced to stop speaking their languages and stop wearing their customary clothing. Dancing, hunting, and practicing their religions were also forbidden, all in an attempt to "modernize" them into the white American culture, which left many of the children traumatized and depressed. Many children died in these schools due to abuse, neglect, malnourishment, diseases, suicide, or other causes.

SIDE NOTE: In 2021, 751 unmarked grave sites were discovered near a former Indigenous school in Saskatchewan, Canada. Such boarding schools operated in Canada from 1883 to 1996, but it wasn't until decades later that government officials recognized the operation of the schools as a *"cultural genocide"* that was also responsible for the deaths of tens of thousands of Indigenous children. In the United States, Native American children experienced similar horrors during the 150 years Indian boarding schools operated here, and unmarked graves continue to be found in this country as well.

The white people who ran the Indian schools used basketball as a means of teaching the children sports, in an effort to assimilate them; however, the kids adapted the rules and playing style to create something of their own. It became a mental and physical outlet and a form of empowerment. Although these boarding schools lasted well into the 1970s in some instances (and even decades later in Canada), by the 1910s and 1920s, some students were returning home and bringing the game with them. Andrea came from a family of talented basketball players, which explained why she had been playing all her life.

SIDE NOTE: Andrea's grandfather attended Haskell Indian Nations University and would tell her a school legend that James Naismith, credited with inventing the game of basketball, used to come over from Kansas University, which is about a mile away, and observed the Native American children playing a game similar to that of basketball. Many Haskell alums tell similar accounts.

Even up against her cousins, Andrea was still the best shooter, so after winning two rounds, we headed in to get some rest. The next morning, we woke up and had a huge breakfast prepared by her aunt and then ventured out to the festivities. Along the waterfront, there were crowds of people and a large fire surrounded by at least one hundred salmon strategically filleted and tied to tall cedar sticks that stood in the ground. The aroma filled the entire beach as the fire slowly baked the fish. There were vendors selling buckskin bread, Indian tacos, woven blankets, and local art, including hand-pulled drums and oars like the ones I saw in Andrea's home.

In the community center, there was a large gym full of drumming and singing, children dancing, and people wearing customary dance clothes preparing to perform. I couldn't believe that this world existed and how little people like me knew about it.

"Do all tribes have reservations like this?" I asked Andrea.

"No, some tribes don't have land at all. Washington has more reservations than most states, though," she replied as we made our way through the gym. She went on to tell me that there are 574 federally recognized tribal nations across the country. "They're not all like this, either. You know that on my mother's side we are coastal Natives; that means our livelihood is traditionally based on the water. That's why we always eat so much salmon, halibut, crab—you've probably noticed that many of my uncles and cousins are fishermen. Our people have always been experts on these waters. We would travel far and trade with most of the nations participating in Tribal Canoe Journey and even farther. But each nation traditionally has a strong tie to the land, so where they are located is important to the traditions of the tribe.

"See over there." She gestured to the left, where a group of young dancers who were dressed in shawls and holding paddles were waiting to perform a dance. "They use the paddles in the canoe dance they are going to do, and on their clothes you can see the whales and salmon designs. You won't necessarily see that with a tribe that doesn't live on the water. Some tribes live in the desert, some live in the pine forests, some live in the Arctic, some live near the ocean or on the river or in the mountains. Our traditional ways often depend on the land we come from."

Andrea and I had a great time watching the dancing and welcome ceremonies, and playing with her cousins and friends. Seeing her know all of the songs that were being sung, wave and greet people by name as she walked through the street, know exactly how the salmon was prepared, and know the stories and teachings passed down from so many generations ago gave me a better lens with which to understand my best friend. I realized that her people have been here doing these same practices since before Europeans even knew this land existed. I took that moment to consider that all of the land we walk about today, in any city or town throughout the country, once belonged to Indigenous peoples, and there were entire ways of life disrupted or destroyed when white people stole this land.

I'd thought I'd understood all of that before coming, but it was different once I was standing there on the Makah Reservation, on the homelands of my dearest friend.

Because of the impact of European colonization, it is not all that common for non-Native Americans to have a connection to the lands that our ancestors originated from, which sometimes makes us unable to empathize with Indigenous peoples and respect—or in some cases even accept—that we occupy their homelands.

In school and as adults, we learn a lot about immigration and the different struggles that various groups have had to overcome to be in the United States. We are taught to revere the early immigrants, those brave pioneers who risked their lives to settle the wilderness of this country. We are even taught that it was the destiny of these colonizers to settle this land—from sea to shining sea. But too often we omit from the conversation whom they harmed in order to build the country to what it currently is. We put aside the utter lack of respect that colonists had for the land itself and for the cultures that were already here. We reject words like **genocide** to describe the deliberate extermination of the Native peoples who got in the colonizers' way, who got in the way of "destiny." And we ignore the lasting impact and continuation of this brutality. In doing this, in teaching only part of our country's history and erasing all the rest, we create educators who teach racist curricula, such as Andrea's teacher who felt it was appropriate to show the movie *Pocahontas* in class. We enable the use of caricatures of Native Americans as school and sports team mascots, and we create a population that is astonished and outraged that anyone might take offense.

It is our responsibility to educate ourselves about whose land we are on, what tribal nations existed where we live before the land was stolen, and what nations are there today. Students may learn that 90 percent of Indigenous peoples in what is now the United States were murdered upon contact with European colonizers—though too many don't even learn that—but they aren't taught about the 2.6 million who remain in the United States today, nor taught to consider what the role of non-Natives is in rectifying the harm Native Americans endure today in order for this country to even exist. To erase Native Americans from present-day conversations about race, social and environmental justice, and politics is to deny the fact that colonialism is current and ongoing. It is the responsibility of non-Natives to support the needs of the communities whose homelands we occupy.

And it's not just Indigenous Americans who need the support of non-Natives. While the issues facing Indigenous peoples vary across the globe, it is vital that their voices be heard and that allies stand with them. Non-Natives must quit stifling the efforts of Indigenous peoples to exercise political power that will allow them to maintain relations with their homelands and wildlife and realizing futures for their families and tribal nations.

An Interview with ANTON TREUER

Author and professor of the Ojibwe language

To gain a better perspective of land rights and modern Native American culture, I spoke to Dr. Anton Treuer, who lives and works in his community on the Leech Lake Reservation in Northern Minnesota. Anton has written extensively on contemporary Native American life and has a lot of knowledge of the relationship between tribal nations and the US government. He also has a nuanced understanding of why there's such a lack of knowledge about Native Americans among non-Natives—and the implications of this ignorance.

ANTON: Native Americans are a small percentage overall of the US population, less than 2 percent. In some areas, you can't avoid us—some parts of the Southwest, Northwest, Plains, some parts of the Great Lakes. But in many other parts of the US, like the whole East Coast and the South, it's pretty easy to avoid us. So many people know very little about Native Americans, and as we look deeper at some of the drivers, we realize that 87 percent of state educational standards required no instruction about anything about Indigenous peoples after 1900.

So the message becomes that we're something that happened in the past. And there might even, among progressives, be the sense there was some terrible injustice—a theft of land, maybe even genocide—but it's still something that happened in the past rather than something that's happening now. It was the precursor rather than a contemporary issue, and so I believe that's always an important distinction to make: that we are ancient and modern all at the same time.

Thousands of years of human history is still in the making, not just something that happened in the past. And certainly land is a big piece of that. So it's a good focal point because one of the defining features of indigeneity is being land-based and connected to land. Although the Indigenous experience is big and broad, with half of enrolled tribal citizens living off reservation and, according to the US census, 70 percent of the self-identified Native citizenry living off reservation. So the Native experience is not just a reservation experience, although those places are special still in the Native sovereignty and psychological frame.

If I had never met Andrea, I may still to this day think of Native Americans in the way I had been taught about them in school, which was only in a historical perspective, and not even an accurate historical perspective at that. History is important, but stopping there doesn't help inform non-Natives on how to interact with and support Native Americans today.

ANTON: Tension between cultural continuity and cultural change is especially pronounced in the Native cultures. So on the one hand, we should have permission to change over time. To be an authentic Englishman, you don't have to worship at Stonehenge and paint your face blue. But a lot of times people expect us to look like we stepped off the set of [the 1990 film] *Dances with Wolves.*

We have the right to change over time. We have cultures that shift and change. How much can people change and still be the same people? That's the tension. I think in Indigenous communities, it's especially profound. So even as we describe

Indigenous land—yes, we were pushed off of our original land-holdings, which was all of it, pushed to reservations. But that doesn't mean the reservations are just horrible places. In a place like Minnesota, Native people maintain land on all of the ten largest lakes in the state, not by accident. They fought to keep what they have. Those are special and sacred places, not just horrible places that they didn't want to be at. So it's complex.

For the Cherokee, they were pushed out of the South, went on multiple trails of tears, were forced to go to Oklahoma. But the land that they have in Oklahoma is still special to them and sacred to them, and it's been home for a long time now, and it's where the community is. So, it's like if every white person in America died from the coronavirus tomorrow and the Cherokee could move back to Georgia, some of them might stay in Oklahoma because they love it. So it's complex.

SIDE NOTE: The Trail of Tears was part of a series of forced displacements between 1830 and 1850 where the United States government expelled Native Americans from their land and placed them on land that was out of white people's way. This was formally called "Indian removal" and it was violent, resulting in the death of many Native Americans. The Cherokee were marched more than 1,200 miles from Georgia to Oklahoma, with guns pointed in their faces and accompanied by seven thousand US troops. The government promised that the land the Cherokee were relocated to would be untouched and that they could stay there unbothered forever. But these assurances would prove to be just more examples of promises broken. Not only was this land already the homelands of other Native nations, but as more white people came and moved westward, the US government began authorizing white settlement of Native homelands.

Expecting Native Americans to be culturally frozen in time is a common misconception held by non-Natives. Another, much more harmful, misconception is that European colonizers landed on a mostly empty continent when they "discovered" America.

ANTON: A lot of people don't even realize that there were over a hundred million people here before Europeans arrived. North and South America were at least as densely populated as Europe at the time of contact. America has a pattern of engineering historical amnesia, and it's a requirement to prop up the mythology of **American exceptionalism**.

SIDE NOTE: For more on the myth of American exceptionalism, see Fred's chapter on the military-industrial complex (chapter 13: "We Have Money for War but Won't Feed the Poor").

Without historical amnesia, there's no way to avoid the fact that for everybody else who came, there actually wasn't room. Their arrival and escape from religious persecution and establishment of a little Pilgrim homeland isn't true. It was stealing, and there's no way to divorce the American experience from that. So it's hard if you want to believe in American exceptionalism, because all you want to do is sing, "This land is your land. This is my land." And you just can't do it.

It's the same thing with the Black narrative. Americans will say, "Yeah, there was some slavery, but we had an emancipation proclamation. How about that Abraham Lincoln?" Or, "Yeah, there was some Jim Crow stuff, but we put an MLK Boulevard in every major city in America. Aren't we great?" And then everybody's confused when they see how upset people are over George Floyd. They're just literally confused—they don't get it.

We cannot have historical amnesia. But that requires America to take a look in the mirror. One of the defining features of colonization is erasure. It's taking one culture and group and using it to erase the others.

What you don't know can hurt in multiple ways. For example: I went to school for thirteen years in my K-12 experience to learn whatever I needed to be successful in the world. And putting aside a few experiences with overt, direct racism from a teacher and getting beat up sometimes by white people just because of my race and that kind of thing, most of the teachers wanted me to succeed. They just wanted me to succeed *their* way. But what hurt was not the mean things they did, but simply the absent narratives, which were screaming at me: *You and yours aren't important, aren't relevant, and don't matter.*

What someone doesn't know can still hurt. It's not just bad intentions and bad actions coming from bad people. It's systems, structures, policies, and erasure. Racism operates at multiple levels. There's the micro level, which is people saying a racial slur. Everyone can identify that and can say, "Okay, that's bad." But then there's the careless racism. And so the problem is you try to point something out and say, "Hey, you know, there is some **cultural smog** or some really unhealthy racist policies and procedures?" And the response often is, "What are you talking about? I didn't do anything bad. I'm a good person." They can't see it. And so how do we see it if we never get a chance to learn even about how we were indoctrinated into it?

I think ultimately, there's *consciousness*, when you know, and you know that you know. Then there's *unconsciousness*, when you don't know, and you don't even know that you don't know it. And then there's *disconsciousness*, where you don't know, but you know you don't know, and you are still not going to pay any attention to that.

Anton's message is powerful. Some of the most harm can be done by people who aren't necessarily intentionally racist but who are unconsciously erasing the Native American experience. It's our responsibility to educate ourselves and to move from unconsciousness to consciousness. It is also our duty as allies to hold the disconscious accountable to the truth. If Andrea was not there to challenge the teacher on *Pocahontas*, it's the duty of those of us who are conscious to not only identify but also step in and refuse to go along with disconscious narratives.

An Interview with ANDREA TULEE

Community leader and volunteer

When considering whom I should interview for this chapter, I couldn't think of a more valuable voice than Andrea herself. Andrea is enrolled in the Confederated Tribes and Bands of the Yakama Nation, from her father's side. She lives on the

Yakama Reservation, in Washington State, where she is also raising four children and running a nonprofit that promotes culture and language revitalization. (I know, real-life super-woman, right?)

Andrea is smart. She's been smart since we were kids, and as a result, has been the one to explain many things to me over the years. Here, Andrea explains sovereignty and why it is so important to nations from her perspective.

ANDREA: Native American sovereignty is very misunderstood by most people. Sovereignty means—very directly—the right to govern yourself and make your own laws.

I'll just reference my own tribe, personally. Our nation actually went to war with the United States government in 1855 after signing a treaty with them because Yakama leaders were upset to see the **treaty rights** be immediately violated. Hostile white settlers were violating the land rights we had agreed to, among many other things, which our leaders didn't agree with. As you can imagine, tensions escalated quickly. The war lasted for three years.

We had negotiated different guarantees in the treaty—the right to hunt, fish, and gather on our usual and accustomed lands. We also agreed to creating a reservation. Part of that treaty also guaranteed the right to govern ourselves, as a sovereign nation.

Tribal nations are sovereign nations and should have a relationship with the United States that functions like a country, nation to nation. But while the US government has a decent record of respecting treaties with international nations, it has a shameful history of violating every treaty it has signed with Indigenous peoples.

ANDREA: Even though we have that treaty that explicitly outlines all of those things that were guaranteed, a lot of people, including judges and politicians, try to question it. For example, they'll try to argue about ways in which treaty language could be interpreted, but one important aspect of treaties is that they are to be interpreted as they were understood at the time of the original signing. Many of our leaders and our people fought, died, gave their lives up to make sure that treaty happened and was upheld. That's why it's really important for us to maintain the treaty, and our rights to sovereignty. We want to be on the right side of that agreement.

Many non-Natives are surprised to learn that tribes are their own sovereign nations. The use of words like *tribes* or *bands*, taught in the classroom or in textbooks instead of the word *nations*, may contribute to this lack of awareness. Whatever the cause, when people learn that each nation is entitled to rights that are independent of the state laws, they oftentimes don't understand and oppose this right to independence.

ANDREA: People feel that it's unfair, because they're not looking at it from a historical context or perspective. I think Americans have this romanticized idea of the United States as a melting pot and they value that. So when they see us, tribal people, fighting our hardest to maintain who we are, our history, our tribal laws, our treaties, they don't want to accept that we might not want to blend into their melting pot and be part of what they created. We all live here and can learn to work together, but our cultures are just as relevant.

Our treaty was established in 1855. That's, honestly, not too long ago. A lot of people have personal stories from those time periods; my great-grandparents were alive. So we take it personally, because we know our great-grandparents; we know our ancestors. We know the stories, the things that they had done, who they were, what they went through. For us to pretend like that didn't happen, and just try to be this melting pot, feels like sacrificing who we are.

This is the same cultural amnesia Anton discussed. Non-Natives and the US government tend to want to quickly move on from history that paints them in a way they don't like, and they expect everyone else to want to do the same.

ANDREA: I think most Americans, they really value the present and the future, so they're kind of missing a big piece of the picture. They really feel, perhaps, that the past isn't valid or important. Many Americans don't care to learn the real history of this country. And even if they wanted to, or were curious about it, it might not even be available to them. Because the history that's taught about Native Americans is incredibly inaccurate when it comes to school.

The reason that the truth is oftentimes not available to non-Natives is because white people were usually the ones writing the history, with little regard for Indigenous peoples' accounts. But just because we won't always find a true depiction of US history in our textbooks, that doesn't mean that Native Americans do not know the real history. As Professor Joshua L. Reid (Snohomish) said to me recently, "Indigenous peoples have their own ways of knowing and remembering the past."

ANDREA: For my tribe, for example, we have cultural leaders here that really know a lot about our history, times of the treaty, and way before that. But what they say is never, ever published. They feel that it's not for textbook understanding, because that's not really who we are or how we learn. We were very careful to always have oral history, and to make sure it was accurate so that it could be passed down. We had certain people who held that position—their job was to remember things as they were. That was something Indian people had always done.

Another reason our ancestors and cultural leaders did not want to print our stories in the white man's literature was because they felt it provided a platform for our oppressors to cut down or challenge what we know to be true, in order to advance their narrative. Rather, they preferred to keep the knowledge within, so as to protect it from those who wish to change the narrative to benefit themselves.

Things are a lot different in our understanding—the understanding that it's our history versus the history the United States teaches. When it comes to, for example, Christopher Columbus, I think a lot of people know that narrative is incredibly inaccurate and romanticized. Really, in all actuality, he was a murderer who hurt children, he was ruthless, but in the textbooks, they celebrate this man as being this great person who did so much for the country. I guess it all depends on who's telling the history.

In Andrea's experience as a member of the Yakama Nation, history is not only important in order to reflect on the past, but is also strongly tied to her present everyday life.

One thing that has always been important to her ancestors is the land, which is still important to her and her family today.

ANDREA: Our land is extremely important. It's vital for us. If you were to hear our elders talk, you would hear them say that we're people of the river. The foods and animals that are natural to the land are our staples. We have extensive resources. We've got our roots here. It's a way of life. Since time immemorial, that's what we did—work with the land. I think that I would really find it hard to imagine, if we weren't allowed on this land, who we'd be.

Some tribes got relocated to places that were completely foreign to them. They had to probably refind themselves. For us, and a lot of us Northwest tribes, our ceremonies, our language, our stories, creation stories—all of that revolves around the land. I can't speak for all tribes because we all have our different ways and different circumstances, but for us, we're proud to be on Yakama land. Some tribes are struggling just to hold on to any little bit that they can, and like I said, some of them have been relocated, so many tribes have a different experience in that way.

Food and resources are important aspects of the land and so it's not surprising that Native Americans are continuously at the forefront of environmental movements. Neither is it surprising, unfortunately, that their rights are often challenged by those who seek to use the resources of their land.

ANDREA: In our treaty, we're guaranteed always to be able to hunt, fish, and gather. But that's constantly being questioned, attacked, and infringed upon—especially by the state.

For example, my great-grandpa, he was fishing—a lot of our people even to this day, that's how they make their life, as fishermen—and they arrested him and put him in jail several times for fishing with a net. He fought that; he went to court several times and made it all the way up to the Supreme Court and won that case. That just reaffirmed the rights that we already knew that we had, that we didn't need a permit. We could fish in those same methods that we always have.

SIDE NOTE: The case Andrea mentions is *Tulee v. Washington* (1942), and it reaffirmed that the original treaty gave the Yakama people the right to fish both on and off the reservation—no permits required. And while the victory was undeniably important, it didn't acknowledge the harm and financial burdens Andrea's family had to endure due to her great-grandfather going to jail numerous times, being torn away from his family and unable to earn his livelihood through fishing, all just to prove what was already reserved and agreed to in the established treaty.

The 1942 case helped pave the way for the Boldt decision,

made in the Supreme Court case *United States v. Washington* (1974), which reaffirmed that Native American peoples of the entire state of Washington could comanage fish harvests, could fish in the places and ways they always had (even if those places are not on reservations), and are entitled to half of the annual fish harvest.

After that, the government still questioned our rights. This was the premise upon which the Boldt decision was made. That involved several of the Northwest tribes, fishing treaty tribes. They fought for quite a while. Billy Frank Jr. (Nisqually), an environmental leader and treaty rights activist, is one of the main people who were featured in that case.

Eventually they won, but it was a really big deal because there are certain things that the Boldt decision reaffirmed, stating that we had the right to half the catch, with the tribes and the state managing the fishery together. Which turned out to be a really good thing for everyone because if you look at some other salmon fishery systems throughout the United States, they're pretty much all depleted because of commercial fishermen, and the ability for non-Indians to come and fish as much as they wanted to. So it's pretty much the Northwest and Alaska that have really healthy salmon fishery systems. It's because of that Boldt decision that we still have that, because if that decision hadn't been made, everything would be depleted by now.

We're still fighting for policies that are going to benefit the health of these ecosystems—dam removal, environmental impacts, we're always taking those things into account. We say when and how much can be done each year, depending on the observations that are carefully taken.

As I mentioned earlier, Native Americans are consistently at the forefront of environmental movements, and their knowledge of their homelands extends far beyond that of the people who have colonized these lands. Native Americans have been in North America for at least fifteen thousand years—well over fourteen thousand years before Christopher Columbus "discovered" America. Yet the United States government still does not trust or consult Native Americans on environmental issues, nor does the government always respect the treaties that allow them to use their homelands and waters in the ways that were agreed upon.

ANDREA: Ultimately, I believe you can question the validity of this country if the United States breaks these treaties. If they didn't make those treaties with us, who's to say they would have any right to be here? So if they break those agreements, then that just undermines their right to be on this land. Treaties are rarely broken when it's country to country, but they think they can break these treaties because we're tribal nations. When they were signed, it wasn't meant to be anything less than a treaty made between countries. We are sovereign nations.

Understanding the history of land transfer from tribal nations to the United States government is important, because that history reverberates to this day. The truth is that Native land was acquired in ways that include deceit and murder. To put it simply, it was stolen. Even when land was "sold" to colonizers, the transactions were unethical and the tribes were often brutally coerced to cede their land. Colonizers would regularly violate the terms of treaties and push Native

Americans off their ancestral homelands to an entirely different area or identify small areas where they would force them
to live. Acknowledging that we are on Native land is not only
something non-Natives need to do out of respect; we need to
acknowledge it because those agreements that our government set with tribal nations are what allow us to even be on
this land.

Native Americans are not just part of the past; they are
here, they are present, and there is still an effort taking place
by the US government to continue colonizing their homelands. Over the years, politicians have found ways to reduce
tribal homelands and impede on them when the government
wants to access natural resources or build, for instance, a border wall. In 2020, Donald Trump revoked reservation status
from the Mashpee Wampanoag Tribe of Massachusetts, which
threatened more than three hundred acres of ancestral homelands where the Mashpee Wampanoag had developed schools,
police, and tribal housing. While the move was overturned in
2021, it's a stark reminder of how perilous things still are for
tribal nations. This is why it is so important to know whose
homelands we are on and what historical and current threats
exist.

Recently, the **Land Back movement** has been gaining
attention, as a call for land reclamation to Indigenous peoples, as well as giving Indigenous peoples decision-making
power over their homelands in this country that they continuously fight to protect. So many non-Natives tell ourselves
that we wouldn't have supported the genocide of the Native
Americans or the theft of their homelands at the time of

colonization. We agree that it was brutal, tragic, and morally reprehensible; however, when we don't acknowledge the stolen land that we are on, or do the work to understand what implications this theft has had and *still* has, we cannot honor those people or stand up for them. The truth is, colonization is not over and acknowledgments alone are not enough. Non-Natives must think critically about what steps we need to take to support tribal sovereignty and self-determination, and we need to pressure our institutions and politicians to do the same. We need to stand with Native American nations and listen to them in order to understand how to protect their land rights and advocate for their sovereignty.

To find out more about how you can help combat Indigenous land theft, visit: BetterThanWeFoundItBook.com.

7
BLACK SQUARES DON'T SAVE LIVES

**Frederick Joseph on Consistently Practicing
Anti-racism and (Re)Learning History
Featuring Dr. Sonja Cherry-Paul**

There are only a few things that I've ever dared to love so deeply that they make me feel like I'm flying, make me feel like I'm free. It's not that I don't have room to love other things; I would certainly welcome the feeling of freedom more often. But as a Black person, I learned early on to always be prepared for this greedy country to take whatever it wants from me at any moment. The fewer things I love deeply, the tighter I'm able to hold them.

I think that's why most Black people I've known love the way they do, with a weighty love. The kind of rooted love that stands tall in a storm. So much has been taken from Black people that sometimes all we have is each other, and maybe that's where that kind of love comes from.

Many years ago, I fell deeply in love with camping. It wasn't something that I grew up doing and not something

I was open to at first, as I hadn't met a single Black person who'd had good experiences in the middle of the woods. But I agreed to go camping for the first time during my senior year of high school with a few friends, and it ended up being one of the best experiences I'd ever had.

On our first night there, I was the last person to fall asleep. I stayed up for a few hours sitting by the campfire and just stared at the night sky, losing myself in the constellations of stars. As I sat there trying to remember what I had learned about Orion's Belt in elementary school, I began to cry. My tears were filled with the realization that in my experience as a Black person in the United States, I had never actually spent time enjoying the land my ancestors were forced to come to, because like so many other Black people, I was always simply trying to survive on it.

On that night I began to understand that the land we occupy is not to blame for what was done to us on it. The trees, the air, the rivers, and the spirit of this place existed long before it was colonized. Long before so many of us were traumatized.

Since that trip, I've gone camping multiple times a year. Doing so allows me to laugh, allows me to remember, allows me to talk, allows me to be with the people I'm holding tightly. But most of all, it allows me peace, which is so rare in my life. One of the most important things I've learned as I've grown older is how important it is to restore yourself in a world that often takes more than it gives. No well is infinite, which is why it's important to pour into yours if you're letting others draw from it.

An added bonus of those trips is not having cell-phone reception or the internet. I believe we as people have become so constantly connected to the outside world that many of us are becoming disconnected from ourselves. Being in nature helps me reconnect to myself.

In May of 2020, I needed to find myself more than ever. The COVID-19 pandemic had been decimating the world, I was still reeling from the murder of Ahmaud Arbery, and Porsche and I hadn't spent time with friends or family in months. We took that trip with my then-eighteen-year-old cousin Novell and his best friend, Mawiyah. I wanted to give them an opportunity to get away, since they were home from school because of the pandemic.

It was a beautifully spent few days. On the final day of that trip, Porsche drove a few minutes away from the campsite where there was internet and cell-phone reception so she could check her emails and texts. As she pulled back up to the camp-site, there was a look on her face that I had seen before. A look of sorrow. Yet, more than sorrow, there was a look of exhaustion.

"What's wrong?" I asked as soon as the car rolled to a stop next to me.

Porsche looked at me for a moment as the regret seemed to boil over. There was something she didn't want to tell me, but knew she had to.

"What is it? Is everything okay?" I asked again.

"It never stops. They did it again, baby," she said simply.

One of the saddest parts about that moment is that I knew exactly what she meant: another Black person had been murdered for being Black. "When? Where?" I asked, already heartbroken for a family I didn't know but was sure was not so different from my own.

"It happened in Minnesota. I didn't see it, but there's a video, and it's supposed to be really bad. Like—really bad." Her voice quaked. In just a few seconds, the joy of the past few days had been replaced with anger and sadness.

I walked over to Novell and Mawiyah and told them what Porsche had told me. I asked them if they were okay, knowing how news such as this always impacts me. ("Always" is such a sad truth about how frequently these murders occur.) They were not okay, but as Black children, they had learned that this is the reality of being Black in America.

We solemnly packed up the campsite and began our two-hour drive back to the city. As Porsche, Novell, and Mawiyah combed through news websites and social media on their phones, my mind was on something else. I couldn't help feeling angry and defeated that while I was away doing what I love, a man who could easily have been anyone in that car was taken from this world. I felt like a fool for believing that I could potentially find peace while so many forces work to keep me from it. For daring to love something deeply. I felt angry with myself for believing that I may find even the slightest freedom as a Black person in such an anti-Black country. *You should have known better, Fred,* I said to myself the entire drive down that lonely highway.

During the days after we arrived home, not only did I hear more information about the murder of George Floyd, but the news of Breonna Taylor's murder became more mainstream as well.

SIDE NOTE: As of this writing, the video of George Floyd being murdered has been viewed more than five billion times on Twitter alone. I'm not one of those views; I've never needed to see people's lives being taken or people being harmed in order to feel compelled to act. Before you watch, like, or share such footage yourself, consider if doing so is really necessary.

I've always likened white supremacy to a fire, something that if not doused or put out, will burn everything in its path. This fire burns all around the world, but it's particularly devastating in the United States, because the fire does not simply exist here—the nation was founded by it. The United States was birthed by the belief that white colonial settlers were superior to the Indigenous people of the Americas who called the land home, as well as the belief that Black people stolen from Africa were subhuman and that as such they could be enslaved and treated as property.

These are the beliefs of white supremacy, the fire that led to the destruction of Black and Indigenous cultures, communities, and lives. The fire that led to the founding of the United States empire and blazed a path for the generational and systemic privileges all white people benefit from in this nation. The fire that burns in the soul of this nation, yet this nation refuses to be held accountable for igniting it, nor does it take actions to douse the flames.

One of the greatest hypocrisies in history can be found in the fact that the United States has a justice system predicated on the idea that if someone is found guilty of doing something wrong, they must face a penalty for the wrong they've done, and yet next to nothing has been done, by the United States to atone for the atrocities it has committed against Black and other non-white people. While laws have been passed and lives have been lost in the name of ending many of those atrocities, there have generally been no penalties for the perpetrators. For example, the companies that took part in slavery haven't had to provide reparations to African Americans, though it would help close the racial wealth gap first created by slavery, and the land stolen from Indigenous people in the Americas has not been given back, though there are various efforts by Indigenous groups to reclaim the land that is rightfully theirs. This lack of accountability and action to right the wrongs committed against various marginalized groups is largely why we are still feeling and seeing the impact of those atrocities every day in the United States.

But during the summer of 2020, that accountability was at the forefront of more minds than ever before.

I have spent much of my life demonstrating against the people and systems that oppress others, but the summer of 2020 felt different. I think the fact these things were happening in the middle of a pandemic that had already left us raw changed everything. Like so many others, I wasn't just ready to protest; I was ready to fight. I was tired of having to look over my shoulder for when America would come take the few things I let myself love. I want to be a father one day, and I want my children to know freedom, even if I never know it.

So Porsche and I went to join the protests that were taking place in New York City, where we live.

SIDE NOTE: Thanks in large part to the amount of media coverage and social media amplification, there were millions of others protesting as well—in more than one hundred cities in more than forty countries around the world.

As I said, I've been to countless protests, but the protests during the summer of 2020 were unlike anything I had ever seen or been a part of. There were people from all walks of life coming together to emphatically tell oppressive forces that the lives of Black people should be valued and treated with respect and dignity—a concept that shouldn't be radical but truly is in a country that not too long ago considered Black people **three-fifths of a human being**, and still often treats us as such. To my left was often someone who looked like they could be related to me, and on my right was often someone who looked nothing like me, but we all had the common goal of ensuring that tomorrow would be better than today.

As the protests continued around the country, cops began committing acts of violence against protesters, regardless of whether the protesters had been demonstrating peacefully or not. Hundreds of thousands of protesters were hit with clubs, shot with rubber bullets—which are devastatingly painful and can cause serious injury or even death if fired at close range—and sprayed with tear gas. But cops resorting to barbaric violence didn't surprise me, as their violence was at the heart of why we were protesting in the first place. In fact, cops being violent shouldn't surprise anyone, seeing as policing in America began as an evolution of **slave patrols**, which were charged with catching enslaved Black people trying to escape.

At the very core of our modern policing is violence and anti-Blackness; therefore it shouldn't surprise us when the police are violent and anti-Black. It should merely make us want to dismantle that violent anti-Blackness.

What did actually surprise me was how many white people seemed to understand how to use their power and privilege in a way that positively supported the non-white people at the protests. As cops became more violent, many white people began physically placing themselves between non-white protesters and cops. In a country that has placed more value on their lives and bodies than on the lives and bodies of non-white people, they used those bodies to shield us from the cops. Seeing that was truly one of the few moments I can remember having hope for what this country may one day become.

Sadly, there were other things that I saw at the protests that spoke to the fact that we have a very long way to go. While some at the protests were putting their bodies on the line for liberation, there were also people putting their bodies in front of cameras for liberation-themed photo shoots. I saw many instances of people who had walked over to the protests to have photos taken of them on their cell phones to make it look as if they were a part of the moment and then walked away from the protests. One morning, before the protests had fully begun for the day, I saw two white women walk over to a few cops and ask them if they would let them sit on their cop cars and hold up their signs while the cops looked angry for a "protest scene." This was mere hours after I had just been tear-gassed by cops who looked just like the cops now being asked to be in this scene.

These people demonstrated a complete disregard for the fact that this wasn't something we protesters were doing for likes or followers; we were in the street being bloodied and battered because we wanted our children and their children to feel a semblance of peace and safety that we had never felt. The same peace and safety many people posing for those protest photos take for granted.

But the photo ops weren't the only frustrating and thoughtless things happening. To show support for Black lives, many people began posting black squares on social media for a day called #BlackoutTuesday, which was apparently created by two Black women and supported by many Black celebrities. While on the surface, the black squares may have seemed like a good idea, there were many issues with them. For starters, millions of the accounts posting black squares on social media used hashtags that protesters, organizations, and activists had already been using to share information and get people help. The black square content from celebrity accounts and their millions of followers drowned out much of the other important content and information. But that's just a logistic point that could have easily been mitigated through planning.

The larger issue is that for millions who posted the black squares, the act amounted to nothing more than **performative activism**. Many people weren't doing it to help create change but rather to make sure that they were a part of the global moment, thus protecting or increasing their own **social capital** or standing. Few of the people or corporations posting black squares had spent time before the moment posting about the issues Black Americans face, and few posted about them after the moment. And far too many were actively harming the very communities they were claiming to support when posting the black squares.

But more important than why people were posting the black squares is the question of what the black squares were intended to do. Posting images or graphics can help draw attention to issues that people aren't familiar with, but that wasn't the case in terms of the black squares. Before #BlackoutTuesday, people around the world were already protesting for Black lives because the stories of the Black people murdered in 2020 were in the media constantly; the video of George Floyd's murder alone was watched more than 1.4 *billion* times on social media in the early days of the protests.

This isn't to say that every person has to throw their body in front of cops to protect protesters, nor that everyone has to take action through physical demonstration. Many people aren't able to participate in these ways. But there are other actions that people can take. Posting the black squares didn't save the lives of countless Black people who were murdered by police after those squares were posted. But posting about policies to protect those vulnerable communities could have saved lives. Making donations to organizations doing work to help these communities could have saved lives. Posting information about the history of policing and what the various visions of change look like could have saved lives.

Black squares were not bringing more awareness to anything other than the fact that people wanted their followers to know that somewhere inside of them they thought Black people deserved better. But the world is only changed for the better when hope and imagination are met with both the actions and learning required to help make it so.

While rampant performative activism has certainly been a hindrance to combating white supremacy, efforts to stop people from learning about the realities and history of white supremacy have been an even greater obstacle. In fact, these efforts played a large part in why many people believed that something as simple as posting a black square could help end white supremacy—because many white and non-white people have never truly learned how widespread, nuanced, and destructive white supremacy is.

As Porsche and I have discussed throughout the book, race plays a part in nearly every issue we face in this world, from environmental justice to the patriarchy. But even as a person who actively writes about race in the United States and globally, I didn't learn about this until I was out of high school. Sadly, my experience is not the exception but rather the rule. Many people in the United States don't have a full understanding of white supremacy's impact or even of the daily lives and cultures of non-white people. That's because most of the things we learn in school, see on television, and read in books are decided by white people and therefore are seen through a white lens.

SIDE NOTE: Nearly 80 percent of public-school teachers are white, though more than 50 percent of students in the United States are non-white.

Which is why our lens must expand.

To dismantle white supremacy, we must learn about the

history, systems, and experiences of those impacted by it, which is why **anti-racism** and **systemic experiential reflections (SER)** are important—and why so many people are against them.

As its name implies, anti-racism is a term for actions, beliefs, and policies that oppose racism. Systemic experiential reflections is a term I've come up with to discuss the importance of learning from firsthand experiences of marginalized people within white supremacy, the patriarchy, and other oppressive systems. I believe we must listen to and platform the voices of people who have been oppressed to find solutions that benefit them and destroy the systems they are oppressed by.

SIDE NOTE: Tiffany Jewell's book *This Book Is Anti-Racist* is an example of anti-racism as it focuses on what actions a person can take to combat racism. An example of systemic experiential reflections is Nic Stone's book *Dear Martin*, which focuses on telling the story of a person who exists within and is impacted by racist systems and beliefs.

No one knows how essential learning is to destroying white supremacy more than the people who are attempting to uphold white supremacy. As support for unlearning what we have been taught by white supremacy and learning how to dismantle its systems has grown since the summer of 2020, so have the efforts of those upholding white supremacy. While some of these people are motivated by racial animus— that is, they actually believe that white people are superior to everyone else and therefore *should* benefit the most from

various systems—many more people uphold white supremacy because they do not or *cannot* believe things are as bad for
non-white people as they are.

Which brings us to the myth of American exceptionalism—the false idea that the United States is inherently different from and better than other countries and that therefore Americans are inherently different from and better than
other people. From our textbooks to our movies, from our
anthems to our slogans, we are told that we live in the best
country on earth. America is the land of the free, the home of
the brave. Americans are the good guys, the heroes.

Without realizing it, I very much adhered to American
exceptionalism myself growing up. I was a kid who loved the
idea of being American. I thought the United States was a better country than others because, I thought, it was one of the
only places that believed everyone should be free and happy.
I believed these things because it's what I had been taught my
entire life.

As far back as I can remember, every school day began with
me standing in front of my desk and placing my hand over
my heart while staring at the American flag hanging from the
wall as the entire school recited the Pledge of Allegiance.

The words to the Pledge of Allegiance are simple yet say so
much: "I pledge allegiance to the Flag of the United States of
America, and to the Republic for which it stands, one Nation
under God, indivisible, with liberty and justice for all."

Before I knew how to properly tie my shoes, I knew that
my allegiance should be to the United States and that it was
a country supposedly devoted to justice and liberty. I was so

propagandized by the Pledge of Allegiance that as a young Black person, I never even thought to ask whether liberty and justice were truly had by *all*.

Another example of how we perpetuate the myth of American exceptionalism can be found in heroes such as Captain America. (Captain America is also used as a means of normalizing militarization, which I discuss later.)

I grew up reading comic books, watching cartoons, and playing with action figures based on this character who constantly saved the world while wearing an America-centric uniform and holding a star shield. He was the embodiment of everything I was supposed to believe that the United States stood for.

We grow up seeing these images and reciting these words about a country that is good, kind, heroic, and filled with people who are the same. Rarely, if ever, are those words and images accompanied by the country's history of genocide, slavery, violence, and economic disparities. Never was my pledge of allegiance to this country as a young Black person matched by accountability for how little allegiance this country has had to Black people.

This is why anti-racism and systemic experiential reflections are important, because they aim to do the work of telling the history and seeing the people who the United States has strategically erased, and to do so in hopes of helping the country evolve into a place where everyone truly has the liberty and justice it speaks of. But to reach that goal—a goal we all share—you must be willing to criticize the country and hold it accountable for its actions.

My first book, *The Black Friend: On Being a Better White Person*, focused on this false perfection in the United States as it pertains to racism. The book reflects my experiences growing up as a Black person in a country that has never come to terms with its history of anti-Black racism. The book was written to give people an opportunity to grow (and to give others the chance to feel seen and respected in their similar experiences), but the very idea that I was challenging the country's moral character made many people angry.

Instead of accepting that my experience as a Black person in a country where legalized segregation ended only twenty-five years before I was born might be different from the experiences of some readers, especially white readers, people attacked me and my book. I received multiple threats to my life and the lives of my loved ones, people spoke at town halls to try to have my book banned from libraries, and I've received countless emails telling me that I am the worst writer in the country. All over a book merely speaking to my experience and the ways that our country can and should be better.

This is the danger in people not learning true history or listening to the experiences of others. When you live inside an echo chamber, anything that challenges your beliefs can feel threatening. Some people react to this threat by clinging to falsehoods, but in extreme cases, this threat can be met by anger and even violence.

An example of the sorts of falsehoods some are clinging to can be found in mainstream conversations and debates around critical race theory (CRT), which is an educational movement and framework that examines the history and impact of race and white supremacy in America and globally to develop equitable and transformative paths to racial justice. Many people have argued that their children are being taught CRT in elementary schools, middle schools, and high schools against their wishes.

> **SIDE NOTE:** "Critical Race Theory is anti-American and lies about our history and the good people we are." This is a quote from an email I received about my own book from someone who was angry that a teacher gave it to her child to learn more about racism.

The reality is that CRT isn't taught at those educational levels; it's taught in graduate school. What some children *are* learning in school is anti-racism, but it's far more difficult for someone to say they are against their kids learning anti-racism without making it sound as if they are pro-racism. So people have appropriated CRT and strategically conflated it with anti-racism to help their efforts to stop people from learning true American history and other people's experiences. In other words, many people are lying and counting on others to believe the lie and help spread it. (A prime example of disinformation!)

Learning and accountability are two of the most important aspects to helping create actual change. We must all find the ability to navigate what may feel like uncomfortable truths—truths like the fact that the foundations of this country were built by people stolen from Africa and forced into **chattel slavery** by **white European colonizers** to create their "new world" on land they stole from Native Americans whose populations they systematically decimated through genocide. Truths such as the fact that while Black people were in chains on plantations and Native Americans were murdered and driven from their lands, white people in the United States spent hundreds of years orchestrating the construction of neighborhoods, businesses, schools, the legal system, the economy, and generally all aspects of life in this country. Those hundreds of years influence every part of our lives today. And while white people made billions of dollars on the enslavement of Africans and the genocide and land theft of Native Americans, Black people and Native Americans have the highest rates of poverty in the United States. This is no accident.

SIDE NOTE: It wasn't just individuals who benefited from and took part in the trade of enslaved people in the United States. Major companies such as J.P. Morgan, Brooks Brothers, Bank of America, and Tiffany also profited from the slave trade. In addition, owners of enslaved people were able to buy insurance policies that would enable them to be compensated if one of the people they were enslaving was injured or died. Many of the companies that sold these policies are still well known today, such as AIG, New York Life, and Aetna, all of which profited on slavery.

Progress has undeniably been made in this country, but even those changes have omitted a full accounting of the wrongs they were righting. Enslaved people were eventually **emancipated**, though they were still not given equal rights, nor did they receive any **restitution** for what happened to them. Civil rights laws eventually replaced Jim Crow laws, which were state and local laws enforcing segregation, especially in southern states. But though many of the racist laws were eventually struck down, nothing was ever done to address the many ways in which non-white people had been affected economically, educationally, mentally, and otherwise by those laws and practices. Indeed, many of today's laws have the same effect as Jim Crow laws, particularly when it comes to voting rights for Black Americans, which means that for all intents and purposes, many of these racist laws still exist.

If we don't acknowledge the mistakes of our past, we will continue to repeat them. Doing the work of unlearning and relearning offers more than an understanding about the lack of accountability in our country; it also allows us to unpack how many of our views and actions are actually influenced by the atrocities that have been committed by our country. If more people had a nuanced understanding of the ways in which Black people have been oppressed, it's likely that fewer people would have been posting black squares in 2020, understanding that the historic marginalization and devastation that Black people have faced would not be cured or alleviated by a social media graphic. Anti-racism isn't just about disliking the idea of white supremacy. It's about understanding what changes are necessary—and *why*—and then acting upon that understanding to make actual change.

Being anti-racist is not a club that someone can just opt into because they feel like it—you have to do the work. This applies to everyone, not just to white people. Regardless of what your background is, many of us have watched the same films, recited the same pledge, and learned from the same textbooks. Each of us in our own way is molded by people who don't want us to understand the realities or complexities of this nation and its history.

This is what makes anti-racism and systemic experiential reflections so important on the road to being actual anti-racists. The more honest we are about how this oppression came to be and how it continues to impact people, the better the solutions we can develop for how we end it.

An Interview with DR. SONJA CHERRY-PAUL

Educator, author, and founder of the Institute for
Racial Equity and Literacy

Dr. Sonja Cherry-Paul is someone I admire greatly for her work in helping educate people so that they may become anti-racists and help bring about the change that many hope to see. An important part of this is changing the way we teach history and current events.

SONJA: I can think back to my own schooling and how there were some things lacking. When I went to college, it was the first time I read Malcolm X's autobiography. And I remember being a freshman, reading this and thinking, *Holy cow, there's so much that I don't know. There's so much that has been missing in my life,* and I wanted to just catch up.

So I took a lot of Black women writers courses and just tried to fill myself with the things that I was missing. I think my parents, they shared what they shared, but mostly I think a lot of it was painful for them to talk about, growing up in the segregated South. So there was a limit on the kind of information that I heard growing up. And it was always just their belief that if I got a good education, things would be better. That was their dream. For sure.

So becoming a mom, I had a different plan about how I wanted to raise my daughter. And then getting into education and becoming a teacher, I had a different plan about how I thought education should go. I just found myself at odds with all of it. And so I guess that really is what got me on the road of thinking about how we teach about race and racism to kids.

Because I truly believe that if we are going to experience an anti-racist world, it begins with those kids who are in the seats of the classrooms that we educators are in and out of. So, that's really what got me into doing this work, is thinking about the profound difference it makes when children learn the truth about race and racism.

Like Sonja, part of my personal awakening to how much I didn't know about the Black American community, and much more, came from reading *The Autobiography of Malcolm X* during my freshman year of college. It changed my life and set me on a path to help create change as well. Prior to college, I had read books and seen art produced by Black people, but very little of it relative to the amount of white-produced art and books I had been exposed to. Like most Americans, I had been educated through a white lens in schools that taught white history and experiences. Therefore, it's important that we expose young people to experiences, art, and culture from people from Black, brown, Indigenous, and other marginalized communities.

SONJA: We do a lot of reactive work, and we need some reactive work when it comes to racism. We need the laws to be put into place when we see the challenges that we're experiencing around this country. But we also need to do this proactive work. We need to help kids really understand what they can do and how they can show up differently. And that will make a difference. We need kids to know that they can educate themselves, that they don't need to rely on the curriculum or their teachers—because white supremacy is in every institution. And that includes education. So we need our kids to know that they have the power to read and to learn.

We need to make sure that they are reading and learning from those who have been most impacted by racism and white supremacy. And that means Black and brown people, and kids don't often know a lot of the Black and brown people that have been doing this work forever to resist racism and white supremacy. And that's part of systemic racism in education. So we need kids reading the scholarship and work of Black and brown people. We need them to think about that proverb in *Home and Exile* by the Nigerian author Chinua Achebe: "Until the lions produce their own historian, the story of the hunt will glorify only the hunter." The entire institution of schooling exists to glorify whiteness. So we need kids to be reading and learning from Black and brown people. And we need to teach kids to open up their worlds to others, to take a quick audit of their own lives, if you will. To just really interrogate themselves: Who are your friends? Who's in your neighborhood? Which TV shows are you watching? What music are you listening to?

Dr. Beverly Daniel Tatum reminds us that our identity is

shaped by all of these factors and more, and you write so powerfully, Fred, [in *The Black Friend*] about the bubble that exists, that we create, when we don't work to open up our lives to others. And we need to teach kids to get involved, to find out about the local activists in their communities, and the local groups. How they can connect with them to learn more about issues that really affect their community, but also the world around them. And so when we do that, we're raising kids in very different ways from how I grew up. We're raising kids to be conscious. And when we raise kids to be conscious, then they'll make different choices and they will show up differently.

We do a disservice to our young people by not having more necessary conversations and teaching them about the history and hardships people face, because if we did, many of them would do whatever they can to make things better. Waiting to do this work until later in life is holding back change.

SONJA: I think some people become more resistant to change as they get older because they'll have to care more about other people's circumstances. And to truly care about other people's circumstances, that means that you sometimes will have to put yourself behind other people. Not in front of them. Because equity doesn't mean equal. And that means centering those who have been marginalized in society and working to change conditions to bring about different and just circumstances.

So for white children, it is particularly important for them to have access to anti-racist education because we cannot do this work on our own. We've all been swimming in this poisoned water, all of us. And so it is incredibly important that each one of us—that includes Black and brown people—do, as my sister Dr. Yolanda Sealey-Ruiz says, "the excavation work." We have to think about the kind of internal racism that lives inside of us as Black and brown people, to identify it, to interrogate it, and to disrupt it. We have to think about the ways horizontal racism plays within communities, the ways in which we oppress others.

That work is also incredibly painful. It's work that can't often be done in the presence of white people, right? It is in affinity spaces where we can come together and really talk about anti-Blackness, really talk about homophobia, really talk about all the things that we need to address in our particular communities, in order to begin to heal from that. So that work is really incredibly important for Black and brown people to be doing.

We have to think about the kind of internal racism that lives inside of us as Black and brown people, to identify it, to interrogate it, and to disrupt it. As I mentioned earlier, there were many aspects of Black history and existence that I didn't know as a Black person, because they had been hidden from me by systems steeped in white supremacy, such as education. Meanwhile, I was fed propaganda about American exceptionalism—which actually reflects *white* American exceptionalism. Sadly, there are many Black people who have been conditioned in similar ways and have yet to unpack and unlearn these things.

SONJA: I think in advancing the work of anti-racism, we need to make sure that we are positioning racism as a right-here-right-now, contemporary, thriving problem. And part of that problem is that racism is experienced in nuanced and different ways based on other social factors. The way that I experience racism as a Black woman is similar, but also different, from the way my partner experiences racism as a Black man. And that is also similar and different from the way someone who identifies as Black and queer experiences racism. And so we have to think about our sexuality and gender and class and language, and all of the social factors that intersect with race to create new levels of racism, different and nuanced levels of racism.

Which is why it's so important that we are in conversation with one another, that we are listening to one another, that we are in constant dialogue, because we don't know what we all don't know. And the way to know is to speak to others who are experiencing varied and nuanced forms of oppression. We can't fight it if we don't know it. And it's willful ignorance to just ignore that and to decide that one's own experience is the experience that we all need to be focusing on.

Black and brown people show up in the world in all sorts of ways. While we may all agree that Black people are facing oppression, it doesn't mean that we have the same lens of what that oppression is. Our various experiences, identities, and privileges deeply influence what oppression looks like to us—and also what liberation looks like. Which is why it's so important that we all continue to unlearn, relearn, and grow.

White supremacy has given us the illusion that we've crossed the finish line, because we are no longer enslaved, because we are no longer legally segregated. But the truth is that we've only taken a few steps in the marathon. As Malcolm X once said, "If you stick a knife in my back nine inches and pull it out six inches, there's no progress. If you pull it all the way out, that's not progress. The progress is healing the wound. . . . They haven't even begun to pull the knife out, much less heal the wound. They won't even admit the knife is there."

Liberation takes courage, vision, and action. Which is why liberating people will always be more difficult than oppressing them. Performative activism is an easy way to make ourselves feel good: posting an image on social media, wearing a T-shirt with a slogan on it, taking photos at a protest. But we have to ask ourselves how those things are actually creating change. The things that are hardest to do are often the things that bring about lasting change. If transformation is easy, then it probably isn't actual transformation at all.

In a country where a Black person can't even have the audacity to enjoy something such as camping out of fear for when the next horrific moment of white supremacy will take place, those in power want you to believe that performative activism can help people become free. These people know that fleeting care and empty demonstration are actually allies of the status quo. Posting black squares didn't save anyone's life; only dismantling and altering the systems that allow Black lives to be taken can do that.

The work may not be easy, but it only takes one strong gust of wind to topple the walls of an empire. Are you going to be part of the winds of change, or are you going to watch as the fire of white supremacy continues to set our society ablaze?

To find out more about how you can help put a stop to racism and relearn history, visit: BetterThanWeFoundItBook.com.

THE MORE
YOU KNOW!

Porsche Joseph on the Need for Education Reform

Featuring **Elizabeth Warren**

Sometimes, it's hard to see things that are right in front of your face. You have to take a few steps back in order to see the big picture. I feel this way about many things when I reflect on the past and growing up, but there's nothing I feel that way about more than my journey through the public education system.

At this point you know that when I was in high school, I wanted to attend the same college as my cousin, in New Orleans. But I didn't always see myself as college-bound. When I was in middle school, I had no desire to go to college. It was less that I didn't want to go and more that I didn't think it was realistic. Going to college wasn't something I could imagine being able to afford, and it didn't seem like something that people like me—poor Black girls with mediocre grades—were expected to do. (It is important to note that today Black women are one of the most educated groups in America, a fact that many do not know.)

But sometimes in life, we are lucky enough to meet those special people who change the way we see ourselves and our place in the world. Ms. Elliott, my eighth-grade English teacher, was that person for me. When I was thirteen years old, she asked me what college I wanted to go to. I will never forget the disappointment on her face when I chuckled and told her firmly that I would *not* be going to college. Graduating from high school was a big accomplishment in itself in my family, so why should I spend a bunch of money I didn't have to continue taking more classes that I didn't like after high school?

Ms. Elliott didn't tell me that I was being ridiculous or try to convince me to change my mind. Instead she gave me extra attention, providing more feedback on my homework and in-class assignments to help strengthen me as a student, and she would casually give me information about different college options—gently, though, so as not to push me away. She eased me into talking about scholarships and grants, and told me about nontraditional programs that she knew I would be intrigued by—ones that gave credits for working a paid job or had nontraditional grading structures, or no grades at all. Looking back, I wouldn't have known about any of these options if not for Ms. Elliott, and I most likely would not have decided to pursue a higher education if she had never instilled in me the confidence to believe that I could.

Thanks in part to Ms. Elliott, by the time I started high school, I was a strong student and ended up enrolling in Advanced Placement courses, where I realized that all of my classmates were only taking those classes because they looked good on their college applications. When I realized that I was getting better grades than most of my classmates—all of whom clearly felt entitled to go to college—I started to feel like maybe I should consider going to college, too. And because of all the work that Ms. Elliott had discreetly done on my self-esteem, I decided that since somebody had to get the scholarships and **Pell grants** she'd mentioned, why shouldn't it be me? The final thing that settled my decision to go to college was that I had a hectic home life—my brother and father were both incarcerated, my mom was constantly working, and we lived in a small, cramped apartment—and college seemed like an opportunity to escape and see something new. But even knowing about the financial aid available, I was anxious that finances would be the one thing that could stop me.

That anxiety around money had been with me since I was very young, as you also know by now. I saw my mom worry about things like light bills and if we would have enough food to make it through the rest of the month, so asking her to help pay for college was absolutely out of the question. I never really concerned myself with how my classmates were going to be able to afford college. It wasn't until my junior year of high school that I discovered that the majority of my classmates had college funds from their families or would have help navigating the finances from their parents. For these people—and for many young people—the expectation that they would go to college had been ingrained in them their entire lives, and their only stress related to a post-secondary education was about whether they would get accepted to their first-choice schools.

"My parents will only pay for me to go to a **public university**," one of my classmates complained to me during class one day. "They said if I want to go to a **private university**,

I'll have to pay for the difference myself or ask my grandparents for money," she continued. "But what if my grandparents say no? This sucks so bad; they're limiting some of my best options!"

"How dare they!" I wanted to say in the most sarcastic tone I could muster, but I didn't know her well enough to joke like that, so I asked a question that seemed reasonable to me: "If it's somewhere you really want to go, why don't you get a job and help pay for it?"

"I can't work while I'm in school! I have to focus all of my energy on doing well in my classes." If the word *duh* was a facial expression, it would've been hers. But she wasn't the only one who was flabbergasted; I had been working two jobs since my freshman year. It was part of my regular schedule to go to the sneaker store at the mall after school, work until the store closed at nine p.m., take the hour-long bus ride home, start my homework around ten thirty p.m., stay up as late as it took to complete it, and wake up and be out of the house by seven a.m. to do it all over again. And on the weekends, I went to my job at a local grocery store. Why did this girl feel it was her inherent right to focus 100 percent of her energy on school and not worry about how anything was being paid for? I wasn't even faced with tuition yet, and I already had to divide my focus between schoolwork and my part-time job in order to pay for the **ACT** prep course I really wanted to take and the college application fees. She and I lived in two different realities. I was thankful when the bell rang, dismissing us from the awkward conversation.

She wasn't wrong about the need to focus, though; I knew that my work schedule was negatively impacting my grades, and I was hoping that I could finesse an explanation for that in my **personal statement essay**.

Later that month, when I began taking the ACT prep classes, I saw the same privilege exhibited in a different way. The ACT (like the SAT) is a standardized test that is a required part of the application process for most four-year colleges. In combination with your GPA (grade point average) and personal statement, these tests make up the typical college application. The test can be important because in some instances, certain scores can be a qualifier for guaranteed admission or for different scholarship opportunities, some covering full tuition.

Prep courses are in no way required, but it is standard procedure for upper-middle-class families to do some form of preparation. Some families pay up to $10,000 for courses or pay private tutors anywhere from $100 to $1,500 per hour. The class I wanted to take cost $800 and took place every Saturday morning over the course of six weeks. My family definitely couldn't afford that, so I spoke to my high-school guidance counselor, who managed to get me a stipend to cover 50 percent of the cost. Four hundred dollars was still a huge amount of money for my family, but fortunately my mother didn't need help with bills or groceries at that time, and I managed to save enough of my work money to pay for the course.

I would show up every Saturday morning, thirty minutes early, and find a seat right in front of the classroom. I'd take notes, ask tons of questions, and regularly stay after class to get clarification on things I didn't understand or ask for assignments that I could do at home. I immediately noticed that many of the students in the class would show up late and barely pay attention. Toward the end of the six weeks, some just quit coming altogether. I didn't understand how they paid *that* much for a class and did not take it seriously. It was as if the money meant nothing to them.

The truth is, for some people, going to college is just a rite of passage—a fun experience, or something they should do because their parents did or expect them to. But for others, it feels like every star has to align for us to be able to access something that can be so basic for others. So many students want to take prep courses like the one I attended but can't afford to, while other people are forced to take them by their parents. These kinds of gaps create added barriers to education. Shouldn't we all have the access to study for a test that can potentially determine our admission to college or ability to qualify for scholarships? Shouldn't we all have the right to learn if we want to, not just if we have the money to do so?

Then again, if your family has enough money, sometimes you can skip these kinds of tests altogether. In 2019, a college admissions scandal appeared all over the news, when it was discovered that a large criminal conspiracy was taking place to influence admissions decisions at several of America's top-ranked universities. Powerfully wealthy parents were found to be bribing exam administrators to cheat or change the scores of their children's college and university entrance exams. These parents were paying hundreds of thousands of dollars, and in some instances millions, just to get their children into elite universities where the children probably would have to continue to cheat their way through if they attended. Most of the parents who were found guilty were given a slap on the wrist and charged with inconsequential fines.

Meanwhile, poor Black parents are treated harshly when

attempting to gain access to an adequate education for their young children who, unlike at the collegiate level, are supposed to be entitled by law to a quality primary and secondary public education. Parents like Tanya McDowell, a Black mother who didn't have stable housing and was charged with first-degree larceny for "stealing" an education when she used her six-year-old son's babysitter's address to enroll him in a better school that was one district over from where they were temporarily staying. Or Kelley Williams-Bolar, a Black mother from Ohio who was convicted of two felony charges and fined $30,000 for using her father's address to enroll her two children in a better school district.

K–12 education is considered a public good—high-quality early education can be a huge factor in how individuals perform in the workforce and on their economic prospects. However, not all public schools are equal. Predominantly white school districts receive $23 billion more in state and local funding than school districts that are predominantly non-white. The playing field is unleveled before we even get to college; even something like where someone attends elementary school can have major implications on their life trajectory. For that reason, parents who cannot afford to live in districts with quality public schools sometimes feel forced to use the addresses of family or friends to get their child into a better school district.

SIDE NOTE: Although less than 2 percent of the nation's students attend private schools, private-school graduates account for 24 percent of the class of 2024 at Yale, 25 percent at Princeton, and 29 percent at Brown and Dartmouth.

Although my family was low-income, we lived in a pre-dominantly white middle-class school district where I had access to a solid education. That, combined with the support of Ms. Elliott in eighth grade and the seriousness with which I approached the prep course, paid off and I was able to score in the ninety-ninth percentile on my first attempt at the ACT, which was the score that I needed to balance out my GPA, which wasn't bad but certainly wasn't in the ninety-ninth percentile. But would it be enough? Since no one else in my immediate family had ever gone to college, my parents had no clue about what this test even was. So I decided to call my cousin Stephanie, who was also graduating that year and applying to colleges.

I was surprised to hear that she had the exact opposite issue: her grades were nearly perfect, but she had gotten an extremely low score on the ACT. Stephanie didn't seem too concerned. She felt sure that her grades would balance out her test score and chalked the poor score up to not having taken the fancy prep courses. She mentioned that her GPA was much better than the average GPAs for the colleges she was applying for, and that our cousin Tanisha had been accepted to schools with a lower GPA and less-than-stellar ACT score. She had a point; Tanisha did tell us that academics aren't everything. But I still wondered how that would work out for scholarships even if she got accepted, as many of the scholarships I'd heard of weighted test scores pretty heavily.

I must have applied to at least ten colleges, out of fear that nowhere would accept me. So I was living on cloud nine when I was accepted to every college I applied to. It was such an important moment for me that my mother still saves some of those college acceptance letters. Every time one rolled in, I felt more assured that Ms. Elliott had been right, that maybe college was for people like me.

Now I had to make the tough decision—where could I *afford* to go? Growing up poor is bound to affect your relationship with money. Either you have an unreasonable amount of fear when you see a large price tag or you don't know how to comprehend the price tag and thus don't know when you *should* fear it. I fell into the first group. Knowing that what my mom made annually wasn't even as much as any of the tuition prices scared the hell out of me. Then, after adding room and board, I nearly had a panic attack. As of this writing, the average cost of tuition and fees (not including room and board) for an out-of-state student at a ranked four-year public college in the United States is almost $23,000 per year, and while the cost of college has increased from when I was a student, it was still astronomically expensive even then. Just the thought of taking out loans to cover *one year* of college nearly gave me a heart attack; I couldn't even fathom how someone's parents could set aside money to pay for four years.

I was so nervous that I wouldn't be able to afford college that I applied to every scholarship I could think of, no matter how small the award amount. Unfortunately, at five eight, I was two inches shy of the height requirement for the Tall Clubs International Scholarship for tall women. (That is an actual scholarship. And there are also scholarships for being left-handed, for competitive pogo stick jumping, creating the best greeting card, playing handball—you name it. I must have researched them all.) All told, I was awarded a good amount of money—enough to cover 100 percent of my tuition, room, and board at the less expensive schools. But this same amount of money barely scratched the surface of the costs of the more expensive schools I had applied to.

I called my cousin Stephanie to see how she was handling this part of the process. She had been accepted to her top-choice school. It was a private school with pretty good academics and the campus life was supposedly fun, so she was ecstatic.

"What about **financial aid**? Did you get any scholarships or grants?" I asked her curiously.

"I didn't apply for any scholarships. I did the **FAFSA** and I qualify for loans and stuff. I'm not going to worry about it right now because I'm going to do my degree in business and make so much money when I graduate, it won't even be a big deal to pay it back. Anyway, my guidance counselor said everyone has to take out loans for college," she added casually.

"But, Stephanie, you had a way better GPA than me. Why didn't you apply for scholarships? You definitely could have gotten some. I know a lot of people do take out loans, but that sounds like a lot of stress owing that kind of money. You could buy a house with that kind of money," I said in a lecturing tone. I could tell that she was annoyed with me, but I had done a ton of research, so I couldn't help but concern myself with her situation. I had a strong feeling that I knew more (or maybe just cared more) than her high-school guidance counselor and didn't want her to be in the dark. But she brushed off my concern about scholarships.

"Well, are they at least subsidized loans?" I asked.

SIDE NOTE: Subsidized loans are loans that don't start accruing interest until you are finished with school. This can be super important because if a loan is sitting for four years, accruing interest, it can end up being much larger than what you originally borrowed.

"Some of them, I think. But they didn't cover much because the school is so expensive, so I had to get **private loans** to cover the rest. Don't worry, though. I've already been approved!" she said happily.

At this point I was so confused as to how we were approaching this situation so differently. I was turning down my top-choice schools to attend the in-state public school that was my most cost-effective option, while my cousin was taking out more than $50,000 in **high-interest loans** with no real strategy to pay them back. She didn't seem to feel the weight of that kind of agreement. But she had made up her mind, so I left it alone and just hoped it all worked out for her.

When I got to college, school felt like a breeze—much to my relief. I had more than enough scholarship money to pay my bills, and I had secured a **work study** position on campus and worked about ten hours a week in between classes. My job was simply to sit at a desk and sign people in as they came into one of the science labs, and it was pretty slow, so I used the time to study. Being able to focus solely on my classes and not on my finances, hectic home life, or after-school job was a total game changer. *Is this how people felt in high school?* I wondered. I could walk to classes—no getting up early to catch the bus—and I had a meal plan, so I could have a healthy meal whenever I wanted. And most importantly, every quarter my tuition and housing was paid and I was even given a small stipend—which seemed big to me—so that I could have money for my books, transportation, or whatever else I needed. I was killing my classes and experiencing less anxiety than ever before.

But not everyone seemed to be having the positive experience I was having. My college was small and the Black student population was tiny, so it was noticeable when Black students kept leaving each quarter. At the end of the school year, I attended a Black Student Union (BSU) meeting where we would be reviewing the year and discussing the challenges we were facing as Black students. One of the first issues that came up was the difficulty of the coursework. First to speak up on it was an outgoing freshman named Courtney.

"I wasn't prepared for how hard the classes were going to be. In high school, I got straight A's. A lot of my classmates in high school were really disruptive and didn't pay attention, so the teachers loved me and the fact that I wanted to learn, but I feel like maybe that didn't prepare me for the kind of work I was going to have here. Looking back, I should have been more concerned that I scored below average on my ACT, but my grades were so good. I thought it was just one bad test. I've spent the whole year feeling like I'm below average, and even though I've been trying my hardest, I still ended up on academic probation by the second quarter," said Courtney very honestly.

A lot of students spoke up and shared the same feelings; they felt like the education they had received in high school didn't adequately prepare them for college. I knew many of the people speaking up had gone to school in lower-income areas, where public schools are traditionally underfunded. Still, it was shocking to hear the consistency in reporting that they didn't feel their high-school educations had prepared them for college. Although my family was poor, the district my high school was in was not, and the significance of that was just now hitting me.

The topic shifted from coursework to the culture on campus. A third-year student named Darius spoke up next. "I felt suffocated by whiteness my first year here. I would feel nervous anytime they would make us do group work or have partners because I knew all these white kids thought that they were better than me. I was also insecure about not understanding some of the material, and I didn't want to prove them right. I chose not to major in biology, even though that had always been my plan. It's mostly lab work, and I was so uncomfortable partnering with white students all of the time, especially when I was struggling. I thought about just dropping out altogether," he said.

I had originally wanted to attend an HBCU, so I was disappointed that there wasn't racial diversity on campus, but it wasn't enough to make me want to drop out. As I said, my high school was also predominantly white, and I am half white myself, so I didn't have some of the same feelings of culture shock the other students were expressing. It was as if for the first time I realized all of my privilege at once. I was always comparing myself to the kids in my AP classes and considering everything I had stacked against me, but I had failed to reflect on just how much more I was set up for success in this system than some others. And not because of my hard work. I felt guilty suddenly for having such a different experience.

My frustration grew when we began to talk about student debt.

"One thing that helped me out a lot was the scholarship I received for students of color," I said.

"That scholarship isn't even enough to cover half of my tuition," said Courtney. "Plus, I lost it when I was put on academic probation." Like many scholarships, the few that were designated for students of color had minimum grade requirements in order to maintain them. "They gave me a lot of loans, but I didn't realize how much it would all add up. They're already accruing interest. If I can't make it through the next quarter, I'll just be back at home, without a degree, and twenty-five thousand dollars in debt."

Courtney's friend Melody chimed in. "My mom lost her job during the school year, so I had to give her my entire financial aid check after tuition to help pay her rent and take care of my little brother. Now I can't even afford my books and I had to discontinue my dining plan, so I don't even have food every day. The scholarship is cool, but I still have to take out a lot of loans just to be here. It would probably be better to quit going for a while and go home and get a job so that I can help my mom out, but like Courtney said, if I don't come back, I'll just be a girl without a degree and a whole bunch of debt."

"I feel you, Melody," said another student, who was a sophomore. "I had some medical stuff going on last year and had to use my loan money to pay for that. I didn't really have any other options. They make it seem like taking out loans isn't a big deal, and maybe it isn't for some people, but I don't have a job waiting for me at some fancy firm when I get out of here. I'm doing my degree in theater and I already have thirty-five thousand dollars in debt. I don't know what job I can expect to find that is going to allow me to pay that back quickly, but if I don't get a really good job, that debt is going to be painful. I wanted to move to LA or New York and try my hand at acting, but I can't even afford to chase that dream if I gotta start paying this back immediately," he said.

Hearing my classmates' stories and watching so many Black students drop out quarter after quarter gave me a dose of reality. I realized how truly fortunate I was. I had already learned how to navigate majority-white spaces—and this was undeniably made easier by the fact that I am biracial—and so the cultural shock and racism didn't hit me as hard as they hit some of my peers. Plus I had managed to scrape together enough scholarship money before entering college that I had financial security. I had only experienced the privilege of not having financial stress for less than nine months, and I had already forgotten how much it can weigh on everything you do.

Sadly, my cousin Stephanie's experience was really not much different from those of the students at the BSU meeting. She had a guidance counselor who didn't do much guiding at all, and no one talked to her about the true burden of taking out student loans. When Stephanie ended up leaving school her sophomore year with tens of thousands of dollars in debt, it became clear to me that this is a common problem.

The United States has $1.5 trillion in federal student loan debt, and the problem is only getting worse. Tuition rates have more than tripled in the past twenty years; meanwhile, wages have barely moved. In a country where women make almost 20 percent less than men, and people of color consistently experience job discrimination, the field is not level when it comes to the ability to repay these loans, either. There is major inequality in the debt burdens for Black, Latinx, and Native American students in comparison to white and Asian students.

SIDE NOTE: One study done in 2018 showed that Black students have nearly *86 percent* more debt than white students. It is astounding that they carry this much more debt into the beginning of their lives than white people.

People from low-income communities, especially Black and brown people, are oftentimes not properly prepared to go to college. This starts at a young age, when they don't receive a quality primary and secondary education, and continues as they go on to college and are given loan amounts and repayment structures that are not to their benefit. This has the potential to build a lifetime of instability and an inability to thrive. In 2017, a study showed that almost half of all Black students defaulted on their student loans, compared with only a fifth of white students and only one-tenth of Asian students. If we want to create more equality, all levels of education, including college, should be considered a public good and thus publicly funded.

SIDE NOTE: In many countries all over the world, college tuition is free. Europe is particularly known for their free tuition models, and some Americans have opted to go there to get an education (although living abroad is not an accessible or affordable option to many, either).

While free college tuition is found to be successful in countries across the globe, we in the United States are holding education hostage and only allowing the elite to access it freely.

An Interview with ELIZABETH WARREN

Senator, professor, and former presidential candidate

Nobody knows more about education funding than Senator Elizabeth Warren. I first heard her speak about her plan to fix the country's education policy when she was running for president of the United States in 2020. During that time, I learned that the senator has a passion for education and was an educator long before she became a politician.

ELIZABETH: Not only did I not start out in politics; it wasn't even on my list of a hundred things I might do someday. Not even close. I've known what I wanted to be since second grade. I wanted to be a public-school teacher. Ever since Mrs. Lee held me close and whispered in my ear, "Miss Betsy, you could be a teacher." It was that moment when my view of myself changed and also I developed direction in my life.

Elizabeth fulfilled that dream with a long teaching career. After teaching children with special needs, she went on to be a professor of law at many of the leading universities around the country. As Elizabeth made her way into politics, she has never shied away from making education one of her biggest focal points.

ELIZABETH: If we're going to build a future as a nation and as a world, the key is education. Everything else we want to do starts with education. To fight climate change, to fight disinformation, to get in every fight we need. I see it as one of the under-explored areas of how we build a future, so think about it this way: We think of education as K–12, and that's our only public obligation. So let's start with the front end. Why is it kindergarten? Why do we start it at age five and say that's where the public obligation begins? The answer is buried in a view from more than one hundred years back that little children cannot learn. So why would you invest any money in trying to help them learn when they're not learners?

But now we've come to see it entirely differently. We know that little children are like sponges, picking up vocabulary and attitudes and enthusiasm for learning. We now know that every dollar of investment we make in education—and I'm using the word *education* broadly here, meaning vocabulary development and development of attention and development of early reading skills, learning to monitor yourself so you don't just burst out when you feel frustrated or when you want to talk; all those things are important!—when we spend on our littlest learners, we can track that through to how they flourish as adults. They go on to get more education, but it's more than that. They're less likely to end up in the criminal justice system. They are more likely to be able to start a business. You want to make that investment. And I want to use both terms, *early childhood education* and *childcare*.

We want to make those investments because a nickel spent there is a dollar saved down the line, if a child gets an opportunity to get on the learning track early. So that's why I've been pushing for **universal childcare**. It's all about early education for these children, getting them off to a good start. So if we want to build a future in this country, let's start investing in the littlest.

The gap in learning and who will be successful or not starts early and can depend on the education that we receive as very young children. But what about the disproportionate ways that education is accessed, and how that affects marginalized populations such as Black and brown communities and women?

ELIZABETH: Children come to our public education system ready to learn, but with different degrees of readiness, partly because of those first five years. How many opportunities have they had? What's been offered to them? Their vocabularies are based on how much they've been read to and how many words they've heard from a beloved parent, from caregivers, from others in their lives. Even by the time they hit kindergarten or first grade, there are a lot of differences.

We've come to learn that children who grow up in households that have lower incomes, or are headed by single parents, have a tougher time in school because they've come from more stressed backgrounds. So my basic idea is that we need to put an extra burst of money into low-income schools so that those children can get smaller classrooms, more equipment, and more computers to try to level the playing field.

So that sounds like a good plan, but because education is funded by local taxpayers, it is hard to find that money in low-income areas. There are a few places where they get some state dollars, but a lot of funding happens right there in your town or school district. So the poorer the households in the district, the less money that's available to go into education. So you've got children who have higher needs, they need a little bit bigger investment, but they're disproportionately in school districts that have less money to put in.

We've just got to stop and acknowledge what's going on in communities of color that have poorly funded school districts. So even if needs are greater, available money is lower. So a gap that starts out big, gets huge. Federal dollars could make up for that. And so this goes back to policy and why I'm always out there fighting for a plan. I have a plan for a wealth tax. Asking those with fortunes of $50 million or more to pitch in two cents would give us enough money—drum roll, please—for universal childcare and early childhood education. But it also would give us about $800 billion over ten years to pour into our K–12 schools. We'd also fully fund IDEA, which is education for our children who have special needs. It would put that money into our public schools so that every child gets an opportunity to flourish. Regardless of the economic circumstances of the family that that child is born into.

SIDE NOTE: IDEA is an acronym for Individuals with Disabilities Education Act, a law that guarantees that students with a disability are provided with free and adequate public education.

So again, you and I are having this conversation about how we build a future. Part of it is let's invest in our babies from the time they're born until kindergarten. But part two is let's invest at the federal level. We can't ask localities to do this. We can't say to families that are already struggling to pay the rent and put food on the table, "You need to quadruple the amount of money you're putting into public schools." Let's say, "No, no, no, this is an obligation of all of us." We all want to see a strong economy. We all want to see opportunities for all our kids.

As I mentioned earlier, many countries provide tuition-free higher education, and the financial model is almost always a national one. If we want to make budgets for education fair, then we need to get on the same page at a national level and make decisions as a country about what kind of education people should be entitled to.

ELIZABETH: So let's start with a little bit of history. Since the late 1800s, people are starting to move from the farms to the cities. As a nation, we begin to understand that it's not enough to have an eighth-grade education. It's not enough to be able to just add and subtract a few numbers and sign your name. To make it in these jobs in the city, you've got to be able to read instructions that are sometimes complicated. You've got to be able to read safety warnings and you have to be able to at least do the basics on a lease or a mortgage to buy a home. Right?

So as a country, we decide more education would be a good thing for everybody and it will boost productivity for all of us. So we made high school free, all across this nation, for everyone. We made a commitment that in every place, no matter where your child was born, there was going to be a high school that was going to offer more advanced education and every child should have the opportunity to do that. In fact, we changed labor laws so that children couldn't be working in factories. They were supposed to be in school. That was the basic idea.

So now here we are early in the twenty-first century and it has become pretty clear that you need more education than just high school. The days when you could make it on a strong back and a willingness to get out there and sweat, God bless, but those days are waning. It's more important for many jobs that you know how to do advanced calculations or you know how to engage in a broader range of skills that you've got.

That means post–high school technical training, two-year college, four-year college—that's what it takes to get a ticket to join the middle class. It's not guaranteed, but a ticket that you might be able to join America's middle class. So what has America done? Instead of saying, "Hey, this is kind of like it was before. It's time for us to make this free and available to everybody," the United States said, "Good luck to you. You're on your own." And what will the government do? It'll lend you the money at interest and then squeeze you dry to pay it back. That's wrong. Just like with our babies, just like with K–12. We want that investment in our young people who are trying to get an education. We want it for them, so that they have an opportunity to flourish, but we want it for our whole economy.

So this is why I believe, first of all, we should make technical school, two-year college, four-year college tuition-free, right? That ought to be the deal. And then, second, we need to get ourselves caught up. The way we do that is we cancel student loan debt for the people who've had to take it on to get here. We can now see in the numbers that student loan debt is holding back an entire generation. People are not moving out of Mom and Dad's house at the rates they used to. They're not getting their own apartments, they're not buying homes, and they're not starting small businesses.

And the consequence of that, we all feel. Think of the number of small businesses over the last ten years that have not been started because somebody said, "I've got a great idea and I'd be willing to live on ramen noodles and have seven roommates while I launch this over the next eighteen months. But I can't do this if I've got to pay $680 a month on my student loan. I just can't." So for me, this is how we build a future: universal child-care, invest in K–12, universal higher education, and student debt cancellation.

We don't know what, as a world, we're going to have to tackle in the next ten or fifty years, or in the next hundred years. But I know this: better-educated human beings will have a better chance at tackling those problems and coming to better solutions. And that's true whether we're talking about criminal justice reform or we're talking about a heating planet. That better education is going to be helpful to all of us.

But I want to make an independent point about what's happening in education. And that is a point about equality. At the college level, Black students have to borrow more money to go to school than white students. They borrow more money when they're in school and they have a harder time paying it off when they get out of school. The cumulative effects of discrimination hit Black college students the hardest.

I'll give you just one example of how this plays out over time. So people who borrowed money in college twenty years ago, they're twenty years into their adult lives now. If you're white and you borrowed money twenty years ago, on average, you're going to still owe about 5 percent of what you borrowed. In other words, you're still paying, but the end is in sight. Now, listen, I think that's pretty shocking that twenty years later, you're still paying this. But if you're white, you only owe 5 percent. If you're Black, on average, twenty years out, you owe *95 percent* of what you borrowed! Folks are going to die with that debt. It's going to be there forever, holding them back. Holding them back when it comes to buying a home and building up wealth through home-ownership. Holding them back when it comes to starting a small business, and they can't do it because they have to meet that minimum monthly payment on their student loans. Every time you start to get your head just a little above water, you've got your student loan debt to drag you back down.

And understand this: the federal government is one of the most aggressive debt collectors out there. There are people who are over sixty-five and collecting their Social Security checks, which are being **garnished** by the federal government for student loans. Think about that. They can't garnish a Social Security check because you didn't pay your credit card bill or you didn't pay your medical bills, but federal law says the long arm of the federal loan program can reach in and take a hunk out of your Social Security check. Even if that means that you're going to have an even harder time putting food on the table and paying your rent.

If President Biden would cancel fifty thousand dollars of student loan debt for individuals, which he has the legal authority to do, it would help close the Black/white wealth gap and Latinx/white wealth gap tremendously between people who borrow for student loans. There is not a single other thing the president of the United States could do by himself to help close those racial wealth gaps to this extent. This is an action that would be a big step toward an America that starts to make a down payment on the promise of equal opportunity for everyone.

So, I say this all the way through: education should be about equality. What's happening is instead of educating our young people being used as an equalizer, it's turning out to accelerate inequality. So here's an opportunity with public policy to begin not only to invest in a stronger economy and opportunity going forward; it's truly a tangible way to invest in a quality of opportunity for everyone. That's the heart of what this is about.

If this country continues along a path of an increasingly unequal education system, it is only going to hurt us more. We need a society of educated people who have ideas and new solutions to problems so that we can continue to be a global leader and have a thriving economy. This starts early on. We need to strive to make K–12 education better and more equitable, so that young people can build the foundations that they need to make change in the world—change that benefits us all. We also need to make higher education free, because providing access to higher education is the only way we can prepare our citizens for the current job market without ruining our economy with more debt.

When I was in seventh grade, without knowing anything about the world, I knew that college wasn't for me, and I knew that had to do with my ability to afford it. Young kids should be able to dream; they should not have to worry that their desire to learn and get an education will be stifled because they were born into the wrong family or live in the wrong school district. We're better than that—or at least, we can be.

To find out more about how you can advocate for education reform, visit: BetterThanWeFoundItBook.com.

9
THE HETERONORMATIVE AGENDA

Frederick Joseph on the Dangers and Ignorance of Homophobia
Featuring **Brandon T. Snider**

For the most part, I really love people. I love the vision, the drive, the hunger to learn, and all that other amazing stuff. But sometimes people suck. Like—a lot. You already know how I feel about bullies, but even people who aren't bullies can sometimes be closed-minded, disrespectful, and, frankly, *mean*. Oftentimes these people are projecting their beliefs and lived experiences onto others in ways that are not only limiting, but destructively—and traumatically—oppressive.

My eighth-grade classmate Doug Delk was most certainly someone who sucked. I'm going to tell you a story about a time when his closed-mindedness actually ruined someone's life. My hope is that seeing how his actions harmed someone else may help others recognize the harm that closed-mindedness can cause—and inspire them to open their own minds, and the minds of others.

Middle school was a terrible time for me. That period of my life was filled primarily with bullies, puberty, unpopularity, and the hope that high school would be much easier (thankfully it was). It would be a grave understatement to say that it was not my finest hour. But there were a few saving graces to middle school, one of which was my eighth-grade music class.

I've always loved music, and was lucky enough to attend a performing arts elementary school, but it wasn't until Mr. Rand's music class that I felt like I really understood how deeply woven into my world music was. Mr. Rand taught us not only how to play and truly hear music, but also the history of it and how to understand what it was conveying.

Mr. Rand was probably in his early twenties, younger than the rest of my teachers—a baby-faced, green-eyed, dirty-blond man who bore more than a passing resemblance to a young Brad Pitt. But as young as he was, I easily considered him one of my wisest and most polished teachers. Mr. Rand was a master of his subject and understood how to perfectly teach it to a group of adolescents so that it was interesting. I'm still not sure why he was teaching at our rinky-dink school, seeing as he had studied at the Juilliard School (a top performing arts school in the world, which to his testament he was never obnoxious about) and could sing, dance, play nearly any instrument, and was knowledgeable about every genre of music you can think of. To this day, I still don't think I've met another person talented enough to play both "The World Is Yours" by Nas on piano and "Human Nature" by Michael Jackson on guitar. All of which is to say, his class was amazing.

One Monday, I came to school and heard a rumor that

one of my classmates, Daisy Wells, had bumped into Mr. Rand over the weekend while she was having dinner with her family at TGI Friday's. (I remember distinctly that it was a Friday's because I love Friday's. That special whiskey sauce— wow.) Anyway, the rumor going around wasn't about where she had seen him, or how odd it must have been to find out that teachers actually exist outside of school, but rather who she had seen him with. Mr. Rand was apparently with another man, and Daisy had seen the two of them kissing. (Though he, apparently, didn't know Daisy had seen them.) Daisy, who was always late to school, somehow managed to be at school early enough that Monday to make sure *everyone* knew what she had seen.

SIDE NOTE: In the early '00s, when this scene took place, homosexuality was even more misunderstood and maligned than it is now. In fact, being gay was seen as such a negative thing that people commonly used the word *gay* to mean "bad," "terrible," "ridiculous," and the like. If someone didn't pass the ball during basketball in gym class, someone would say they were "playing gay." If someone received a bad grade on a test, they might say "This grade is gay."

At the time, most of us using the word in this way did it unthinkingly, often not even making a conscious connection between our use of the word and homosexuality. But looking back, I'm horrified by the way we thoughtlessly wielded the word, and the damage it did to all of us—most especially our LGBTQ+ friends and classmates, many of whom hid this part of their identities because of such blatant homophobia.

Though Mr. Rand's presumed homosexuality was the only thing most people seemed to be able to talk about, I didn't really think or care much about it, personally. Whether he was gay or not didn't change the fact that he was the only person I had ever heard play a harmonica as well as Stevie Wonder. Nor that he was the only teacher who had ever asked me how I was doing, knowing that I was bullied a lot. But based on what ended up happening, I was apparently the only person in the entire school who didn't have Mr. Rand's sexuality on their mind.

Before Daisy saw Mr. Rand at TGI Friday's, our class had been learning about musical theater. While musical theater has historically been one of the more safe and supportive spaces for many members of the LGBTQ+ community, one needn't be a member of this community to love musical theater—though you wouldn't know that from the way many people talk about musical theater. When Mr. Rand walked into class that Monday, he began his lesson as he often did, by telling us how he had failed us by not having yet taught us about a musical genius or genre. "Per usual, I've done a grave disservice to all of you. We've spent the year talking about the greats of jazz, rock, orchestra, and now musical theater. But I have failed you, because we haven't yet talked about Stephen Sondheim! How can I ever forgive myself? Does anyone here already know who Stephen Sondheim is?"

The room was silent. No one seemed to have heard of the great Stephen Sondheim. But I had. However, I didn't raise my hand. I hadn't raised my hand the entire year, even though I knew most of the answers to the questions Mr. Rand would ask. As much as I loved the class, I wasn't going to gain any points with my classmates for being Mr. Rand's star student. More than likely, people would see me as a know-it-all, and I'd be bullied even worse than I was already.

As I said, I was deeply unpopular and though Mr. Rand tried to make that class a safe space, there was one problem—Doug Delk was in my class.

Doug was an extremely popular kid who came from a mega-wealthy family, one so wealthy that they were rumored to be third cousins or something to the Rockefellers.

SIDE NOTE: John D. Rockefeller—as in the Rockefeller Center in New York City, and a whole bunch of other stuff—was mind-blowingly wealthy, even wealthier than Jeff Bezos and Elon Musk. Be sure to check out Porsche's chapter on the wealth gap (chapter 4: "Let Them Eat Cake") for more about the historic disparities in income in this country.

But Doug wasn't simply known for being wealthy and popular; he was also known for being cruel. Like, really, really cruel. Raising my hand would draw Doug's attention to my existence, and the last time Doug had realized I existed was in sixth grade, when he and his friends put gum in my then-long hair (which hadn't been long since). There was no way I was going to be the one person in class who knew how utterly amazing Stephen Sondheim's career in musical theater had been.

Mr. Rand stared at me for a second; obviously he was hoping I would speak up. He knew that I had attended a performing arts elementary school and that I was a fan of musical theater, among many other genres. But he also knew that I almost never spoke in class—and he knew why. Eventually, he got the hint.

"Well, then, since all of your parents and the American educational system seem to have done the same disservice to all of you as I have, let me fill you in. Stephen Sondheim is a brilliant composer and lyricist behind hit musicals such as *West Side Story*, *Sweeney Todd*, and *Into the Woods*."

I remember wanting to chime in and say, "Whoa! What about the brilliant show *Company*?" (To this day, the song "Being Alive" is my *jam*.) But of course I said nothing—though someone in the back of the room did speak as soon as Mr. Rand was finished.

"Of course you would know this type of gay stuff." The statement was said low, but loud enough to make a few kids in the back of the room giggle while getting the attention of the rest of the room, including Mr. Rand.

"Excuse me, Douglas? What was that?" Mr. Rand asked.

"I was just saying that my dad says any guy who likes musicals has some 'sugar in his tank,'" Doug responded, with the arrogance and vileness of a kid who puts gum in his classmates' hair.

"That is extremely disrespectful and homophobic, Douglas," Mr. Rand responded, sounding shocked and frustrated. "Also, a person's taste in music does not reflect their sexuality."

Daisy glared at Doug as if she was trying to burn a hole through him. Doug caught the look and loudly said, "What?! It's not my fault he's a homo!"

Mr. Rand slammed his hand on his desk. "That's enough! Stay after class, Mr. Delk."

When the bell rang, Doug stayed behind to receive whatever punishment was coming his way. I was praying that Mr. Rand would lock him in a guitar case and throw the case into the ocean, but I knew he was probably just going to get a stern talking-to and maybe an in-school suspension.

I arrived the next day at school to find another rumor going around about Mr. Rand—this one an obvious (and vicious) lie.

Apparently, after staying to speak with Mr. Rand, Doug went to baseball practice and joked to his teammates that Mr. Rand had probably wanted to kiss him. Those jokes ended up spreading around and turning into rumors that Mr. Rand had tried to kiss Doug when they were by themselves after class. It was a hateful rumor started by a thoughtless jerk—but it would change everything.

Later that day, we sat in music class waiting for Mr. Rand to arrive, but instead the assistant principal walked in with a person I had never seen before. "Hello, everyone," Assistant Principal Burns began. "Mr. Rand won't be teaching this class today. Instead, Ms. Powell will be your substitute for now. In the coming days, some of you may be asked to come to my office so that we may speak about a few occurrences said to have happened. Your parents will all receive a phone call about this, and a letter will be sent to your home as well." With that, he walked out of the room. The substitute proceeded to roll in a TV cart and play a documentary about orchestral music.

The next few weeks were a whirlwind of interviews, accusations, allegations, and lies—all based on homophobia. Upon learning of the rumors about Doug and Mr. Rand, the school administration had launched an investigation. According to the letter and phone call my mother received, the administration was investigating to make sure that students were "safe." But what they weren't saying—though what was clear to anyone familiar with stereotypes based on homophobia—was that Mr. Rand's sexuality would be what determined how "safe" students were around him.

SIDE NOTE: One of the many false and repugnant narratives about the gay community is that its members are more prone to predatory behavior. Let's be very clear here: there is no correlation *whatsoever* between sexuality and child molestation, or between sexuality and sexual violence. But these false narratives have long been used to justify oppressing and/or persecuting members of the LGBTQ+ community, as was the case with Mr. Rand.

The interviews were conducted by the principal and a group of people who had been sent by the school board. I hated speaking to them, as their questions seemed like they weren't focused on what you were saying as much as on what they wanted you to say:

"So, Frederick, we've learned that you and Mr. Rand sometimes met up after class. Did Mr. Rand force you to stay after class with him?"

"No."

"Well, what were the two of you doing after class?"

"Talking about music."

"You had that in common. Sounds like the two of you were close. Did Mr. Rand ever become physically close to you?"

"No."

"I just want to let you know that you can trust us. We are here to help you and protect other children. So you can tell us if Mr. Rand ever touched you in a way that felt inappropriate. Did he ever do that?"

"No."

"So you're saying that you spent all of that time after class, just the two of you, and he never once tried to physically touch you?"

"He never touched me. Mr. Rand is cool. If I'm being honest—"

"Yes, be honest!"

"Well, if I'm being honest—Doug Delk is a dick and you should be investigating him." (Yes, I actually said that.)

Needless to say, if they were trying to build a case against Mr. Rand to give them an excuse for their homophobia, I wasn't going to help.

Eventually—reportedly after some pressure from a group of girls who had once doodled Mr. Rand's name in their notebooks—even Doug caved and admitted that Mr. Rand actually didn't do anything to him or make any advances and it was just a joke that got out of hand. While the star witness recanting might have ended the investigation into whether Mr. Rand had been physically inappropriate with Doug or other students, it didn't stop the school administration, school board, and countless parents from doing everything in their power to derail Mr. Rand's career.

Though Mr. Rand was found to have done nothing wrong, he still wasn't allowed to come back to school. In the eyes of many people, he was still guilty—not of acting inappropriately with a student, but of being gay. Upon hearing about the investigation, many parents took issue with Mr. Rand being in the same school as their children, even parents who didn't have children in any of Mr. Rand's classes. When the results of the investigation were found to be in favor of Mr. Rand, those parents began not only writing letters but also showing up to school with signs protesting Mr. Rand and the idea of children learning from an educator who is gay. Students actually began fighting in school over Mr. Rand as well. Many students loved him and were trying to stand up for him, while other students and their parents attempted to destroy his life and image.

One of those fights is what ultimately gave all the people against Mr. Rand an excuse to let him go without it technically having to be because he was gay. But the fight wasn't between students—it was between parents. And it wasn't a fight as much as a brawl.

There was a school hearing held for parents, Mr. Rand, and others to share their perspectives and vantage points about—well—Mr. Rand's existence, I suppose. At that hearing, someone's father took the lead on saying many ignorant things: "I don't want my son learning from him, and he shouldn't have to. The Bible says that homosexuality is wrong!"

Someone's mother, a more progressive and learned parent, then responded, "There is nothing *wrong* about homosexuality. Right or wrong would imply a choice, and homosexuality isn't a choice; it's a part of who people are. You have no idea what you're talking about." To which the first parent doubled down on his hateful ignorance and said a few more homophobic things.

SIDE NOTE:

▶ In case you were unaware, homosexuality, like hetero-
sexuality, is not a "choice." Modern science contradicts
the notion that sexuality is in some way a choice and
indicates that it is instead based on genetics and biology.

▶ There is nothing "unnatural" about homosexuality. Plenty
of other animals practice homosexuality—more than
1,500 species, in fact.

▶ Also, if we were all made in God's image, as the Bible
says, aren't people who are not heterosexual also made
in that image?

Instead of giving facts as I just did, the woman called that
man a few names that might not have been nice but were completely on point, which made him feel inclined to call her a
few names back. In response, that woman's husband walked
up to the man and punched him in the mouth. The man then
proceeded to punch the woman's husband, and soon all was
chaos: chairs were thrown, black eyes were given, Band-Aids
were needed. Eventually the police were called.

As I mentioned, Doug Delk, the kid whose homophobic "jokes" had started the entire chain of events, was from
a very wealthy family, and as is often the case with people
who are wealthy, they were also very influential. That fight
gave Doug's homophobic father just what he needed to make
a case against Mr. Rand remaining at the school. In the days
after the brawl, Mr. Delk used his power and influence behind
the scenes to convince the people in charge that Mr. Rand's

presence had become a "distraction that endangered the lives of students and fellow teachers" by creating "a tense and hostile environment." At least that's what it said in the letter that was sent to every parent in the school district within days of the fight. It should have said, "We've found a loophole to fire Mr. Rand for being gay without firing Mr. Rand for being gay."

Mr. Rand wasn't simply let go from our school but from our entire district. A man had lost his job and students lost an amazing teacher, all because he had kissed a man instead of a woman at a TGI Friday's.

> **SIDE NOTE:** Though this story is from the early 2000s and may seem like ancient history to many of you, it actually didn't become illegal for someone to lose their job for belonging to the LGBTQ+ community until 2020. In June 2020, the Supreme Court ruled that an employee can't be fired for being gay or transgender. This was a massive win for LGBTQ+ rights, as nearly half of the states in the United States did not have legal protection for LGBTQ+ employees. But it is also heartbreaking to realize that such protections didn't already exist.

I wondered for a long time how Mr. Rand's being gay disqualified him from teaching music, especially when he was one of the few teachers I'd ever had who actually seemed to love what they did. But of course his sexuality *didn't* impact his ability to teach. It was never really about that, regardless of what the administration might've said. Instead, his life was destroyed because some people didn't like the fact that he was a man who cared for another man. It's as simple—and deeply messed up—as that.

> **SIDE NOTE:** Having teachers with various lived experiences actually benefits students. There is much to gain from simply being around people who have differences from ourselves. In that way, parents were hindering their own children's ability to grow.

As time has gone on, I've also wondered how incidents of homophobia, such as what happened with Mr. Rand, impacted my classmates who were a part of the LGBTQ+ community themselves or were maybe figuring out what community they belonged to. To my knowledge, no one in my school was openly part of the LGBTQ+ community, but there were people I went to middle school with who came out years later (some even waiting until adulthood for their own safety). The public persecution and destruction of a good man—and a great teacher—for simply being himself would likely make anyone fearful of being themselves.

Unfortunately, that type of persecution didn't just happen in my school, and it didn't just happen in the past. It happens every day in countless situations. It is at the root of why young people in the LGBTQ+ community are three and a half times more likely to attempt suicide than heterosexual youth and why 76 percent of LGBTQ+ youth felt that the political climate during Donald Trump's presidency negatively impacted their mental health or sense of self. The ignorance that may have destroyed a phenomenal teacher's career is also destroying the lives of the very children people are claiming to protect.

An Interview with BRANDON T. SNIDER
Actor, author, and comedian

I can't speak to the horrors and lasting impact of being a victim of homophobia, but my friend Brandon T. Snider can. Now in his forties, Brandon is still navigating the homophobia he started being subjected to as early as elementary school.

BRANDON: We moved to Terrace Park, Ohio, when I was in third grade, and that's where things really changed for me, because these kids were an extra layer of cruel. I was different in a town that deeply valued uniformity. I stayed as bright as I could, but that's when I started to internalize a lot. It's when I started to not communicate all of the things that I was going through, because I was just trying to get a bead on it. I went from an elementary school where everyone was friends to one where there was a hierarchy shaped around class. There were multiple instances in elementary school, junior high, and high school of popular boys in positions of power who would make fun of me.

It's weird because over the years, I've said *make fun of me*, I've said *bully*, and I've also said *abuse*, but I can't really communicate the fullness of it. Saying *make fun of* sounds too light. No description seems to be enough. It felt like mind games, really, of people calling me names, calling me the f-word in public, and then in private saying, "Hey, let's hang out." I had to deal with this DL behavior from my peers a lot over the course of my youth.

It was in elementary school when I started to become aware that the perception of being gay was negative and how that perception was going to paint my entire life. I knew I wasn't like the other children, but I didn't even understand what being gay was—I was nine years old. And unfortunately, I looked around my world and didn't see any gay anything. I had no references. All I knew was, "I'm just a kid. This is me."

The impact of people viewing me negatively started early, though. I had a poor self-image, weight issues, and much more. It was all this big tangle, and I didn't know how to articulate my trauma . . . I mean, I was a kid. All of these traumatic events caused me to have a really skewed view of things. I had to fight for clarity more often than not.

One of the greatest issues in our society is that we teach people that other people's identities are wrong. From the music we listen to and the films we watch, so much of what we're exposed to is riddled with homophobia, which normalizes hatred based on sexual orientation. It's important to understand how young some people are when they begin internalizing and perpetuating homophobia, and thus how young some people are when they begin being victimized by it. If we truly want to address this issue, we need to reach kids at the earliest stages of life.

BRANDON: I went to college for theater and still did not see myself as gay. Any of the feelings I had just sort of existed in this space of, "Well . . . maybe this will go away?" I didn't give it a ton of thought, but I knew I was afraid to go too far into it. I didn't really see too many gay people around me. There weren't gay role models. So there wasn't a community I felt I could access. I didn't really know what was best to do or best for me, and there didn't seem to be anywhere to find out. I was a small-town Ohio boy who was consumed with fear.

In college, I thought how I felt was going to pass, or was part of a process because I still had feelings for women, I still had attraction to women. But looking back, I think of those feelings as a socialized sort of viewpoint where it was like, "I think women are beautiful. I think women are great." I had feelings for men, too, though. It was a jumble. I couldn't really figure it out.

I remember a female friend of mine told me that some guys were trying to start a chapter of a fraternity. And she said I should do it. I told her I didn't really feel like a frat guy. And she was like, "No, it will be fine. It's really good guys. They're all recommended. You have to be recommended by somebody, too; you can't just join." I figured that meant there was some level of quality. And I was like, "Cool." I went to a couple of meetings and then one morning something horrible happened.

My freshman year I lived in a beach house because I couldn't get on-campus housing. This guy that I met at orientation found us a place then left second semester, so it was just me in a beach house. It was nice to have the place to myself.

One morning, at around six a.m., I got a phone call, and this guy left me a message on my answering machine. When the phone rang, I woke up and heard the whole thing. He said, "You f*&%ing f*$#%ot, I'm going to kill you." Among other things. I knew he was one of the dudes I had gotten to know from the fraternity and apparently he thought I was gay. It made him angry, I guess? He said, "I know where you live," and began naming things around my house. I was really shaken in a way that I never reconciled until years later—what that really meant to me, to feel unsafe where I lived. To feel like there was nowhere I could exist.

I went to the head of the fraternity and I said, "So this

happened. I think it's this person. But I don't know." All he said was, "I'm so sorry, man. That's not us. That's not what we're about." With a shrug. But he didn't really recognize what really happened. He didn't care. So I just decided that frat wasn't for me and moved on. Another unreconciled trauma to add onto the pile.

I don't think I truly reconciled any of my trauma until I met my partner, Travis, in my thirties. I didn't even know I *was* traumatized until I met someone I cared about enough to reconsider my poor self-image. I spent so many years thinking, *I will get to this later. I am not worth the healing because I'm just going to die alone.* I would tell myself these things in my head. *I'm not worth it. I'm never going to meet anybody. Who cares?*

And then when I went to college and I found alcohol, all of a sudden, I had an escape. I had a way to "relax" and let go. But of course that wasn't exactly the reality. I would have a great time . . . until I didn't. I was talking about this the other day because I've been putting ideas together for a memoir and thinking about old times. Parties where I would be having a great time and then suddenly it would be like, "Why is Brandon weeping on the balcony?"

At the time I couldn't identify what was going on inside me. I knew there was a fine line with alcohol where I could forget everything in the moment, but then later my brain was like, *Oh no, no, you're not going to get away with this. You're going to go home and you're going to weep into your pillow until you pass out.*

Imagine spending your entire life being told that you are wrong for simply being who you are—so much so that you question whether you're ever going to have happiness. All because people who have nothing to do with you, and whose lives are in no way impacted by your life, have chosen to torture you because you don't share their sexuality.

Unfortunately, for too many of you, you don't have to imagine what this is like—you live it every day. And you absolutely deserve not to.

BRANDON: When I met Travis, he saw somebody that I didn't see. He saw value I told myself I didn't have. He had the patience and the kindness to allow me to sit in my thoughts so I could finally take a step back and go, "Why do I feel this way about myself? How did I get here?" Because it's not just, "Oh, I have weight issues." It's not just that I'm insecure or self-conscious or whatever it is. It's this tangle of things.

And it wasn't until he gave me space that I could line up the pieces. These traumatic events—these things that I think about frequently apropos of nothing . . . there's a reason that happens. Now I know why I think of that football player whipping his penis out in science class and telling me to suck it. I think of that instance because it was traumatic. Do you know what I mean? These events in my brain where I thought, *I don't want to think about this*. But I did think about it. And I would think about it at weird times. And now I could finally identify this trauma and address it. Travis gave me the space for that. My parents were great, and have supported me, but in my brain I was afraid to tell them the bad stuff as it was happening. I used to tell myself, *Don't worry them*. So, yeah, I didn't really share a lot of those traumatic events until Travis.

I came out a year and a half or two years after we met. I told my parents, "Hey, just so you know, my friend Travis that I've talked about—he's actually my partner." And my parents were over the moon because they've been together since they were teenagers. They understand commitment and partnership so they were ecstatic I'd found someone to love who loved me back. It feels like I've always been out. And it meant a lot for me to talk to them about my trauma and let them know the reasons why it took me so long to be this honest with myself and them. It wasn't because of anything they did.

We live in a society where we don't always share enough about our pain. I think it's really brave and amazing when people share about the things that have shaped them, the painful things, because that's how we all heal. I mean, we share things so that we can all collectively heal. In sharing my story I've been able to understand a lot of the woundedness in the gay community. It's heartbreaking.

Creating safe spaces for people in our lives who have various lived experiences is vital to creating change and supporting others. Dealing with the trauma of oppression is inherently difficult, but even more so if a person feels like they must face it in a silo.

BRANDON: It reminds me of this therapist character that Al Franken used to play on *Saturday Night Live*. He would look in the mirror and say, "I'm good enough, I'm smart enough, and doggone it, people like me." That was his daily affirmation. My daily affirmation was the opposite of that. When I was in a bad headspace I'd think, *You ugly piece of crap.* I did that constantly and would often vocalize it.

Travis has heard me say things like that out loud to myself during moments of frustration and has told me, "Don't say that.

Stop it." He had to remind me I wasn't this broken thing. But it was so easy for me to be super cruel to myself because I was so used to others being cruel to me throughout my life.

One of the most damaging aspects of oppression is how often oppressed communities internalize their oppression. If you are told negative things about yourself and see false or harmful representations of your community on a regular basis in media throughout your life, there is more of a likelihood that you will begin to believe those things. Challenging this toxic conditioning is essential to creating real, lasting change.

BRANDON: Sometimes when I watch gay media, I just bawl. There are two things I distinctly remember bawling at: *It's a Sin* on HBO and *Moonlight*. I wept so hard. There are certain things that just trigger me in lots of different ways, and it's cleansing. I feel like I've been through a lot of processes since I came out.

I came out when I was thirty-five—I'm forty-five now. But it still feels fresh sometimes. Things will trigger me in a way that makes me think, *Oh. I guess I'm not out of the woods yet. Will I ever fully be healed?*

Coming into this interview, I was nervous because I wondered, *Am I still in these processes more than I thought?* I've tried to heal myself, move forward, and use my work as a way to heal and help heal others by putting distinctly personal things in my stories, especially for younger readers, that I hope taps into some of the things that have made a difference in my life. Am I in a different place? I think I am. I feel like I'm doing what I was meant to do. I have love. I have friendship. I have a body of work. I'm in the best place I've ever been in my life. But I'm often reminded of

**that dark thing that knocks on the back of my brain, reminding
me of the past. Sometimes it takes effort to tell that thing, "No.
Not anymore. I'm worth it."**

I am grateful to Brandon for joining me in conversation
because as he said, we don't share enough of our pain, and
the reality is that homophobia creates pain. It has been a long
time since Brandon was a child being bullied in elementary
school, or since he was a young man being threatened in college, but the wounds are there. The wounds are deep. The
wounds are life-altering.

Homosexuality and a spectrum of sexual identities have
existed long before the systematic efforts to create purely
heterosexual societies—long before homophobia became
enshrined in law. But regardless of how homophobia may
have started, there are no arguments for it other than perpetuating hatred. The most basic truth is that who a person is
attracted to or wants to be with has NOTHING TO DO WITH
ANYONE ELSE. Whether someone is with a woman, a man,
or someone who doesn't conform to gender binaries, it doesn't
harm anyone and thus it simply shouldn't matter.

While some progress *has* been made in the treatment of
LGBTQ+ people in this country, we're still miles and miles
away from anything approaching full acceptance, equality, or
systemic equity. Consider, for example, that America didn't
legalize same-sex marriage until 2015.

SIDE NOTE: Currently, only 30 of the 195 countries in the
world have legalized same-sex marriage: Argentina (2010),
Australia (2017), Austria (2019), Belgium (2003), Brazil (2013),

Canada (2005), Colombia (2016), Costa Rica (2020), Denmark (2012), Ecuador (2019), Finland (2017), France (2013), Germany (2017), Greenland (2015), Iceland (2010), Ireland (2015), Luxembourg (2015), Malta (2017), Mexico (2020), the Netherlands (2001), New Zealand (2013), Norway (2009), Portugal (2010), Scotland (2014), South Africa (2006), Spain (2005), Sweden (2009), Switzerland (2022), Taiwan (2019), the United Kingdom (2014), the United States (2015), and Uruguay (2013).

As I write this, seventy-one countries still have laws making same-sex relationships illegal—*seventy-one!*—and in eleven of those countries, the death penalty may be imposed for same-sex acts. Let that chilling fact sink in: *Eleven countries can impose the death penalty for same-sex sexual activity.*

Imagine someone having the power to legally murder you because you were born with brown hair instead of black. People are being murdered and having their lives ruined simply because they were born different from the people in power—a difference that again has nothing to do with anyone else.

But as with any type of bigotry, homophobia isn't just about people losing their jobs or being murdered. It's so much more nuanced. It's in the words we say, the things we assume, and the problematic expectations and limitations we place on people. The good news is that these are things we can change. We can all do our part in changing the culture around LGBTQ+ identities. We can all do our part in saving and protecting lives—and ensuring that everyone has the freedom to be themselves.

To find out more about how you can help put a stop to homophobia, visit: BetterThanWeFoundItBook.com.

10
THE PRICE OF LIFE

Porsche Joseph on the Importance of Health Care Reform
Featuring **Anna Paquin** and **Jesse Katz**

In the spring of 2021, I took a trip to our local Target to pick up some toothpaste and other household items. "Other household items" is basically code for "permission to roam the store, combing every aisle in order to not miss any random thing, and tossing stuff in my cart that I didn't even know I needed until I saw it." These kinds of Target visits typically take place on days when I have nothing to do and nowhere in particular to be. Consequently, these are also the kind of moments when I am open to friendly banter and casual small talk—as opposed to more intentional trips, where I need to get in and out quickly.

On this particular day, I found myself in front of the shower curtains, staring indecisively, trying to choose between stripes or polka dots. Suddenly, I heard an older woman's voice behind me. "Go for the stripes!"

I laughed. "You know, that's what I was leaning toward! Thanks for helping me make such a tough decision," I responded in a friendly tone, turning toward the woman. She was in her late fifties but looked weathered and tired. Her hair was gray and she was wearing an oversize T-shirt and worn-out jeans. I noticed she was buying cleaning supplies, so in an effort to be friendly, I told her how much I loved the product she had in her hand and how we live by it in our household. When our eyes met, I sensed a heavy sadness and immediately knew that she was not at Target that day with a carefree agenda like I was.

"Yeah, I'm making a trip to my son's apartment to do some cleaning and get it ready for him to come home. He's leaving the hospital tomorrow. He just had a procedure; he had to have his leg amputated," she said as her eyes brimmed with tears.

I felt a rush of concern and wanted to comfort this person I didn't know at all, but I wasn't sure how to respond. *Do I hug her? Should we sit down somewhere so she can tell me more?* One moment I was spontaneously redecorating my bathroom, and the next I was sobered by a stranger's unexpected story. "I'm so sorry to hear that" is all I managed to reply.

"It's okay," she said in that way that means it wasn't okay at all. "He's only twenty-seven. I just never envisioned this for him when he was a child. He has diabetes and I kept him on my insurance as long as I could, but he couldn't stay on anymore after he turned twenty-six. That's the law. When he lost the health care coverage, he couldn't afford his medications anymore and had to stop going in for his checkups, and within less than a year we ended up here, having to remove his leg."

Diabetes is a disease that occurs when blood sugar levels are too high, and at its very worst, unmanaged state, it can lead to an amputation. Many people in my family have diabetes, so I was all too familiar with the threat of amputations.

SIDE NOTE: Diabetes is fairly common in America, affecting more than one in ten people—and more than one in five people over the age of sixty-five. People of color are disproportionately affected.

I asked the woman if there was anything I could do to help, though I knew that this family needed more help than I could possibly provide. She told me they had a GoFundMe fundraiser that they were hoping would help with the $45,000 surgery, so I asked for the details and made a donation. My contribution felt minuscule, but the woman was very grateful. We chatted a bit more after that, and as we parted ways, I wished her luck and thanked her again for the shower curtain suggestion. As I made my way toward the checkout area, I felt a deep wave of depression set in, faced with the reality that my brother, father, and most of my nieces and nephews had no health insurance.

When I got home, I told Fred about the conversation with the woman I met. As he listened to me rehash the story, he sighed deeply and asked for the fundraiser website.

SIDE NOTE: More and more, people are looking to these crowdfunding platforms to help pay for medical needs, because average people cannot afford the costs. Nearly one-third of GoFundMe campaigns are created to help pay for health care expenses, which comes as no surprise when considering that 28.9 million people in America lack health insurance, with 4.3 million of that number being children. However, even people who have decent health insurance often come up short when they need to pay their **co-pays** and **deductibles**.

I have too many personal stories to count about how the health care system has failed me and people around me, but nobody's story sums up how dire the issues with our health care system are more than that of a young woman I met a few years ago named Regina.

Because of the gaps in the health care system, there are a lot of nonprofits that work to support different health crises, whether that be diabetes, HIV, Alzheimer's, lupus, you name it. At the time that I met Regina, I was working for a nonprofit that was dedicated to helping those with cancer. One of the things the organization did was offer free lodging for cancer patients undergoing treatment in the area. Many people have to travel far to receive treatment, so this alleviated some of their costs, since staying in a hotel or an Airbnb can be really expensive. Some of the patients stayed for only one or two days, while others stayed for an entire year.

One of the perks of my office was that it was located in the same building as the patient lodging. There was a community floor with a kitchen, TV room, and board games and books where patients commonly hung out when they didn't feel like being in their rooms. When I was drained and overworked, I would go to the community floor, make a strong cup of coffee, and usually meet some amazing people who were there because they were fighting cancer, and be reminded of who it was that I was working so hard for.

One day, I was having an unusually slow day at the office and decided to take my lunch over to the community room to eat and say hi to whoever was around. I was also secretly hoping that someone had baked cookies or brought desserts and left them out to share, as occasionally happened. But there were no sweets and nobody was around, so I decided to spend my lunch break working on a jigsaw puzzle. (Confession: I am really bad at puzzles. I knew I was bad when my six-year-old niece told me, "Hey, you're really bad at puzzles." But for some reason I never let that stop me.)

I had been struggling to separate out the border pieces when a young woman came over, introduced herself in a thick southern accent, and asked if she could sit with me and help.

"I'm off to a slow start; I could use all the help I can get," I responded.

Regina was a whiz. She began zooming through the puzzle as I contributed about one piece for every ten she connected. At one point I apologized for not carrying my weight. "My six-year-old niece actually told me that I'm really bad at puzzles," I informed her.

Regina laughed. "Ah, six-year-olds tend to think that it's their official job to tell everyone about themselves—even when nobody asks them." We laughed. "I used to teach first grade, so I know *all* about that."

As we chatted, I learned that Regina was from a place in Georgia not far from where some of my family lives and that she was a twenty-eight-year-old proud mother to a two-year-old boy named Donte. Unfortunately, she'd had to leave Donte at home with his father while she underwent her treatments. Because her chemotherapy and radiation treatments left her immune system extremely compromised, she couldn't leave the facility for anything but doctor's visits and treatments, which meant she was not only lonely but also bored. And so we set up a regular lunch date where we'd work on a puzzle and eat lunch and chat a bit about our lives.

Regina would always wind up doing most of the puzzle, while I did most of the eating. We would talk about how much she missed her family and her plans for the future. It soon felt like we had known each other for years. Puzzles evolved to watching cheesy TV reruns and I even helped Regina pick out a wig when she began to lose her hair. Eventually she confided in me about her cancer diagnosis and how it came to be.

Regina had been complaining to her doctor about the pain in her abdomen for more than a year before the cancer was detected. Doctors assured her that everything was fine and that the pain was probably related to her menstrual cycle. She found it unsettling that they seemed to dismiss her numerous reports that something didn't feel right and began to think it had something to do with the fact that she was a Black woman and that all of the doctors she saw were non-Black, and mostly men.

She told them that the pain would come and go, but when it was there, she could barely get out of bed. One of the doctors joked that he would love to stay in bed every time he didn't feel well, and went on to tell her about how bad his knees were from years of skiing. He was treating her like she was exaggerating, and she began to convince herself that maybe she was. He gave her a prescription for high-dosage pain pills, but when she began needing to double the prescription just to make the pain subside, she knew she needed to see a different doctor.

She went to a woman, and the doctor entertained Regina's concern with an X-ray and other lab work and assured her that she was fine and that they didn't see anything to be concerned about. The doctor told her it was normal to have pain and that she was sure that "a young woman like her" could manage. She went on to pretty much accuse Regina of being a drug addict for developing a high **tolerance** to her pain pills and told her in a really rude tone that she wouldn't be able to give her any more and warned Regina not to try to get more pills because that was her final answer. "She said she wasn't going to 'support that habit,'" Regina told me. "I was so humiliated. I had never even asked for more pills! I didn't want to take them, either. I just wanted to know what was actually wrong!"

Recounting Regina's story makes me cringe. There is a huge issue with racism and sexism in the medical field, and numerous studies have shown that health care professionals are commonly guilty of **implicit bias**. One such bias is the racist assumption that Black people have a higher tolerance for pain than white people, which can lead doctors to undertreat their Black patients for pain. Another bias is the sexist assumption that women are prone to overreaction—what doctors used to call "hysteria"—which makes them unreliable assessors of their own pain. Because of these biases, nonwhite people and women receive inferior health care—and Black women receive some of the worst care of all.

SIDE NOTE: In the United States, Black women are more than three times more likely to die while pregnant or giving birth than white women. The majority of these maternal deaths are preventable. This is not a unique circumstance: the National Academy of Medicine has determined that "racial and ethnic minorities receive lower-quality health care than white people—even when insurance status, income, age, and severity of conditions are comparable."

"At some point, the pain went away for a few months, so I figured whatever it was, it was getting better," Regina continued. "I thought that maybe it had just been something related to giving birth to Donte that my body naturally resolved. That was around the same time my husband was in a really bad car accident and couldn't continue working. As a teacher, I was only taking home about $2,500 per month, and suddenly I was the main source of income for the family. There was just no way that I could afford to pay almost $1,000 each month, which is what the health care coverage through my job was costing me. So I had to give it up, just until we could figure out our issue with income."

Regina's situation isn't unfamiliar to many Americans. The majority of GoFundMe campaigns that are created to help with the costs of health care are made for people who *have* insurance. The monthly **premiums**, the cost to just *have* an insurance policy, are often just too high. In Regina's case, it is illogical to think that anyone on a regular teacher's salary can afford such an exorbitantly expensive premium and still be in a position to provide for their family. Premiums can also be particularly tough when the patient's medical condition renders them unable to work.

SIDE NOTE: In 2020, the average annual premium for family coverage was more than $20,500. Those who participated in their employers' medical plans contributed, on average, nearly $7,000 and the employer pitched in the rest. Considering that the median household income is less than $70,000, this would make the contribution about 10 percent of the family's yearly income. And that's often the best-case scenario; for those with lower employer contributions, or none at all, the premium might be completely unaffordable.

High premiums are unsustainable for many, especially since most insurance plans still expect you to pay a portion of the bill *and* meet a deductible. If you don't have any known medical issues, you are expected to pay into something that you may not even use, and in the meantime you are supposed to disregard how helpful that money could be if spent elsewhere, paying down debt or going toward necessities like rent or food. As a result, many people have to decide if having insurance is even worth it.

Besides those mystery pains, Regina considered herself a generally healthy person. Then one night she became extremely sick. A few months after the pain stopped, she woke up in the middle of the night with the worst pain she'd ever felt in her life shooting through her stomach. "It hurt so bad that I was screaming and eventually fainted," she said. "I felt like I was going to die. Finally, when the doctors figured out what was wrong, they came to me and told me I had stage four colorectal cancer and it had spread to my ovaries and liver. The doctor said I have about a 14 percent chance of survival, but if I would have caught it earlier, I could have had a better **prognosis**. But now I'm here, just hoping to survive for Donte."

Regina couldn't work, and although she now had insurance, she still can't afford her treatments, so she was putting everything she could on her credit cards. "I can't really worry about it right now because I know I may not live to see tomorrow, so I just need to make it through one day to the next. We'll likely end up filing for bankruptcy; there's no other option. I'm happy they're letting me stay here for free; this is the doctor I really needed to see because she's one of the few who have experience with my specific type of cancer and I could never have afforded to live here for months to get treatment, so I am thankful for that. I try to remind myself of that when I miss my family, but it's still hard."

I felt terrible as I listened to Regina's story. *Nobody should have to deal with this kind of stress,* I thought, *let alone a twenty-eight-year-old mother who should be able to focus on fighting for her life.* Instead she was overwhelmed with the idea that her survival might cost her son his next meal or the roof over their heads.

I have always been someone who feels like there has to be a solution to every problem; however, in the case of medical emergencies and illness, there is often no controlling the situation and sometimes, there is no answer. But oftentimes there *are* answers and there *are* things we can do—if we have access to proper care. Too often there are roadblocks in the way of that care—roadblocks that have been set in place by our government and by corporations. One of the biggest roadblocks is the cost of health care. In addition to trying to deal with the emergency itself, the financial burden can be devastating. For millions of Americans, a medical emergency can financially shatter their entire life.

I don't know what happened to Regina's finances—I don't think that there was much hope for that aspect of her story—but after being away from her family for months, she returned to Georgia to continue her treatments. Although her outlook was grim, her spirits remained high, and I missed seeing her during my lunch break.

A few days after the trip to Target that had really gotten me down, I received an email from Regina. I hadn't heard from her since she'd left—people often promise to keep in touch and then life gets in the way, and Regina certainly had plenty on her plate—but it couldn't have been better news or better timing. "I beat the odds! My cancer is in remission and continues to be stable." I nearly dropped my phone.

Hearing from Regina reminded me that people are resilient. There is new cutting-edge technology and brilliant research being done every day, and if we can figure out a way to give everyone access to those resources in an equitable way, then there is hope.

More than twenty-six thousand people die each year in the United States because they don't have insurance and avoid going to the doctor because they cannot afford it. *Twenty-six thousand people.* This is wrong. Health care is one of the most profitable industries in America, but it is failing the customers it is supposed to serve—existing as the leading cause of bankruptcy. While there are business executives in the health care industry getting rich, millions of people in this country struggle to afford the most basic care. People are held hostage by their health insurance plan and have to make decisions about their health based on what insurance will cover.

It doesn't have to be this way. Other countries successfully provide health care to their citizens without spending as much as individuals in the United States do. The privatization of hospitals in America means that the services cost much more. Because there are so few regulations on how much companies and hospitals can charge, care and medication costs vary greatly, making the price of a simple doctor's visit completely unpredictable.

SIDE NOTE: A CT scan, which shows images of internal body parts, costs less than $100 in Canada but nearly $900 in the United States. Differences in costs can be even more drastic when it comes to medications. Some years back it made headlines that EpiPens—medicine for emergency situations to treat life-threatening allergy attacks (think a severe peanut allergy or bee sting)—were not being covered by many insurers in America and cost around $600, compared to $69 for the same medicine in the United Kingdom.

And what's worse, the United States is consistently ranked low when it comes to health outcomes. So while our health care costs much more and access is very limited, it's not even necessarily better than other countries'.

The system is broken, and people's lives are on the line because of it. It's crucial that changes are made so that health care can be more accessible and more equitable.

There are many places around the world, including most other wealthy and high-income countries, that provide health care to their citizens for free, or for a very low price. It's important to acknowledge that no country has the perfect solution and that there are always flaws, but I believe that looking at these countries is the best way to learn how the United States can create better options for general coverage.

An Interview with ANNA PAQUIN

Academy Award–winning actress and activist

To gain a different perspective on health care, I wanted to talk to my friend Anna Paquin, who is Canadian and grew up in New Zealand—two countries that offer universal health care. New Zealand's health care system is funded by the national government through public taxation. Although people have the option to use private health care, everyone has access to health care paid for by the government. The country is also pretty healthy—it has one of the highest life expectancy rates in the world.

Anna is a mother, and the child of two teachers. She says that the assurance her parents felt knowing that they and their children would always have access to health care, no matter the circumstance, was invaluable.

ANNA: When I was growing up, my mum taught in high schools—she's an English teacher—and that's as poorly paid in New Zealand as it is in America, but as far as the things that we were exposed to and choices that were made on behalf of us by my mother, our **socioeconomic group** seemed much higher than what living on that salary might look like here in the US. My mum prioritized things like music lessons—she felt exposure to the arts was extremely important—organic food, things that people might have a difficult time accessing without money here. Because even if we didn't have any money to do anything else with, that's where she channeled the resources into.

Obviously New Zealand's is not a perfect system and people still gripe about the specifics, but I think it's often from a position of privilege. Some people aren't even aware of what it's like to live without universal health care and how much privilege they have for having access to that health care. The first question when you walk into a doctor's office or an emergency room isn't "What's your insurance information?" It's "What's wrong? How can we help?"

I often think about the **Hippocratic oath**, in which doctors pledge to do everything in their power to help their patients. How does sending sick people home because they can't pay align with that? It must be pretty infuriating if you're a doctor or a health care provider. They go into this career to help people and there's this third-party entity (insurance) telling them if they can or can't.

Health insurance companies act as a barrier between doctors and patients, for no other reason than to profit. They don't have a product; they just take a cut of the services health care professionals offer and somehow stand as a $1.1 trillion industry in the United States. Doctors and nurses have to argue with insurance companies on behalf of their patients, and beg and prove that patients deserve to be covered for services they prescribe. Meanwhile, these insurance companies are almost never led by people who are trained health care workers. In 2020, the highest-paid health insurance CEO made $25 million, not including his $14.9 million in stock awards. He collected this kind of money while people were struggling to survive

COVID-19 and going broke trying to afford these insurance plans in one of the worst economies in recent history.

ANNA: Having done enough bouncing back and forth to the US for work, it wasn't like I didn't know conceptually what I was getting myself into by moving here, but it still frankly blows my mind that health care and education are not fundamental human rights in this country. Instead it is based on privilege and class. In that way, I have been in culture shock going on twenty-five years now. If you've lived anywhere else where health care is not a hugely politicized debate, it's just impossible to get your head around. Why would the bottom line of providing help to people be profit?

And in addition to corporate greed, there is a fundamental belief held by a lot of people that, "If I earn it, it's mine, and I don't need to share it with anybody else." Culturally, the idea that either we all feast or we all starve and that wealth should be distributed to not just the person who earned it but to the people who surround them—that's just a cultural value that doesn't seem to have prevalence in America. That idea seems to make people not just uncomfortable, but incredibly defensive of their right to hang on to their own possessions. I don't know how to argue with that, because this mythical idea that it's only lazy people who are unemployed or unhoused or uninsured or whatever gives absolutely no real assessment of how those people's situations came to be or what needs to be done to solve it.

One of the worst things about the current health care situation in America is that our government has fooled people into believing that the current system is in their best interest.

Although some polls show that around 70 percent of people living in the United States describe our current health care system as being "in a state of crisis" or having "major problems," many of those same people are still reluctant to turn to universal health care.

During the 2020 democratic primaries, presidential candidates Elizabeth Warren and Bernie Sanders proposed plans to implement universal health care, which they term "Medicare for All." Warren's plan promised to stay away from taxing the middle class and focus on getting the money to pay for health care from corporations and the very wealthy. Sanders's plan, on the other hand, was less detailed but proposed ideas such as a tax to employers per employee, and a lesser tax on employees. There have also been ideas about how to transition to a Medicare for All system by using the existing Medicare program, which provides health insurance to those over sixty-five, as a launchpad and decreasing the age annually until everyone is covered, or to implement universal health care one state at a time.

ANNA: I just don't understand the downside of universal health care. I have lived with and without it, and I simply can't understand who wouldn't want that kind of safety net. Yet somehow it has been sold that that's a bad thing, that you will never get to pick your own doctors or you'll never get access to good care. There will still always be private health care. In New Zealand, you are covered through public health, but you can also still, if you are privileged, pay for privatized health care. It's not like that's not an option to you if you have the means. I just think it's such a fundamental human right to be able to access *something*.

In addition to having a global perspective on health care, Anna also has experience with unionized care. She belongs to the Screen Actors Guild–American Federation of Television and Radio Artists (SAG-AFTRA) union, which provides health insurance to about sixty-five thousand union members and dependents. Anna's experience during the pandemic sheds light on **unionized health care**.

ANNA: Disproportionately, most of our members are not able to financially support themselves on a living wage by acting only. So fundamentally, there are those that are being carried by those of us who are privileged enough to get to earn our living exclusively by doing the thing that we love to do, and I'm good with that. That aligns with my morals. That aligns with my sensibilities as a human.

What a lot of us were not aware of is that there was no clause for the pandemic, so when that hit, per our union, we weren't allowed to work. But you are required to meet minimum hours of work or a certain amount of pay, and so people are being kicked off their health insurance plans because we no longer meet the work requirements, even though we aren't allowed to work. And we've all been paying into this for years and years, so to take insurance away during a pandemic just makes no sense. There's no rollover of past hours worked, and there was no pause button.

Luckily, my husband and I are in a position of privilege in that we had enough hours, but many people whose entire families and livelihoods relied on that insurance were just systematically informed, "You are no longer insured . . . but you also can't work."

Fundamentally, unions do a ton of great stuff, but they are

not perfect, and that was a massive hole in our system that most of us had frankly just never even considered. Who was actually expecting there to be any reason for all production around the globe to stop for an entire year? But other unions paused their plans' requirements so that union members weren't left entirely compromised. Because as a country, there's no safety net.

Before our conversation, I had never thought about what options actors have for health insurance or how their benefits might be affected when they're unable to work due to a worldwide health crisis. Anna and her husband are both extremely successful actors; I can turn on any major streaming service and see one or the other of them anytime. But even they were almost unable to meet the hours of work required by the union during a global pandemic, which would have left not only them uninsured but their two young children as well. However, if they were in New Zealand or Canada, they wouldn't have to worry about it because they would be covered by public health care.

Earlier in the conversation, Anna mentioned that her mother prioritized feeding her organic food and exposing her to the arts. Anna's entire life could be different if her mom was unable to do this—if her mom had been expected to pay high monthly health care premiums like some teachers in the US.

ANNA: I imagine if we'd lived here then, we would not have had the ability to pay for good food and activities such as music lessons—that would not have been where the money could go. Whatever health care we would've had to opt into probably would've meant that those things would have been sacrificed. People don't know what an immense privilege universal health care is until you walk away and you see how vastly different it is in other places.

Having to choose between things that are just fundamentally so crucial to producing competent, good, healthy adults is ridiculous. Having to pick which is more of a priority, education or medical care, or having to think, *Oh, we can't afford both medications, so what sickness is going to hurt you worse?*—that just feels like an intensely wrong way to have to raise your family. Also, it's one of those things that people on the **far right** get a bit touchy about, asking, "Well, who's going to pay for it?" Well, I'm happy to pay a larger share. Yes, I earn more money, and yes, I absolutely should be taxed more. I'm completely comfortable with that. I think that's appropriate.

Much of Anna's perspective and willingness to pay taxes have been informed by her experience growing up in a country where the approach to health care and other social services is different from the approach in the United States. Here, there is a lot of stigma around people paying taxes for services that may benefit another individual more than ourselves. However, it is rarely acknowledged that the majority of Americans believe that the government has the responsibility to provide health care coverage for all. And the support for universal health care is growing. The barriers to figuring it out are oftentimes more political than logistical. Taxpayers are discouraged by politicians who tell us it is too complicated for us to understand, and meanwhile, those large companies (health insurance providers, hospital systems, pharmaceutical companies) that stand to lose have major political power and spend a lot of money on lobbying to ensure things don't change.

ANNA: Young people should know that what they're going to be taught about health care in school is definitely not going to be the full picture. I urge them to look at the way it's done in other countries, and what the health statistics and numbers are like in those countries. It doesn't have to continue to be this way, but it does start with things like access. I don't know how you get around the fact that in the present state of this country, access is handed out on a basis of socioeconomic and racial privilege. Young people need to know that they are the next generation of voters, and the kind of issues on the ballot are going to be ones that they really can change if they get involved. The culture of elitism is not working. Whether we like it or not, we are all in this together.

Fundamentally, we all learn the importance of sharing in our formative years of education, and then somewhere along the lines, it becomes about, "It's mine. You can't take it from me. I don't have any obligation to share." We spend so much time as parents teaching children about sharing and inclusiveness and those ways, and then . . . I don't know where the switch gets flicked, but it completely goes the opposite direction once people become adults. But the fact is, people are struggling, people are dying, people are in pain, and it should be one of our top priorities to help these people, because it could easily be any one of us at any moment.

We may learn that this country was founded on principles of religious freedom and new chances, but the fact is what drove America to fight for its independence from England was taxes. America was founded not long ago, and it was founded specifically on principles of capitalism and financial profit. So it is not surprising that this country and its politicians would seek to commodify and profit from anything and everything.

An Interview with JESSE KATZ

Entrepreneur

Jesse Katz, contrary to Anna, was born in America and moved to Canada at a young age, experiencing a different kind of culture shock. Jesse is an entrepreneur (he owns a clothing company called Roots of Fight, which makes some amazing gear). Entrepreneurs and people without traditional employers are some of the main people in the United States who don't have health care coverage. For Jesse, health care is very important to him and his family.

JESSE: I had problems with my health growing up. It turns out, I have an autoimmune disease: I have reactive arthritis, but nobody knew what it was. So all of a sudden in my late twenties, early thirties, things just started to go wrong with my body. Tissue would tear; my back would be aching, right through to the core of my spine. Growing up an athlete, I had broken bones, had stitches everywhere, I had sprains, and so I knew what pain was and these pains were not normal. Nerve pain is just different in how it gets to you. And so I was on a journey to really understand it.

Living in Canada, we have an incredible health system here, but it's not perfect. It's like anywhere: there are issues. But the incredible thing is that nobody's left behind; you can always get care here. For myself, I've really had to research and learn to take a holistic approach in treating my disease, meaning diet changes, eating well, lower stress, cutting back on alcohol and certain foods.

As a person living with a chronic illness, having health care is extremely important to Jesse. Knowing that he will not lose his care, or be required to make huge monthly payments, allows him to focus on providing the best preventive care for himself, including stress management, eating organic foods, and taking supplements, rather than scraping together all of his money to pay for basic prescription medications.

Jesse's wife is an artist and they have two teenage children. In America, his family would be responsible for finding and paying for private health insurance that would cost tens of thousands of dollars per year in premiums.

JESSE: It's something we think about all the time. Everybody talks about how "health is wealth," but for my family, it comes down to security—*security is wealth*. Being able to get access to the health care that we need if something goes wrong, and feeling secure that our kids will never have to worry about it, is extremely important to us. Especially as someone living with a disease and with an aging parent. The way we see it, basic health care is a human right. If you are in a country that has access to the wealth that the countries that we live in have, everybody should have basic health care.

My mother, who has Alzheimer's and is in a wheelchair, has private care. She's in an apartment and she has care workers that come in and it's an incredible amount of money to do that, but there are options. Sometimes Americans act as if it will take away all of their autonomy to opt into universal health care, but that's not true in our case. I think that having access to health care allows me and my wife to focus better on our work. It gives us more choices as to what we want to spend our money on—so if that's on my mother's private care, that is our decision, not our only option.

There're certain things that I just can't change, stress-wise: I have aging parents, teenage kids, COVID stress, work stress. But having that ability to make more decisions when it comes to our health care, not to have to avoid having a procedure done or visiting the doctor because of costs—it really does help us control our stress and work on the things we're passionate about.

Healthy eating and access to a healthy, low-stress lifestyle is one of the most important aspects of **disease prevention**. In America, socioeconomic status is strongly correlated to health, and some researchers argue that it is one of the most influential factors in determining an individual's physical and mental health and life expectancy. The burden of financial stress associated with the current health care system only adds to mental health issues such as depression and anxiety.

JESSE: Mental health is as big an issue here as it is anywhere in the world. But I feel there is a different level of accessibility. Like most major cities, our city is battling complexities of homelessness, mental health issues, and drug abuse and how they intersect. So I want to acknowledge how large and complex the issues around mental health are. But I think on the surface, I feel confident about accessing care if we need to. There are quality care providers and it's not going to be unaffordable like I know it is in some places.

I know family health is accessible and I would assume that once you get into lower socioeconomic groups, access becomes worse; people may not know what they have access to. But with the public system, outside of those very real and unfortunate barriers, once people do navigate the system and access mental health support, there's one less barrier of having to figure out how to pay for it.

America is not doing enough to help those with mental health needs. Many mental health diseases have characteristics that deter people from seeking professional help, that make it difficult to keep a job, or that can make it feel overwhelming to navigate complex insurance regulations. Nearly one in five US adults experience mental illness each year, yet more than 43 percent of adults are uninsured or underinsured, with plans that don't cover many mental health services. Imagine how many people we would be able to reach if we made mental health care more accessible through universal health care.

JESSE: I pay very high taxes here, and I don't love that, but I like that way better than living in a place where people don't have basic needs met and basic access to good education, health care infrastructure, or whatever is needed to have a society that is functioning at least at a base level. People deserve to have an opportunity to take care of themselves and their families and live a decent life. I have an American passport and citizenship, but I choose to live in Canada and I choose for my family to be raised here. There are so many things I love about America, but mentally and emotionally, I'm much happier being here. I feel safer, and I feel my family is safer.

For Americans, it may be strange to hear people say they are happy to contribute money to helping other people in their country. However, in other parts of the world, there's an understanding that supporting safety nets such as health care and education creates a happier and healthier society that benefits everyone.

As Anna and Jesse noted, the health care systems in New Zealand and Canada are not perfect, and I don't want to paint any other country as having the ultimate solution. Furthermore, providing universal health care does not absolve these countries of their own issues with systemic racism, sexism, and other prejudices that show up in medicine. But we can look to them as examples and see that we have options when it comes to creating a more financially accessible health care system for everyone.

It is abundantly clear that the American approach to health care is not working for the majority of us. Our entire way of life is based on the concept that in order for one person to prosper, another person has to go without. But that's a lie. In the case of health care, we will all benefit from a better, more equitable system that takes care of the sick and provides adequate preventive care that can help people identify problems before it's too late. The cost of diabetes medication is much cheaper than the cost of performing an amputation, and avoiding the need for an amputation frees up one of our valuable doctors to deal with other things. Identifying colorectal cancer at stage two gives someone a 75 percent chance of survival versus identifying it at stage four, which has only a 14 percent survival rate and costs much more to treat.

If the system is so obviously flawed, why haven't we changed it? In part, I think this comes down to the adage "Better the devil you know than the one you don't." While many of us may not like the current system, we're used to it. Change can be scary, and the fear of the unknown is enough for some people to cling to the way things are. Ironically, those who might benefit the most from universal health care are also those who may be the most reluctant to embrace it because of the false belief that it will cost them more money than private insurance. Paying for universal health care very likely means raising people's taxes, and while the bulk of the expense will be borne by the super-rich—those who can easily afford an increase in taxes—the rest of us would likely pay a slightly higher tax rate, too. But we wouldn't be paying for health care premiums, nor would we be paying out of pocket for deductibles or to cover the balance of the hospital bills that our insurance doesn't cover. Without those expenses, the average American would save money under a universal health care system—even if they paid a bit more in taxes.

Health care should not be a political issue but should instead be viewed as a human right. America is failing the people in this country miserably, and it is costing people their lives. A system that is based on short-term profit will never prioritize helping those in need. Health care should not be left in the hands of corporations, because our lives are worth more than medical bills.

To find out more about ways to promote health care reform, visit: BetterThanWeFoundItBook.com.

11
YOU, ME, US, THEM

Frederick Joseph on Respecting Gender Identities
Featuring **Charlotte Clymer** and **Ben O'Keefe**
Trigger Warning

I'M GOING TO TELL YOU A LOVE STORY. It's a story my friend Veronica asked me to tell, though I'm just an ancillary character in it. Veronica asked that I tell this story in hopes that it may save a love, and more importantly—save a life.

Like most love stories, this one is nuanced. It's a story about loss, hope, and trust. Not every love story has a happy ending, and this one certainly doesn't. (And please note that this story comes with a trigger warning.) But one of the beautiful things about love is that even when you've lost it, there's a good chance it can be found again. As has been the case for Veronica.

But I'm getting ahead of myself.

As so many great love stories have begun, this one started immediately following a date, during a period I refer to as "the wow." "The wow" is the period between when you leave a first date and when you see the person again. If the date was good enough, the first thing you'll think when it's done is "wow," and all you'll hear from your friends when you tell them about everything that person did and said during the first date will be "wow." There are few better feelings than the wow, and if you're lucky, the wow period can actually extend well beyond the first date—so much so that one day you find yourself planning a wedding and clearing out your life savings to get the perfect flower arrangements.

I lived with two roommates my junior year of college: Teddy and Jeremy. One night early in the fall semester, Jeremy came home from a date, and not only was he in the wow—he was in "the holy smokes," which is basically the maximum level of the wow. It's when the person you were just with has seismically shifted your entire world and you know that there is no way anything will ever be the same again.

Jeremy walked into our dorm room, closed the door, and stood his six-foot lanky frame directly in front of the television where Teddy and I were playing *NBA 2K*. "What are you doing?! Get out the damn way!" Teddy and I shouted, trying to peer around him and get back to our game.

But Jeremy ignored us. "We love all the same music! The same movies! She's a Knicks fan!"

"We get it: you had a good time," I responded irritably. "We'll see how you feel in a few weeks," I added. Jeremy had a history of falling hard and fast—and just as quickly *unfalling*.

"She offered to pay for dinner!" Jeremy said.

This was enough to pique the interest of two broke college students. "Oh, wow." Teddy placed the game controller on the table next to him. I followed his lead, and in an annoyed but curious tone said, "Fine. Tell us all about it."

Over the next two hours, Jeremy told us every detail about his date with Veronica. A date that was never supposed to happen.

Veronica, Jeremy, and I had been in student government together for about nine months, and it had been obvious since about the first moment they met that there was romantic chemistry between Jeremy and Veronica. On the surface, they were very different. Jeremy was a good-looking Korean guy who had grown up in a very sheltered home in the suburbs of Massachusetts. His style was very suburban-chic, so basically hoodies, cargo shorts, and Nike slides, while Veronica was a fashion-forward white woman who had grown up in Manhattan and was raised by parents who were former hippies turned wealthy art dealers. In spite of their differences, something just seemed to click when they were around each other. So, after a few weeks of building up the courage, Jeremy asked Veronica out on a date. Teddy and I told him that it would be easier if he did it over text, but Jeremy didn't agree. "She's not a girl you text. I want to look her in the eyes and tell her how much it would mean to me to be able to take her out."

"It's not like you're asking her to marry you," Teddy quipped. "It's just a movie and maybe Applebee's."

"But it's not just one date. It's her. I know it. She's—different. Other girls haven't mattered since the moment I met her," Jeremy said, as if he was floating in a dream by himself.

"Okay. You're doing too much," Teddy responded.

"I'm not. Fred knows what I'm talking about," Jeremy quickly replied.

He wasn't wrong. I've always been a sucker for a good

romantic story, so I suppose I did know what he was talking about.

"Yeah—he can't text her. She could be his future wife," I chimed in.

Teddy rolled his eyes as Jeremy smiled at him and darted out the door to head across campus, where Veronica's class would soon be ending. Jeremy made it just as Veronica was walking out of class.

"Hey! What are you doing on this side of the world, Jeremy? And why are you all sweaty?" Veronica said, surprised but happy to see him.

"I was running here to ask you something," Jeremy said as he gasped for air.

"Why didn't you just text me?" Veronica asked.

Jeremy laughed slightly. "I didn't want to text this, and if I waited any longer, I would have just kept psyching myself out and not doing it."

Veronica stood silent while nervously clutching the straps of her backpack.

Jeremy caught his breath, then let it out in a rush: "Veronica, I'd really like to take you out on a date. I know how much you're into Murakami, so I figured maybe we could go to the Brooklyn Museum—they have an exhibit with his work. I don't know much about art, but I like anime. He's kind of like anime-based, right? Anyway, maybe after we could get some food? What do you think?"

Veronica stared at him for a moment, then shook her head. "I can't. I'm sorry," she said concisely.

"Oh. Okay. It's just that, I thought you said you didn't have a boyfriend, so I figured maybe—"

"I said I can't. Let it go!" Veronica said as she hurried away.

When Jeremy arrived back at our dorm room, he said nothing to us. Instead, he lay on his bed and sank into his disappointment. Teddy, being the jerk he was, thought that Jeremy's obvious rejection was funny. So he took a photo of Jeremy in bed with his head under his blanket and posted it on social media with the caption: "So much for getting married. Ha!"

While Teddy's intention was solely to get a laugh, he actually helped accomplish something unexpected. One of the people who saw Teddy's post was Veronica, who was the only person besides the three of us who understood the context of the caption and photo. She was in her dorm room wallowing in the fact that as much as she had wanted to say yes, she felt that she had to tell Jeremy no. After seeing the photo of Jeremy with his body and head tucked under the covers, Veronica decided to call her mother and ask for advice.

Veronica's mother was also her best friend, and the only person she trusted to be honest with her about what she should do. After Veronica had been speaking for about an hour, her mother said plainly, "Sweetheart, you've been talking about how amazing this boy is since the school year began. If he's as kind and thoughtful as he seems to be, or likes you as much as you like him, then it will be fine. But even if it's not, you have to give people a chance to succeed or fail."

As soon as she got off the phone, Veronica texted Jeremy asking if he would meet up with her on the bleachers at the soccer stadium. An hour later, Jeremy texted back agreeing to meet. (He would have responded much sooner if he hadn't listened to Teddy telling him not to seem "thirsty.")

When Jeremy arrived, Veronica was already there, sitting alone and staring at the sky.

"I've never been here when there isn't a game going on," Jeremy said as he sat down next to her.

"Yeah, most people haven't," Veronica responded. "I like finding places where people constantly spend time, but I know what it's like to be there all alone. Kind of what it's like to know a place when it's sleeping." She stared down at the field reminiscently. "This is the first place I came to when I visited the school as a high schooler. I was supposed to play soccer here."

"Really? Why didn't you?" Jeremy asked.

"That's a long story. One that I hope I can share one day," she said. "But I wanted to apologize for what happened earlier."

"You don't have anything to apologize for. I get it. We can just be friends."

"But that's just it. I like you. I *want* to go on a date with you, but I feel like I shouldn't," Veronica said, still staring at the field.

"Why not?" Jeremy asked, deeply confused.

Veronica sighed. "If we go on a date and we have fun, then we will go on another, and then another, and we will probably fall in love."

"Okay? Are you against love? Wait—are your parents racist or something?" Jeremy asked.

Veronica finally turned her gaze upon Jeremy. "No! Gosh! No! Overly optimistic, annoyingly thoughtful, painfully hippie white, sure. But definitely not racist. They would probably love you. The problem isn't them; the problem is me. I don't want to get close to a person and let them really see me, only for them to hurt me."

"Well, if you go through your life avoiding being hurt, won't you also miss out on the chance to be pleasantly surprised?" Jeremy asked matter-of-factly.

"You sound like my mother," Veronica responded.

"So—is that a yes? You'll go with me to the museum?" Jeremy asked.

"That's a yes. On one condition," Veronica cautioned.

"You name it!" Jeremy quickly responded.

"If I ever show you all of who I am—if you ever get the chance to fully see me—you don't have to love me; just try to respect me," Veronica said, staring in Jeremy's eyes.

"I promise," Jeremy replied in a heartfelt and firm tone.

So, Jeremy and Veronica went on their first date at the Brooklyn Museum, where she taught him all about Japanese artist Takashi Murakami, and afterward he introduced her to his favorite Thai restaurant in Brooklyn. Throughout the date they laughed, talked, and shared information about themselves. When that date was over, they were both in "the holy smokes," which didn't change after the next date, or the next one, or the countless dates, text messages, and walks to class that followed.

Eventually, the two of them were inseparable. Jeremy began bringing Veronica around me and his other friends. As I said, I knew her from student government, but I didn't really know her until she started hanging out with us. I had thought Veronica was simply a perfectionist kind of student who was a part of student government and other extracurriculars because she wanted a strong résumé for an eventual career in law, which was also why she was always so stylishly dressed. (Regardless of the situation, Veronica dressed as if she was on a runway. Even when simply hanging out with us in our dorm room, she would show up in makeup and heels, wearing an outfit that looked as if it had been plucked right out of *Vogue* magazine.) But I didn't know that Veronica was a huge basketball fan, an avid video game player, and a classically trained jazz pianist. All of which led to her and I becoming close friends as she and Jeremy blossomed into something timelessly beautiful.

They were similar in all the best ways, and where they were different, they found opportunities to learn and grow for each other and themselves. That's difficult to find in any relationship, let alone in a relationship where both people are so young. Many people in relationships struggle to figure out how to stay who they are for themselves while making space to also be something else for someone. They had that part mastered from early on, which is why theirs was one of the few relationships I've seen in my life where I genuinely thought two people were perfect for each other.

They were two people who clearly loved being in love with each other. But after months of dating, they still hadn't actually said "I love you" to each other—though it was painfully obvious to everyone who had been around either of them that they did. I remember one night we were all hanging out at a place that had a digital jukebox where you could choose a song, and someone asked Veronica and Jeremy what their song was, and they realized at that moment that they didn't have one. While that wouldn't have been a big deal for most couples, it was a big deal for them (because every couple should have a song).

Later that night, I received a text from Veronica asking me a bunch of random questions about Jeremy to help her choose the perfect song to represent him. Little did she know, at the same time she was texting me, he was combing through his iPod trying to find a song to send her that he thought reflected their relationship. I told each of them what the other was doing, which may have ruined the surprise, but I hate when people don't know how much someone else cares. (Also, I was trying to sleep, and this was going to get her to stop texting me and get him to stop asking my opinion on songs.)

Neither of them could settle on a song. So, of course, they did what any reasonable couple would do: they started sending each other a different song to listen to every day for weeks until they found one. The song they settled on was "Like Someone In Love" by Chet Baker, which Teddy thought was repulsive but I thought was one of the sweetest things I'd ever heard. I also could see between the lines as to why they consciously or unconsciously chose a song about seemingly being in love but still not openly saying so.

"So, when are you going to tell her how much you love her?" I asked Jeremy as soon as he told us what their song was.

Jeremy looked at me as if he was astonished. "It's that obvious?"

"Yeah," Teddy and I said at the exact same time.

"I've been trying to figure out the best way to tell her. I want it to be special. I don't know who hurt her before, but I want her to trust me when I say I love her."

"Just tell her," Teddy responded. "She's a girl—she'll just be happy you said it."

SIDE NOTE: I'll come back to this problematic comment later.

"Shut up, Teddy," I said, exhausted by his nonsense. I turned to Jeremy. "Look, she's special to you. And realistically, if she's as special as I think she is, this may be the last time you say 'I love you' to a woman," I continued.

"You're both girls. I'm going to get some food; I can't be around this Nicholas Sparks stuff anymore," Teddy said as he walked out of the room.

SIDE NOTE: I'll *for sure* be coming back to those problematic comments!

Teddy was right: it was some romance novel stuff. But romance is a good thing, and we weren't going to let toxic masculinity get in the way of Jeremy finding the perfect way to tell Veronica how he felt.

So we went to a Redbox and rented a bunch of romantic movies. After hours of research, a few tears, and a long argument about whether Monica should have snuck out to spend time with Quincy when he found out his dad was cheating on his mom in *Love & Basketball*, we finally came up with an idea for how Jeremy could tell Veronica he loved her.

As soon as we figured out what he should do, Jeremy texted Veronica, "Sunday morning. Me and u at 6am. Early but worth it. Details soon." Veronica agreed to meet up, so Jeremy and I got to planning and calling in a few favors.

That Sunday, Veronica met Jeremy outside her dorm at six a.m., then followed him to the student parking lot where I was waiting in the driver's seat of my friend Adam's car to chauffeur the two into Manhattan. (Adam owed me a favor for letting him cheat on a political science exam.) As we drove,

Jeremy placed a blindfold on Veronica. She was apprehensive about not knowing or seeing where we were going, but he asked her to trust him, so she did. Maybe that's what love is all about—caring for someone enough to trust them, and them caring for you enough to be worthy of your trust.

We arrived at our destination and Jeremy carefully helped a still-blindfolded Veronica out of the car and through a sliding door, where they were greeted by a security guard and a man in a suit (who we would later learn was a fellow executive at the company Jeremy's dad worked at—a company that had office space at our destination). The two men escorted Veronica and Jeremy to an elevator, where they headed up for what felt like forever. Jeremy could see that Veronica was nervous, so he grasped her hand to let her know she was safe, and she squeezed his hand so that he knew that she felt safe with him.

The elevator stopped and a final security guard escorted them to a door that, when opened, sent a sudden whoosh of air through Veronica's hair, but she kept walking and kept trusting.

Finally, Jeremy stopped Veronica and removed her blindfold. "We're here."

Veronica couldn't believe her eyes. She and Jeremy were alone at the top of the Empire State Building, looking out on what felt like the entire world below. She looked at Jeremy in awe.

He smiled. "You said you like being alone places everyone else usually goes to, knowing what those places are like when they're sleeping. I figured what better place to watch sleep than New York City?"

Veronica didn't say anything. She just stared out upon

the city, closed her eyes, and thought, *I love him so much.* Though in her heart she already knew the answer to the question, she turned to him and asked anyway: "Why did you do all of this?"

Almost before she could even finish asking the question, Jeremy said the words that had been yearning to lunge from his lips since the night he came home from their first date. "Because—I love you."

Veronica closed her eyes again and let the words she had always been afraid to hear, but wanted to receive more than anything, wash over her like the first light of morning through the curtains of a window. She wanted to say it back so badly that it hurt. But she knew that true love also meant being honest.

"I . . . I . . ." Veronica tried to speak but was choked up.

"It's okay! You don't have to love me! I mean—maybe it's too much right now. I'm sorry, it's just how I feel—and maybe you'll love me eventually. But maybe you won't—and that's okay, too!" Jeremy said in the painfully frantic tone of someone trying to navigate what it means to love but not be loved in return.

"It's not that, Jeremy. I . . . I have something to tell you." Veronica stared at the floor, unable to look Jeremy in his face.

"What is it?" Jeremy asked nervously.

"Well, remember how I said that I was supposed to play on the school soccer team but it was a long story why I didn't?" Veronica asked, still staring at the floor.

"Yeah, I remember. Why?" Jeremy responded, deeply confused.

"The . . . The . . . The reason I, uh, didn't play is because I wasn't eligible to play with the women's team. My high school was more accepting, and uh, I was allowed to play with the girls' soccer team. But when I got to college, they said the reason I was so good was because I had an unfair advantage, which wasn't true. But, uh, yeah . . . I . . . ." Veronica stumbled through her words.

"Why wouldn't you be able to play with the women's team? Were you on steroids? I'm confused. What are you talking about?" Jeremy asked.

"Jeremy. I want you to see me. All of me," Veronica said as she began crying.

"What are you saying to me, Veronica?" Jeremy asked in frustration.

"I'm trans, Jeremy," Veronica said through a river of tears.

"What? Wait—what?" Jeremy asked while backing away from Veronica.

"I've always been a woman, but I was assigned male at birth. I'm transgender, Jeremy. I began my transition two years before college. I should have told you sooner, but this is me. I'm me," Veronica said, reaching out to Jeremy.

"Don't touch me!" Jeremy yelled in a tone Veronica had never heard from him before, but was too familiar with. "You lied to me, Veronica—or whatever your real name is. You let me fall in love with you! You knew I wouldn't . . . I should . . . Dammit!"

"I'm sorry I didn't tell you sooner! Please! Just listen! This is me! I'm who you fell in love with!" Veronica exclaimed.

"Leave me alone!" Jeremy yelled as he began to walk away.

"Jeremy! Please! Please! I didn't say anything because I didn't know if it was safe! But I trust you! I love you! Please!" Veronica yelled as her world felt like it was crumbling.

"Don't say those words to me," Jeremy said. He walked through the doors and onto the elevator as Veronica fell to the floor and broke down.

When Jeremy came back to the dorm room, he didn't tell us what happened, but he was angrier than we had ever seen him, so we left him alone. I was concerned as to why he wasn't with Veronica, but when I texted her to find out what happened, I didn't receive anything other than, "Don't want to talk." I texted her a few more times over the next few days to see if she was okay, but I didn't hear anything back. Neither of them showed up to our student government meetings over the next two weeks, and I didn't see Veronica anywhere on campus.

Eventually, I found out from her roommate that she had barely left their room in weeks and was hardly eating. At that point, I began to pester Jeremy about what had happened until he broke down and told me, but begged me not to say anything. He had been researching the transgender community and had learned about the dangers of being "outed." He told me that just because he didn't want to be with Veronica, it didn't mean he wanted her to be unsafe.

If given the chance, I would have told him that it sounded like he still loved her, and maybe that was worth something. Maybe that's bigger than other things. But I didn't get the chance.

What we didn't know was that Teddy was in the common area of our suite and had overheard much of our conversation. Though he promised not to say anything, it wasn't long before we found out that Teddy had no intention of keeping that promise. He not only told people that Veronica was trans; he posted about her on social media. The night he posted it, we found out because Veronica came storming to our dorm after her roommate told her she no longer wanted to live with her.

"How could you do this to me?" Veronica yelled at Jeremy after I let her in our room.

"I didn't!" Jeremy replied.

Tears filled her eyes. "But you did! You said you would respect me! You promised!" She slammed our door and left.

After she left, Jeremy set out in search of Teddy—and eventually found him. But no matter how many times he hit Teddy, it wouldn't change the fact that friendships ended that day over ignorance. It wouldn't change the fact that two people who might have been perfect for each other would never know because of transphobia. Most of all, it wouldn't change the fact that Veronica ultimately had to transfer schools because she was being harassed, had lost friends, and was receiving death threats for simply being who she was.

Before she left, Veronica was forced to change her phone number and delete her social media pages. When she was packing up to leave campus, Jeremy asked if I would check on her. Knowing that this would likely be his last chance to communicate with her, I asked him why he didn't go do it himself. What he said speaks to the heart of transphobia—to the fear, ignorance, and hatred we sometimes feel about people we perceive as being "different." He said, "I hope she's okay, but I can't. What will people think?"

Whether many of us realize it or not, a great deal of the ways we act and the things we believe are based on what other people might think. In reality, when it comes to the choices we make in our own lives, the most important thoughts should be our own.

Jeremy's response is a prime example of not only how destructive prioritizing the thoughts of others can be—but also of what an inauthentic reflection it often is of your own thoughts and feelings.

Though Jeremy ended up breaking Veronica's heart and frankly traumatizing her, she later told me that she believed that he truly did care about her. That's one of the saddest parts about being conditioned to care about the opinions and thoughts of others—how often we stop ourselves from pursuing our happiness or being our total selves out of fear of ridicule from others.

But to stop loving someone because the world judges you might mean you never loved them at all.

I did as Jeremy asked and went to check on Veronica as she was leaving. We talked for a while about how heartbroken she was that Jeremy couldn't even muster the courage to be a friend to her through all of this. She understood him not wanting to be with her, but she was hurt because he promised to respect her, and he hadn't even done that.

A few hours later, Veronica left the school, and the boy she had fallen in love with.

But not every love story is the story of how you met your true love. It took Veronica a few years to learn to trust someone again, but ultimately, she did and that man proved to be worthy of her trust, and her love.

Veronica ended up attending law school and is currently a lawyer focused on trans rights. How do I know? Because

Veronica and I have stayed great friends ever since I went to check on her. We have grown together in how we both fit in this world, and she has helped me better understand how I might be able to support the trans community.

Which is why when I told her I was writing about this subject, she asked if I could tell the story of the love that was lost because some people decided that she was not worthy of it because of her identity. (Though she had long since realized that what she had with Jeremy wasn't true love at all—and that he wasn't worthy of her.)

Beyond being a story about love lost, the story of Veronica and Jeremy is also a story about a **social construct**—a belief shared by a group of people within a society that is treated as a fact, even though it is not objectively true. A person's sex is typically determined by their reproductive organs at birth (though there's a bit more to it than that). People can be born **intersex**, which means they are born with reproductive or sexual anatomy that isn't typically male or female. But gender is something societies have invented.

Gender often encapsulates societal expectations of behavior (how someone acts or reacts), roles (the things a person does in society and in their relationships), and presentation (how a person dresses, how they wear their hair, how they speak, and so on). These gender expectations can be rigid or they can be relaxed, depending on the society or community.

But it is simply not true that one's sex determines one's gender. Your sex might determine what gender *people feel you ought to identify as*—and these expectations can have very serious implications, to be sure—but only you can determine what, if any, gender you are.

How a person identifies in terms of gender is about a feeling, something true and honest about their existence and personal experience. Your gender identity or lack thereof shouldn't be a matter of what has been assigned to you, but rather a matter of who you feel you are.

While Jeremy didn't take Veronica's **coming out** to him well, she notes that he responded far better than many people, which tells you just how far we as a society have to go toward dismantling our rigid gender expectations. Many transgender people face violence when revealing that they are trans—even from those who claim to love them, such as friends and family.

SIDE NOTE: In 2020, forty-four transgender or gender-nonconforming Americans were murdered—the deadliest year on record for the trans community.

But this violence is not only manifested in physical acts; it also takes the form of attacks against a person's rights. In the first five months of 2021, there were more than one hundred **anti-trans bills** introduced in state legislatures throughout America, which is a record number. Elected officials are using their power to try to strip trans and gender-nonconforming people of their ability to simply be who they are.

While I'm grateful that Veronica gave me the opportunity to share her story on her behalf, I believe it's always important to hear directly from the people who are a part of the communities you're learning about. Which is why I've asked my friends Charlotte Clymer and Ben O'Keefe to lend us their voices on the topics of gender identity and transphobia.

An Interview with **CHARLOTTE CLYMER**
Writer and activist

Charlotte Clymer is not only a brilliantly caring and thoughtful person; she is also a trans woman who is an LGBTQ+ activist, thought leader, and writer around trans issues and rights. There are few people more outspoken about gender identity, and that made her a perfect person to interview.

CHARLOTTE: I grew up in central Texas, in a mainly conservative environment, and I knew from an early age that something was different. I just didn't know how to explain it. I didn't know the word *transgender*; I didn't know about **gender dysphoria**. I just knew from a very early age that I wanted to be a girl. And my reaction to that was to lean into masculinity as much as possible. So I was a kid who didn't rebel. I got straight A's. I listened to the adults in my life. And a part of that was this thought that I needed to cleanse myself of this need.

No matter how much I pushed, it just didn't go away. I played football in high school. I ran for city council. I did all this stuff with the church—it just did not go away. And so I joined the army, mostly because I wanted to serve, but the second reason was that I felt, *Okay, this has got to be it. If I go and serve, this is the height of "masculinity." To serve in a military uniform.* And it was a wake-up call. It was a reality check on so many different levels. Not only did it reinforce this idea that I was kind of denying the central authentic part of myself, but it also exposed me to a lot of aspects of the world that I didn't have as much experience in, like systemic racism, misogyny, ableism, to some extent—all these areas of advocacy that we all need to pay more attention to, but which those of us with privilege don't see as much.

As mentioned in the chapter on homophobia, because oppression is often internalized by people in oppressed communities, it can be difficult for people to fully explore or be honest with themselves about who they are, let alone admit it to others.

CHARLOTTE: I didn't come out as trans until, gosh, 2017. November 29, 2017. And for the three years before that, I was identifying as **nonbinary**. Going by *they/them* pronouns. Because I didn't have—I don't want to say *the courage*, because that's probably not the right framing. But I feel like I didn't have enough support yet to come out as a trans woman. And after the election of Trump, I broke up with my partner because her parents forced her to choose. "It's either us or this very weird **genderqueer** person that you want to see."

And I thought, *Well, I don't want to die tomorrow not being my authentic self. I can't do that anymore.* And so I wrote this long coming-out post and posted it on Facebook, posted it on Twitter. By then, I was "known" to people on social media, but posting it was revelatory. Because I did not expect the reaction I got. I honestly expected a lot of people to get weirded out by it or to maybe distance themselves from me over time (back when "socially distanced" meant something else). And instead, I was embraced by all my friends, and a lot of people who I hadn't talked to in years reached out to me to congratulate me and offer me support. And it's been such a long journey navigating the progressive space and, more specifically, the LGBTQ space and all the intersecting issues that come with that, whether it's fighting white supremacy, trying to get health care access for all people, fighting for **reproductive health care**, all this stuff.

I'm a trans woman. So I do face transphobia, misogyny, and homophobia to some extent, but I'm also white. I'm able-bodied. I'm not a religious minority. I have financial security, more or less. And so I have all these privileges that correspond with myself, even though I do face oppression. And one thing I think it's so important for all of us to embrace is the idea that experiencing a form of oppression is not a race. The benefits we get from an unearned privilege that we have—that doesn't absolve us. Our oppressions do not absolve us of our privileges.

Charlotte didn't feel comfortable coming out as a trans woman until she was in her thirties. That's a great deal of her life spent having to dilute aspects of her existence because she felt that she was going to be treated negatively. People shouldn't have to deny the truths of themselves and/or fear for their lives because of the ignorance and hatred of others. This is particularly important to recognize for people who live at multiple intersections, such as Black trans women, who face societal oppression not only due to being trans but also due to being Black and women. To deepen our understanding of this lived intersectionality, it's essential that we learn from the perspectives and experiences of trans activists and thought leaders of color, such as Marsha P. Johnson, Miss Major Griffin-Gracy, Andrea Jenkins, and Sir Lady Java.

CHARLOTTE: There are so many issues that come with being out: acceptance by your family and friends for one, and you could expose yourself to violence or discrimination. All these factors really keep people **in the closet**. I would not be where I am were it not for all the people who came before me and made it easier for me—LGBTQ people in general, no doubt, but primarily trans people who came out before me and kind of paved the way. And specifically trans women of color who really did so much of the groundwork of advocacy and pushing for better policies.

I live in DC, which is the most trans-friendly place in America, hands down. I mean, I would say even more than San Francisco in some ways. Well, I don't know, maybe that's debatable, but here's what's true: we have more trans people per capita in DC than anywhere else in the country. We have five times the national rate of trans people in the district. And part of the reason is that there are legal protections in place that only came about because of mainly Black trans women who fought for those policies.

I would not be out of the closet right now were it not for the trans people who were proudly out and themselves and their authenticity, and showing the world that this is something that is completely natural and we need to embrace it. But most places don't have those protections, and that is not the reality for most trans people, especially non-white trans people who face transphobia and racism.

While Washington, DC, is not perfect, the legal protections that exist there show us that such pro-trans policies are possible elsewhere. And if many Americans support legal protections for trans people, why hasn't more progress been made?

CHARLOTTE: On the larger level, we have an issue of complacency right now. So, when same-sex marriage was legalized by the Supreme Court in 2015, it was a big event. We were very happy. But a lot of activists were worried that most cisgender heterosexual people would believe that "Oh, so that's it. LGBTQ rights are no longer an issue, this is solved." And in fact, that's exactly what happened. A couple of years ago, Reuters did a poll of voters and asked two questions. The first one was: Do you support nondiscrimination protections for LGBTQ people? And like, 75 percent of respondents said yes, including half of Republicans, right? So the vast majority of the country supports LGBTQ rights, hands down. The second question was: Do LGBTQ nondiscrimination protections exist at the federal level? (Referring to Congress-made laws protecting LGBTQ people.) And half of respondents said yes. And in fact the answer is no.

There are basically no LGBTQ protections at the federal level. There's this Supreme Court case for marriage. And there was a Supreme Court case in 2020 for employment—so basically, LGBTQ people cannot be denied employment or be fired for being LGBTQ—but that's it. That's all. In most of the United States right now, LGBTQ people face discrimination in housing, credit, public accommodations, education, jury service—all across the board, every aspect of the public square in most of the United States.

In something like twenty-eight or twenty-nine states, there are very few protections against discrimination for LGBTQ people. Now, I want to be literal about this. If I live in Missouri right now, in most of Missouri—and there might be some municipalities that have passed local laws—but in most of Missouri, it is legal, or at least it's not protected, for a landlord to deny me housing because I'm transgender. They can say, "Oh, actually we don't want to rent to you because you're transgender." And that's it; I take my ball and I go home. And I think there are a lot of people who don't realize that right now, because they see that big Supreme Court case. They're like, "Oh, same-sex marriage is the whole ball game." And in fact, it's an important but very small piece of the overall picture.

And primarily what so many people don't realize is that the people most affected by this are LGBTQ people of color, and LGBTQ people who are disabled, and LGBTQ religious minorities—the folks who are already marginalized in certain ways because of xenophobia, racism, ableism, whatever. They have this added-on structure to them that they have to lift up, that they can't because it's too heavy. And so, when you look at homeless rates, when you look at unemployment, when you look at housing discrimination, jury discrimination, being denied credit, these primarily affect LGBTQ people of color, and more specifically trans people of color. And unless we address this with legislation like the **Equality Act**, we're not going to get anywhere. And that's why we're fighting for the Equality Act.

SIDE NOTE: The Equality Act is a bill that would ensure that LGBTQ+ individuals are protected from discrimination in essential sectors such as work, housing, credit, education, public spaces and services, federally supported programs, and jury service. Although this law would be welcome and beneficial, my dear friend trans activist and author Raquel Willis recently reminded me that the larger ask beyond policy from many trans people of color is that trans allies help protect the trans community on a personal level, which includes getting involved with local trans-led organizations and stepping in when we see harm taking place.

Now, let me say one more thing real quick, because there's been a little confusion. So President Biden signed an executive order in January 2021, and it banned discrimination in the federal government against LGBTQ people. However, the federal government does not control state laws, right? Separation of powers. So although a federally funded program cannot discriminate against someone like me, I can still be discriminated against in most of the United States. If I started driving from New York to Sacramento, I'm going to drive through some kind of state, county, something, where as a trans person, I do not have equality.

There should be *no* place in this country where transphobia and other forms of LGBTQ discrimination are legally sanctioned. Thankfully, many Americans agree with that statement. Now we just need the people in charge of making the laws to listen to us.

An Interview with BEN O'KEEFE

Activist, Forbes 30 Under 30 producer, writer

It was important to me to speak with Ben O'Keefe because he exists at the intersection of many identities, as so many people do—even those who don't realize it. He is a brilliantly creative person, but more importantly, a brilliantly inclusive and intersectional trans ally whose partner is transfeminine.

BEN: I use the pronouns *he, him, his*. I'm a queer man, but I identify as cisgender, meaning that I align with the gender that I was assigned at birth. And so when I use my pronouns, when I'm showing my pronouns, it's less about people **misgendering** me and more about signaling to others that we should be aware of the fact that people do have pronouns and identities. And by me sharing mine, it helps normalize when someone might use *they/them* pronouns, or *ze/zir* pronouns, or any of the many other pronouns. I'm trying to create space by normalizing the behavior.

By posting our pronouns, we challenge the idea of the gender binary—something Ben went on to discuss in more detail.

BEN: The gender binary is a belief that there are two genders and you can be only one or the other, male or female, and being male means that you have to subscribe to all of these different ideas about what it means to be a man. Being female, or being a woman, means that you have to identify with all of these different ideas of what it means to be a woman. They are constructs, like most things in our society.

Race itself is a construct. Race is actually just about the way that people look. It's not scientific. It's not based on ethnicity. That's a totally different concept. Race is just a construct, as is gender. So many people have realized that just because they were born with certain genitalia didn't mean that they felt most aligned with the way that society describes who someone should be because of that genitalia.

The gender binary is this way of keeping people in boxes. We like to do that. We like to keep people in boxes because it makes it easier for us to understand people as opposed to doing the work of finding out who other people are and finding out who we are ourselves. Looking outside of the gender binary is an amazing thing that all of us should consider doing because it means I get to be who I am without being told who I am. I don't have to subscribe to what society says it means to be me. I get to live my truest, most authentic self. I get to wear clothes that make me feel like my truest, most authentic self. I get to have a personality that makes me feel like my truest, most authentic self.

There's a lot of pain that's associated with being forced to be someone that you're not. There's a lot of real struggle to exist in the world and not be seen for who you are. I am someone who has embraced femininity, someone who believes that masculine energy can also exist with feminine energy. Masculinity to me is strength. It's support. It's just being a force. And it's about being that strength for others. That's what it means to me. Femininity to me is about empathy. It's about maternal energy and *mothering* as a verb, which I think men can do as well.

When I finally learned that I could be myself after years of growing up Catholic in a conservative space, being queer, gay, part of the LGBTQ community, embracing different identities throughout that and finding myself—it gave me permission to be myself. And in doing that, I can help other people learn how to live the most authentic life that they can live, because we deserve that. And when we live authentically, we make a much larger impact in the world because we're not trying to be anything but ourselves. And when people are themselves, when people feel they're valued and they have agency just in being who they are, that's when we can really make transformative change in the world.

The social constructs of gender and sex assignment don't just impact people who are trans and nonbinary. They impact everyone. We are all limited by how characteristics, behaviors, and interests are assigned and assumed based on the constructs of masculinity and femininity. Remember how I flagged some problematic comments of Teddy's and told you I'd come back to them? Well, let's take a minute now to really consider what he was saying when he called me and Jeremy "girls" for our interest in romance. Teddy, like many of us, had been socialized to believe that romance and its associated emotions—love, tenderness, thoughtfulness—are feminine in nature. And that same socialization tells us that femininity belongs only to women. But the fact that Jeremy and I are die-hard romantics proves that these traits don't "belong" to women. And plenty of women have no interest in romance, which goes to show that one doesn't have to like traditionally "feminine" things to be a woman.

Emotions, interests, behaviors, mannerisms—these things don't belong to any one gender or any one sex. Those who claim otherwise are wrong, and those who *insist* otherwise are not only wrong but are also scared by anything or anyone that doesn't conform to their narrow and rigid expectations. Your existence is limitless and should not be defined by boxes that someone else has created.

BEN: I think social constructs are all about power. It's all about who decides what is "right." And so we have something called the dominant culture. Dominant culture is a really important construct to understand. The people who have the most power—and in our society, that's straight white males, primarily, right?—those people who have power get to set the precedent. It's one reason that we've seen Black people and women historically underrepresented in certain industries.

It's systemic. It's about this overarching system, how our world works, who has the power and then who calls the shots. So to overcome social constructs, it's about not saying, *What have I been taught?* but it's about saying, *How do I feel?* and *How do I feel that I should be showing up?* Not *How do other people feel that I should be showing up in the world?* These social constructs—hey, they're not real, right? We use them as a tool to help us understand each other, but they don't have to define how we understand ourselves. And there's no better person who understands ourselves than us. So it's about understanding that constructs exist, knowing that they can be a tool to navigate the world, but knowing that they don't have to define us.

We don't have to exclude. We can just get to know people for who they are. It's fitting that we've seen so many gender reveal parties quite literally blow up in people's faces—it's because we don't get to reveal someone's gender because we don't know their gender. We know their genitalia, their sex assigned at birth, but we don't know who they are. And so much of life should be about letting people discover who they are. For example, when we see parents who let kids pick their own clothes and let kids express themselves and their gender in their way, those kids likely turn out to be happier people. Just being themselves.

I think that so much of how we operate is by trying to put people into boxes, by trying to define people. We don't have to define people's identity to respect them as people. We don't have to fully understand someone or fully prescribe something onto someone. We can let them tell us who they are. We can let them tell us what makes them feel good. And so I think it's important that we start thinking about the ways that we project these things. So many people, including people who maybe even have trans friends or who might know nonbinary people, will still have a gender reveal party because that is just what we've been taught. But I think we've just got to start living in a post-gendered world where your genitalia doesn't describe your opportunity, it doesn't describe your personality, and it doesn't describe how you are treated in the world.

I've always believed that everyone has a right to exist as their truest self, and the strategic attacks on and erasure of the trans and gender-nonconforming community aim to make that impossible for them. Why? Because someone isn't like you? Because someone wasn't born identifying as you identify? Because someone dares to be purple in a world that says that you may only be pink or blue?

Simply put, people are being oppressed because someone else wants to decide who they should and shouldn't be—and it doesn't have to be that way. No one should have to fear a life of obstacles or violence or even death for simply being themselves.

Since gender is a cultural construct—since "normal" is a cultural construct—we get to decide what it means, or if it even exists. The new normal can be that everything is normal, that people are people—complex, dynamic, and ever-changing.

Being inclusive and supportive of individuals who are unlike you doesn't mean you have to change how you identify or who you date. Jeremy didn't have to continue dating Veronica once he knew she was trans (though maybe he would've wanted to, if he hadn't been socialized to think there was something wrong with being trans). He just had to treat her with respect, to acknowledge that she was as worthy as he was of being treated with kindness. Being inclusive simply means you have to find ways to show up for others so that they know they are respected and have the space to safely be themselves.

Using pronouns, learning more about people who are transitioning or have transitioned, learning about misgendering, learning to respect other people's experiences and existences, and beginning to stop assigning behaviors and interests to genders are all ways we can begin to open those boxes we've all been forced into. And one day, we can get rid of the boxes altogether.

To find out more about how you can help put a stop to transphobia, visit: BetterThanWeFoundItBook.com.

12
HOME IS WHERE THE RENT IS (OR ISN'T)

Porsche Joseph on the Need for Housing Security

Featuring Julián Castro

When you're twelve years old, going into junior high feels like the most important thing you've ever been through. Forget about taking the training wheels off your bike or learning cursive. The idea of going to a new school with new kids and a long list of firsts—first lockers, first class periods, first time trying out for school sports teams . . . Even thinking about it now triggers my preteen angst!

I was a horrifically shy kid at that age (though many people probably just thought I was awkward) and the thought of junior high filled me with anxiety. I had been going to the same elementary school since kindergarten and had managed to collect a couple of friends. I would have been happy staying in the little world I had built for myself until it was time to graduate high school. Sadly, it was time for a fresh start, whether I wanted one or not. But I was tormented by the unknown. *Would I fit in? Would people tease me? Would I be forced to hide in the bathroom during lunch?* I still liked to play tag and had a collection of troll dolls with jewels on their bellies on a shelf in my room—how on earth was I supposed to go to school with fourteen-year-olds? But as I would come to learn, it was a privilege having to worry only about things such as starting school.

I had spent the summer before junior high taking any jobs that I could. Sadly, there wasn't much work out there for a twelve-year-old, so I stuck to the usual suspects: babysitting and doing chores for neighbors. I did get a chance to attempt to deliver newspapers, but that was short-lived. (It requires a lot more coordination than you'd imagine.)

See, my mom was a single parent of three and we didn't have "back-to-school shopping" money. My older brother, Darnell, was heading into his sophomore year of high school and my younger brother, Preston, was starting kindergarten that year. So, between supporting the eating habits of a fifteen-year-old student athlete and clothing a six-year-old through his many growth spurts, my mom's minimum-wage income was stretched to its limit. If I wanted back-to-school clothes and supplies, it was up to me to pay for them.

I desperately felt the need for some cool new clothes to help me in this social experiment of leaving elementary school. If people thought I dressed well, maybe they wouldn't know how poor my family was. If I was dressed in cool clothes, maybe they wouldn't know that I still had a giant *Beauty and the Beast* poster above my bed. I wouldn't be an easy target, and they wouldn't know how utterly nervous I was.

Looking back on it, getting "cool clothes" wasn't really that important. But at the time, if I didn't have Adidas shell-toes and a Baby Phat coat, I could have sworn I would die. I had spent the whole summer either working or in the house watching music videos, and it was the year of Missy Elliott and Nelly. (I am well aware that for many of you that may mean nothing, but if you know, you know.) So I scraped together all of the cash I had earned over the past few months, hit the nearest Coinstar with my piggy bank, and asked my mom to take me down to my favorite store, TJ Maxx. (I am still a Maxxinista to this day, and am also in love with the sister store HomeGoods, which you may be too young to appreciate but will surely learn to one day.)

For those of you who may be used to spending a couple hundred dollars on a single outfit, you may think that a couple hundred dollars couldn't get you far, but there is an art to shopping on a budget, and I learned it early. That day, I was on a shopping *spree*!

After the exhausting yet gratifying task of spending every penny of my summer savings on my new "cool clothes," we finally headed home. When we got to the house, my mom told me she had a surprise for me. She went to her closet and pulled out a brand-new pair of Adidas. My heart exploded! They weren't the most expensive sneakers in the world, but they were the sneakers I had been wanting all summer and had determined would go with all of the outfits I had put together in my head. Because I couldn't justify spending a large portion of the money I had saved on one pair of shoes, I had resigned myself to wearing my old sneakers with my new clothes. Now suddenly there they were, right in front of my eyes—and an entire size too big, because if you've ever been a kid in a household with a limited income, you know all about buying things with "some room to grow." My mom knew how badly I had wanted those Adidas, and even though she couldn't afford them, somehow she made it happen for me. My wardrobe was complete!

"Honey, you've been working so hard all summer and I am sorry I can't do more for you," she said. "But I want you to know how proud I am of you and how excited I am for you to be moving on to a new school and a new chapter of your life."

I was always an anxious kid, with an overwhelming feeling that something was going to go wrong, which probably came from the fact that it always seemed like my family was working tirelessly just to get through one thing or another. But that day felt good. That day felt like nothing could go wrong. Everything was in place and I was ready to start school in a couple weeks.

Maybe this new-school thing would go better than I thought.

The next week, I was having one of those lazy end-of-summer days. School was starting in less than a week and my brothers were out enjoying time with their friends. My mom was taking a nap, something she hardly ever had the opportunity to do, and I was sitting in the sunshine on the porch, painting my nails blue and listening to TLC's new *FanMail* CD. (Yes, you read that right, a CD.) I didn't realize anything was wrong until I heard the alarm and then the smell of things burning. At first it smelled like a bonfire, but as the fire grew, the smell of chemicals and melting plastic burned my nostrils and eyes. It is a smell I can never forget.

It's difficult to recall everything that happened next. All I remember is running into the apartment and seeing it filled with smoke as my mom dragged herself out of her bedroom and past the flames coming from mine. My mother was chok-ing on the thick ash in the air, her face already covered in soot, but she managed to crack a desperate smile of relief when she saw me standing unscathed in front of her. I had been ren-dered motionless by the pure shock of it all, so she grabbed my arm and pulled me to the front door.

When we got outside, we caught our breaths and then just stood there, tears rolling down our faces, as we watched my childhood home go up in flames with all of the things we had worked so hard for inside of it. Things we needed, things we loved, things we didn't have the money to replace. Things we could never replace, even with all the money in the world.

The only word to describe how I felt is *broken*. We had already barely been making it; things were going to be impossible now. I can never imagine what was going on in my mother's head at that moment—a single mother working long hours at a low-paying job who was now left with noth-ing and had to figure out how to make things okay for her three children. I felt so sad for the position she was in, and wished with all my might that I could help her solve this. But there was no number of hours I could babysit that would fix this.

After the fire was put out and the firefighters completed their inspection, we were told that the fire had begun in my room and quickly spread to the rest of the house. Before I had gone outside, I had lit a candle in my room—which I'd totally forgotten about. I still don't know how the fire actually started, but I do know that it was because of me and that one moment of thoughtlessness.

Luckily, we weren't in any legal trouble since the fire was

deemed an accident. But that was about as far as our luck went. We had no renters insurance, no savings, no place to go. All that worrying about starting junior high and my silly school clothes seemed so far removed now. On that hot August day just a week before school was to start, I had nowhere to live. Suddenly, we were houseless.

SIDE NOTE: Although the term *homeless* is still used by many people, including those in the government, I chose to use the word *houseless* because it better encompasses the many circumstances in which someone might be without traditional housing, rather than the stereotypical idea of homelessness.

There is a common stereotype that people make the choice to be houseless, either directly (because they're lazy and refuse to get a job) or indirectly (because they're unstable or have an addiction problem). But I'm living proof that there are any number of reasons an individual or a family might end up houseless—most of which have nothing to do with choice.

The firefighters gave my mom the number to the American Red Cross, who offered to put us up in a motel for a few days. They also gave us vouchers and gift cards to get some new things, which were a godsend. Somehow, there we were, sitting in a motel room with nothing but the clothes on our backs and no safety net or plan for what to do next.

It was now two days before school began, and my mom was busy hustling, trying to get us everything we needed. She was going to churches, applying for every assistance program she heard of, and working on finding a more permanent housing solution (and probably many other things I couldn't even comprehend).

We had a neighbor who saw what happened and put together some of her daughter's hand-me-downs for me. She didn't speak any English and we had never had a single interaction with her before, but she was the sole reason I had a few shirts and pairs of pants at the start of the school year. They were no Baby Phat, but she was an angel and I wish I knew her name so that I could publicly thank her now. I have held on to one of her daughter's sweaters to this day.

We had a gift certificate to Walmart from the Red Cross and I was able to get some more things—hair products, school supplies, pajamas—but by our last night in the motel, we still had no place to live.

Luckily, I have an aunt who made space for us to all sleep in her living room. Needless to say, it wasn't how I envisioned starting middle school. But when I woke up on the first day of school in a sleeping bag on my aunt's floor, I felt thankful. Thankful to be out of that motel. Thankful to know I had a mom who was pouring herself into solving the problem. Thankful for my aunt. Thankful for the Red Cross and those vouchers. Thankful we hadn't been forced to resort to living in our car. Thankful we *had* a car. Looking back, I am also thankful for my mother's mental health and ability to stay strong and find the energy to take on the task of rebuilding our lives while my siblings and I were fortunate enough to go to school (something many children in similar circumstances may not be afforded the opportunity to do).

I don't remember much about those first days of junior high that I thought would be so important. I do remember hiding in the bathroom during lunch with chipped blue nail polish, avoiding eating my free school lunch in front of everyone and giving them the chance to notice that I only had enough outfits to get me through three days. (My mother washed my clothes every other night so they were clean, but I knew that wouldn't be enough to protect me from being teased or bullied.) All of the other formerly terrifying aspects of starting at a new school now seemed so irrelevant.

I did the best I could to avoid being noticed, but one day one of the most popular boys in school started making fun of my sweatshirt. The sweatshirt had come from the bag of clothes gifted by my neighbor and it was the only sweatshirt I owned at the moment, so I wore it pretty much every day. (It's too cold for T-shirts in the fall in Seattle.)

This boy started teasing me, saying that my sweatshirt probably smelled like [insert anything unpleasant here]. That was the game that day: name anything and everything that stinks and say that's probably what my sweatshirt smelled like because I wore it every day.

My sweatshirt was washed often and it didn't actually smell, but seventh-grade boys can be cruel and a couple of them joined my tormentor in the creative little game for the next hour of class. Honestly, it wasn't really uncommon to get teased by immature boys in junior high, and I was hardly their only target; they did stuff like this to a different person nearly every day. But because of what I was going through outside of school and my insecurities around people finding out, I was utterly humiliated. It made me wish I could disappear that very moment and never return.

A few weeks into the school year, Ms. James, my guidance

counselor, called me into her office, pulling me out of my fifth-period math class. Ms. James was popular among the students because she was young and pretty and seemed to have a good relationship with many of the popular students. I was excited that she was assigned to me but unsure of why she was calling me into her office. Students usually only met with their counselors at the end of the semester or if they were in trouble.

"Hi, Porsch," she said with a very fake smile. "Come in."

If I hadn't already been wary, her calling me "Porsch" would've made me so. That's not my name, and I hate when people shorten my name without permission. But I didn't feel comfortable correcting her. She was very much in control of this interaction, and we both knew it.

Ms. James had perfectly straight hair and a bright-white smile that complemented her polished look. All the other counselors, especially the younger ones, wore casual clothes, but Ms. James was always in trendy business attire, with everything in perfect place. I recall her wearing a black pencil skirt and pumps that looked brand-new that day. She had a bright-pink blazer hanging on the back of her chair, and she was wearing the same shade of lipstick.

She didn't waste any time. "Why don't you tell me about what's going on with you?" she asked.

This was clearly a loaded question—she obviously thought something was "going on" with me—but I had no idea what she meant by it. I knew it wasn't about the sweatshirt teasing incident, because the boys were careful to do that out of the earshot of the teacher and no one would dare rat them out (hence having a new target every day). Had I done something wrong? Was this about my math class? I knew I wasn't very good at math, but we hadn't even had a test yet. How badly could I be doing?

I should have asked her what she was getting at, but all I could spit out was a simple avoidant answer. "Not too much. I'm just trying to do well in all my classes," I replied, without making eye contact.

She probably attempted to make some small talk then, but what I remember next was the line of uncomfortable questioning. She had a notepad out and jotted things down here and there.

"Where are you sleeping? Is there enough food where you're at? Do you feel safe? Does your mother ever leave you for long periods of time? Do you ever see people drinking or doing drugs around you?"

While these might have been good questions to know about any and all kids, I was confident that this wasn't protocol. I had been singled out for this interrogation, and I felt scared in that room with that woman, whom I had never met before and who appeared to want to paint my mother as an unstable parent. She was making assumptions about my mother, implying that she was neglectful or had a drug or alcohol problem, simply because we were experiencing a moment of houselessness, instead of allowing us our humanity and offering support.

As I sat there trying to answer her questions as briefly yet politely as possible, I felt ashamed. What had I done to be singled out? Had my teachers noticed that I repeated the same few outfits or that I was often late to school? (My aunt lived really far away and on days that my mother couldn't take me to school, I had to take a public bus and walk about a mile just to get there.)

Regardless of how Ms. James had learned about my living situation, this was a conversation that she should have had with my mom, not me. Or I should have been spoken to by a qualified social worker who understood how to be sensitive with the situation—not abruptly pulled out of fifth period, interrogated by an unsympathetic stranger, and then sent back to class. When I was finally dismissed, I stopped at the bathroom instead of going directly back to class. I went into a stall—my safe place—and bawled my eyes out as silently as possible, hoping no one would come in and hear me. Did everyone know I didn't have a home? And did teachers and students talk about me behind my back and wonder about all those things Ms. James had asked me about?

Fortunately, within a couple of months, my mother was able to secure housing. We had no furniture and had to start from scratch, but she is a superwoman and by the second half of the school year, we had restored a sense of normalcy to our lives. I collected more clothes, and our home was furnished piece by piece. It's estimated that more than four million children and young adults experience houselessness each year. That's about every thirty children in America. That means the odds are that you are or have been in classes with students without a safe, stable place to live. And this number does not improve as children become young adults; in fact, one in every ten people age eighteen to twenty-five experience houselessness every year. Which means you probably know someone who is or has been houseless, even if you don't realize it. As it was in my case, you can't always tell if a person is houseless.

While houselessness can mean living on the streets, in a shelter, or in a car, houselessness can also refer to those who are living **doubled up** with relatives, **couch surfing**, or in an unsafe or substandard housing situation.

Although the causes of houselessness vary greatly, one major driver is **gentrification**. While the federal minimum wage has not increased in over a decade, well-paid professionals have overtaken neighborhoods where people used to be able to afford to live on working-class salaries. San Francisco is a prime example. When the tech industry grew and San Francisco became the unofficial capital of the industry, well-paid developers and tech entrepreneurs who could afford to pay a lot for housing drove the prices up. Meanwhile, wages for other sectors did not increase and quickly became inadequate to meet the increasing housing prices. This meant the artists, the bakers, the teachers, the construction workers, and other blue-collar families were priced out of the market.

Another common cause of houselessness is health issues. From physical health to mental health, health problems can create major barriers to working and having stable and sufficient income to afford housing. Additionally, large medical bills can be a huge obstacle for those struggling to afford housing. Unfortunately, social programs that are supposed to help those with disabilities do not provide nearly enough support to afford housing.

Solutions have been suggested to create more equitable housing—from increasing public housing to housing voucher programs, from incentives to develop more affordable housing to implementing **rent control**. But until society and policy makers can agree that people deserve to be paid a **living wage** (particularly those who are undervalued in the workforce or are unable to participate in the workforce) and that housing is a human right, we cannot expect the problem to be tackled in a meaningful way.

The danger of misconceptions or stereotypes around houselessness is that they create apathy around fixing the issue. If people believe that houselessness is a choice or a result of someone's choices, it discourages them from helping houseless people or investing in their well-being and opportunities. People often hesitate to give money to a houseless person on the street, worrying about where their five or ten dollars will go. But how often do those same people stop to question the tax dollars they give to the government and how they are spent, or why our tax dollars aren't doing more to help our houseless population?

Studies conducted all over the country have shown that it costs less to house people than it does to police them and pay for emergency room visits. To put this in perspective, one study in Florida showed that policing nonviolent offenses of houseless people cost three times as much as it would cost to get every houseless person a shelter and a social worker. This country has enough resources and housing for everyone. We just need to commit to allocating these resources directly to the people who need them the most.

In the summer of 2021, the Pacific Northwest experienced unprecedented heat waves that are estimated to have resulted in the deaths of eight hundred people, many of whom were people without housing or with inadequate housing. That is just one example of why housing is a human right. People's lives are at stake when they cannot access adequate housing.

Beyond protection from extreme weather conditions, housing also offers access to sanitation and hygiene that reduces the chance of illness and disease.

Government spending should never prioritize anything over the well-being of people, because the people are what the government exists for. Countless excuses have been made for why the funding can't be found to end houselessness, but we see that whenever a capitalistic opportunity arises, like finding money for businesses to stay open during the COVID-19 pandemic, those excuses disappear and the money is made available. Billionaires' cumulative wealth rose by nearly four trillion dollars during 2020, the first year of the pandemic, while almost fifteen million Americans were behind on rent and facing eviction by the summer of 2021. The money to address the problem of houselessness is there—we just have to convince people to use it accordingly.

An Interview with JULIÁN CASTRO

Former US secretary of housing and urban development; former mayor of San Antonio, Texas; and former presidential candidate

Few people have thought more critically about and worked harder to advocate for housing rights than former secretary of housing and urban development (HUD) Julián Castro. When he joined President Obama's Cabinet in 2014, he was the youngest member at thirty-nine years old. During that time, he helped make plans to create a more equitable housing market, as well as draft policy to support communities affected by natural disasters.

I wanted to learn more about what has driven Julián's

passion to make change since an early age, and particularly for people from marginalized communities.

JULIÁN: People don't live in silos. People's lives are shaped by all sorts of different policies that help them, that hurt them, that advantage them or disadvantage them. From housing to education to job creation, and, of course, everything that intersects with that, whether we're talking about racism or sexism or other biases—all of these things intimately impact the ability of somebody to live up to their full human potential. And so when we're thinking about policy or when we're thinking about how to make sure that people can live with dignity and how they can have a real shot at opportunity and reach full equality, then we need to think about policies and those policies' impact on them.

We need to think about it in not just one silo, but across the board, how all of those things work together. That's what I tried to do as mayor and tried to do at HUD. At HUD, we really did that in full, under the Obama administration. Especially with things like affirmatively furthering fair housing and programs like ConnectHome and even efforts like Choice Neighborhoods to connect the dots of policy.

HUD's ConnectHome program is an initiative that was launched in 2015 to help students in grades K–12 living in public and tribal housing access technology by providing Wi-Fi and related devices.

SIDE NOTE: More than 3.5 million families with school-age children don't have reliable access to the internet—putting these students at a severe disadvantage during the COVID-19 pandemic when most schools were forced to switch to remote learning.

Choice Neighborhoods aims to increase property value and revitalize neighborhoods by creating opportunities to blend different income levels into high-poverty neighborhoods, increasing affordable housing, as well as investing in public schools.

SIDE NOTE: Bienville Basin in New Orleans was one of the first Choice Neighborhoods. Since the redevelopment was completed, the crime rate dropped by one-third, and 80 percent of residents who were assigned case workers to help them find jobs reported "positive outcomes."

These kinds of budget decisions and pilot programs are ways of looking at issues of housing and poverty holistically by identifying the communities that are struggling the most and determining what barriers can be alleviated. Critical to crafting such policy is recognizing historical and present-day drivers of inequity.

JULIÁN: There's no question that in this country, including in the twentieth century and even today, that people of color, especially Black Americans, were disadvantaged by the laws that were put in place around housing, from local laws that redlined neighborhoods to all sorts of other types of restrictions. So with the Obama administration, when it came to housing, we were taking a sober look at that entire history and doing what we could to untangle it and right some of the historical wrongs and make housing policy actually work for people of color and other disadvantaged communities. We know that discrimination is too often baked into our housing policy. The legacy of that discrimination still impacts the ability—especially of people of color—to live in certain neighborhoods, to be able to go to certain schools, access certain tools, and to be able to fulfill their potential.

We wanted to change this on a system-wide level, not just case by case, which too often is the way it is done now. For most families, their home is their greatest source of wealth. However, historically, the fact is that many people of color, especially Black Americans, were effectively shut out from owning homes for a long time. Even when they could own homes, those homes were valued less than similar homes owned by whites. And throughout the years, predatory banks and other financial institutions have taken advantage of people, especially people of color. All of that has added up to a huge wealth gap overall, but especially when you look at housing wealth.

This was made worse by the Great Recession of 2008, which decimated Black wealth. A lot of wealth was lost in housing value or the outright loss of their homes. And so in the Obama administration, we were trying to pick up the pieces of that and bring that wealth back. On top of that, there was a stigma that was associated with pushing home ownership in general, because of the narrative that conservatives had sold—that it was the fault of people who bit off more than they could chew with these home loans and it had caused the whole economy to crack. Well, you know, that wasn't the whole story. It was these banks that were taking advantage of people, and also other instruments that they created, that accelerated that financial collapse.

While the recession of 2008 was painful for everyone, the Black community was hit particularly hard. One reason is because home ownership often makes up a larger portion of Black communities' wealth. Poor people and people of color were also more likely to be the target of predatory lenders who convinced them to take on high-interest mortgages that were almost impossible to pay back. Because of this, Black and Latinx homeowners were far more likely to have to foreclose on their homes, leaving them housing insecure or houseless.

Unfortunately, this is just one of many instances throughout history that have made it difficult for Black and Latinx people to achieve homeownership. For that reason, we must address race when discussing housing stability and policies that can reverse historic housing discrimination toward certain communities.

JULIÁN: Oftentimes the most vulnerable people in our country, and really around the world, don't have real input into policy making. They're not the ones with lawyers and lobbyists that are paid to represent them in front of Congress. Too often, they're not the ones whose voices are heard at the ballot box. So I created a podcast, called *Our America*, that tries to shine a spotlight on people who are hurting and on ways policies and investments can lift them up. We've covered everything from our foster care system, which is habitually ignored by policy makers and underfunded, to homelessness.

We need to reorient the image that we have of a homeless person. A lot of times the image that we have of a homeless person is a young or middle-aged man, but the story of the last generation is more often that the homeless are families, including children. It's not just somebody sleeping on the street; it can be families that are sleeping in their vehicle or doubling up at another family member's apartment or a neighbor's house. So we need to update our sense of who our homeless are.

There's also a lot of work we have to do at the federal level to better serve children who are homeless. For instance, when I was HUD secretary, we were working with the Department of Education to better sync up how we define homelessness. Every year the Department of Education releases this figure on the number of students who are homeless and it's always a lot higher than HUD's, based on the different definitions of homelessness. So people wonder, "Well, why is HUD saying one number and the Department of Education saying another number?" We need to get our act together at the federal level, and also dedicate the resources necessary to end homelessness generally and especially among children.

At the end of the Obama administration, President Obama put forward an $11 billion plan that over ten years would end family homelessness. Of course, that was ultimately not funded by Congress, but at least it was a marker for the future. In the Reagan era and the post-Reagan era in our country, too many people got too comfortable blaming folks for their poverty, blaming people for living on the street or being down-and-out, as if it was only their problem and assuming they all must be addicts or lazy or bad people.

I hope the COVID-19 pandemic has really drilled into people's heads that oftentimes, it's not their fault. People, for different reasons, find themselves living in poverty and facing bad circumstances, and that's especially true of children. But it's never a child's fault when they find themselves hungry or homeless or downtrodden. We need a commitment in this country to provide for all of our children robustly and intensely, to make sure that they have a real shot at fulfilling their potential. However, we're still a long way from that.

Misconceptions around houselessness start at an early age and often focus on a reason or person to blame, justifying it as a unique circumstance that is far removed from us and our children. But it's not. Even if you do not experience housing insecurity firsthand, it is more than likely that you will have classmates who don't have stable housing or have experienced houselessness. I was a classmate who was housing insecure and easily could have become a child experiencing chronic houselessness if not for some of the support systems my family was able to access.

JULIÁN: We need to focus a lot more on what our children are taught from the very beginning about different groups of people. Right now, we raise a society of people who tend to put more value on certain types of folks and less on others, which creates bigotry. It creates the ability to ignore the needs, especially, of people of color or other vulnerable communities like the LGBTQ community. I'm convinced we need to focus on what our children are learning in school.

I didn't know, before I became HUD secretary, for instance, that in many communities, up to 40 percent of teens who were homeless come from the LGBTQ community. For various reasons, but oftentimes because they're kicked out by their family or their family makes it so uncomfortable living there that they feel compelled to leave. That goes to the lack of acceptance still in our society, among many people, for someone who is gay, who is lesbian, who's bisexual, transgender, and we need to change that. We need to change attitudes going forward; that's going to help a lot with better outcomes and also better policy and better investments for disadvantaged communities.

Educating ourselves about different identities and communities may create empathy for other lived experiences outside of our own. And when that happens, people may start to look at this as our national problem, not just someone's individual problem. Developing this level of empathy is what will allow people to pull together collectively and support policies and programs aiming to eradicate housing insecurity.

It is important that we acknowledge that in order to end chronic houselessness, in addition to access to affordable housing, we will need to provide support services that help people with addiction, disabilities or health issues, and other barriers to maintaining stable income and housing. **Permanent supportive housing** is often proposed alongside the concept of "housing first." These two ideas together mean that there should be a focus on getting houseless people into stable, independent housing and provide supportive services that help them maintain that housing, rather than the current system of requiring people to go through extensive processes to prove their readiness or worthiness for housing.

JULIÁN: I believe it's possible to end homelessness, and there would be an astronomical return on investment that would go well beyond the people who are homeless. It would benefit the entire country economically and in every other way. I'm confident that we could do it because we saw how successful the right policy and the right investments can be in significantly reducing homelessness. In 2010, President Obama released a blueprint for ending homelessness called Opening Doors. And the first goal was to end veteran homelessness by 2015. Now, look, we didn't end veteran homelessness by 2015, but between 2010 and 2016, we reduced it by 47 percent. That is substantial. I believe it is very impressive, in such a short amount of time, to almost cut it in half, and if we had more time to keep going, I believe that we could have done even better than that.

If we can do that with veteran homelessness, we can also do that with family homelessness, with chronic homelessness, with teen homelessness, and so forth, because we know what works. What works is an investment in permanent housing with supportive services. An approach that doesn't blame someone who's homeless, but commits to working with them to get them into permanent housing and provide the resources that they need to address other issues that they may have in life. For example, if they haven't finished their education and want to get their GED. Or a lot of people have been in the working world and they're out of a job—how can we help them get employment?

I reject the notion that homeless people are just people who are addicted or have a mental health issue, but some people do have those challenges and so we want to be able to provide mental health resources and resources related to addiction. All of those things, panoramically, can help have a major impact on solving homelessness. But we need the political will translated into investment and smart policies to do it.

Ending houselessness is an achievable goal and a moral obligation. If we can change minds about houselessness and come to the understanding that the situation is not far removed from everyday people, we can come together to put forward creative solutions and financial support. As a child, I didn't understand what I was experiencing or how common it is. Houselessness can be that teenager that you know who's sleeping on a friend's couch or that family staying with their cousins until the parents find work or otherwise get back on their feet. It might be the woman who leaves an abusive relationship and is forced to sleep in her car or someone with mental health issues that make it difficult to hold down a job and thus afford an apartment. There are a number of reasons, but there is no good reason that anyone should not have access to safe and reliable housing.

The sad truth is that for most of America, we are all just one house fire, health issue, pandemic, or other unforeseen circumstance away from being houseless. Even in the case where houselessness is the result of an individual's choices, no choice, however poor it might seem, should result in a person losing access to housing. As I said earlier, housing is a human right.

It is up to all of us to destigmatize the issue of houselessness and demand solutions, and to evaluate what roles our communities and government play in solving the issue.

To find out more about how you can help put a stop to housing insecurity, visit: BetterThanWeFoundItBook.com.

13

WE HAVE MONEY FOR WAR BUT WON'T FEED THE POOR

Frederick Joseph on Understanding the Military-Industrial Complex

Featuring Amed Khan

When was the last time something blew your mind—really, truly astonished you? Was it when you found out that Froot Loops are all the same flavor, or that it's impossible to hum while holding your nose (go ahead and try), or that before toilet paper was invented, Americans used to use corncobs to wipe themselves? (Corncobs!)

> **SIDE NOTE:** Major shoutout to my friend Marlisse at *Reader's Digest* for getting that list of facts to be at the top of my Google search.

But as mind-blowing as those facts are, they're pretty inconsequential—trivia, basically. When was the last time you found out something that was not only astonishing, but that had major implications on everything around you? For me, it was when I learned about the **military-industrial complex**.

The military-industrial complex (or MIC) is essentially the relationship between a country's military and the industries that manufacture and supply military weapons. This relationship is conceptually quite simple: the country needs and/or wants weapons, and companies supply them in return for money. But it's not that simple. Far from it.

Let's back up a little and explain how the MIC came to be. America didn't always have the mighty military that's ready for action at a moment's notice (or always in action) that it does today. At one point, when war or some other conflict threatened America, the country would enlist people and companies in the creation of weapons, planes, and other things necessary to respond to the conflict. In other words, a factory that made bicycles before a war might now have to instead make tanks. But America realized two things after **World War II**: first, the old way of doing things—pivoting manufacturing in response to conflicts—was no longer sufficient to meet the needs of this modern era of warfare, and second, wars are very lucrative. So much so that when America built the most powerful military in the world during World War II, it also became the wealthiest country on the planet.

In 1961, then-president Dwight D. Eisenhower, a former general himself, foresaw the potential issues with the military-industrial complex and tried to warn Americans about how much of an impact the MIC was going to have. On January 17 of that year, President Eisenhower gave his final speech from the White House, in which he explained that a union of armed military forces and defense contractors—the companies or people that provide goods or services to a government's military or intelligence agency—was a threat to American democracy:

> *In the councils of government, we must guard against the acquisition of unwarranted influence, whether sought or unsought, by the military-industrial complex. The potential for the disastrous rise of misplaced power exists and will persist.*

Eisenhower realized that the military and the people and companies who provided the military with services and tools were going to potentially gain power and influence well beyond what is needed to protect the country. So much power and influence, in fact, that if allowed to persist, the military-industrial complex might become more powerful than the democracy it's supposed to be protecting. Sadly, in just the few generations since President Eisenhower's speech, his worst fears are coming true, and we have all been impacted by it.

I didn't learn about the military-industrial complex until I was in college, but my first surface-level understanding that it exists happened when I was ten years old and told my mother how "cool" it would be to become a navy SEAL.

SIDE NOTE: The United States Sea, Air, and Land (SEAL) teams are a special operations force of the navy that is composed of some of the most talented and skilled members of any military worldwide. They are the elite of the elite, if you will: the top 1 percent of military personnel.

I had learned about the SEALs from watching the cartoon *G.I. Joe*, which is one of the most famous toy, television, and film franchises in history. What I saw in the *G.I. Joe* characters were strong and skilled men (there were a few women characters, but the vast majority were men) defending their families and friends from evil. They didn't have superpowers or come from other planets; they were regular men, just like I would be one day. I wanted to defend my friends and family from evil.

"What are you here watching? *Hey Arnold!* again?" I recall my mother asking me.

"No, *G.I. Joe*. I'm going to become a SEAL, just like the guy in the show!" I replied.

"A SEAL?!" she yelled with a horrified look on her face. "I want you to get any ideas of the military out of your head! The military is no place for a Black man!"

"But why, Mommy?" I asked, genuinely confused. I saw the military as the people who were out protecting me and her at that very moment.

My mother ran into the living room and started rummaging through some things. She returned with a VHS tape of *Boyz n the Hood*, put it in the VCR, and hit play. Little did I know, it was going to become one of my favorite films of all time—and more importantly, be the beginning of my understanding of just how powerful the military-industrial complex is.

It's a phenomenal film and you should definitely watch it if you haven't seen it. For those who haven't, *Boyz n the Hood* takes place in the 1980s and centers on the character of Tre Styles, who moves to South Central Los Angeles to live with his father, Furious Styles, when he's ten years old. The neighborhood at that time is riddled with drugs and violence. As Tre grows up, he learns lessons in self-worth, friendship, and how various systems in America are strategically conspiring against Black people while benefiting white people. Systems like the military-industrial complex.

There are various moments in which the characters interact with military propaganda that is intended to both normalize and incentivize people into supporting or joining the military. For instance, one of Tre's best friends is Ricky, a star high-school football player who is being recruited by multiple collegiate programs. Ricky has a bright future ahead of him, but he also has a child, which makes him feel pressured to be financially stable. One day, while Ricky's watching a football game on TV, a commercial comes on telling viewers about the financial benefits of joining the military. You can see in Ricky's eyes that he's interested in the prospect because it may be an easy way to change his current inability to support his child financially.

There are other scenes such as this throughout the movie, where characters consider the merits of joining the military to help alleviate their burdens of poverty. But what many of the characters fail to examine—and what much of the military propaganda doesn't show—are the realities of military service, such as war, death, and being away from family. What these commercials and marketing by the military also don't show is that more times than not, Black and brown people who join the armed forces are often ultimately sent to places where they have to fight against other Black and brown people. All in the name of powerful decision-makers who have their own goals and agendas that usually don't include helping the oppressed Black and brown people who are fighting one another.

Legendary boxer and activist Muhammad Ali spoke to this point when explaining why he refused to fight in the Vietnam War:

> Why should they ask me to put on a uniform and go ten thousand miles from home and drop bombs and bullets on brown people in Vietnam while so-called Negro people in Louisville are treated like dogs and denied simple human rights? No, I'm not going ten thousand miles from home to help murder and burn another poor nation simply to continue the domination of white slave masters of the darker people the world over. This is the day when such evils must come to an end. I have been warned that to take such a stand would put my prestige in jeopardy and could cause me to lose millions of dollars which should accrue to me as the champion. But I have said it once and I will say it again. The real enemy of my people is right here. I will not disgrace my religion, my people or myself by becoming a tool to enslave those who are fighting for their own justice, freedom and equality. . . . If I thought the war was going to bring freedom and equality to twenty-two million of my people, they wouldn't have to draft me, I'd join tomorrow. . . . I have nothing to lose by standing up for my beliefs. So I'll go to jail, so what? We've been in jail for four hundred years.

After watching *Boyz n the Hood*, I became more aware of the military propaganda around me. There were shows like *G.I. Joe*, for starters, which glorified the military, as well as popular Marvel superheroes such as Captain America, Iron Man, Captain Marvel, and the Hulk, each with ties to the military. And then there were the recruiters . . .

After 1973, America stopped forcing people to enter the military through the **draft**, meaning they had to find people who actually wanted to become soldiers. How did they do that? Well, for starters, they began to strategically make the military seem appealing through marketing and media. (Like with *G.I. Joe* and the Marvel superheroes. Who wouldn't want to go fight bad guys in the military like Captain America? Of course, no one ever mentions that those "bad guys" are just people who are poor and wanting to support their family, just like you.)

Another example can be found in film, as fourteen of the top thirty highest-grossing films of all time have positive military representation. Whether that means the military fighting terrorists or helping superheroes fight aliens, or a person in the military driving really fast cars in a franchise that has gone on far too long (I'm looking at you, Fast & Furious), positive representation of the military is all around us. You can also see it in many of the most popular video games in history, such as *Metal Gear Solid*, the *Call of Duty* franchise, *Gears of War*, and *Battlefield*—all wildly popular games that place players in the role of soldiers who are completing missions and murdering people along the way. There is a direct correlation to many people's thoughts on the actions of our military and the hours they've spent playing video games where they themselves are going around blowing up supposed terrorists and enemies of the US government.

But beyond making some people believe joining the military is cool, the government also made it appealing in other ways, by offering incentives like travel and college tuition. Let's say you're a young person who comes from a middle-class family that can afford to go on family vacations and can afford to send you to college. The military wouldn't necessarily appeal to you because it wouldn't be offering you opportunities. But if you're a kid from poverty who has never had the chance to travel, and you don't know how you'll pay for college or what you're going to do after high school, the military positions itself almost as if it's doing you a favor.

Which brings us back to recruiters, who historically target low-income areas in hopes that people living in poverty will be more susceptible to their recruiting tactics and promises of gaining educational and financial opportunities.

SIDE NOTE: Studies have found that Junior Reserve Officers' Training Corps programs exist predominantly at schools with larger populations of Black students and students who qualify for free or reduced lunch.

Growing up in a poverty-stricken neighborhood, I would often see military recruiters standing outside of stores, barbershops, and parks with pamphlets that told us how we could travel, see the world, and, after a few years, be given money to pay for college. But just like in the movie *Boyz n the Hood*, they failed to tell us any of the negative aspects of joining the military.

In addition to exploring military propaganda, *Boyz n the Hood* also explores the impact of the military-industrial complex on American neighborhoods and lives. There are numerous scenes in which characters threaten people with military-grade weapons such as submachine guns, which were invented during World War I and are widely used in America by SWAT and counter-terrorism teams. Tre's father, Furious, makes a point of addressing not just how violent the acts are that these young people are committing but also the logistics of how teenagers got access to such weapons in the first place.

Despite already having the largest and most advanced military in the world, America purchases new military weapons on a regular basis. Many of the weapons that are no longer being used by US soldiers or haven't been sold to other countries sometimes fall into the hands of weapons dealers and America's enemies, who sell weapons to various types of customers, including people our government considers terrorists and criminals. In response, American military and law enforcement use the fact that those terrorists and criminals are heavily armed as the reason they must continue to upgrade and advance their own weapons. For example, many police departments in America now have advanced weapons such as drones and tanks because they feel they need to keep up with the weapons of criminals—weapons that originate from the police and military themselves. This cycle is at the center of the military-industrial complex, as it creates a constant supply and demand.

As mentioned before, war is a very lucrative business. But not all wars are fought with other countries; whether it's a war on terror or one on gangs or drugs, there is money to be made for those profiting from the MIC. In Eisenhower's worst nightmares, he likely couldn't have imagined how out of control the MIC would become. In 2019, America spent more than $730 billion on the military, which is more than China, India, Russia, Saudi Arabia, France, Germany, the United Kingdom, Japan, South Korea, and Brazil *combined*. That number is an increase of more than $300 billion since President Eisenhower warned Americans about the growing power of the military-industrial complex.

That's a ton of money, and the argument can't be made that it's necessary in order to keep us safe, as we are so far beyond any other country in military power and influence. The reality is that the military is an industry no longer focused on simply protecting us; now, like most other industries, it's focused on growth and profits. By the looks of things, business is booming. But because the business of the MIC is violence and war, it does far more harm than good.

Some people argue that we should keep the budget as is because the military creates jobs and opportunities for people. But the truth is that you could slash the military budget in half, still have the most well-funded military in the world, and take the remainder of that money and create jobs in other sectors—sectors not invested in violence and war, but instead invested in humans. Because of the lack of resources invested in its citizens, the United States is not even ranked among the top twenty-five countries in education or health care. You could put hundreds of billions of dollars into infrastructure, renewable energy, or even tax cuts for working people and create more jobs than you do with military spending.

So why don't we focus on spending money on children instead of bombs? Because the people who are making money on bombs would no longer make that money if America focused its resources elsewhere, which is why those people have also invested a great deal of money in keeping things the same—or worse. As President Eisenhower warned, the military-industrial complex holds a great deal of political power through the donations and support they give to elected officials who will vote for policies that are friendly to the MIC. They also pay lobbyists to influence or persuade the people who write laws into making sure those laws benefit the people profiting from the MIC. Hundreds of millions of dollars are spent annually by defense contractors who are lobbying lawmakers. Simply put, other sectors focused on making people's lives better don't have the resources or finances to compete with that.

But the bloated military budget and the political influence of the MIC aren't the only issues. Another part of the growing danger is that the MIC is also involved with things that have nothing to do with war or violence, which gives the MIC more power over us and knowledge about our lives, making it far more difficult to extract ourselves from the MIC. For example, defense contractor Lockheed Martin is known for building bombs, submarines, and missiles. But they are also one of the companies that developed some of the FBI fingerprint database technology—used at the airport by anyone who signs up for Clear or TSA PreCheck. They also help the IRS process our taxes, and have helped the US Census Bureau process data. Even companies such as AT&T have huge billion-dollar contracts with the military and department of defense. (Personally, I use AT&T, and finding that out made me consider using a carrier pigeon for my future communications.) Basically, almost every part of life is impacted by the military-industrial complex.

But the impact of the MIC on civilian life is hardly new. Charles Wilson was once the president and CEO of General Motors (GM) until he became the United States secretary of defense under President Eisenhower—the same president who used his last address to warn the nation about the dangers of the MIC. During his confirmation hearing, Wilson said he believed "what was good for our country was good for General Motors, and vice versa," not seeing—or more likely not admitting—that the interests of the government and GM might sometimes be in direct conflict. GM ultimately became a major defense contractor, then later also became a mortgage lender and nearly went bankrupt after giving people fraudulent loans that financially ruined many families. Though it had acted wrongfully and harmed American citizens, the US government gave the company a bailout loan to stop it from going bankrupt—a loan that was given with taxpayer money, and a loan that GM has yet to fully repay. So even though GM didn't act in the best interest of the nation, it was still the nation who had to pay for how GM acted.

The growing influence of companies in America is alarming. Unlike elected officials, companies don't have loyalty to you, me, or even to democracy; they have loyalty to profit.

SIDE NOTE: These profits fund things like a **congressional caucus** that exists specifically to try to figure out how to get the military to buy and use more drones. And yet as of this writing, there is no congressional caucus for children, health care coverage, green energy, or senior citizens. In a country draped in the military-industrial complex, the motto is apparently "In profits we trust."

So, what do we do? How do we stop something that's a part of the cartoons we watch, the movies we enjoy, the census we fill out, and innumerable other parts of our daily lives?

Well, to stop something, you must first understand it. Then you empower those who may be able to make changes.

An Interview with AMED KHAN

Humanitarian, investor, activist, and political adviser

There are few people on this earth who have the wealth of knowledge and understanding about the military-industrial complex as well as many other aspects of global militarism, capitalism, and imperialism that my friend Amed Khan does. He has seen it all, from firsthand, on-the-ground experiences to being on the policy end of things while working with President Bill Clinton. Amed is a voice brilliantly positioned to discuss this topic.

AMED: I worked with the US government in the '90s and I worked for international **NGO**s, and one of the places I worked was in Rwanda for an organization called the International Rescue Committee, which is a refugee support organization.

At that point, I got really interested in the cause of refugees. I worked with refugees after the invasion of Iraq. And again after the Syrian war. So having spent, let's say, twenty-five years working with refugees, at some point you start to see a pattern. A large part of the military-industrial complex is what countries receiving refugees have done to countries sending them. When you start to ask yourself *Why are there so many refugees?*, you can draw a straight line toward militarism as a policy. And so it's a strange thing because there's a bizarre narrative that refugees are victims: *We should feel bad for them, maybe we should help them out.* And it's kind of upside-down because the reality is that there is a relationship between the sending country and the receiving country. And it's not a good relationship. Very often the receiving country has caused immense amounts of damage to the sending country.

I've heard many Americans speak about the "illegal" migrants from Honduras. But how many Americans know that we've invaded Honduras six or seven times? How many Americans know that we destroyed the economy of Honduras? How many Americans know that anytime there was a government that was standing up for the rights of Honduran people, we'd go and wipe that government out? And now Honduras is a failed state, and the people are just looking for safety and the children are looking for safety. What do you do when you just can't be safe? You run. The same thing goes with regard to Afghan refugees or Syrian refugees or Iraqi refugees, Somali refugees. Each of those places has been a theater for Western destruction. So I got into ending US "forever wars" and looking into US militarism and asking, *Why are we like this?*

It's important to understand that people are only refugees because a country created the situation that made them so.

This point is also addressed by Porsche in the immigration reform chapter (chapter 16: "No Human Is Illegal").

SIDE NOTE: Unlike most wars throughout history, over the past few decades a large number of wars have taken place with no clear-cut, tangible objective and thus we have "forever wars" like America's war in Afghanistan, which lasted nearly twenty years.

AMED: I don't even know what Dr. [Martin Luther] King would think of where we are now. Because in 1967, he named the three giant triplets of essentially what's wrong in America and they were racism, militarism, and extreme materialism. And it's interesting because Dr. King was connecting the three, and he said you couldn't really deal with each one of them without dealing with all three of them. And so we have the murder of George Floyd last summer, and we were dealing with racism and that's great, but we're leaving out the rest. And that's a problem because if you track the rise of militarism in American foreign policy, you will also see the rise of militarism with regard to our police, domestically. And I don't need to tell you that the numbers are off the charts in terms of Black and brown people being the targets of militarized police.

The United States' annual budget spent on militarism—it's called national security, but it's really not—the numbers are wild. And again, back to Dr. King—I'm just always amazed by Dr. King and Malcolm X and so many of the leaders of the '60s, when defense spending was only a fraction of what it is now. They saw all this coming. And here we are in 2021, and it's multiples of what it was back then, but they all pointed out that if you are spending money on what you call national defense— more money than you are on social justice or social causes, like our broken health care system, our education—you aren't going to have much of a country. And you're going to have a violent country. It's going to be difficult.

We know where we are and why it happened. But what were the mechanisms that made it possible? America didn't just one day dump billions of dollars into the military, so how did this happen?

AMED: We have something called the National Defense Authorization Act, or the NDAA. And that is the annual budgetary process for the Defense Department. So the Defense Department budget is roughly around $800 billion. There are other national security matters within the United States' annual budget, which comes to about $1.2 trillion annually.

Now, if you're talking about the big number, you're talking about a lot of interests. And half of those interests are probably defense contractors. So now if you're a contractor making money off of this large annual budget, it is in your interest to make sure that that large annual budget stays intact, and that's been the process of what's happened since Eisenhower's farewell speech when he said to beware of the military-industrial complex. What we have now is various entities that make money on the military-industrial complex needing there to be a reason for it to exist, so they've helped America become a place where we are in search of things to spend money on, in search of enemies to justify this massive dragon of a military growing and growing and growing. Which is why the United States spends more than the next nine largest economies in the world combined on what's called "defense." Because it's in the best interest of wealthy and powerful people to do so.

The United States has more than eight hundred military bases outside of the United States. There are 195 member nations of the United Nations. So that means there are four bases for every nation that exists outside the United States. Why is that? The country that's second, I believe, is France, with nine. So it's literally a different world of size and scope and it's become our default mechanism to police places around the world. For example, we were attacked on September 11, 2001, and our answer back was to attack indefinitely. There was an Authorization for Use of Military Force vote, which gave unprecedented power to the executive branch, a few days after September 11. There are 535 members of Congress between the Senate and the House, and there was one leader, named Barbara Lee, who was the only person who voted against any of it. She voted against it immediately. And I think it passed 420 to 1 in the House and 98 to 0 in the Senate, but she saw what was coming—which is that we would keep finding places to use force. And that's what happened.

The US is actively deploying lethal drone strikes in over ten countries that we know of. Active military is engaged with local forces, and it just grows and grows. But you come back to follow the money. And no one is actually ever looking for an audit of how we spend that money. There's this massive footprint in so many countries: Iraq, Afghanistan, Syria. There's a move to reduce it. But are we looking at weapons systems? How much money do we spend on weapons systems? Or what do the systems do? And who makes the money off these systems? These sorts of things are kind of the questions that really, really need to be asked going forward.

For people who make a lot of money off of war, winning a war or finding peaceful resolutions to conflicts would actually be bad business, as that would result in the loss of potential profits. To keep making money, these people need to make sure there is always a reason for bombs, tanks, spy satellites, and all sorts of other means to surveil or destroy people. But how do we stop it?

AMED: You would need a foreign policy that promotes diplomacy and human rights and mutual respect and prioritizes climate change. Instead, they built up a system with lobbyists so the defense contractors have made up stories on why it's so important to job creation. Now, if you were ever to look at our weapons contracts and see how many jobs were created—you would have been better off giving the money directly to those people, rather than creating these weapons of mass destruction that go and kill people in corners of the planet that most Americans don't even know exist. Is that the greatest way to create jobs in the United States?

We have a crumbling public health system. We have a crumbling domestic infrastructure system. We have a crumbling education system. I mean, these are the questions that need to be asked by advocates and activists and young people. Rather than creating weapons that pad the pockets of defense industry executives, couldn't we better utilize that money to educate our people, to make sure our people are healthy? And by the way, health is a national security objective. Health is not going to be achieved by funding more weapons systems.

So there is without question a much better use of the mass amounts of funds that we spend on national security. There are much better uses of those funds in public health and public education. And you could go on and on—domestic infrastructure, airports, roads, hospitals, et cetera.

But the opposition to this stuff has done a masterful job of keeping people distracted. I think we have to do a better job, perhaps as activists, because what we're up against is so well organized and funded. There's a massive lobbying system. They've co-opted Hollywood, for example. All of us have watched these films where we're raining missile strikes, and everybody's cheering like, "There's bad guys. We've been fighting the bad guys."

So the defense industry has done a remarkable job of making sure we sleep and they go off to the races. It was kind of a funny thing because when Mitt Romney was running for president, he said, essentially, everything is on the table in terms of the federal budget, except for the Department of Defense. And I was thinking, *That's the place where you're going to get the money from, but you want to cut the Department of Education. Are you kidding me right now?* And this is nuts because really what it is, is it's money spent in foreign places, and they've done a great job of propagandizing us that they're keeping us safe. And they've also done a great job of making you feel unpatriotic if you are against Defense Department spending.

But a tiny fraction of that money actually goes to supporting the troops. They don't really get paid that much and the health care system for veterans is horrible. The mental health care system for veterans is horrible. The money goes to weapons systems and defense contractors, and the numbers are enormous. And if we were all looking at defense CEOs and found out they have multiple boats and multiple villas and multiple homes and private planes, and they literally never fly commercial, then one would think we'd be outraged, but they've got a remarkable propaganda system and it keeps us all sort of distracted and quiet.

Back to refugees, there's this meme that says, "If you don't want more refugees then stop causing them." Right? These are commonsense things. Why are we building jet fighters that can bomb people in Yemen but our bridges are terrible? I mean, how does that help us? But they've done a great job of making sure we all remain quiet and accept this as just the way it is.

Well, I mean, we'll keep spending and spending and spending and our national debt will keep growing and we'll create more disruption and more wars and more people will keep moving, and we'll ignore the climate. There are now war refugees, and there will be **climate refugees**. There actually already are in parts of Africa, and there will be more and more. And if we keep going along this route, the future is not bright; it's simply not. It's unsustainable. We cannot have this large percentage of our federal budget going toward military activities when we are neglecting our own citizens. If we continue to ignore diplomacy and human rights, and continue to look at all our solutions as military, we'll spend ourselves into oblivion.

To stop what's happening, we have to take control of our

money and put people in power to do the right things with it, or this nation will fail. There needs to be an audit from people willing to ask how and why we are paying for all of this, and then take that money and reallocate it in a way that benefits humanity, not a few mega-wealthy war criminals.

This money that we need to control is *our* money. The record spending that's being done to uphold the military-industrial complex is being done with our taxes—your money, my money, your parents' money. We have to look closely at what we are seeing around us, investigate how that money is being spent, learn which political candidates align with our needs and wants, and then help those candidates get elected.

The other way of taking back our democracy from those loyal to profits instead of people is to stop supporting companies that are benefiting from and upholding the military-industrial complex. There is a great deal of power in our collective dollars, power that can influence change.

The truth is that my generation, your generation, and the coming generations have inherited immense debt due to no fault of our own—and also no benefit to us. They are the debts of people whose only focus was war. National debt, student loan debt, health care debt, and mortgage debt are all things that are worse than they would have been if taxpayer dollars had been allocated differently, and we are paying the price. These people have led our nation to a collapsing infrastructure, a pandemic- and climate-ravaged country, and a polarized political culture. We have to outperform previous generations. We must hold companies and lawmakers accountable for their roles in the military-industrial complex and demand investment in *people*, not profits.

We must stay politically engaged and understand the agendas and goals of our international engagements—and hold our leaders accountable to these goals. Above all, we must demand that the directions and investments of America are ones that center peace and dignity, as opposed to war and money.

To find out more about how you can help put a stop to the military-industrial complex, visit: BetterThanWeFoundItBook.com.

14
AMERICA'S MODERN SLAVERY

Porsche Joseph on Dismantling the Prison-Industrial Complex

Featuring Nic Stone

I spent much of my childhood visiting family members in prison. The prisons were so familiar to me, sometimes they felt like a second home. Some of my earliest pictures of me and my father show him sporting a khaki jumpsuit and standing in front of the kind of cheesy backdrop that so commonly graces visiting rooms for the purpose of family photo ops—in this case, a fantastical nature mural painted by inmates on one of the walls. Since before I can remember, I knew the dress code for visiting hours: no jewelry, no skirts, no colors affiliated with gangs. I grew up accepting so many collect phone calls from prisons, I can still hear the operator in my head: "An inmate at the XYZ state correctional facility is attempting to make a call. If you accept, press one."

Though it had directly impacted me throughout my childhood, it wasn't until my freshman year of high school that I truly began to learn about the **prison-industrial complex**—and then it came to live at the forefront of my mind. That was the year my seventeen-year-old brother Darnell went to prison, the year that changed my life and my family's lives forever.

Darnell had a friend named Jesse who I had only met once or twice. He was a gangly twenty-year-old who lived down the block with his grandmother, an elderly Latina woman who I would see sitting on her porch when I walked to the bus stop. I remember she had a kind smile.

Desperation often breeds bad decisions, and Jesse was in a dire situation. His girlfriend was expecting a child soon, and he and his grandmother were facing eviction from their apartment. Their home had been broken into a month earlier during a string of thefts in the neighborhood, all believed to have been committed by the same person. Multiple cars and homes had been broken into and robbed, and although many people had a good idea of who was responsible, there was no way to prove it. The only money Jesse had to his name had been stolen during the break-in and he couldn't afford to pay the rent.

Two white guys Jesse knew from the other side of town said they knew where the guy who robbed Jesse's house lived, and they had a plan to retaliate and rob him. They invited Jesse to join in and get his rent money back. According to them, no one would be home and no one would get hurt. It would be a simple in-and-out job. The white guys had robbed plenty of people before, so Jesse trusted they knew what they were doing.

Jesse and Darnell had been hanging out often, so when Jesse told Darnell about the plan and begged him to come, it didn't take long for Darnell to say yes. Darnell wanted to help his friend out—and maybe help out our family as well.

The big plan went south when they entered the apartment and found two people inside. My brother and Jesse asked the two white guys who'd organized the break-in not to hurt anyone, but one of them punched one of the residents in the face. Meanwhile, the other resident panicked and jumped off the third-floor balcony, breaking his leg. Ultimately, all the two white guys, Jesse, and Darnell got out with was a PlayStation and some other random personal belongings. They didn't find the money they were expecting and certainly didn't get what they needed to pay Jesse's rent.

The four of them weren't caught immediately, but it was pretty easy to track them down with the security camera footage from the building. (Desperation breeds people who make bad decisions—not necessarily criminal masterminds.)

It was a cold February morning when the police barged into our home with guns drawn and no warrant. They shoved their way past my eight-year-old brother Preston, pinned Darnell to the floor, and placed him under arrest. It was the type of moment I hope none of you ever have to go through. The police stayed there for hours, ransacking our apartment looking for evidence, while taking and destroying anything they pleased along the way. I'll never forget the look of utter heartbreak and confusion on my baby brother's face as the cops tossed his video game system onto the floor. The same video game system my mother had saved all year to buy him for Christmas just months earlier. They carried on like this into the afternoon, and my mom was forced to watch them take away our few items of value in evidence bags, items that she knew would never be returned.

In hindsight those material things were of little

importance, but it's one example of how expansive the collateral damage is that comes along with having a loved one in the criminal justice system. And because so many of the people who are charged with crimes come from poverty, the economic hardships that incarceration can cause are often devastating. Many financial burdens exist even before a person is formally convicted of a crime. An example of this is paying for legal counsel. A good defense attorney is expensive. Even a not-so-good attorney is expensive. Frequently, the **public defender** that is provided is handling hundreds of cases each year, so depending on what crime you've been charged with, your life could depend on having the financial means to afford an attorney who is invested in your case. Another hardship for people in poverty is paying bail. Bail is set while someone is waiting in jail for trial. They have not been proven guilty—and remember, in our legal system you're meant to be considered "innocent until proven guilty"—but what determines if they will stay in jail or not isn't what kind of crime they've been charged with or even how likely it is that they committed the crime. Instead, it's a matter of how much money they have. All too often, poor people experience the inequity of the bail system, sitting in jail awaiting trial while people with the money to pay bail walk free.

Beyond the awfulness of being behind bars itself, there are countless consequences to remaining in jail while awaiting trial—a process that might take a few months or even a few *years*. If you can't report to work, you might very well lose your job—even if you're proved innocent once you go to trial. The loss of a job itself can profoundly impact an individual and their family, as it means a loss of income and sometimes a loss of health insurance. If you're a single parent, your child or children could be taken in by Child Protective Services and it could be incredibly difficult for you to get back custody even if you're proved innocent.

In our case, we couldn't afford an attorney or bail. So my brother sat in jail during the final stretch of his senior year, while I tried my best to keep up whatever normalcy I could. Before his arrest, I wouldn't have hesitated to describe myself as a good student. I had always done well in school, and after being encouraged in my studies by Ms. Elliott the year before, had even started to set my sights on college. But when Darnell was arrested, a deep depression set in and I went from being an A+ student to someone who was failing most of my classes and hated getting out of bed each morning. I was struggling just to get through each day, but I didn't know how to navigate my mental and emotional health, and unfortunately the signs and symptoms were lost to the adults in my family, who were preoccupied with the chaos of my brother's troubles. So I suffered silently.

While most of my classes couldn't hold much of my attention, I became engrossed in learning about the criminal justice system. Although I was only in the ninth grade, I felt like it was my duty to understand the system that was destroying my family, especially because with Darnell gone, I was the most educated person in my family. When Darnell was arrested, I felt as if my family all depended on me to provide some sort of special knowledge on my brother's case. They'd ask me to translate legal jargon, talk to attorneys and advocate for him, and essentially act as an adult to weigh in on his legal matters. It was exhausting.

Aside from the added pressure to help make sense of the legal logistics, I was also having a difficult time reconciling how my big brother could go from being my best friend and a person I admired very much to being in the system—seen by the courts as just another inmate ID number. He was the person who had taught me how to ride a bike, read me bedtime stories, and made me bologna sandwiches after school. He loved playing chess and was the first-chair bassist in the school orchestra. Every Sunday night, I would braid his hair while we watched cheesy action movies from the '80s. He was the kid who never hesitated to defend others from bullies. He was a brother, a child, a friend—and then suddenly he was an inmate, property of the state, a statistic.

Darnell had never been in any real trouble, apart from a fight here and there; however, it seemed like punishments always found him differently from the way they found his white peers. Like the time he hit someone in the back with a rubber band in the fourth grade and was permanently expelled from school. Meanwhile, that same year a white classmate of his brought a gun to school, and the only discipline from the school was a request that the student attend counseling. Or there was the time Darnell was twelve years old and was stopped by the police while walking home and handcuffed for not having an ID, while white kids rode their bikes through the streets of the same neighborhood without a care in the world. For my brother, racism loomed over all of his experiences with discipline at the hands of those with authority. This moment was no different.

Mass incarceration is a national problem, but the disproportionate impact on Black and brown folks is truly staggering—especially on those living in poverty. While Black people make up just 13 percent of the total US population, they constitute nearly 40 percent of people in prison and jail.

SIDE NOTE: Latinxs and Native Americans are over-represented in prisons and jails as well. Latinxs experience incarceration at 1.3 times the rate of whites, while Native American men are four times more likely to go to prison than white men, and Native American women are six times more likely to go to prison than white women.

Darnell was the only minor involved in the crime, but he was also the only Black person in the group. When the prosecution started offering **plea bargains** some months after the incident, racism became an obvious factor. My heart stopped when the prosecutor first offered Darnell forty years (*forty years!*), and his public defender told him that was a great deal that he would never be offered again. I knew that he had committed a crime, but I couldn't reconcile how he could deserve to sit in prison until he was almost sixty years old. As the plea bargains for the other young men involved began rolling in, what was happening became clear: the two white men, who were well into their twenties and years older than Darnell, each received less than a year in jail—and each agreed to testify against Darnell and Jesse. Jesse took a plea for seven years.

Though Darnell was a minor, the prosecutor charged him as an adult and was not willing to budge on their offer. My brother was doomed to be in prison for the next four decades. I was angry. I felt helpless—I felt small. How was my best friend's life treated so worthlessly over one bad decision? I knew what he did was wrong, but the punishment seemed drastic and disproportionate.

Darnell spent his eighteenth birthday in jail—and then his nineteenth, and then his twentieth—all while awaiting trial. Eventually, the prosecutor offered him a similar deal to Jesse's, stating that if he didn't take this offer, they would ask the judge for sixty-five years at trial. My brother took the deal.

My family weren't the only ones who knew about my brother's situation. At school, people would callously ask me about how the star football player had become a criminal. When the local newspaper ran a story about the incident, kids kept sliding the article to me during class, asking me if I had seen it. Yes, I had seen it. No, I didn't want to talk about it. Some parents would no longer let their kids hang out with me; they said my mom must not have been a good parent. Even teachers treated me differently.

But as painful as it was at school, it was even worse at home. There was no music, no laughter, no joy. Almost every week, my mom would make Preston and me do the three-hour drive with her to visit my brother, while she racked up credit card debt in order to pay for gas and expensive collect phone calls. My mother could barely sleep anymore. She had extreme anxiety about how Darnell was being treated by the guards and about the fact that her teenage son shared a cell with a man who was a serial killer.

My mom has described that time as a kind of purgatory. She said it felt as if her child had died, but there was none of the closure that comes with death; she couldn't bury him or hold a service. She just had to pack up his letterman jacket, guitar, and all the rest of his belongings and mourn him alone silently. Her home would never feel the same, and the next time she would get to hug him, he would no longer be a child.

By the time I graduated high school, I was no longer the shy girl I was when I was younger, the girl who hoped to fly under the radar. What happened to my father had changed me, what happened to my brother had changed me, what happened to countless other Black men had changed me. I had returned to getting straight A's, though teachers were reluctant to give them to me because I was outspoken and didn't bother displaying what they considered a positive attitude. They didn't like that I played devil's advocate and challenged their curricula, identifying much of it as racist. I had seen how unfairly my brother had been treated, being shuffled from school to prison, and came to the conclusion that none of these teachers cared about kids like him, so I cared very little about their opinions of me. It wasn't the best way to feel as a kid, but it drove my desire to change these systems, and I couldn't wait to get out of there and find my place in the world.

Darnell was still in prison when I went to college, but the fire his situation lit in me influenced everything from what I studied to where I volunteered. I knew that I wanted to study pre-law, so my freshman year, I took a course in criminology. I showed up to the first day of class not knowing what to expect. I had very strong views on the law, and because of my experiences with my teachers in high school, I highly doubted the middle-aged white man who was teaching the course would agree with those views.

When we all were seated, he gave us a prompt for a very untraditional icebreaker: "I want everyone to take out a piece of paper and write down the most illegal thing you've ever done," he said. "This is completely confidential; don't write down your name. When you're done, please fold the paper and come put it in the box on my desk."

We all took a moment and scribbled something down. When everyone's paper was in the box, the professor dug through it, randomly selected a piece of paper, and unfolded it. "'Drinking and driving,'" he read, with no comment. "'Smuggling drugs across the border.' Interesting," he responded. "'Shoplifting thousands of dollars' worth of clothes,'" he continued. The list went on, ranging from stealing a library book to vandalism to arson. I looked around the room, trying to imagine what the hell these seemingly nice kids did outside of the classroom.

The professor looked around the room. "According to most of these responses, many of you should be in prison right now instead of sitting in this classroom. Do you think society would be safer if half of the students in here were in prison right now instead of college?"

A young white man quickly raised his hand. "No," he answered confidently.

"Why not?" asked the professor.

"Well, everyone has done *something* illegal, but it doesn't mean we're, like, criminals," said the student.

"Ahh, okay," said the professor. "And if you look around the class, you'll notice about ninety-five percent of you are white, while thirty-four percent of incarcerated people are Black. Is that just coincidence?" he asked somewhat condescendingly.

The young white man was quick to respond. "Well, there's

a lot of Black-on-Black crime due to gang violence, so that could somewhat explain the difference."

There was a silence for about five very awkward seconds, until a young Latina woman spoke up. "I don't think that's true. A lot of people who aren't white do a lot less than some of the things you just read from the class and they end up going to prison for a really long time. I think you definitely get harsher treatment if you're not white."

The professor nodded in agreement. "Before the Civil War, Virginia had seventy-three criminal offenses that would result in the death penalty for slaves, and only one for whites. Slaves were considered criminals for doing things that white people were completely free to do—something as simple as learning to read. Even after the war, as late as the Great Depression, it wasn't unusual for cities that weren't doing well economically to round up Black people for violating random vagrancy laws, which included things like smoking in public or speaking too loud, and they used the prisoners for labor such as sanitation work. Do you think there's a through line to today?"

My hand shot up. "Absolutely. I see prisoners working on the side of the freeway picking up trash all the time. I've had family members in prison, and one would work all day making military uniforms. They get paid almost nothing," I said.

The professor followed up: "Many of you wouldn't think about this, but prisoners produce garments, furniture, do farmwork; they're even used as call center employees—and they receive literal pennies for their work. It's not just the government that uses prison labor; some of your favorite companies like Victoria's Secret, JCPenney, probably some of your phone providers, have had people laboring for them inside prisons.

"There's a loophole in the United States Constitution that allows for slavery as a punishment for a crime. This results in inmates working unreasonably long hours, with no sick leave, no vacation, and no rights to breaks. If they don't work, they can be punished with solitary confinement," he said.

This guy knows what he's talking about! I thought. Although I had been thinking a lot about the inequities in the legal system over the years, I hadn't made this direct connection between the history of slave labor and the systemic design of the law—which included the police, lawyers, and judges, in addition to the actual prisons. Suddenly, a light bulb went off in my head. Those laws for slaves and recently freed slaves that were meant to keep Black people under the control of white people, and essentially keep them laboring for free, never really went away; they just evolved.

And they're still evolving. In 1971, President Richard Nixon declared a "war on drugs," making drug crimes a main focus of law and order. This made drug crimes exponentially easier to prosecute. The main target? Black and brown communities. Two years later, the governor of New York passed the Rockefeller Drug Laws, which were some of the harshest drug penalties in the United States.

SIDE NOTE: The Rockefeller Drug Laws were said to target kingpins but mainly led to the incarceration of nonviolent, low-level, first-time offenders. Possession of relatively small amounts of drugs held minimum sentences of fifteen years, and policing was heavy in Black and Latinx neighborhoods. Despite the fact that people of all races use and sell drugs at similar rates, by the early 2000s, Black and Latinx people made up over 90 percent of the drug offenders in New York state prisons. The Rockefeller Drug Laws weren't substantially reformed until 2009.

In 1982, President Reagan recommitted to the war on drugs as one of the focal points of his campaign. One of his major "accomplishments" was passing acts that expanded upon the Rockefeller Laws at the federal level, removing judges' discretion for sentencing and requiring mandatory minimum sentences that were extremely long and severe. Along with this, he made harsher sentences for drugs that were used more often in Black communities and substantially increased policing in Black neighborhoods.

"Ronald Reagan is widely known for improving the American economy," my professor said in class that day. "He made his plans clear: he wanted to reduce government spending, reduce taxes for businesses, and have less government regulation. So it's no surprise that one of the first things he did was privatize prisons. Meaning, he allowed private companies to come on the scene and open up and run prisons, which had previously only been operated by the government. These private prisons can be contracted by other corporations to supply labor. And who do you think will have to do this work?"

The professor quickly answered his own question: "Yes, the inmates. It's easy money for the private prisons. They're getting money from the government to house and feed the prisoners, and they're getting money from companies to produce air filters, furniture, clothes, you name it. They only pay the inmates about fifty cents per hour, on average—*before* taxes. Enough money to make a handful of phone calls a month or buy a five-dollar bag of Doritos from the prison store, basically giving the money right back to the prison. It is a pretty sweet deal for these businesses—I mean prisons."

He was right. What my professor was referring to was the prison-industrial complex—the symbiotic relationship between for-profit prisons, the government, and corporations. From the mid-1970s to the mid-1980s, incarceration in America doubled, and that number doubled *again* from the mid-1980s to the mid-1990s. What that really means is that America increased the invisible workforce. Today, America has 5 percent of the world's population but *25 percent* of the world's prisoners. If Black people and Latinx people were incarcerated at the same rates as whites, prison and jail populations would decline by almost *40 percent*. The prison-industrial complex is a multibillion-dollar industry that we continuously need to feed. It is America's way of salvaging the classic slavery model.

The professor gave us some reading assignments and ended class by encouraging us to all consider some of the policies and underlying causes that feed Black and Latinx people into the US prison system and to consider what other alternatives could be implemented.

What the professor didn't know was that I had been doing that assignment subconsciously for the past four years. Mental health treatment, drug rehabilitation, community service, fines and restitution, house arrest, and halfway houses are just a few of the viable alternatives to incarceration, especially for minors. What we often see instead is Black and brown youth encountering the legal system early on, and being primed to enter the **school-to-prison pipeline**.

SIDE NOTE: Black and Latinx students make up 70 percent of those involved in school-related arrests or referrals to law enforcement. Consider the story of my brother being expelled from school for shooting a rubber band at a fellow student while a white classmate was sent to counseling for bringing an illegal weapon to school. The preferential treatment of rehabilitating white kids but sending Black and brown kids to prison instead is obvious. It's as if society has decided that Black and brown kids would be more valuable in the invisible economy—the legalized slavery—that is prison labor.

The probability that a Black man without a high-school diploma will be imprisoned by the time he is in his midthirties is nearly 70 percent; that's 53 percent more than for a white man. However, instead of helping incarcerated people succeed in school, the government has only made it more difficult. There is War on Drugs–era legislation that still exists today in many places that bans any student with a drug conviction from receiving federal financial aid for college. This added financial barrier for people who have already had a rough start prevents many of them from pursuing an education that could be life changing.

In addition to being barred from college financial aid, legislation was put in place in the '90s that places a lifetime ban on anyone with a felony drug conviction from receiving federal welfare benefits, such as housing assistance and food stamps. No other offense, not even murder or rape, results in the loss of aid. While some states are opting out of or modifying the limitations of these bans, the federal ban still stands today.

This type of policy is counterproductive to safe **reentry**. When someone is released from prison, these types of benefits can be critical to their ability to survive as they work to secure employment, which is challenging enough due to the fact that most job applications require a person to disclose previous convictions and employers oftentimes use that as an automatic disqualification for hiring. Withholding assistance only increases the likelihood of a person returning to crime in order to provide for their family. America's current policies don't just punish offenders; they also trap them and their families in a lifetime of struggle.

> **SIDE NOTE:** The incarceration rate of women has been growing at nearly double the speed of men since the 1980s. The vast majority of these women experience poverty, and without access to these programs, their children can suffer greatly.

From the point of entry to release, the prison-industrial complex is detrimental to society. It doesn't just target individuals; it targets entire communities. It tears families apart, takes away Black voting power, inhibits people from finding adequate work, and forces Black and brown people to walk through life in constant fear of what a run-in with the law could mean.

> **SIDE NOTE:** It's estimated that nearly 5.2 million Americans are restricted from voting due to conviction laws. One in sixteen African Americans of voting age is disenfranchised.

While the inequity and injustices of the criminal justice system have long existed, and while Black and brown families have long been forced to have discussions about racism in the legal system, the conversation has finally made its way to the mainstream—making it harder and harder to deny the urgent need for change.

An Interview with NIC STONE

Best-selling author

My friend Nic Stone has tackled issues of race and the American justice system in her best-selling book *Dear Martin* and its sequel, *Dear Justyce*. One of the things I love most about her writing is that she sheds light on the experiences of Black people who so often get lost. I wanted to speak to her and gain her perspective on the legal system and the prison-industrial complex, and how she came to incorporate these topics in her writing.

NIC: When my agent and I sent my first book proposal out on submission, an editor wrote back asking if I was working on anything else. So I wound up writing a proposal for *Dear Martin*, which is what set me on this trajectory. Similar to Angie Thomas,

I was terrified of writing a book about race and racism—especially one involving police, because I grew up with a cop in my house.

My dad was a police officer for the first twenty-three years of my life. And he actually wound up being very helpful, because I just needed to understand the mechanism behind the deaths of all of these Black boys, because I had just given birth to a Black boy and was like, *What is happening? Why are these things happening to these kids? What are the things driving this in our society? What is it about our thinking that we're not even realizing are there that are causing people to pull the trigger so quickly? So Dear Martin* started a trajectory that I would've never expected to be on.

Nic's personal experience of having Black children and growing up as the daughter of a cop is an interesting one. On the one hand, she has children who she feels are in danger if placed at the hands of the police, but she was also raised by someone who loved and protected her and *was* the police.

NIC: Even though I did have a police officer for a father, I definitely fall in line with the idea of the abolition of police. Really the abolition of the prison and getting rid of common policing as we know it now. And that does come from having a police officer as a father who completely agrees with me.

The first thing that I learned when I was working on *Dear Martin* is that police officers are people. I think part of the issue with the way that we interact with each other in this country is that we tend to elevate the role over the humanity of a person. So in coming to recognize that, *Wait a minute, this dude, his brain is just as fallible as anybody else's,* was one of the first things that helped me to understand that police aren't heroes by virtue of being in a uniform.

Helping kids to understand things differently from their parents is where things get tricky. I find that a lot of the kids I interact with, when I start explaining to them that there are ways of handling things like "crime and justice" without the use of brute force, it's like they don't even understand. It makes no sense to them. Helping kids imagine the world differently is where we start to make the world different.

As Nic says, police officers are just people. People panic, people have biases, and people screw up. Putting on a uniform doesn't absolve anyone from that. So why do we continue to support the notion that police can be trusted to use their discretion when deciding whether or not to use force during a routine traffic stop for a broken taillight or expired tags? How many lives need to be lost in such scenarios before we accept that the system is broken?

NIC: The thing is the higher you go, the broader you go, systemically. So then you just have to deal with more and more people who have more and more ideas. I am super, super appreciative of a lot of the **juvenile justice reform** that's going on right now. But it's those systems that we've got to attack. I think about attacking it from both ends, so you're changing the legislation at the top, but also working with the individuals at the bottom.

It is ridiculous to cut human beings off from other human beings, to lock them away. Totally ridiculous. And I think about it, again, from the perspective of a parent. I have two sons. I can send one of my sons to their room, but he's not going to be in there very long—forty-five minutes, max. I'm not a cut-you-off-from-everything-and-everybody-as-a-form-of-punishment kind of parent, because it doesn't actually teach you anything. It doesn't help you.

When I think about the way policing works now, even without the history involved, policing is a system based entirely on punishment, completely. It's all about people who have the authority to punish you, to take away your rights, to take away your freedom, if you don't fall in line. If you were to apply that concept to literally anything else, it would never work. So why we think it'll work in this way, I have no idea. Clearly policing as it stands has not changed the number of people who are incarcerated. It has not changed the number of people who "break the law." If anything, there are more people, if you look at numbers in prisons.

So when I think about prisons, when I think about the ways in which we try to get people to do things the right way, I think about all of the things that lead people to do things the wrong way, and correcting those things. Correcting things like economic inequality. Correcting things like inequality when it comes to educational systems. Correcting things like the ridiculous amounts of relative poverty in this country in comparison to the amount of wealth that's here. There are so many other factors that play into why people do the things that they do. And a lot of the time, it's just to get something they need. So how about we just make sure people are getting what they need? Maybe that would actually cut down on some of this.

There is no positive reinforcement for not committing crimes, only punishments for committing them. This isn't an approach that people take anywhere else in society, whether it be in terms of parenting or in the workplace. Studies have shown that spending time in prison actually increases the likelihood that a person will reoffend.

Providing access to basic needs would have more impact on reducing crime than the threat of incarceration. In fact, some people are in such desperate situations that they intentionally go to jail just to seek shelter from the cold or gain access to health care they can't otherwise afford. If we could provide shelter, food, and health care to people, crimes would go down drastically. But this is a system that benefits the business of prison by sacrificing the poor to modern slave labor.

NIC: Let's just throw it all the way back to 1619. From the moment Black bodies existed in this country, we have been seen as commodities, ways for white people to make money. That has not changed literally throughout the course of American history, hasn't changed at all.

So the shift from slavery to "Okay, we're just going to throw you all in jail and make you work and we're going to get money from these people for keeping you here, and because we keep you here, we got to buy beds, we got to buy all of this stuff. So let's make sure that you're here. We've got to populate this place so that people are making money"—it's just so frustrating to me. Especially when I see my orange-jumpsuited brothers— because if I see a prison crew cleaning on the side of the road, the majority of them are Black. Every single time, in their orange jumpsuits, picking up trash off the side of the road, it's free labor.

This sounds familiar, right? You have these people cleaning the cities, these prisoners cleaning the city, right? I'm paying my taxes to make sure that the city stays clean, yet instead of paying people with my taxes to make sure the city is staying clean, they're pulling these people out of jail to make them do the work for free.

Maybe Nic was sitting in on my criminology class, because this was the exact point my professor was making. It's important to know that Black bodies were brought to America as commodities of labor—and that concept didn't end when slavery ended. Convict leasing, what you might think of when you hear the term "chain gang," forced prisoners to perform free labor and allowed prisons to profit from outsourcing labor to private parties, such as plantation owners and corporations. This practice was widespread in the southern United States after the Civil War and primarily used African-American men. This is not much different from what my professor explained is happening today. Companies and government profiting from using Black bodies for labor has a direct through line from slavery and the postwar responses to the abolition of slavery.

If you're appalled by the concept of slavery, you should be appalled by the prison-industrial complex. Prisons should never be for-profit and, more importantly, prisons *don't work*. Incarcerating more people than any other country in the world has not reduced the crime rate here in the United States. We must recognize that the system is not designed to help reform offenders or reduce crime, and challenge our government to implement alternatives to incarceration, as well as address the racial disparities that treat being non-white in America as a crime.

NIC: I think about charging young people with, Hey, you care about people.

I can see that you care about people. You care about yourself. How do we turn that care about yourself into care about other people using empathy?

Find your people. Get together with the people who think the way that you do, who see the world the way that you do. I think about the group of six girls who started all of the protesting in Nashville in 2020. These girls didn't even know each other. They came together and were just like, "You feeling this? You, too? Okay, let's get it. Let's do this!" Seeing that there are young people who do these things empowers us all. But we've got to believe in young people first.

More than any other generation in history, young people today have the tools and the access with which to understand and mobilize against racism and systemic injustice. Each of us has what it takes to practice anti-racism and to speak up and educate others on how racism exists in modern policing and the law—and what we can do about it.

Many people think that the answer to solving racism in policing is to hire more racially diverse cops, but it is the system of policing itself that is broken, not simply individual cops. If a Black neighborhood has been designated as a location to be over-policed, then having diverse police will not help the fact that more arrests will take place in those neighborhoods while the same crimes go unmonitored in white neighborhoods.

We need to reimagine options to reduce crime—options that do not involve the police. Redefining laws is a great start.

For instance, Portugal, Switzerland, the Czech Republic, and the Netherlands are just some of the countries that have **decriminalized** drug use and have instead invested in programs to reduce addiction rates and the harm caused by drug use. In 2020, Oregon became the first state in the United States to decriminalize the possession of all drugs, a move that acknowledges that the threat of jail does not deter drug users from using drugs. Tax dollars that would once have been used to arrest and incarcerate drug users will instead be used toward drug treatment or public safety. With one-fifth of incarcerated people in America serving time for drug offenses, the approach that Oregon is taking could have major implications if expanded nationwide.

Policy to reduce crime is just one thing we can consider, but we also must reimagine what alternatives we have to policing itself. If someone is having a mental health crisis, wouldn't everyone be better served if we could call a trained specialist or social worker to de-escalate the situation rather than police?

Justice should serve to rehabilitate and heal rather than punish and destroy. If we can begin to reimagine the criminal justice system and prioritize people's well-being, we can not only reduce crime rates, but we can also redirect the current government spending to other programs that help create healthier, stronger communities.

To find out more about how you can help put a stop to the prison-industrial complex, visit:

BetterThanWeFoundItBook.com.

15
IS EVERYONE REALLY WELCOME?

Frederick Joseph on the Dangers of Ableism

Featuring **Keah Brown, Natalie Weaver,** and **Greg D'Amato**

Whether most of us realize it or not, we all have a morning ritual. The things we do just about every single day like clockwork that help kick off the morning. For some it's waking up and making breakfast while Alexa plays their favorite playlist, for others it's checking social media to see if that selfie they posted before bed was liked by their crush, and for Porsche it's turning the air conditioner off in the morning even though she knows I run hot and I hate waking up feeling like I fell asleep in the middle of a humid Florida swamp (yes, I'm shading you, Porsche).

About ten years ago, I used to wake up every morning and do three sets of push-ups, pull-ups, and crunches, then drink a protein shake all while listening to Kanye West (my favorite artist at the time). But that ritual has changed—and not just because I canceled Kanye a few years ago. (Remember the way he said early in his career that George

Bush doesn't care about Black people? Well, apparently neither does Kanye, based on his support for Donald Trump.)

Over the past five or so years, this has been my morning ritual: I wake up and flex my hands repeatedly to make sure they aren't stiff and that they are working well enough for me to use that morning. Then I close my eyes, take a deep breath, and try to make sure I can recall what I did the day before and what I have to do that day. Finally, I get out of bed and pace back and forth next to the bed a few times to make sure my legs have the strength I need to walk regularly.

The reason I do all of this is because I have multiple sclerosis (MS), which is a central nervous system disease. MS causes the immune system to attack the protective layer around nerve fibers, which results in inflammation and lesions. This makes it difficult for the brain to send signals to the rest of the body. Symptoms of MS vary by individual, but they often include cognition difficulties, such as memory loss and concentration issues; vision issues, such as blurred eyesight and potentially blindness; fatigue and the potential of being more worn out than normal; heat sensitivity; bladder problems; general pain throughout the body, such as the feeling of pins and needles; motor difficulties, such as issues walking or using hands; and a host of other symptoms.

There are multiple types of MS: relapsing-remitting MS (RRMS), secondary progressive MS (SPMS), and primary progressive MS (PPMS). The type I have is RRMS, sometimes just called relapsing MS, because the symptoms aren't constant. New symptoms can occur while old ones go away, and sometimes I have no symptoms at all. (This symptom-free period is known as remission, or, as I call it, "peace.") When symptoms do arrive, it's known as an attack, relapse, or flare-up. Roughly 85 percent of people with multiple sclerosis are initially diagnosed with this type of MS. Secondary progressive MS (SPMS) is a condition in which the disease tends to progress more quickly. There are two stages of SPMS—active and non-active. Primary progressive MS (PPMS) is a condition in which disability tends to worsen over time without an early relapse or remission.

MS is a very difficult disability to live with because it basically does whatever it wants whenever it wants to. No two days are alike, and no two people have identical symptoms and experiences. My morning ritual has evolved over time to match my ever-evolving symptoms. I flex my hands because oftentimes when I wake up, they are so stiff from the way MS impacts my nerves that I can hardly grasp my phone to check the news. I take a breath and try to recall my days because there have been numerous occasions when I woke up and could barely recall what I was supposed to be doing that day or had done the day before. I pace back and forth to confirm that I am able to walk because there have been times that I've climbed out of bed and into the shower only to end up falling out of the shower and onto the bathroom floor, or falling in the shower and hitting my head on the ceramic tub. In other words, my morning ritual is designed so that I never experience some of the worst moments of my life again.

Most people don't assume that there is anything wrong with me, as I am six foot three, in decent shape (too much Ben & Jerry's), and am living with an **invisible illness and disability**. I'm not telling you any of this for you to feel sorry for me; I live a wonderful life, as do many people with disabilities or illnesses, invisible or visible. I'm telling you this because I want us to talk about people's experiences and truths that we don't necessarily see and thus haven't done enough to support. Sixty-one million American adults live with a disability, and 10 percent of Americans live with an invisible illness that could be considered a disability. I didn't realize all the simple things that were missing from the world around me that could make the lives of people with invisible diseases and disabilities safer and more comfortable—until I needed them. Things such as rails in showers, which could help stop people from falling when they can barely stand on their own, yet I've never seen one in any place I've lived.

I found out that I have MS when I was in my early twenties, and when I did, my life changed forever. Though it wasn't until recently that I realized how my life had changed in many ways for the better. For a long time, I was the kind of person who thought I was invincible. If I had the flu, I would try to sweat it out with a run. If I dislocated a shoulder playing a sport, I would pop it back into place and keep going. If I was tired from a long day of work but wanted to hang out with friends, I would drink an energy drink and go party. In other words, I thought taking care of my body simply meant lifting weights and jogging. Because of that, I probably wouldn't have received my diagnosis until much later than I did if I wasn't encouraged to visit a doctor by my friends, and the only reason they knew something was wrong with me was because they watched me nearly die.

When I was younger, my friends and I would get together every year to play football on Thanksgiving. We called it the Turkey Bowl. I'm not sure when the tradition started, but it always ended in the same way, with a bunch of us arguing over the score and most of us hurt from tackling and being tackled without pads on. While there was an immense physical toll that came along with that tradition, it was always worth it. Though none of us would've admitted it, what actually made that day special was getting to spend time together, even if that time was doused in testosterone and male egos; such time was becoming rarer as the years went on. I think about those Turkey Bowls often, not having realized at the time that the last one I played in would be my retirement game.

During that Turkey Bowl, things were pretty much going the way they normally did: people were getting injured, touchdowns were being debated, and no one was admitting just how sore they would be later that day. But there was one thing that had been a bit different all day. For some reason, I had been having trouble moving my left leg, which was making it difficult to walk and run.

Earlier that morning, on my way to the field, I felt a pins-and-needles sensation in my leg, sort of like when you sit down for too long and then suddenly stand up. But regardless of what I did, the sensation wouldn't go away. Right before I reached the field, it stopped, though, so I didn't think much of it until it became worse while we were well into playing. What had begun earlier as pins and needles had evolved into a feeling of numbness and occasional sharp pains. At times I couldn't feel my leg, and when I did, it hurt in ways I had never felt before. Eventually, I had to sit out because I couldn't walk or run on it at all.

When people asked me what was wrong, I attributed the issue to being hit during the game. I didn't really know what else to say, and in my belief that I was Superman, I figured the issue would go away on its own. After sitting for a half hour or so, the numbness and pain actually *did* go away. My leg felt completely normal, and so of course I decided to continue playing. While I was concerned about what was going on with my body, I was more concerned with going home with a win, which we did. (There go that testosterone and ego again.)

After the game, a few of us walked to the Metro North train station so we could all head to our families' homes to celebrate the rest of the holiday. As we stood near the tracks and waited for the train, my left hand began to have the same feeling of numbness my leg had had earlier, and then I felt a pulsating pain in it. Again, I attributed it to hurting myself while playing football, or maybe lifting wrong in the gym. I switched the bag I had been holding to my other hand and said nothing to my friends, though one of them could see that I was grimacing in pain.

"Fred, you good?" my friend Terry asked with a concerned look on his face; it was rare for me to show that I was in pain.

"Yeah, I just hurt my hand playing ball. You know, it's not easy catching all of those touchdowns," I quipped, half smiling through the pain.

"Whatever. Do it again next year!" Terry said, rolling his eyes.

"Don't worry, I wi—" I began to respond, when all of a sudden, my right leg lost all sensation and I fell forward.

Life happens very fast; you blink and the next thing you know, much of it has come and gone. But as I fell forward, I swear everything around me seemed frozen in time, as if life itself had stopped for a second to teach the young man who thought he was invincible just how mortal he truly was. There was a train coming and I was now on the train tracks in front of it, unable to stand up. It was all happening so fast and yet so slow at the same time.

"Fred!" "Get up!" "Stop the train! Stop the train!" "Fred!"

That's all I remember hearing besides the sound of the train horn ringing in my eardrums as it grew closer, and the screeching of train brakes that sounded too close to help spare me. The sounds of the train had grown so loud, I could barely hear myself think; the only thing louder may have been my racing heartbeat. I was sure that I was going to die.

Then I heard a voice say something that seems sensible now, but sense is the last thing I or most of the people looking on had during a moment of such fear:

"Roll! Roll out the way! Roll to your right!" a woman on the opposite platform exclaimed just seconds before the train was about to introduce itself to my weakened body. With all the effort I had in me, I rolled to my right and toward the opposite platform, out of the way of the train. I never got the woman's name, as various people rushed to get me off the tracks and then I was escorted out and eventually driven home, but she saved my life.

By the time I got home, my body felt normal again, but now I knew something was definitely wrong. I went to two doctors to try to find out what was happening to me. The first doctor ran very few tests and claimed my symptoms were likely because I wasn't fully taking care of my body, even though I worked out often. She made a few awkward comments about me partying too much so I wasn't getting enough rest, though I never mentioned anything to her about my lifestyle and rarely partied. She told me to get more rest and not to worry about it, claiming that I was too young and in too good shape to have anything seriously wrong with me. "You're a big strong guy," I recall her saying as she squeezed one of my biceps in a way that made me feel extremely uncomfortable.

Her lack of interest in truly helping me find out what issues my body was facing taught me an important lesson that I'm going to pass along to you all now, in the hope that none of you ever have to learn this the hard way: doctors are humans, and no human is perfect. And so it's important to be the primary advocate for your own health. If something feels wrong, even after getting a doctor's opinion, get a second opinion—which is exactly what I did, though only after a friend of mine convinced me to go see her sister, who was a doctor. Her sister ran a multitude of tests—none of which the first doctor had run—and eventually I was diagnosed with multiple sclerosis.

I spent the first few months after my diagnosis navigating symptoms that were becoming worse and living through a deep depression as I tried to figure out what having MS was going to mean for me, my family, and the trajectory of the rest of my life. Eventually, I came out of that depression and started taking medicines that helped alleviate many of my daily symptoms. I decided that I was going to begin figuring out how to live a life that wasn't spent simply trying to survive with MS, but one that was fulfilling despite having MS. This is when I quickly started realizing just how ill-equipped and under-resourced the world was for people who were living with disabilities and symptoms from invisible illnesses. This is also when I learned about the discrimination and prejudices disabled people face and how that **ableism** manifests all around us and in our daily lives and interactions.

When I told most people that I had MS, they did one of two things: they either felt sorry for me or they shunned me. I understood why people might feel sorry for me, though that's not what I wanted and I think oftentimes it's not what many people want. I remember one of my good friends researching MS and asking me whether I was "going to end up in a wheelchair." I told her that it was a possibility and I wasn't worried about it. She seemed taken aback, even horrified by the prospect, which is a deeply ableist reaction. But I truly wasn't worried, and I'm still not. If I am in a wheelchair, does that mean I'm no longer alive? Does it mean I can no longer experience joy? Does it mean I'm no longer me? Of course not. If I do end up in a wheelchair one day, I'm less interested in being around people who feel bad for me, as much as people who are going to help push the chair when I don't have the energy to roll myself. I think this is what many people want.

While I didn't want anyone to feel bad for me, I also wanted people to try to understand that my life might be different, but I still wanted to live a full life. But for some people, *different* is not something they want to deal with or have the capacity for dealing with. I found out pretty quickly that the workforce is often one of the spaces that exists without a capacity for difference. While there are many laws against disability discrimination, such as the Americans with Disabilities Act, the reality is that we need many more laws in place to properly address and prevent discrimination.

SIDE NOTE: The Americans with Disabilities Act (ADA) was signed into law in 1990 and was focused on prohibiting discrimination in employment, salary determination, and termination. It also required businesses to provide reasonable accommodations to disabled workers, such as wheelchair access. However, one unforeseen issue with ADA was that employers worried that making these accommodations could be expensive and feared the potential of being sued if accommodations were not met. Because of this, the employment rate for disabled people fell dramatically.

As I mentioned before, there are many symptoms of MS, and those symptoms make it difficult for me to work some days. But there were various ways that I could navigate those symptoms while still being able to do my job, including working from home and/or extending my work hours depending upon how I was feeling. I would still be able to produce the same work and meet my deadlines. I just wouldn't always be doing so in the typical nine-to-five, in-office framework. My bosses were uninterested in making those accommodations, however, and thus I was put in a position where I was unable to do my job as effectively. Which led to me not having a job.

As I searched for other positions, I told many of the hiring managers about my MS to ensure that they not only had accommodations my prior employers hadn't, but also to avoid dealing with the trauma of being treated as if I was a liability if I informed them later. While they couldn't legally end my candidacy based on it, the only positions I received job offers for were the ones where I hadn't mentioned having MS. Sadly, my experience wasn't the exception, but rather the rule: 12.6 percent of Americans who have a disability are unemployed. Though I ended up working for multiple companies while living with MS, I ultimately never found a position where I felt sufficiently comfortable or safe. In fact, I had to work twice as hard as my colleagues just so I wouldn't be judged for the days that I might not be feeling well.

It's not just about the workforce, though; it's about an entire world existing that doesn't account for the millions of people who are living with disabilities and invisible illnesses. I briefly had to drop out of graduate school to figure out how to get a handle on my MS before I could return, because there were no guidelines or safety measures in place to help people such as myself be able to attend school. In fact, only about 16 percent of disabled people over the age of twenty-five have a bachelor's degree or higher. This is largely because our society and its spaces were built to ableist standards, which makes it nearly impossible for people to access certain opportunities or achieve certain successes if they don't meet these deeply ableist standards.

Only 5 percent of tables in new restaurants must have seating that is accessible for people with disabilities, so if a restaurant has twenty tables, only one person needing an accessible table can eat there at a time. Even in a major transportation hub such as New York City, only 25 percent of the subway is accessible for people with disabilities, meaning that millions of people have difficulty with or can't even ride the subway. As of 2011, less than 5 percent of homes are accessible for individuals with mobility difficulties, and less than 1 percent of housing is accessible for wheelchair users. As I said, our country is ill-equipped and under-resourced for the millions of people who are living with disabilities and invisible illnesses.

But ableism isn't just about the lack of accessible, comfortable, and safe spaces for people with disabilities. It's also about the erasure of the disabled community and the lack of respect afforded to its members. I asked myself recently how many times I had seen a television show or film starring or featuring a disabled person whose story line wasn't solely about them suffering because they are disabled. The reality is that such representation is rare, and as is the case with any community, the erasure or omission is particularly damaging for people living with disabilities, because so many spaces are already seemingly trying to erase us by not being accessible, thoughtful, or safe.

Lack of respect for disabled people takes many forms, including **ableist language** and **ableist ideologies**. Some examples of ableist ideologies are: treating disabled people as if their disability is the totality of their identity; acting as if people who have various needs because of their disability are somehow a burden to us; assuming that because we can't visibly see someone's disability or its impact on them, it is less important or worthy of respect; and making assumptions about how someone feels about their disability. To the last point, I've been guilty of doing this in the past and have heard many people do the same. It is wrong to assume that anyone living with a disability would prefer to not have that disability. While this may be true of some people, it is not true of all people. Disabled people are just as varied and dynamic as anyone else, and we shouldn't project our own beliefs on people with different lived experiences.

Ableist language is language that insults people with disabilities and consciously or unconsciously upholds ableist ideologies. For some people, when compared to issues like accessibility in physical spaces, ableist language may seem unimportant. But like other forms of discrimination, words are signals as to who is respected, welcomed, and treated fairly—and who isn't. Ableist language, like any other **microaggression**, can have a deeply harmful impact.

Because ableism is so woven into the fabric of our society, we don't even necessarily know how to identify it when we see it or are perpetrating it. For much of my life, I didn't know what words were ableist and so used them without thinking. And there were some words that I *did* know were ableist but I used them anyway, because I didn't think it was a big deal. Now that I know better, I've removed these words from my personal vocabulary. It took me a while to get used to adjusting my language, but once you make a commitment to being better about this, you'll find that it's surprisingly easy.

While ableism may be a new concept for some, many of the qualities and skills needed to fight ableism are also needed to fight racism, homophobia, sexism, and other forms of bigotry. So developing an intersectional skill set for combating oppression is key, because all of these forms of ignorance, discrimination, and oppression feed off of and uphold one another. Which is something I spoke about with my dear friend, author, actor, and creator of the hashtag #DisabledAndCute, Keah Brown.

An Interview with KEAH BROWN

Disability activist, author, journalist, actor, and writer

Keah Brown is not only an activist; she's also a dazzling writer and the author of *The Pretty One: On Life, Pop Culture, Disability, and Other Reasons to Fall in Love with Me*, which I suggest everyone read, as it offers her wonderfully intersectional perspective as a queer, disabled Black woman.

KEAH: The first time I saw *Crip Camp*, that was the first time that I watched a movie where I was like, *Oh, so we can have happiness and joy and not spend an entire movie being like, "No, how could you love me? I am disabled."* That was the first time that I was like, *Oh, so it's possible for us, too.* I've spent my entire life loving pop culture and finding bits and pieces of myself within other things because I had to, you know? We had such a plethora of fantastic stuff for Black people in the '90s, when I was growing up. And we lost that. The reason I'm as vocal and as honest as I am about what it means to live in the world as a Black disabled woman is because I'm not seeing it from anybody else who looks like me. And those of us who are doing the work are not seeing the recognition and the platforms that we deserve.

I think what happens now with pop culture is there's the token person a lot more. There's never been much representation of disability in pop culture, but there used to be more representation of Blackness, at least. When I was younger, you would see more Black people so that it was a larger swath of an experience. There was *Family Matters*. There was *The Fresh Prince of Bel-Air*. There was *That's So Raven*. There weren't enough options, but there were options in a way that we don't have anymore. The Black people that they have on a lot of shows today aren't just underdeveloped; they also all look the same. They're super skinny, they have a certain type of hair, they look a certain way. So they're Black, but they also fit into this idea of what is safe, I think, for white people. What they can recognize. What they can understand. You're not seeing darker-skinned Black women in these roles and given the same sort of agency and attention that the people who fit the Eurocentric beauty standards are going to get.

Which is one of the reasons I wanted to write my debut book, *The Pretty One.* Not only to focus on being Black, but on being a Black disabled woman specifically. Before I wrote the book, I asked myself, *What is it that you want to talk about that you don't often get the chance to talk about?* And so I allowed myself the room to expand beyond the idea of asking humanity, like, "Please care about me a disabled person, because you or someone you know might be disabled." Instead, I let myself talk about things that matter to me, as a disabled person and as a person. I talked about ableism and how exhausting it can be and why it needs to end and what a world free of ableism looks like. But I also made it a point to simply talk about the world I live in and enjoy. Because I think a lot of times when you're marginalized in any way, such as with Blackness and disability, people only expect you to talk about how hard it is and painful and exhausting, and it is those things and I did talk about them. But it isn't only those things, and I didn't want *The Pretty One* to be only that.

So I didn't just talk about disability issues, but rather my experiences as a person who is disabled. Things I dislike and things I love, pop culture, my love for rom-coms, cheesecake, and how I love languages.

Keah makes a point here about how people from marginalized communities, including the disabled community, are often seen simply through the lens of their struggle. But that often only further marginalizes people. It's important to understand the realities of the obstacles people face, especially because of systems and beliefs that impact their daily lives, such as ableism. But people are so much more than their marginalizations. Keah's work helps place the dynamism of the disabled community in the forefront. Why do so many people expect her to talk only about her disability as opposed to her passions, interests, and joys? Because we don't do enough work to represent, normalize, and celebrate the spectrum of existences of the people in the communities she belongs to.

KEAH: I try to remind people that if you are speaking to somebody in any marginalized community, not everything is going to be the same. For instance, I personally prefer the term *disabled* over euphemisms, like "handy capable" and "different abilities" or any of the other host of them. I'm not really interested in the comfort of people who don't share my lived experience. I'm more interested in what makes me feel better and feel good and feel most like myself, and less in what somebody is going to take from me saying I'm a disabled person.

I find that often, if I get a compliment, especially from people with no sort of background with disability at all, they will say something that's in the family of, "Oh, yeah. You're so pretty for a disabled person." When I was growing up, a bunch of people said to me, "Oh, you would be pretty if . . ." You know? It was a lot of people being like, *There's a caveat to your prettiness* or just saying my disability somehow cancels out any sort of attractiveness that I might have. People would be like, "If your hand wasn't like that, you'd be so much prettier." Or they would be like, "You just have to find the person willing to look past your disability." And it's always this caveat where either I'm "pretty for a disabled person" or I'm not ugly, but I'm never just *pretty*, because I don't fit into Eurocentric beauty standards of being white, thin, having curves in the right places—or able-bodied.

I walk through the world with a limp and in a Black body, and many people deem me unworthy because of it. For example, on dating websites, people have said, "Oh, I googled you and I'm just not interested," because they saw full-body pictures of me. Or they'll be like, "I didn't even know that you were disabled until I saw you move" or they treat disability in some way like it is the biggest aspect of my world and completely defines me.

The ubiquity of these able-bodied, Eurocentric beauty standards is really damaging. What happens is these beauty standards tell you that you'd be so much happier if you look this way. And though I know better, even I buy into it. Even I buy into the idea that if I had different hair and my hair was longer and if I was skinnier and I wasn't disabled, I'd be happier.

And so what the standards actually do is make you never feel satisfied with who you are. Which is wild, because the people that we're supposed to be idolizing don't even look like what we think they look like. You'll see a celebrity on the cover of a magazine and they look great, sure, but nobody looks like that all the time. And it's just the idea that if we're as close to the

Eurocentric model as possible, if we're as close to able-bodied as possible, that means beauty and that means access and that means privilege and that means a whole host of things. It gets you all these things that will always allow you to have an advantage in a way that I think a lot of us, whether we are ready to admit it or not, are clamoring for.

I caught myself the other day because I posted a picture on Instagram and I was like, *Oh, I look cute. I'm posting this.* And I posted it and people were really nice about it, and then I was looking at the numbers and getting caught up on the difference between a post that I made after that that had way more likes than the picture of me. And I'm like, *Are you ugly?* And then I'm like, *No. You're not ugly.* And I said the four things that I like about myself to get myself back on track. But it is really easy to feed into that idea when you're seeing the highlights on people's Instagram and you're seeing the bodies that you're constantly told are beautiful and you look at your own and you're like, *Well, mine isn't like that, so does that mean I'm less worthy?* And the answer is no, but it's hard to remember that in the moment.

This point that Keah makes is extremely important, because it speaks to the fact that we have been taught to chase not only Eurocentric or white standards, but able-bodied standards as well. We are strategically taught by society that we should look like people in magazines and on social media who don't even look like that themselves more times than not. We are taught that beauty is not inclusive of certain groups—the disabled community being one of them.

KEAH: I think that people don't want to talk about ableism because they don't want to talk about disability. It's this weird idea that to talk about something less makes it less real. Which is obviously never the case. If you see a disabled person in any sort of beauty campaign, they're almost always shuffled to the end of it. Or they're just in the background. And you always see the same type of disabled person—who is a wheelchair user. And as much as I think this representation is important—it's not enough. I feel like when we don't challenge even the types of disabilities we give the public, we see the scraps of disability that we get in fashion and beauty. Not adding different types of disabilities that are represented broadly is why we see such a lack of disabled people being included in these great conversations about body positivity, about making sure that we show people who aren't just white and thin and aren't just your "standard" idea of beauty. Making sure people aren't always just able-bodied should be included as well. It's weird that we often look at disability in general as like, "You got one. There's some random person there. That should be enough for you." The same way we treat Black people, Latinx people, any marginalized people. It has to stop.

And I think that young people are the ones pushing the needle forward. If it wasn't for young people, we wouldn't have the progress we have, I think. They're the ones rejecting the idea of what we're supposed to aspire to. That this is what we're supposed to want to look like, or what we should want to wear, what we should want to do, and who we should want to be. I think that young people, in particular, are absolutely the ones putting the work in to be like, "No, we reject everything that has come before us," or "Maybe we'll keep some scraps of it, but we want something else." They want something that's more inclusive, more fair.

If we are going to end ableism and give disabled people the space, platform, and humanity we deserve, I truly think young people, our future decision-makers, are going to do it. Keep rejecting anything that isn't equitable.

As Keah says, it's important for everyone to play a part in helping dismantle ableist standards. One of the people doing this work from the perspective of an accomplice is disability rights activist Natalie Weaver, who spoke not only about the work she's doing, but also about her late daughter Sophia, and the importance of us all tearing down the systems and beliefs of ableism.

An Interview with NATALIE WEAVER
Founder of Sophia's Voice, activist, and writer

When I think of strength, Natalie Weaver is one of the people who comes to mind. What she has dealt with publicly over the past few years has been so tremendous and daunting, I can't imagine what she has gone through in private. She fought for her daughter's rights as a disabled child right up to the moment Sophia passed and then continued to fight for other people with disabilities. While it's critical to listen to the voices of disabled people themselves—which is something Natalie talks about—Natalie's journey to becoming a disability rights accomplice is one that I thought was important to share, as the work of creating a less ableist society requires the effort of communities that are and aren't directly harmed by ableism.

NATALIE: Sophia was my first child, and she was born with profound disabilities and facial differences. As an able-bodied white woman, I could blend into the world, so when I started to take my child out, I was very naive. I knew that there would be stares, but I didn't expect the hate and the reactions, or to be experiencing discrimination. As a woman, I had some experiences with discrimination. But this was on another level. This was pure hatred. This was fear. This was really difficult to deal with. I decided to be more private because of people's reactions to her conditions. That was more comfortable for me than dealing with hate and discrimination.

Meanwhile, I started to learn that I had to speak up and I learned to become an advocate, kind of on a personal level, fighting for my child, for her health care, for the services that she needed. I learned, "Hey, I'm good at this. I feel a charge when I fight for my child and I actually get her everything that she needs." So I had the experience of advocating personally, but then on our state level, they were going to take away about 60 percent of a special Medicaid service—it's home- and community-based services—from my child. People didn't understand that Medicaid also serves people with disabilities and it helps them to be able to stay in the home because **institutionalization** is the other option. And for my child, losing services was a matter of life or death.

So at that point, I had to make the decision to say, "I can't be private anymore." I kind of lost that privilege and I had to speak out, advocate on a public scale for people who weren't being given the opportunity to advocate for themselves. Through my work with able-bodied and disabled people combating able-ism, we were able to stop our state from decreasing those services by going on the news and raising awareness and getting people to care. And what I learned is that I have to tell people my story. I have to; I can no longer be private. I have to have them care about my daughter the way that I do, so that they will fight for her and fight for others like her. And so I did that. And then Donald Trump was elected. He wanted to ravage Medicaid, so I had to speak on a larger scale.

I began to speak in front of hundreds of people. I never knew I could do these things. I gave interviews and just pushed and pushed and probably was annoying. But I wanted everyone to know our story, to understand it, to hear it, to care about Sophia, to see her as the human being that I did. And as I was doing that, I began to receive vicious hate. Lies being made up about my child, assumptions being made, being told to murder my child, her being made fun of on social media platforms. That's when I realized I had to shift and advocate on an even bigger scale.

I began to share the voices of disabled people because in situations where people are fighting for community and equality, disability is constantly left out. So I wanted to make it a priority to share disabled activists' work. Because so often, when there is light shed on the necessary work of combating ableism, it's able-bodied caregivers and parents whom the light is placed on. So I started Sophia's Voice because I realized there was a direct need for medical support, financial support. And so I started to directly help people with disabilities by providing them with that type of support, but then also supporting disabled activists and the work that they do because that's the critical work. And that's the work that actually helps everyone.

One of the reasons I wanted to share Natalie's story is that while she became a very prominent and influential activist for the disability community, she didn't start out as any sort of expert in these spaces. She had to educate herself—and continues to educate herself—and she also had to push herself way outside of her comfort zones in order to be the best advocate possible for her daughter, and for others in the disabled community. And, critically, Natalie realized that one of her responsibilities as an accomplice is to make sure the voices of those she's advocating for are being heard.

NATALIE: When I started out, I was a stay-at-home mom, and I didn't know what I was doing. And I just did it out of my passion to protect my child. I had never even heard the word *ableism*, and I think that's important to state because going into advocacy, you're not going to be an expert at any of this. There are people that have been doing the work for decades, and it's okay to not know something. But when you do learn, you realize how acceptable ableism is in society.

When I changed Twitter and had them include disability among their abuse reporting options, someone was like, "So now you're taking away my ability to make fun of disabled people. That's not right. I have a right to." It is widely acceptable in our society to mock disabled people, to not be accessible. I mean we have events for equality and justice, and yet these events don't have an interpreter or don't have a ramp.

I can't speak for disabled people and I won't. I can only speak about my experience as a mom of a disabled child, but I would post something about my child and underneath my posts people would be discussing why I didn't kill her, why I didn't abort her. People viewed her as having a low quality of life without knowing anything about her life, just because she had facial differences and profound disability.

So devaluing disabled people is just pervasive and it's considered acceptable. And I've noticed in the course of doing this work that people are starting to realize that and address it, and that is important, but it's just been so widely accepted to devalue disabled people. And to view them as less than. It's ingrained in all of us, including in our language. How many of us use words like *dumb* and *crazy*, or the words *lame* or *psycho*? Those words are in so many songs. We're not perfect. But if we learn that our language is harming someone, I would just think that we would want to change that. It's really just as simple as saying "Okay, I say the word *crazy* a lot. What are five words that I could replace this with?" and just start practicing. I remember when my husband and I decided, *Oh my gosh, this is bad.* Once we learned this, we would always be like, "Oh, you said the word." We would help each other try to change because it was very important to us, especially after having a disabled child.

Like many oppressive forces, ableism is woven into our daily lives in ways those not directly impacted by it may not even realize. A person who doesn't live with disabilities may not think about a place not having a ramp for people who use a wheelchair or need a walking aid. They may not think about how certain terms are harmful to people. They may not think about the exclusion of disability from the abuse reporting options on social media, or any of the other daily manifestations of ableism a disabled person encounters when they try to simply exist. This is in large part because we don't talk about ableism—which is something Natalie confronted with social media.

NATALIE: Someone was using Sophia's image to promote abortion, and there was nowhere to truly report it. I looked into hate speech on most social media platforms and they listed gender, race, religion as protected groups, but they didn't list disability. Many disabled people that have reached out to me would report hate toward them, people making fun of them for being who they are. And there was just nowhere to even report that. I kept getting, "Oh, this doesn't violate . . ."—you're telling me, someone could tell me that they want to kill my child and this doesn't violate anything because she's disabled?

This isn't okay. It was in the policy not to discriminate against people with disabilities, but it was not being followed because there was nowhere to report it. Seeing a huge social media platform not have those types of protections was just unbelievable to me. So you could see how it was widely accepted and how once again, disability was forgotten.

It wasn't too long ago that if you had a disabled child, a child with facial differences, deformities, or any of that, the doctors would say they have to go into an institution. And they would be kept in a hospital setting in these little tiny beds and just kind of thrown away, out of view from society.

And then we had **eugenics**—and it wasn't just Germany that did it—trying to wipe disabled people off of the planet.

While forced sterilization and forced institutionalization are no longer legal, I've seen firsthand how disability is frowned upon in society. Many people don't just treat people living with disabilities as if we're different; they often treat us as if we shouldn't exist. There is an erasure of the reality that people with disabilities are as much a part of society as anyone else. We need to change that.

NATALIE: I think that people's fear and willful ignorance of disability are what's behind this kind of *Out of sight, out of mind* approach to disability. When it comes to facial differences, people often look the other way. Which is why we need to make disability a part of people's lives and in their faces and in Hollywood. Part of my work is normalizing disability, profound disability, specifically, for my daughter, and facial differences. But you don't see people on TV shows or in movies with profound disabilities or facial differences just walking by without it being a big deal. We're not even to that point yet. It's not a part of daily life. So it's out of sight, out of mind. Nobody wants to think about it.

Part of some of the work that I do on Sophia's Voice is I created a series "Grow with Sophia" so that you could learn about Sophia, and children could watch and they could see a child being loved and living her life with facial differences.

So this is what I ask parents and caregivers to do: please start at home with kids as young as one or two, when they can really understand differences, and show them. There are so many amazing disabled people online that share their lives and educate and take the time to help people understand.

So do your part and make a commitment to normalize

facial differences and disability. And you do that by sharing it. You do that by teaching your children about it; you do that by correcting their language when they're using the wrong words or calling someone ugly or things like that.

And it could be very simple, just going online and learning about people, getting to know them. They share wonderful things, just regular, everyday things about their lives. And it's so easy now because of social media. So there should be no excuse. Get books about disability. They make them for children.

All of those things, you just have to make it a priority and care about it.

SIDE NOTE: Be sure to check out Keah Brown's picture book, *Sam's Super Seats*, illustrated by Sharee Miller.

It shouldn't take being disabled ourselves or personally knowing someone who is disabled for us to care about members of the disability community, and to want to work alongside them to make the world more welcoming to them. It starts by checking your own ableism and continuing to listen to and learn from others in the community—people like my good friend Greg D'Amato.

An Interview with GREG D'AMATO

Philanthropist, entrepreneur, and researcher

Greg D'Amato is a dear friend of mine, someone I appreciate for his perspective and worldview who in many ways is different from me. But there is one way in which we are the same: we both live with multiple sclerosis. I wanted to talk to Greg and for you to hear about his life, because it shows you how living with MS is different for everyone.

GREG: I had a good life growing up, what some might call a "normal" life. But it had an interesting element, too: my dad had MS, which was a heavy part of my childhood, a memorable part—good, bad, and ugly. But it was a good childhood.

I think in my personal life, given my demographic as a white man with relapsing-remitting MS, I have layered privilege. Having an invisible disease sometimes can be a privilege and sometimes it cannot. For people like us, we're lucky enough where sometimes we don't have to talk about it. We don't have to address it unless we want to, it's necessary, or we're comfortable in doing so. Some people are not as lucky.

While there are undeniable privileges of having an invisible disease and potential invisible symptoms from that disease, one negative is that most people don't know to make spaces accessible or comfortable.

GREG: I live in a beach town now, and there are times when it's hot as hell. Some days in the summer where people think it's beautiful, I'm not going outside—because I know that's going to trigger vision problems; it's going to give me a hard time. And there's a fine line between letting somebody in and explaining that to them and thinking that they're going to understand and take it at face value, and somebody thinking that I'm making excuses. It's really the nuance of just looking out for yourself, because you know what those things are based on your own lived and learned experiences, where you're like, *It's ninety-nine* *degrees. I'm going to have a whole week's worth of problems if I go outside today.*

But I can't be mad at people for not realizing this; it's an issue systemically. Someone shouldn't have to have a visible disease or disability to have resources to take care of themselves or be respected. Those should exist regardless, but they don't because we don't place an emphasis on them. I think it goes all the way back to everybody's beginning. It's really those core lessons you learn as a kid: be kind to others, treat others as you want to be treated, and understand that at the end of everything, somebody with a disability, without a disability, with any type of complex or issue—they want to be seen, they want to be understood, just as much as you do.

Just like Natalie, until I was directly impacted by disability, I had never heard the word *ableism.* Think about that for a second. The word is nearly as old as I am, but spending twenty years of my life in school and living in the digital age, I had never encountered this fundamental term until it impacted me. That's not because I wasn't interested; it's because it was never made important. If the word itself isn't important, is it any wonder that creating access and resources for people dealing with ableism hasn't been made important enough, either?

GREG: I think it goes back to just the teaching and the learnings and the desire of parents today to teach their children about empathy, about equality, about acceptance. In my household, we do everything we can to teach those core values and things we believe in that are for the greater good and doing what's right. We talk to our daughter, Elle, about how to respect people and understand differences. Because it has to start early. There's never an age too early to build empathy and respect. That's why my wife, Jacki, and I talk to her about it. It helps her understand that when Dad's having a bad day, it's nothing she did. I'm just not feeling well. We want the moments in our household to help inform her moments and engagements outside of our household.

Beyond what I've already mentioned, I think one of the most impactful things we can do is create environments where everyone feels comfortable being themselves. As we all are on a constant journey of self-acceptance, I want to see an environment where self-acceptance, regardless of ability or disability, is okay. Understanding that some of us need a bit more from certain environments to feel comfortable, and most importantly, safe. And for me personally, having a daughter, thinking about her future, thinking too about the hereditary potential of MS—it's not proven that it's necessarily hereditary, but in this family tree, I know that it is and it can be—so just building a legacy I'm proud of, knowing that I want her to have a world where she is safe and comfortable no matter who or what she is. I want my daughter to inherit a legacy of bravery and openness. A lineage she can be proud to belong to and pass down, if she so chooses. A family whose spirit and name are known for dedicating our lives to creating soft and safe places for people whether they are disabled or belonging to any other marginalized group.

Young people are the key to all of it. When you think about cultivating these types of environments, they're going to be the ones that are going to do it. I like to think that our generation is a piece of that puzzle, but I really think the generation behind us, and the generation behind them, are going to be the ones that move it forward. And I think that because in so many ways they are challenging the status quo. You have these young people coming into these companies having these thoughts, desires, and ideas that they want to see structurally in these organizations and too often they're being dismissed. But they're correct about a lot of it.

Having multiple sclerosis has been one of the most difficult obstacles I've ever faced, but it's also been illuminating, for which I'm incredibly grateful. I've learned to consider how society often lacks safe and equitable spaces for people who are disabled or living with illnesses, as well as how I've been conditioned to normalize these issues. From ableist language to expectations of who a disabled person is and what they can do, we all play a part in how society erases these communities.

One billion people worldwide live with some form of disability, and it's up to us to make sure that they are not only welcomed in society, but that they know that this society belongs to them as well. Dismantling ableism starts with developing respect for the experiences and needs of others—and then we must turn that respect into actions. Actions like being considerate of how our words may traumatize others. Actions like being thoughtful about whether spaces are accessible for everyone—and working to make them so if they're not. Actions like continuing to educate ourselves and unlearning what is and isn't "normal." We can be better—and so we should.

To find out more about how you can help put a stop to ableism, visit: BetterThanWeFoundItBook.com.

16
NO HUMAN IS ILLEGAL

Porsche Joseph on the Impact of Immigration Policy
Featuring Daniel Alejandro Leon-Davis

That moment when summer is winding down and fading into fall has always been my happy place. The weather becomes comfortable as the temperatures drop and the humidity subsides, and as the days become shorter, my mind has always seemed to naturally prepare to let go of frivolous summer habits like staying up late watching crappy movies and sleeping in the next day. The fall ushers in a feeling of readiness to get back to school. The summer after graduating high school, I was particularly ready for fall to come because I would be able to leave the suburb I had spent my entire life in, quit my job at the local grocery store, and venture out on my own to something new.

After giving up on my dream to attend school in New Orleans, I was disappointed that I wouldn't be with my cousins during college. However, I had been awarded a full scholarship to a university in Washington, so I was adamant about finding the silver lining.

The college I would be attending was the exact opposite of Xavier University, in Louisiana. It was only a couple of hours away from home, in a slow college town about twenty miles from the Canadian border. I was nervous that I wouldn't make any friends, but the one thing that made me feel less apprehensive about the situation was knowing that Ana would be there alongside me.

In first grade, Ana moved with her family from Mexico City to my neighborhood in the outskirts of Seattle, and she and I quickly became friends. Although we didn't go to the same elementary school, because the one I attended didn't offer **ESL**, we would often do homework together after school, and I can credit her with single-handedly teaching me my multiplication tables.

Ana moved to a different neighborhood a few years later, but she was still nearby and we would hang out every once in a while. We weren't the closest of friends during high school, for no other reason than the way people naturally drift apart when at different schools, but we both worked at the grocery store that summer and I found out that she had been accepted to the same university I had and would be attending that fall.

We quickly rekindled our friendship over our shared excitement to start college and agreed that we would take it on together. We must have spent that entire summer discussing our plans. Ana would text me pictures of the tacky furniture she bought for her dorm room (a clear inflatable chair and a lava lamp), and in return I would show her the tacky posters I purchased and planned to hang (a monochrome picture of a young Notorious B.I.G. and Tupac—RIP). Ana and I discussed which dining hall meal plan we would select and registered for as many classes together as we could.

Ana had always been at the top of her class and was

in every Advanced Placement course her school offered. Fortunately, we had managed to register for two of the same college classes together, which was a huge relief because not only was I looking forward to her company, but it was good to know I had a friend who was incredibly smart that I could work with if the coursework was difficult.

One thing I never thought much about was Ana's **legal status**. I knew she was born in Mexico, but in my eyes she was also American. After all, we grew up together and worked together. However, I would soon find out that one small thing—where we were born—set us apart more than anything else.

Bellingham, Washington, where our college was, had a population of fewer than eighty thousand and was over-whelmingly white. The town was chock-full of vegan cafés, secondhand shops, and the kind of hipsters who managed to wear expensive clothes yet still look like they belonged in a grunge band. This place had a lot of plaid, Birkenstocks, band Ts, and the occasional white person with dreads. Ana and I had some good laughs over the ridiculousness of it all. (Life update: I now have a pair of Birkenstocks and I get the hype—most comfortable sandals I own.)

Many of the residents of Bellingham were students at the university or worked at the university in some capacity, and the college was widely known for being the most lib-eral in the state. Even so, the US Immigration and Customs Enforcement (**ICE**) had a heavy presence in Bellingham, and the **immigration raids and arrests** that took place around the area were supported by many of the county residents. The targets of these raids and arrests tended to be places that employed a number of Latinx immigrants.

While I was turned off by the lack of diversity on campus, as a **US-born citizen**, I didn't have to think much about the consequences of ICE or anti-immigrant racism near the border. I was just excited to be close to Vancouver and to have easy access to a bigger city with more diversity.

Ana and I had quickly befriended two girls in our classes, Amara and Stacy. After surviving our first month, we were preparing tirelessly for our first college midterm exams. I wanted to plan a visit to Canada for the four of us. Amara, who was of Middle Eastern descent, quickly declined, informing me that crossing the border would be hell for her. Even though this was years after September 11, there was still a strong anti-Muslim sentiment in the country. The bigotry they endured was heightened when traveling, and they were often treated like suspected terrorists. Ana agreed with Amara; she, too, wanted to avoid racial profiling from ICE at all costs.

It speaks to my own privilege that I hadn't considered that they would feel that way. Because Bellingham was so close to the border, I met *a lot* of Canadians at school, including our friend Stacy. Many of them mentioned how easy it was to obtain a **visa** that allowed them to study in the United States and said that they never had any issues crossing the border or run-ins with ICE. The difference between them and Ana and Amara was that they were white.

The majority of people who cross the Canadian border into Washington State are white. Before September 11, Americans and Canadians could pass freely at many of the checkpoints, sometimes being asked to present a state-issued ID, but oftentimes not. By the time I attended college, years after September 11, there was still no requirement for a passport—simply an ID and a photocopy of my birth certificate would do—but what counted as valid ID was regularly left to the border patrol's discretion. For someone like Stacy, a blond-haired, blue-eyed, white college student, she might be able to pass through with just her student ID.

At any rate, Stacy told us she had lost her ID months ago and hadn't gotten around to replacing it, so we all agreed to scrap the trip and stay in and order pizza after the big test day. We decided to meet at Stacy's dorm room that night.

Amara was the last to arrive. She walked in and immediately suggested a change of plans. Apparently a girl from our class, Gina, was having a party. "She says we should come!"

"I'm in," said Stacy without pause. "I've had a terrible day; I know I bombed that test. Maybe we could salvage it with my first college party!"

I had never been to a college party, either, but I wasn't especially eager to change that. Many of the kids I had met seemed to think college was their own personal Woodstock festival, sprinkled with weekend ski trips expensed to their parents' credit cards. They were a bit delusional and unknowingly pretentious. Best-case scenario, we would be standing around a bonfire, drinking kombucha while discussing the best thrift stores in town.

Ana, too, was hesitant. "I don't know. We've had such a long day and I'm not much of a party person." But Stacy and Amara pleaded, and before we knew it, Ana and I were agreeing to go along—on the condition that we stay no longer than an hour.

When we arrived at the party, it actually didn't seem so

bad. It was mainly people standing around talking. Lil Wayne had just dropped a new album and it was playing loud in the living room while a handful of people danced offbeat. If nothing else, I figured I could do some great people watching. Amara said she wanted to go find Gina, so Ana volunteered to go with her while Stacy and I found the bathroom.

Before we even made it to the bathroom, people started pouring out of the apartment, as a number of police officers were stopping people at the door in an attempt to bust people for underage drinking. Stacy and I went to grab Amara and Ana, but we couldn't find them in the house. We decided to head outside and give them a call to tell them where to find us.

As soon as we got to the door, an officer approached us. "Ladies, we'll need to see some ID," the officer said.

Stacy flipped her long blond hair over her shoulder and grunted. "Why? Are you detaining me?"

He laughed. "I like your confidence. No, I'm not detaining you." He sighed. "Look, you seem like a nice girl; you remind me of my wife when we were young. You're not the kind of person we're looking for. Get back home, okay? Do you need one of my men to escort you for safety?"

Stacy rolled her eyes. "No, thank you. That won't be necessary."

I was shocked. I had never seen someone speak so boldly to the police. "How did you do that?" I asked when we were safely out of earshot. "You just put that cop in his place. You scared the crap out of me, though! I thought you were going to get us arrested!"

"I have an uncle who's a cop. I know they can't just ask

for my ID for no reason while I'm in someone's house. I don't even have an ID, anyway, so he was wasting his time," she said casually.

Neither Ana nor Amara were answering their phones. Our dorms were only a few blocks away, so we continued walking toward home while calling them repeatedly, though we weren't too worried. We knew they weren't drinking or doing anything else illegal and assumed they would make it home just fine. Stacy and I said good night once we reached our building. Enough time had passed after I was back in my dorm that I was relieved when Amara finally called.

"Hey, are you home?" I asked anxiously.

"No, I'm walking there now, but the police took Ana!" she said frantically.

"What do you mean they took Ana?" I said, leaping to my feet.

Amara explained to me that the police had asked for their IDs, the way they had asked for Stacy's and mine, and kept them both there for a long time before they told Amara she could go. I told Amara there must be some mistake and that surely they would let Ana go home soon, too.

We didn't hear from Ana that night. Or the next. I checked the online jail registry nonstop to see if there was a record of her arrest—though I couldn't imagine what they might've charged her with—and I began sending countless Facebook messages to random family members I had never even met before who were tagged in pictures on Ana's page, asking if they'd heard from her. Days went by and I heard nothing from anyone. I'll never forget the panic I felt during those days. I could barely sleep or eat with the guilt I felt that my friend had disappeared on my watch, and I had no idea if her family even knew what was going on.

Finally, a cousin I had messaged asked for my number and gave me a call. She thanked me for reaching out to the family and told me that ICE had become involved somehow that night. Even though the state passed laws in 2019 that banned local law enforcement from contacting ICE or even questioning people about their immigration status except in limited cases, those laws are still frequently violated today and didn't even exist at that time. And although I didn't understand the vague information her cousin was giving me, I understood immediately what I had never thought to ask—Ana was not documented. But it still didn't make any sense to me how this could happen to her, or even what was happening to her. She wasn't a criminal; she wasn't out causing trouble. She was just a college student who had gone to a totally benign college party. A college student who had been in this country most of her life. Ana's cousin asked me not to speak to anyone about it, and I agreed. I didn't understand much, but I understood that I shouldn't ask too many questions. Legal status can be very private for people in undocumented communities. Sometimes people don't even know or understand their own legal status, and the information is often not disclosed to people without good reason.

And just like that, less than six weeks into the school year, one of my only friends at college was gone and I couldn't even talk about it.

I felt terrible. Why had I allowed us to go to that party?

She didn't even want to go! But the truth is, she hadn't done anything wrong by going to a party after acing her first college exam. She wasn't doing anything wrong by existing in a place that she was brought to as a young child.

Around the time of Ana's arrest, Washington State had just passed a law that allowed undocumented students who had been in the state for at least three years and had graduated from a local high school to qualify for in-state tuition prices. But the bill still did not allow them to apply for financial aid, which meant they couldn't get student loans or other forms of assistance, nor did it give them legal status or create a pathway to citizenship. It pretty much allowed undocumented students to attend college for the same price as a citizen but gave them no protection against deportation.

It wasn't until 2012, years after I graduated from college, that President Barack Obama would announce DACA (Deferred Action for Childhood Arrivals). DACA was created to protect eligible immigrants who came to the United States before the age of sixteen from deportation. Although it does not provide a path to citizenship, DACA gives young immigrants a temporary legal status for two years (which can be renewed) and allows them to apply for driver's licenses and work permits.

SIDE NOTE: A survey in 2017 found that 97 percent of DACA recipients were employed or enrolled in school and that recipients' hourly wages had increased by 69 percent on average upon obtaining DACA status. While the majority of people in the United States support DACA, it is under constant attack from anti-immigration politicians and judges.

DACA is just one program, but it serves as evidence that immigrants contribute greatly to this country, and even more so when given the opportunity to do so legally. DACA recipients pay taxes on that 69 percent pay increase and circulate money back into the economy every time they buy groceries, pay rent, fill their gas tank, and so on. The students go on to make great contributions to advancing our country and helping others—in fact, of the Nobel Prizes in science given to people affiliated with US universities, one-third are earned by immigrants.

Here's the thing: apart from the compelling humanitarian case for welcoming immigrants, we *need* immigrants. More than half the people in this country are over the age of forty and the current huge wave of retirees is going to peak in the next decade, when the last of the **baby boomers** reach retirement age. In the coming decades, the country will be in even more dire need than we already are of new taxpayers to help fund Social Security and Medicare, and a workforce to take the place of retirees as well as health care professionals to care for these elderly people. This issue has prompted many politicians to speak up to encourage Americans to have more children, acknowledging the benefits to a growing younger population. But why do we need more births when so many young people, many who are already here, would like to participate in the US economy?

SIDE NOTE: In a 2019 *Time* magazine article, Suketa Mehta wrote, "In 2008, Bill Gates stated before Congress that for every tech worker the country lets in, five American jobs are created. Over half of all billion-dollar tech startups have an immigrant founder. Today they employ half a million Americans. Immigrants or their children founded 43 percent of the 2017 Fortune 500 companies, which employed more than 12 million people worldwide in 2016."

Immigrants have always been the backbone of the American story. They start businesses at twice the rate of those born in the United States, and they bring a creativity and work ethic that fuels the American dream. Restricting immigrants does not preserve our precious US resources; it stifles them and keeps us stagnant.

About a year or so after that night with Ana, I took some courses on how to file immigration paperwork so that I could volunteer with a nonprofit that held workshops and provided free lawyers, paralegals, and translators to assist people in completing applications for their path to citizenship. It was in that volunteer work that I realized how common deportation is and the incapacitating fear it places on individuals, families, and communities. ICE agents would stalk the people who would come to use our services, staking out the places where we held our workshops, fully knowing that these people were there in an attempt to do things the legal way. They would harass them and sometimes arrest them as they left the building. People would be forced to hide in the building until the ICE agents left. As an American, it did not feel to me like protection; it was terrorizing. ICE was targeting community members, coworkers, peers, and friends.

While we should treat immigrants humanely because it's the right thing to do, we also need to accept our role in all of this. It is important to understand that mass immigration is often a result of the unlivable conditions in other countries that United States has contributed to causing. It is critical to acknowledge the role that more than a century of US-supported military coups, economic meddling, corporate corruption, and destruction of resources has played in creating much of the poverty and violence that exist in some of the main countries whose citizens seek refuge in the United States. Those countries include Guatemala, El Salvador, and Honduras, whose often-desperate residents come to the United States by way of Mexico. The United States has pushed these countries into less-than-beneficial trade agreements that prioritize the market over the people. The United States has also regularly backed wars in these countries by providing troops, high-grade weapons, and billions of dollars in funding. This leaves countries war-torn and has taken hundreds of thousands of lives, yet there is little effort to assist the refugees and asylum seekers created by the wars we support.

We need to be wary when the US government proudly boasts that they have struck trade deals that are firm on benefiting the United States, because quite often these America-first deals force farmers and agriculture producers in other countries out of business because they can't compete with big US companies. The trickle-down effects of this situation can be drastic; the loss of jobs for small farmers increases rural migration, which our economists know. If we continue to make these deals, we need to consider expanding the number of immigrants we accept from these countries or help create other ways to boost their economies so that the exchanges are more equitable instead of complaining about the migration that comes from our actions and demonizing the people we have displaced or put out of work for trying to better their life by immigrating. People like Ana's family. And people like my dear friend Daniel Alejandro Leon-Davis.

An Interview with DANIEL ALEJANDRO LEON-DAVIS
Designer and cultural architect

Daniel Alejandro Leon-Davis is not only a brilliant creative force, but he also has had the experience of living in the United States as an undocumented person. Daniel worked on a #RentRelief campaign that helped raise and distribute $20,000 for undocumented people who were struggling to make ends meet during the pandemic, many who did not have access to stimulus checks due to their immigration status. Daniel also helped lead the I Stand with Immigrants Initiative, a creative campaign that brought together celebrities, influencers, and organizers to highlight the beauty of immigrant communities.

Daniel has done a lot of work to educate others on immigration. In some ways, his story is similar to Ana's, so I asked him to share his experience and his thoughts on immigration policy in the United States. I didn't understand the full scope and legal logistics of immigration when I was younger, but Daniel helped shed light on the wide range of difficulties of immigration in the United States and his firsthand experience of going from being undocumented to having full legal citizenship status.

DANIEL: We moved to the States from Venezuela when I was six. Like every other immigrant kid, I was told to focus on school. For me, that worked. I was totally the straight-A kid who just grew up loving being in school and also loving the arts. My mom had built an entire career in Venezuela—she was an interior designer, a fashion designer, and was very well known in her craft. When my mom and I moved to Miami, she went from being very high up in her industry to working three jobs—everything from being a janitor at a movie theater (which I thought was dope as hell because I got to watch movies for free) to sewing garments. I always go back to that starting point for me because I actually didn't even realize my immigrant status. I knew I was Venezuelan and my mom only spoke Spanish, but I didn't realize the impact it would have in my life.

Like a lot of DREAMers or undocumented young people— especially in the era when I graduated from high school, which was 2008—I actually didn't find out I was undocumented until after I applied to college. That was the moment that I became super politicized. Like everyone else, I grew up saying the Pledge of Allegiance, playing sports, going outside and playing, and being focused on school and my hobbies, but it wasn't until I was seventeen that I would find out that I actually didn't have access to all the things that my peers had access to, simply because I didn't have some little piece of paper.

SIDE NOTE: The DREAM (Development, Relief, and Education for Alien Minors) Act sought to give citizenship to young immigrants who were brought across the border as children. The DREAM Act never was passed, but it paved the way for DACA, and the movement that was created around the act was important. People from this era of youth activism who hoped to be recipients, and frequently went on to be recipients of DACA, are commonly referred to as DREAMers.

So many people, like Ana and Daniel, come to this country at a very young age. They do not make the choice to come here—in Daniel's case, his older siblings were already here and his mother wanted to give him more opportunities as well as be near her other children, even if that meant giving up the successful career she had built in Venezuela—and they often don't see the difference between themselves and the kids they play with at recess or on their soccer team; just like their classmates, they're growing up as Americans. However, the little piece of paper Daniel referred to is a permanent residency card, often known as a green card, and it can make all the difference. Immigrants can apply for a green card if they enter the country legally, although it's not guaranteed that they will ever receive it. It essentially allows immigrants to be here more permanently and apply for full citizenship. In Daniel's case, his mother put in applications for them both at the same time, and while hers was granted after only a couple of years, he never received a response.

SIDE NOTE: About the only things people with a green card can't do are vote and have a US passport. But with this card they can do important things such as legally work, get a driver's license, open a bank account, and access health care plans.

DANIEL: My mom, in trying to protect me, didn't tell me I was undocumented. When I wanted a car at the age of sixteen, she convinced me to wait until I graduated. Then when I asked her why I couldn't get my license, she made up something about her being afraid of me crashing. Even when it came to work—all my friends got summer jobs and I wanted one, too, and she'd respond, "Come work for me." But I never put the pieces together that I actually couldn't do any of those things. I couldn't go get my license. I couldn't go get a regular job.

I think her hope was that my residency would come in before I graduated high school and she would never have to tell me, or if she did, she could say that this used to be an issue but it's solved. I got into some of the top colleges in the nation and got offered full-ride scholarships, and I didn't find out I couldn't take the scholarships until they told me I had to fill out FAFSA, and as an undocumented person, you can't fill out FAFSA.

When Daniel speaks of his residency coming in, he is referring to the green card/permanent residency application that was submitted by his mother when he was a child. This application process often takes many years.

DANIEL: My permanent resident application was actually in the process for fourteen years before I ever became a resident, so when people talk about, "Oh, just get in line. Oh, do it the legal way," I'm an example of how that doesn't work. During all that time I was undocumented, we had lawyers advising us. My mom actually became a resident during that time.

The concept of "just get in line and wait your turn" isn't as simple as people make it sound. The backlog for green card applicants is extremely long. And although "lines" do exist, many people are not eligible to be in them—and even those who are may wait decades to see any advancement.

> **SIDE NOTE:** While the process to becoming a naturalized citizen is relatively quick, you are first required to have a green card, which is often the part that makes the process incredibly drawn out.

DANIEL: After high school, I ended up having to take a gap year. In that gap year I went into a really deep depression. Everything I knew—my excitement around going to one of the top schools and the life I knew being focused on school, school, school—was done. I had come out as gay my junior year of high school, and in my senior year, here I was having to keep a whole new secret, because at that time it was just the beginning of people talking about being undocumented and not being afraid of the consequences.

I remember when my mom told me I was undocumented, she sat me down and said, "You can't tell anybody. You can't tell anybody because you're going to get deported." That was always the fear.

Just like Ana, Daniel knew this was something he couldn't share with anyone. Even though it was the biggest thing that had impacted his life thus far, he had to deal with it on his own. This can cause a lot of turmoil for immigrants, as at any moment their lives can be completely disrupted and destroyed. At eighteen, Daniel was supposed to be at a prestigious university with a full scholarship, and instead he was stuck at home, unable to work or even drive, and couldn't even explain why to the people closest to him.

DANIEL: During my gap year, I continued to struggle with depression and spent the first six months thinking, *Okay, I don't know what to do. I don't even know how to go to school. Am I even going to go to school?* In the second six months of the year, I decided, *I can't let this stop me*, and I had to do something that I was really ashamed of—I had to get a fake license and Social Security card, and I had to find a way to make money, in order to survive. Did I want to do this? Of course not. But I knew I needed to do it in order to survive.

The moment that I think about all the time was when I was stopped by the police while I was driving. I've only been stopped once in my life. At the time, I was a teacher at a local dance studio. I got stopped maybe not even a minute away from my school, and I'm freaking out. The cop came and asked, "Can we see your license and registration?" And I said, "Yeah. The car's registered to my sister. She just let me borrow it. Here's my license." I handed her the license, she went and checked it, and it was a fake license. I was so scared to see what was about to happen. She came back and said, "It's not going through. Is there something wrong?" I just said, "No, there should be nothing wrong." But every time she went away, I was in tears because I knew this was going to be the moment I got deported. There was no other way out of it.

She came back and she's like, "Where are you from?" And I knew exactly what she meant by that—she was trying to figure out where I had emigrated from. My fake license was from

Tennessee, so I said, "Oh, I'm from Tennessee. I haven't changed my license over yet." We went back and forth for a while and she eventually escalated it to the point that she asked me to step out of the car. So I asked, "Ma'am, is there a reason that you're asking me to get out of the car?" She screamed, "Get out of the car!" When I got out of the car, she handcuffed me and I was literally just crying. I hadn't had the chance to text my mom, my sister. I just knew I was getting deported. There was no other end in sight.

She called for backup and when they showed up, I could hear her telling them what happened and when they walked up, one of the officers said, "Daniel? Man, get this guy out of handcuffs." It happened to be the dad of one of my dance kids.

I think back to that moment all the time because I would have 100 percent been deported. That was the closest I came to that fear of truly believing the life I had created for myself was all over. The reason I tell that story is that it's the fear that people live with every single day, and all because of not having a piece of paper that says you belong here.

The fear Daniel must have felt that night is unimaginable to me. But as he said, it's a fear millions of people live with every single day. And some of them aren't as fortunate as Daniel was. For those who grew up here and get deported, the relocation can make them feel much more like an outsider— like an immigrant—than they ever felt living in the States. In Daniel's case, almost all of his family got residency before him, even though he spent his childhood here and in his words is the "most American."

DANIEL: I was lucky enough to grow up bilingual, but I know a lot of immigrants who don't even speak their native tongue. I still have a lot of family in Venezuela, but if I was deported, I wouldn't have known what to do. It would have completely uprooted my life. My nuclear family was all here in the States.

Immigration violations have become a large part of the US criminal justice system. Some immigrants are not immediately deported, but detained without the same rights as citizens.

DANIEL: You can't talk about immigration in America without talking about mass incarceration. Immigration detention surely is incarceration. I grew up with ICE, or La Migra, always being talked about even though I didn't know I was undocumented. I think in immigrant communities in general it's something that gets talked about often, especially having grown up in the '90s when there was such a big surge of ICE raids. There were a lot of people who were working under the table and basically, ICE would organize raids to go into these workplaces and make sweeping arrests—everything from the restaurant industry to the fashion industry—to try to gather as many undocumented immigrants as possible, hold them in detention, and then be able to deport them.

Every time I think about ICE, the first thing that comes to my mind is my mom grabbing me. ICE takes up so much space in the minds of immigrants in this country. For example, we would go to the mall and if my mom saw the mall cop, she would grab me really tight and hold me by her. Once I found out I was undocumented, I realized my mom, like so many immigrants, basically thought that anyone with a badge could deport me.

And now, over the last couple of years, it's gotten really murky because there are cities and states where the police can actually report you to ICE, and then there's cities and states which we know as **sanctuary cities or states**, where the police cannot do that. Even if you get stopped by the police for a traffic infraction, like my own, they won't report it to ICE because they don't work together.

There's a conversation about policy and immigration in which some people claim that when immigrants commit real crimes, outside of immigration violations, the country can't enforce the law on them and so we have to deport them, and that's just false. In places like sanctuary cities, you can actually enforce the law without someone getting deported for something like a traffic stop.

Crimes related to immigration and/or immigration status make up the majority of all federal criminal arrests. One of the first issues Donald Trump raised when he began his campaign for presidency in 2015 was immigration—when he made it clear he considered immigrants to be synonymous with criminals. In one of his infamous speeches, he claimed that undocumented immigrants are dangerous. "They're bringing drugs. They're bringing crime. They're rapists. And some, I assume, are good people," he said. Contrary to his statement, research repeatedly confirms that undocumented immigrants are far less likely to commit crimes than US-born citizens. In fact, studies show that US-born citizens are twice as likely as undocumented immigrants to be arrested for violent crimes, two and a half times more likely to be arrested for drug crimes, and more than four times more likely to be arrested for property crimes.

Given that immigrants contribute so much value to this country, why are they so often vilified?

DANIEL: Immigration in this country has always been about white supremacy. The Naturalization Act of 1790 established the first rules of national citizenship. In the Act, it said that free white persons of good moral character were granted citizenship after two years of residence in the US. That's literally how immigration started in this nation. It's so fascinating to think about the fact that we live in a country that heralds itself on the idea of diversity and multiculturalism—of basically being the "melting pot"—but the true focus is on keeping Black and brown people out, and oppressing the Black and brown people that are already here.

When you look at the immigration numbers, the highest ratio of application to acceptance rates are from white countries. When it comes to immigration for non-white folks, the fact is that it has always been about labor. Policy makers obsess over how Black and brown immigrants fit into the country's labor needs.

Unless you are Black and your ancestors were brought here through slavery or you are Native American, at some point somewhere down the line, your family immigrated here. Slavery itself was forced migration.

The idea that the United States welcomes diversity often is not borne out in our approach to immigration. Politicians demonize non-white immigrants by claiming that they come over and steal all of the jobs. In reality, often there are not enough people to do all of the jobs in this country, and moreover, immigrants tend to compete for jobs with other immigrants. Although politicians have stoked fear around the idea of immigrant competition, they have no problem with companies outsourcing the same work overseas where labor is not regulated, or to prisons where they pay little to nothing to fill jobs. And despite President Trump asking why the United States would want "all these people from sh*thole countries," referring to places like Haiti and Africa, he did not fail to request hundreds of temporary immigrant labor visas for hospitality workers to work at his golf club in Florida. The kicker: most of these employees came from "sh*thole countries."

There is so much fearmongering around the idea that Black and brown immigrants are going to steal our jobs or rob our houses, yet these thoughts and feelings rarely come to mind when considering European immigrants. Due to visa allotments, it is easier for immigrants coming from countries with largely white populations to obtain legal status in the United States; however, that does not mean that their dreams or motivations for being in the United States are any different than those of immigrants who come from countries that are predominantly Black or brown. So while some might argue that it's appropriate for ICE to target Black and brown immigrants because it's statistically more likely for those immigrants to be undocumented, we need to be aware of the racist policies that make it easier for immigrants from majority-white countries to obtain legal status in this country—and work to change them.

DANIEL: When talking about DREAMers or young undocumented people in general, you have to consider that the majority of these young people have already been invested in. For example, what would it have looked like to deport me as a young person? As someone who went to public school in the US since first grade, I had a lot of taxpayer dollars invested in me. If I were deported, we wouldn't even get the chance to see the return on that investment.

Especially now during the pandemic, you can't talk about immigrants without talking about essential workers. A very large portion of essential workers are actually DACA recipients or immigrants. The pandemic would have been very different without having access to that workforce. I hate justifying immigration with labor, but the reason that it works, policy-wise, is because there's this huge misconception that undocumented people don't contribute, don't pay taxes, and that is extremely untrue. I myself paid taxes while I was undocumented.

Immigrants contribute to the US tax base and would contribute even more if they could become documented and therefore have better access to work opportunities that are not paid under the table. While undocumented, they cannot access most benefits, including many options for health care, and oftentimes can't even go to the doctor without the fear of being deported. This results in many deaths and injuries that could be prevented.

DANIEL: One of the biggest losses for undocumented immigrants is access to health care. In California, undocumented people do actually have access to health care, and that was a really big policy win for us. I didn't grow up going to doctors and I think about the fact that if anything ever happened to me or one of my friends, more often than not we had a community doctor who was a friend of our family try to help us out, and the worst-case scenario was that we went to the emergency room and had to pay out of pocket.

Daniel's path to citizenship took a surprising turn when the courts overturned the Defense of Marriage Act, which meant same-sex marriages would be recognized at the federal level.

DANIEL: Right after I graduated college, in the summer of 2013, the Supreme Court came down with a decision on the Defense of Marriage Act. This is actually before same-sex marriage was legalized everywhere. But what few people realize is that when the Supreme Court made that decision, for any state that had already legalized marriage, it allowed the marriage to be recognized federally.

Anyway, people were super excited about it. And I remember being on the steps of the Supreme Court when the decision came down and literally having tears come down my face, and not because of the marriage piece, but because for the first time ever it meant that a same-sex couple not only had to be recognized federally, but could actually petition for immigration. Until that point you couldn't be a same-sex couple petitioning. My now-husband couldn't have petitioned for me. A couple of months later, he proposed to me and that's when I started my process around my residency.

I remember when I got my permanent residency card and I

was so upset. Everybody else gets really happy. I literally got so angry and I called my mom. Obviously, she was excited I'd finally become a resident, but I was pissed because I thought, *Wait, all of this for this ridiculous little card? This card signals that I can be here all of a sudden?* It made me so mad.

For Daniel, that little piece of paper meant his entire life was changed, although he was still the same person he had been while waiting the majority of his life for his turn to come up in line. If the Defense of Marriage Act had not been passed, Daniel might very well *still* be waiting.

DANIEL: I think that everyone deserves to be treated like a human, and the immigration system is the most dehumanizing thing I've ever gone through. I went to therapy for it. I think the fact that we live in a country that continues to prioritize the oppression of Black and brown people just shows that it's not a country that's actually living up to its values.

Since its founding, this country has been in a struggle to find its identity, to marry its stated values with its actual laws and practices. Much of this identity crisis has taken the form of debates over whether we are a nation of immigrants or a nation of laws. But what if we made laws that support our current immigration needs? Laws that create avenues for immigration, and prioritize keeping families together? Laws that recognize the need for workers, while ensuring that people are employed in humane and legal ways? We need laws that recognize the important role we must play in providing asylum for refugees, particularly those from countries where we have been an active presence. We need to take a more nuanced view of what constitutes a "good" trade deal for our country. And most importantly, we need to create better-functioning paths to citizenship.

Although the American dream has historically not applied to many groups, we have the opportunity to change that by educating ourselves on immigration policy and challenging the systems that fund ICE, detention centers, and deportation and divert these dollars to increase pathways to citizenship instead.

It is important to understand that borders are created by people. And just as borders can be changed, so, too, can laws. People are not illegal, and immigration is only illegal if we uphold the laws and policies that make it so.

We have always had more to gain from immigrants than we've had to lose. It's time to treat them as the vital members of society that they've always been. It is time to treat them like humans.

To find out more about how you can fight for immigration
reform and help immigrants, visit:
BetterThanWeFoundItBook.com.

The End:
WE CAN BE HEROES

ON SEEING EACH OTHER'S HUMANITY

An Interview with **FREDERICK JOSEPH** and **PORSCHE JOSEPH**
Writers, activists, and philanthropists

A Note from the Book's Editor, Kaylan Adair

I first met Fred and Porsche in February of 2020, when they were in town for a wedding. Fred and I had just wrapped up the edits on his debut book, *The Black Friend: On Being a Better White Person*, and while we had gotten to know each other reasonably well over email, phone, and through the surprisingly intimate process of editing, I hadn't yet met him in person—nor had I met his then-fiancée, Porsche—and so I jumped at the chance to finally do so.

Meeting Fred and Porsche in person was like being reunited with two old friends. They were instantly warm and generous, so ready to welcome me fully into their world. One of my favorite experiences of that afternoon was sitting on the patio of their Miami hotel and listening to the two of them talk—about race, about TV shows, about publishing. They had this amazing dynamic, each speaking freely and with confidence, pushing back against each other when they disagreed, amplifying each other when they agreed—all of it grounded in mutual love and respect. It was amazing to behold, and the impression of that moment has stayed with me.

It was that moment that we wanted to try to replicate for the ending of *Better Than We Found It*, and I'm so glad that you, our reader, will have the experience of being welcomed into Fred and Porsche's world, of sitting down with these amazing individuals and listening in as they engage in conversation.

So, pull up a seat and enjoy. We're so glad you're here.

Let's start with the basics: What does a better world look like to you both?

PORSCHE: I think that a better world comes down to giving people opportunities to live peacefully. A better world looks like creating something that's more accessible so that people are able to thrive at their highest self and are able to do what they want freely, and are empowered to be who they want to be in a world that also supports them.

FRED: I think for me, a better world looks like the freedom to be anything anybody wants to be that doesn't harm others. I think that if that's the baseline of existence, that everybody has equitable and equal opportunities to be free, then the world is better.

Do you feel like your answers to that question have changed through the writing of this book—and if so, for better or for worse?

FRED: I think in working on this book, my answers haven't necessarily changed as much as my urgency has. I think there are moments that I was working on certain chapter topics or Porsche was working on certain topics and a new article or an update would come out about that specific thing. Like, oh, you're writing about gun violence, and you hear there was another mass shooting, or there were fifteen more mass shootings. I'm watching Porsche write about climate justice and also a United Nations report is released about the climate saying that things are far worse than we could have imagined. So, it hasn't changed. It's just more crucial, more vital, more urgent for me.

PORSCHE: I think that I have a strong understanding of how things are intersectional, but in writing this, I could truly feel how it's all connected. It was difficult to even focus on one thing at a time. How race, gender, disability, and all of these subjects are so tied to one another. It further makes the point about how important it is to find solutions for them all and not just one thing, and how urgent it is that those solutions come sooner than later.

You crafted this book very deliberately for a younger audience, for people who mostly can't vote yet. What was the thought process like in deciding the audience for this book, and what are you really hoping this audience takes away from the work?

PORSCHE: There is beauty in the way that young people get fired up about things. And I feel the older people become, there is a natural inclination to become more apathetic. If we can engage young people and really lean into the fact that many are fired up about things and reimagining how the world works, we can make lasting change. We see it working—look how many people are engaged thanks to people such as AOC and Ilhan Omar, the types of politicians I didn't see growing up. Especially because they are women of color meeting people where they are. Let young people see themselves as vital changemakers and they will make vital change.

FRED: I feel like we owe a service to young people to give them as much information as we can that's the correct information. And to equip them with the tools to do something about it. It's not that somebody who's thirty, forty, fifty, sixty, et cetera, can't learn, or doesn't want to learn. But why not reach people earlier, before they go down the roads and make the mistakes? I don't think that people have to necessarily walk the path and then go back and be like, "Oh, I messed that up." It's like, wait, we can do something about it before you get there, if you're willing to listen.

How did you two decide who would work on which topics? What was that like for you both, and were there things about the process that really surprised you?

PORSCHE: When we first drafted the list of the topics that we wanted, we drafted that list, and we sat with it for a while. Then we came to the table to discuss the logistics of who would write each chapter. We were like, "I've been thinking about that. Actually, I have a great story for that." We know each other well, so one of us might be like, "Hey, you feel pretty passionate about that. You should take that one." Or, "I know you dealt with that. You've told me stories about that. You should definitely write that. That's now your story." So I felt like it was pretty natural. And then also pretty, I guess, strategic in some ways of being like, *When and where can we challenge ourselves to step up?*

FRED: There was a large conversation about why it was important for readers to see one of us discuss a topic. For instance, with the chapter on feminism, we knew that many readers have heard women speak about the importance of feminism, the importance of womanism, and so on. But the work is not just women's to do. The work of unpacking and dismantling the patriarchy is work for men to do as well. And I think the same thing goes for white supremacy. The work is not for Black and brown people to do solely; it's also for white people to do.

So how did the interviews come about? When you drafted the list of topics, did you have people in mind already? Were you searching out people? How did that come together?

FRED: I think that for certain topics, we had people in mind, there were certain people who we were like, "Oh yeah, we definitely want that person." And for others, you start kind of looking around to see, at least for me, for some of my chapters, I wanted to see who offers a perspective that I either didn't or couldn't. Because I don't think that this book could accomplish its aim if everything is just an echo chamber of our voices and our experiences.

PORSCHE: Fred and I partnered and brainstormed together for all of the chapters and figured out who would be great. A lot of names came to mind at first, so we just kind of had a free brainstorm of like, "This might be a little bit of a reach, but I would love to talk to this person." And then even just down to people we personally knew, like, "This might not be a name that a lot of people know, but I know this person and their story moved me."

Each individual chapter and story is so powerful and impactful. My hope is that when young people read this book, they feel deeply moved to take action on all of these things that they finish the book with a desire to make good change in their spheres for each of these topics. But the book covers so much ground; how do you address someone who wants to do it all, knowing that that's not going to be possible? What advice would you give?

FRED: My advice is do something and do what you can. What one person can do is not necessarily what another person can. It might be as simple as saying, "Oh, I am this cisgender person who is going to not only reevaluate, but actively stand up for the trans and gender-nonconforming communities." I want people to grow and make the changes that are possible for them.

PORSCHE: Yeah. I completely agree. I don't think that people should have to feel unrealistic about being able to do every-thing. Sometimes it is just learning and having a mindset shift. To Fred's point, if you've never been around a trans per-son in your life, at least please have the empathy and under-standing to not let people say transphobic statements around you. You have to assess what you can do, and understand that you will make mistakes—but try.

We have friends who are extremely passionate about the environment and do so much throughout their daily life to address climate change. And not everyone is able to do as much as them, but that shouldn't stop you from doing *some-thing*—that shouldn't stop you from recycling or composting or taking a shorter shower.

Fred, one of the things you mentioned in The Black Friend *is the fear of bringing kids into this world. How much of writing this book has to do with making the world better for the children you and Porsche hope to have, and what do you hope this current young generation does for the one coming next, which might include your own children?*

FRED: No matter who you are, if you're paying attention, you should have a fear for what kind of world that we're going to leave for coming generations. What kind of world are we going to leave in terms of safety—thinking about things like gun violence? What kind of world are we going to leave in terms of housing security, health care, and all these things? And we take all that, and then you add in the fact that it's all exacerbated by, "My kids are going to be Black."

I definitely have a great fear, but I believe in the perseverance of change. And I believe in people. On a regular basis, people step up, show up, stand out in ways that make me keep going. And I'm hoping that young people do that, honestly, for themselves. We say in the book, essentially, we're the ancestors of tomorrow. As much as I'm sitting here, responding to this question, I'll be gone before you know it. As will the people reading this book. So, you ask yourself, what's your legacy going to be?

PORSCHE: To echo what Fred said, I think that it can be scary and overwhelming, the current state of the world and people in general. It's easy to feel down and to doubt that there's goodness and that that goodness can ultimately save us and be a world that we would be happy to bring children into. But there are good people out there who want more. And so if you feel that way and you feel overwhelmed, I think all we really can do is work toward creating a better future generation. Fred and I speak often about what we want for our children and about expectations of our children. Our expectations really do align in wanting them to make a better world, be good people, be people who have strong morals. So if we can shift back into that and lean into that and somehow create a place where that's where our priorities lie, then I am hopeful.

I'd love to circle back to that idea of legacy. In the process of writing and editing this book, we've talked about the idea of "Better than you found it" being not just a book, but an ethos—leaving the world better than you found it. In that regard, the work is not done with this book, the work continues. So, what does the continuation of this work look like for you both? Not just in terms of book projects, but life projects, life goals—what comes next?

FRED: Well, I think you said it: "Better than we found it" is an ethos, and it's not just our ethos, I think it's one of the reasons why we're all a team, including yourself; we're just putting a name to it. It's how we all want to parent. It's how we all want to be friends, it's how we all want to be significant others, it's how we all want to be customers at a store, it's how we all want to be citizens of the global web, it's how we all want to exist. I think that the reality is that we're just beginning, we're just getting started.

I'm coming into myself, not just as an author, but as a human being, because the same things that we're talking about in this book are many things that I had to unpack and unlearn, and I feel almost reborn. So now it's not about "What's next?," because I'm looking at everything. Everything is next, and everything kind of exists with that ethos of *Better than we found it* at its core. The work continues in all ways: books, social media presence, conversations, and love.

PORSCHE: This is totally unfair, because I was going to give that butterfly/reborn analogy as well! I am coming into myself. And I think that I'm reset. I think that ultimately it feels good to be able to create something, to put something out into the world that feels like a reflection of my ideals. And so that is something that I can continue to do in different creative ways. That would be the goal. As Fred said, there is no next—it's kind of like looking at a bigger picture, like how to continue to contribute to the world in a way where we can be used and needed.

One final question: We've talked a lot as a team about acknowledging our individual identities and lenses—Porsche, as a biracial woman; Fred, as a Black man living with an invisible disability; me, as a white woman. These identities shape how we approach various topics, how we think about them, write about them, and edit them. I'm curious to know how you've changed each other, from when you first got together—learning about each other, loving each other—and then how that has influenced the work you've done together on the book and beyond?

PORSCHE: I think that it's been important for me in my growth as a person to understand that I have a different lens than not just Fred, but many people in this world, and that my lens needs to be able to shift and change. That's at the core of what will make me the mother I want to be, the daughter I want to be, the sister I want to be, and the me I want to be to myself. Growth is a part of self-care. Becoming more today than you were yesterday, and becoming someone you couldn't even imagine tomorrow. But for that to happen, you have to accept that sometimes the ways that you think you're doing things right, quite frankly just are not. Accountability is the first stop on the road of growth. There's been a lot of missteps in understanding who I am since I was young until this day. And I'm okay with that. And at peace with it.

FRED: Porsche and I are imperfect, and I don't think that either of us came into this thinking that we were perfect, but I think that considering yourself not perfect and actively understanding that you are imperfect are two different things. We're all in progress. And I mean that in the truest sense of that statement. We are all on a road. We are all on a journey. We are all going, we're all coming. We are all leaving at all times. And I've come to realize as we've started talking about having children—and I never thought about having children before, but when I started thinking about wanting to be a parent and wanting to go on that journey with her, I realized that even when I'm gone, that won't be the end.

I might never meet my grandchildren's grandchildren, but they are a manifestation of everything that we have done and everything that we brought into this world. And therefore, I think that more people need to see that. You're not just your own progress. You are the progress of everybody that comes after you, as I'm the progress of everybody who came before me. We either stand on the shoulders of giants or we stand on the shoulders of nobody. And I think that the people reading this book, the people who are here, are all giants whose shoulders the future will stand upon.

THE DICTIONARY OF CHANGE

ableism: discrimination and societal prejudice toward people with disabilities and/or people who are considered to be disabled

ableist ideologies: views that are offensive to or disparaging of individuals with disabilities

ableist language: terminology that is offensive to individuals with disabilities; often terms that are disparaging, harsh, or unpleasant, such as *crazy*, "turn a blind eye," and "falls on deaf ears"

accomplices: people who takes action in support of oppressed communities rather than simply hoping for progress; the term is inspired by a line from Black feminist author Mikki Kendall about supporting Black people against racism: "We don't need allies, we need accomplices."

ACT: a standardized test used for college admissions in the United States (the acronym stands for the company that produces it, American College Testing); equivalent to the SAT (Scholastic Aptitude Test)

alt-right: a collection of far-right beliefs, organizations, and individuals that feel that "political correctness" and "social justice" are weakening white people and "their" culture

American exceptionalism: the belief that the United States is special and superior to other nations based on the country's values, history, and political system; this belief also implies that the United States is entitled to be a world leader and should be acknowledged as such by the rest of the world

anti-racism: a set of views, behaviors, and policies aimed at combating racial prejudice, structural racism, and the oppression of particular racial groups

anti-trans bills: proposed legislation intending to limit transgender people's legal rights

assets: anything of worth, or a resource of value that may be converted into cash

assimilation: the process by which a minority group or culture acquires (sometimes forcibly) the values, practices, and beliefs of another group, whether wholly or partially

baby boomers: people born between 1946 and 1964, during the post–World War II jump in the US birth rate

bailout: government provision of money and/or resources to a failing enterprise in order to help avoid the negative effects of the company's probable demise, which could include bankruptcy and financial collapse

bill: a proposed new piece of legislation

bond: a fixed-income security or investment; usually taken out by an individual from a borrower such as a company or the government; the borrower uses the investment to fund its operations

chattel slavery: the enslavement and ownership of human individuals and their offspring as property that can be purchased, sold, and compelled to work for no pay; used to distinguish ownership enslavement from other forms of forced, unpaid, or low-wage labor

cisgender: used to describe a person whose gender identity is the same as the sex they were assigned at birth

climate change: the shift in weather patterns due to the long-term global increase in temperatures; the main driver of this shift has been human activities, including the burning of fossil fuels such as coal, oil, and gas, which produces heat-trapping gases such as carbon dioxide and methane

climate deniers: people who refuse to acknowledge the science that proves the earth is warming and global climate is changing

climate refugees: people displaced due to climate change

CO_2: the abbreviation for carbon dioxide, a heavy, colorless atmospheric gas that occurs naturally and as a result of human activity; most animals (including humans), which exhale carbon dioxide as a waste product, are natural sources of carbon dioxide; carbon dioxide emissions that are caused by human activities come primarily from burning coal, oil, or natural gas for energy

coming out: a shortened form of the phrase "coming out of the closet," a metaphor for LGBTQ+ persons revealing their sexual orientation or gender identity for the first time. *See also* **in the closet**

communism: a political and economic ideology that promotes a classless society in which the means of production are collectively controlled and private property is either nonexistent or severely restricted

congressional caucus: a group of members of Congress who get together to work on common legislative goals

co-pay: a payment made up front (usually for health services) by an insurance policyholder in addition to the payment made by their insurance provider

cost of living: the amount of money required to pay for basic expenses such as housing, food, taxes, and health care; the cost of living is frequently used to compare the expense of living in different cities

couch surfing: staying temporarily in other people's homes, typically making use of improvised sleeping arrangements; often entails short stays in a series of homes

cultural genocide: the destruction of the culture of nations or ethnic groups by forcibly eradicating spiritual, national, and cultural practices and knowledge

cultural smog: subconscious exposure to misinformation based on stereotypes and prejudices; the term was coined by psychologist Dr. Beverly Daniel Tatum

debt-to-income ratio: the percentage of a person's gross monthly income that goes toward paying debts; this ratio is often used by lenders to determine the risk of loaning money to an individual

decriminalize: to remove or minimize the criminal categorization or status of a law

deductible: the amount of money an insurance policyholder must pay for services before an insurance company will pay a claim

disease prevention: targeted, population-based, and individual-based treatments for early detection of diseases with the goal of reducing impact and risk factors

disinformation: a type of propaganda that spreads incorrect information with the intent of deceiving people

doubled up: sharing the housing of friends, family, or anyone else due to loss of housing and/or economic hardship

draft: the mandatory enlistment of citizens in the armed services; since 1973, the United States military has not had a draft and has been entirely made up of volunteers

ESL: English as a Second Language; a language acquisition curriculum

emancipated: liberated from another's control, restraint, or authority

enrolled or **enrolled tribal citizen:** someone who is recognized as a member of a federally recognized Indigenous tribe or nation; each tribe or nation has the sovereign authority to define who their members are and who is eligible to be enrolled

Equality Act: a bill in Congress that, if passed, would expand the Civil Rights Act of 1964 to outlaw discrimination based on gender, sexual orientation, and gender identity in employment, housing, public accommodations, education, federally supported programs, credit, and jury service

equity: a sense of fairness or justice in the way people are treated

eugenics: the science of arranging reproduction in a human population to promote the incidence of the arranger's desired heritable qualities; developed primarily by Sir Francis Galton as a method of improving the human race, eugenics became increasingly discredited as unscientific and racially biased during the twentieth century, particularly after the Nazis adopted its doctrines to justify their treatment of Jewish people, disabled people, and other minority groups

FAFSA: Free Application for Federal Student Aid; used by colleges to make decisions regarding the distribution of student financial aid

far right: used to describe politics, ideologies, and beliefs that are more extreme than mainstream political conservatism, especially in terms of being anti-communist, authoritarian, ultranationalist, and often racist

fascism: a far-right, authoritarian ultranationalism that rose to popularity in early-twentieth-century Europe, marked by dictatorial control, brutal repression of opposition, and strong regimentation of society and the economy

fearmongering: attempting to scare people into believing, unreasonably, that something (such as a public policy) will cause them or others terrible harm

federally recognized tribal nations: Indigenous groups that have a government-to-government relationship with the United States; some tribal nations continue to seek federal recognition

financial aid: supplemental funding to an individual, usually used in relation to students enrolled in a post-secondary educational institution in the United States

financial capital: wealth (such as savings) that is available to be used to generate further wealth

financial crisis: a time of great instability and insecurity in the economy. *See also* **Great Recession**

garnish: to seize, by a legal procedure, some portion of a person's or company's earnings or capital for the payment of a debt

gaslight: to repeatedly present a false narrative that causes another person to doubt their own observations to the point of becoming confused and distressed

gender dysphoria: a feeling of anxiety caused by a mismatch between a person's biological sex and their gender identity; a sense of alienation from oneself that can have severe effects on a person's daily life and well-being

genderqueer: used to describe someone whose gender identity exists beyond the gender binary of male and female

genocide: the intentional murder of a large number of people from a specific nation, gender, class, or ethnic group with the goal of destroying that nation or group

gentrification: the process of wealthier people moving into an area, renovating housing, and luring new companies there; the result is that the character of the area is changed, costs are driven up, and existing residents are displaced

golden parachute: a large payment made to a company executive when they are dismissed, in lieu of their facing any sort of penalty

Great Recession: a significant economic slump that began in the United States in 2008 and resulted in a great deal of poverty and job and home loss; the downturn began when the housing market collapsed due to corrupt mortgage lending practices, causing many people to default on their home loans

green card: a permit that allows an immigrant to live and work permanently in the United States; it is officially known as a permanent resident card, and holders are known as lawful permanent residents or green card holders

gun-free zones: areas where unauthorized individuals are not allowed to carry firearms

gun sense candidate: someone running for political office who has committed to governing with gun safety in mind

HBCU: Historically Black College or University; a college or institution that was formed specifically to educate Black students

heterosexual: a person who is sexually and/or romantically attracted solely to people who are a different sex or gender from themselves

high-income countries: developed countries with a mature economy that are able to produce a large number of goods and have a technologically advanced infrastructure compared to other nations

high-interest loans: loans that charge a relatively large percentage of the amount borrowed; such loans are often difficult for the borrower to pay off

Hippocratic oath: a sworn statement outlining a doctor's responsibilities and proper behavior, once made by people entering medical practice

hoax: an act that is purposefully created to deceive or dupe others

housing projects: *See* **public housing**

ICE: Immigration and Customs Enforcement; a division of the US Department of Homeland Security

immigration raids: a practice in which immigration agents invade a space, unannounced, with the intention of finding and deporting people without legal immigration documentation

implicit bias: the assumed attribution of particular qualities to a person based on beliefs about a social group they belong to

in the closet: used to describe a person who wants or needs to hide their sexual orientation. *See also* **coming out**

institutionalization: placing a person in the full-time residential care of a specialized hospital or other institution

intersectional: involving the coexistence and/or collision of two or more experiences, identities, and/or elements

intersex: used to describe individuals born with any of various combinations of female and male sex traits, such as chromosomal patterns, gonads, or genitals

invisible illness and disability: a disabling chronic illness or condition that is not immediately obvious but often considerably affects a person's regular everyday activities

Jim Crow laws: state and local legislation that enforced racial segregation across the United States, especially in southern states

juvenile justice reform: improvements to laws, regulations, and practices relating to young people involved in the criminal system

K–12: kindergarten through twelfth grade

Land Back movement: a movement to return public lands to Indigenous peoples and increase their political decision-making power on a national level

Latinx: a gender-neutral alternative to *Latino* or *Latina*

lawful permanent resident: *See* **green card**

legal status: the standing of a person in relation to a national government; people may be citizens, permanent residents, temporary visa holders, undocumented persons, or fall under other designations

LGBTQ+: an inclusive initialism that encompasses lesbian, gay, bisexual, transgender, intersex, queer, questioning, and asexual

living wage: a wage that enables the earner to afford basic necessities such as rent, food, clothing, and transportation

lobbying: the process of attempting to influence the actions, policies, or decisions of government officials, most commonly legislators or members of regulatory agencies

lobbyist: a person who takes part in an organized attempt to influence the actions and beliefs of government officials

low-income housing: *See* **public housing**

marginalized group: a community that is excluded from mainstream social, economic, educational, and/or cultural life; groups may be excluded due to ethnicity, gender identity, sexual orientation, age, physical ability, language, immigration status, or other qualities

microaggression: an act that exhibits indirect, subtle, or inadvertent discrimination or bias against members of a marginalized group, such as a racial or ethnic minority

military-industrial complex: the enmeshed relationship between a country's military and the defense industry that supplies it and has a vested interest in influencing public policy and opinion

minimum wage: the least amount of money that a business can lawfully pay its workers

misgender: to refer to someone using a pronoun or a form of address that does not accurately reflect the gender with which the individual identifies

misinformation: information that is erroneous, inaccurate, or misleading but not necessarily intentionally so

misogyny: extreme negative feelings, including hate, disdain, or deep prejudice, toward women

Mothers Against Drunk Driving: a nonprofit that aims to put an end to drunk driving and impaired driving and provides support for those affected by drunk driving

National Rifle Association of America (NRA): a gun rights advocacy organization

net worth: the total wealth owned by a person, company, or household, based on all financial assets and liabilities

NGO: non-governmental organization; a non-profit organization that works on humanitarian and/or environmental causes around the world

nonbinary: used to describe someone whose gender identity or identities exist beyond the gender duality of male and female

oligarchs: wealthy business leaders, sometimes with criminal ties, who wield undue political influence

over-policing: maintaining more police presence than is necessary to keep the peace, often including forcefully responding to minor possible offenses

PAC: political action committee; formed to raise and spend funds in order to elect or defeat candidates

Pell grant: a federal stipend that is distributed based on financial necessity to students who are pursuing post-secondary education; these grants are not required to be repaid

per capita: per person

performative activism: activism done for the sake of increasing one's social capital rather than for the sake of a cause

permanent supportive housing: housing assistance that combines affordable housing with services to support the needs of chronically houseless people; services provided focus on building independence and might include resources such as addiction treatment, community reentry support, health care and disability assistance, or employment support

personal statement essay: an essay used for college admissions that explains why the applicant should be selected or gives perspective on the applicant's transcript

plea bargain: a response to a criminal charge by which the defendant accepts a lesser charge than the original one; plea bargains often place defendants in difficult situations, tempted to plead guilty to a lesser charge even if they aren't actually guilty of it in order to avoid the risk of a more serious charge

political ideologies: the ideals and principles of a group, such as a social movement, institution, class, or party, that reflect how members of that group feel society should function

political party: an organization that supports its candidates for elected office; members of a political party are likely to share views, and parties may also advocate for certain ideological or policy goals

premium: the price paid for health insurance

primaries: a process through which voters express their preference for a candidate from their political party in an upcoming general election, municipal election, or by-election

prison-industrial complex: the rapid growth of the inmate population in the United States under the political support of private prison companies and businesses that profit from supplying goods and services to the government and for-profit agencies

private loans: loans from a lending organization that is not controlled by federal government guidelines; such loans often entail higher interest rates and conditions that can be predatory, increasing the original debt by large amounts

private university: an institution for higher education that is not run or principally funded by a government entity

prognosis: the prediction or likelihood of an expected development of a disease

public defender: a state-assigned defense lawyer paid for by the public and provided when a criminal defendant cannot afford representation

public housing: housing subsidized by the government for eligible low-income families, elderly people, and people with disabilities; also called *housing projects* (or *projects*), *low-income housing*, or *subsidized housing*

public university: an institution for higher education that is funded and run by a government entity or receives substantial public funding

redlining: the practice of denying inhabitants of certain areas home loans or similar financial support due to their race or ethnicity; both a historical and current phenomenon

red-flag laws: gun control statutes that allow police or family members to petition a state court to have firearms temporarily removed from individuals who may pose a danger to others or themselves

reentry: transition into the community after serving a long prison sentence

regulatory bodies: government agencies charged with exercising power over a certain part of human activity in order to license and regulate it; the Food and Drug Administration is an example

rent control: a set of laws that aims to ensure the affordability of housing by regulating rent prices so that they don't increase drastically

reproductive health care: wellness services related to a person's reproductive and sexual organs and systems during all life stages

restitution: compensation paid to a victim by a criminal offender according to a court order for losses or injuries sustained as a result of the criminal offense

Sandy Hook: a shooting that occurred on December 14, 2012, at Sandy Hook Elementary School in Newtown, Connecticut, when twenty-year-old Adam Lanza shot and killed twenty-six people, including twenty children and six adult staff members

sanctuary cities or states: cities or states that limit cooperation with ICE and other federal efforts to enforce immigration laws

school-to-prison pipeline: the funneling of children, often those who are living in poverty and/or who are Black or Latinx and/or disabled, out of public schools and into the criminal justice systems rather than providing them with social services and other supports

segregation: the systematic division of people into racial or ethnic groupings, allowing only some groups to have access to certain places, services, or amenities

slave patrols: organized groups of armed men who tracked and captured enslaved people who attempted to escape from bondage

social capital: a person's or group's power or influence within social circles or in the general public sphere

social construct: a concept that is often assumed by people in a society to be innately true or fundamental but that has, rather, been developed, accepted, and perpetuated by a society's citizens

social safety net: social welfare programs that provide services and basic necessities to those in need

socialism: a political and economic framework by which society as a whole owns or manages the means of production, distribution, and exchange; the goal is to spread wealth evenly and build a society based on principles of fairness and equality

socioeconomic group: a grouping related to its members' social and economic rank or class; can take into account education, income, and occupation

"stand your ground" laws: laws that give individuals the right to use "reasonable force," including deadly force, to protect themselves from a perceived threat; originally intended to apply to the protection of one's home, these laws have expanded in scope to include things like parking lot disputes and have been challenged as inherently racist, given that immunity is granted overwhelmingly to white shooters of Black people

state legislatures: the groups responsible for enacting laws that apply to a state within the United States

subsidized housing: *See* **public housing**

systemic experiential reflections (SER): a term coined by Frederick Joseph that refers to portrayals of or responses to firsthand experiences of marginalized people within white supremacy, patriarchy, and other oppressive systems, often conveyed through art and/or storytelling

three-fifths of a human being: an agreement made during the 1787 United States Constitutional Convention that, for the purposes of determining a state's population, an enslaved person would be counted not as a full human being, but rather as three-fifths of a human being; the population counts would be used to determine how many seats in the House of Representatives each state would have and how much each state would pay in federal taxes

tolerance: used in relation to pain medication to mean that the medication becomes less effective over time; used in relation to pain to refer to the ability to put up with or accept physical discomfort with little outward expression

transphobia: beliefs and actions that include a variety of harmful and/or dangerous views, feelings, or behaviors toward transgender individuals

treaties: contractual agreements between two or more parties, usually sovereign states, that are formal and legally binding; in the United States, treaties are ratified by the Senate and considered the supreme law of the land, according to the US Constitution

treaty rights: already held, specific rights reserved by Native authorities as a result of negotiated and signed treaties with the United States; such rights often include hunting, fishing, gathering, and management of Native communities and resources

unionized health care: a system by which workers, represented by their trade union, negotiate health benefits with their employer; in this way, the workers have more power in decision making than if they were negotiating on their own and are committed to keeping health care expenses down

universal basic income (UBI): a system by which every adult citizen receives a predetermined amount of money on a regular basis from the government, with no exchange of labor or services

universal childcare: childcare and early learning paid for by the public, through use of taxes

universal health care: systems in which all residents have health insurance or access to health care for little to no cost

urban Indian: a Native American, Alaska Native, or Canadian First Nations individual who lives in a city setting

US-born citizen: someone who is entitled to US citizenship by virtue of the fact that they were born in this country

wealth: an abundance of available money and of financial assets and/or physical possessions that could be turned into cash

wealth gap: a wide difference between two groups' assets and net worth

white European colonizers: white European countries that gained full or partial governmental and societal authority over other nations and areas, forming colonies, filling them with settlers, and exploiting the areas and their people culturally and economically by violent means; some of the countries most known for colonization are England, Spain, Portugal, and France

white supremacy: the belief that white people are a superior race that should rule society, usually to the exclusion or disadvantage of other racial and ethnic groups, particularly Black and Jewish people

work study: a government-financed program that helps students pay for post-secondary education through on-campus employment

World War II: a global multi-front war waged from 1939 through 1945, involving all of the world's great powers, which formed two competing military alliances: the Allied forces and the Axis forces

SOURCE NOTES

1: Not All Information Is Created Equal

p. 2: When attempts were made to research the company . . . : Max Fisher, "Disinformation for Hire, a Shadow Industry, Is Quietly Booming," *New York Times*, July 26, 2021, www.nytimes.com/2021/07/25/world/europe /disinformation-social-media.html.

p. 15: the first disinformation department existed in Russia as far back as 1923: Marko Mihkelson, "Disinformation: Russia's Old but Effective Weapon of Influence," International Centre for Defense and Security, June 16, 2017, icds.ee/en/disinformation-russias-old-but-effective-weapon-of-influence.

2: We're the Planeteers; You Can Be One, Too

p. 30: one of the deadliest hurricanes in US history: Eric S. Blake, Christopher W. Landsea, and Ethan J. Gibney, "The Deadliest, Costliest, and Most Intense United States Tropical Cyclones from 1851 to 2010," National Oceanographic and Atmospheric Administration, August 2011, https://www.nhc.noaa.gov /pdf/nws-nhc-6.pdf.

p. 35: up to thirty thousand New Orleans residents had sought shelter in the Superdome: Christine Rushton, "Timeline: Hurricane Katrina and the Aftermath," *USA Today*, August 28, 2015, usatoday.com/story/news /nation/2015/08/24/timeline-hurricane-katrina-and-aftermath/32003013.

p. 36: "To listen to politicians thanking . . . who are very upset": quoted in Elizabeth Jensen, "An Anchor Who Reports Disaster News with a Heart on His Sleeve," *New York Times*, September 12, 2005, www.nytimes.com/2005 /09/12/arts/television/an-anchor-who-reports-disaster-news-with-a-heart -on-his.html.

p. 37: an action the chief of police continued to defend: John Burnett, "Evacuees Were Turned Away at Gretna, La.," *Morning Edition*, NPR, September 20, 2005, https://www.npr.org/templates/story/story .php?storyId=4855611.

p. 37: nearly a hundred thousand people: Sarah Pruitt, "How Levee Failures Made Hurricane Katrina a Bigger Disaster," History.com, August 27, 2020, www.history.com/news/hurricane-katrina-levee-failures.

p. 38: The communities that were affected the worst were the Black neighborhoods . . . : Gary Rivlin, "White New Orleans Has Recovered from Hurricane Katrina. Black New Orleans Has Not," Talk Poverty, August 29, 2016, talkpoverty.org/2016/08/29/white-new-orleans-recovered-hurricane -katrina-black-new-orleans-not.

p. 38: the 2020 Atlantic hurricane season was the most active recorded to date: "2020 Atlantic Hurricane Season Takes Infamous Top Spot for Busiest on Record," National Oceanic and Atmospheric Administration, November 10, 2020, www.noaa.gov/news/2020-atlantic-hurricane-season-takes-infamous -top-spot-for-busiest-on-record.

p. 39: During the Great Mississippi Flood in 1927 . . . : John Barry, *Rising Tide: The Great Mississippi Flood of 1927 and How It Changed America* (New York: Simon & Schuster, 2007).

p. 39: During Hurricane Betsy in 1965 . . . : "Hurricane Betsy," Louisiana State University Libraries, Research Guides: Louisiana Hurricanes, updated April 21, 2021, guides.lib.lsu.edu/Hurricanes/Betsy.

p. 41: 27 million acres, an area larger than Portugal: Brian Resnick, Umair

Irfan, and Sigal Samuel, "Eight Things Everyone Should Know about Australia's Wildfire Disaster," *Vox*, updated January 22, 2020, https://www.vox .com/science-and-health/2020/1/8/21055228/australia-fires-map-animals -koalas-wildlife-smoke-donate.

p. 42: hundreds of millions of people will be permanently displaced by the rising sea levels: Scott A. Kulp and Benjamin H. Strauss, "New Elevation Data Triple Estimates of Global Vulnerability to Sea-Level Rise and Coastal Flooding," *Nature Communications* 10 (October 2019), www.nature.com /articles/s41467-019-12808-z.

p. 42: most parts of densely populated Shanghai, China, are expected to be covered in water in the next thirty years: Denise Lu and Christopher Flavelle, "Rising Seas Will Erase More Cities by 2050, New Research Shows," *New York Times*, October 29, 2019, https://www.nytimes.com/interactive/2019/10/29 /climate/coastal-cities-underwater.html.

p. 46: Texas senator Ted Cruz left Texas during a deadly winter storm in 2021: "Texas Senator Ted Cruz Flew to Cancun, Mexico, amid Weather Crisis," BBC News, February 19, 2021, www.bbc.com/news/world-us-canada-56117800.

p. 49: almost 90 percent of the drinking water was imported from Northern California and the Colorado River: "Water Supply," City of San Diego, www .sandiego.gov/public-utilities/sustainability/water-supply.

p. 50: the Flint River has been heavily polluted and poisoned for over a century: Tim Carmody, "How the Flint River Got So Toxic," *The Verge*, February 26, 2016, www.theverge.com/2016/2/26/11117022/flint-michigan -water-crisis-lead-pollution-history.

p. 50: residents were complaining of smelly, poor-tasting, and discolored water: Melissa Denchak, "Flint Water Crisis: Everything You Need to Know," NRDC, November 8, 2018, www.nrdc.org/stories/flint-water-crisis -everything-you-need-know.

p. 50: "Exposure to lead . . . children has been identified": "Prevent Children's

Exposure to Lead," Centers for Disease Control and Prevention, National Center for Environmental Health, https://www.cdc.gov/nceh/features /leadpoisoning/index.html.

p. 51: more than thirty million Americans drink water that is in violation of safety rules: Justin Worland, "America's Clean Water Crisis Goes Far Beyond Flint. There's No Relief in Sight," *Time*, February 20, 2020, time.com /longform/clean-water-access-united-states.

p. 52: the negligent governmental response to the Flint water contamination was a "result of systemic racism": "The Flint Water Crisis: Systemic Racism Through the Lens of Flint," Report of the Michigan Civil Rights Commission, February 17, 2017, www.michigan.gov/documents/mdcr/VFlintCrisisRep-F -Edited3-13-17_554317_7.pdf#page30.

p. 52: for more than two million Americans . . . : Frances Stead Sellers, "It's Almost 2020, and 2 Million Americans Still Don't Have Running Water, According to New Report," *Washington Post*, December 11, 2019, https://www .washingtonpost.com/national/its-almost-2020-and-2-million-americans -still-dont-have-running-water-new-report-says/2019/12/10/a0720e8a-14b3 -11ea-a659-7d69641c6ff7_story.html.

3: Sledgehammers and Glass Ceilings

p. 85: women earn an average of 82 cents for every dollar a man makes: Robin Bleiweis, "Quick Facts About the Gender Wage Gap," Center for American Progress, March 24, 2020, https://www.americanprogress.org/issues/women /reports/2020/03/24/482141/quick-facts-gender-wage-gap/.

p. 85: Globally, sixty-two million girls are denied education: "Let Girls Learn," USAID, www.usaid.gov/sites/default/files/documents/1869/USAID_LGL _FactSheet.pdf.

p. 85: in 2021, only twenty-four countries around the world had a woman as the country's leader: "Facts and Figures: Women's Leadership and Political

Participation," UN Women, updated January 15, 2021, www.unwomen.org /en/what-we-do/leadership-and-political-participation/facts-and-figures# _edn7.

p. 85: ten countries in the world . . . give equal legal rights to men and women: "Women, Business and the Law 2021," World Bank, 2021, www.worldbank .org/content/dam/sites/wbl/documents/2021/02/WBL2021_ENG_v2.pdf.

p. 85: A study done between 2010 and 2013 showed that for every female character in films, there were 2.24 male characters: Dr. Stacy L. Smith, Marc Choueiti, and Dr. Katherine Pieper, "Gender Bias without Borders," Geena Davis Institute on Gender in Media, 2014, seejane.org/wp-content/uploads /gender-bias-without-borders-full-report.pdf.

p. 85: Of forty-one studied countries, the United States is the only one that does not provide any form of paid maternity leave by federal law: Gretchen Livingston and Deja Thomas, "Among 41 Countries, Only U.S. Lacks Paid Parental Leave," Pew Research Center, December 16, 2019, www.pewresearch .org/fact-tank/2019/12/16/u-s-lacks-mandated-paid-parental-leave.

4: Let Them Eat Cake

p. 96: about 45 percent of businesses fail altogether in the first five years: Michael T. Deane, "Top 6 Reasons New Businesses Fail," *Investopedia*, February 28, 2020, www.investopedia.com/financial-edge/1010/top-6-reasons-new -businesses-fail.aspx.

p. 97: there is no place anywhere in America where a full-time minimum- wage worker can afford to rent a two-bedroom home, and in only 7 *percent* of counties . . . : "Out of Reach: The High Cost of Housing," National Low Income Housing Coalition, 2021, 4, nlihc.org/sites/default/files/oor/2021/Out-of -Reach_2021.pdf.

p. 97: minimum wage has increased by only about two dollars per hour . . . :

"History of Changes to the Minimum Wage Law," US Department of Labor, 2020, www.dol.gov/agencies/whd/minimum-wage/history.

p. 98: When adjusted for inflation, being paid $7.25 an hour in 2021 is like being paid $5.70 per hour in 2009: "Why a Dollar Today Is Worth Only 78 Percent of a Dollar in 2009," Inflation Calculator, updated September 14, 2021, https://www.in2013dollars.com/us/inflation/2009?amount=1.

p. 98: the majority of minimum-wage workers adults who work full-time . . . : "Low-Wage Workers Are Older Than You Think: 88 Percent of Workers Who Would Benefit from a Higher Minimum Wage Are Older Than 20, One Third Are Over 40," Economic Policy Institute, 2013, www.epi.org/publication/wage-workers-older-88-percent-workers-benefit.

pp. 98–99: half of all people in the entire country share less than 2 *percent* of the nation's wealth: "Distribution of Household Wealth in the U.S. since 1989," Federal Reserve, updated October 1, 2021, www.federalreserve.gov/releases/z1/dataviz/dfa/distribute/chart.

p. 99: on average, white families have *ten times* the wealth of their Black counterparts: Kriston McIntosh, Emily Moss, Ryan Nunn, and Jay Shambaugh, "Examining the Black-White Wealth Gap," Brookings Institution, February 27, 2020, www.brookings.edu/blog/up-front/2020/02/27/examining-the-black-white-wealth-gap.

p. 99: *six times* as much as Latinx families: Neil Bhutta, Andrew C. Chang, Lisa J. Dettling, and Joanne W. Hsu, "Disparities in Wealth by Race and Ethnicity in the 2019 Survey of Consumer Finances," FEDS Notes, Board of Governors of the Federal Reserve System, September 28, 2020, https://www.federalreserve.gov/econres/notes/feds-notes/disparities-in-wealth-by-race-and-ethnicity-in-the-2019-survey-of-consumer-finances-20200928.htm.

p. 100: according to the Federal Reserve, in 2016 the average homeowner . . . : Jesse Bricker et al., "Changes in U.S. Family Finances from 2013 to 2016:

Evidence from the Survey of Consumer Finances." *Federal Reserve Bulletin* 103, no. 3 (September 2017): 13, doi:10.17016/bulletin.2017.103-3.

p. 100: Black applicants are denied by mortgage lenders at a rate 80 percent higher than white applicants: Diana Olick, "A Troubling Tale of a Black Man Trying to Refinance His Mortgage," CNBC, August 19, 2020, www.cnbc.com/2020/08/19/lenders-deny-mortgages-for-blacks-at-a-rate-80percent-higher-than-whites.html.

p. 100: Homes in neighborhoods that are non-white are valued much lower . . . : Courtney Connley, "Why the Homeownership Gap between White and Black Americans Is Larger Today Than It Was over 50 Years Ago," CNBC, August 21, 2020, www.cnbc.com/2020/08/21/why-the-homeownership-gap-between-white-and-black-americans-is-larger-today-than-it-was-over-50-years-ago.html.

p. 102: the United States actually spends more per capita on health care than any other industrialized country in the world: "Healthcare Spending: International Comparison," Peter G. Peterson Foundation, July 7, 2020, www.pgpf.org/chart-archive/0170_international_health_spending_comparison.

p. 103: Reducing or forgiving student loan debt would also be meaningful for people who are struggling to make ends meet: Elizabeth Warren, "I'm Calling for Something Truly Transformational: Universal Free Public College and Cancellation of Student Loan Debt, " *Medium*, April 22, 2019, https://medium.com/@teamwarren/im-calling-for-something-truly-transformational-universal-free-public-college-and-cancellation-of-a246cd0f910f.

pp. 103–104: the group who received the payments found more full-time work . . . : Rachel Treisman, "California Program Giving $500 No-Strings-Attached Stipends Pays Off, Study Finds," NPR, March 4, 2021, https://www.npr.org/2021/03/04/973653719/california-program-giving-500-no-strings-attached-stipends-pays-off-study-finds.

p. 107: If a person works full-time . . . $13,000: Dani Arbuckle, "The Tax Rates

for Minimum Wage," Bizfluent, updated September 26, 2017, bizfluent.com
/info-7890463-tax-rates-minimum-wage.html.

p. 107: The average annual rent in America is $9,477: Sterling Price, "Average
Household Budget," ValuePenguin, April 26, 2021, www.valuepenguin.com
/average-household-budget#housing.

p. 108: a woman in the United States makes only 82 cents for every one dollar
a man makes . . . : Robin Bleiweis, "Quick Facts about the Gender Wage Gap,"
Center for American Progress, March 24, 2020, https://www
.americanprogress.org/issues/women/reports/2020/03/24/482141/quick
-facts-gender-wage-gap.

p. 108: over a forty-year career, a Latinx woman is paid over $1 million less
than a white man: LySaundra Campbell, "Latinas Lose More Than $1.1 Million
over a 40-Year Career Due to Wage Gap, New NWLC Analysis Shows," National
Women's Law Center, November 14, 2019, nwlc.org/press-releases/latinas
-lose-more-than-1-1-million-over-a-40-year-career-due-to-wage-gap-new
-nwlc-analysis-shows.

p. 108: The gap is even wider for transgender women: Jamie Wareham,
"Transgender Pay Gap Revealed: Cisgender People Paid 32 Percent
More," *Forbes*, November 17, 2021, https://www.forbes.com/sites/
jamiewareham/2021/11/17/transgender-pay-gap-revealed-cisgender-people
-paid-32-more/?sh=1edf601217b2.

p. 117: *forty million* Americans live in poverty: "Poverty Estimates, Trends,
and Analysis," US Department of Health and Human Services, Office of the
Assistant Secretary for Planning and Evaluation, aspe.hhs.gov/topics/poverty
-economic-mobility/poverty-estimates-trends-analysis.

5: We Shouldn't Be Afraid to Leave Home

p. 129: As of 2018, there were over 393 *million* guns in civilian hands in
America . . . more than 40 percent of guns: Aaron Karp, "Estimating Global

Civilian-Held Firearms Numbers," Small Arms Survey, June 2018, 4, www
.smallarmssurvey.org/sites/default/files/resources/SAS-BP-Civilian-Firearms
-Numbers.pdf.

p. 130: More than 300 people are shot in America every single day . . . : Brady
Campaign to Prevent Gun Violence, "Resources: Key Statistics," https://www
.bradyunited.org/key-statistics.

pp. 130–131: Black Americans experience ten times the gun homicides . . . :
"Impact of Gun Violence on Black Americans," Everytown for Gun Safety,
everytownresearch.org/issue/gun-violence-black-americans.

p. 134: much of it is also supported by the majority of Americans, including
gun owners: "Majority of Americans, Including Gun Owners, Support a
Variety of Gun Policies," Johns Hopkins Bloomberg School of Public Health,
September 9, 2019, publichealth.jhu.edu/2019/majority-of-americans
-including-gun-owners-support-a-variety-of-gun-policies.

6: You Can't Discover a Place If People Are Already There

p. 145: "Nation, race, and class converged in land": David A. Chang,
*The Color of the Land : Race, Nation, and the Politics of Landownership in Oklahoma,
1832–1929* (Chapel Hill: University of North Carolina Press, 2010), 7.

p. 151: "the story that Disney tells is a complete lie": Vincent Schilling, "The
True Story of Pocahontas: Historical Myths Versus Sad Reality," *Indian Country
Today*, updated September 13, 2018, indiancountrytoday.com/archive/true
-story-pocahontas-historical-myths-versus-sad-reality.

p. 152: Along the journey, they cover up to three hundred miles: Crystal Paul, "30
Years after the Paddle to Seattle, Tribal Canoe Journeys Represent Healing and
Revival," *Seattle Times*, August 11, 2019, www.seattletimes.com/life/30-years
-after-the-paddle-to-seattle-tribal-canoe-journeys-represent-healing-and-revival.

p. 155: In 2021, 751 unmarked grave sites were discovered: Nora McGreevy,
"751 Unmarked Graves Discovered Near Former Indigenous School in

Canada," *Smithsonian*, June 28, 2021, www.smithsonianmag.com/smart
-news/751-unmarked-graves-discovered-near-former-indigenous-school
-canada-180978064.

p. 155: "cultural genocide": quoted in Ian Austen, "Canada's Grim Legacy of
Cultural Erasure, in Poignant School Photos," *New York Times*, July 30, 2021,
www.nytimes.com/2021/07/05/world/canada/Indigenous-residential
-schools-photos.html.

p. 162: The government promised that the land the Cherokee were relocated
to would be untouched . . . : "Trail of Tears," History.com, updated July 7,
2020, www.history.com/topics/native-american-history/trail-of-tears.

p. 167: a shameful history of violating every treaty it has signed with
Indigenous peoples: Vine Deloria Jr., *Custer Died for Your Sins: An Indian
Manifesto* (Norman: University of Oklahoma Press, 1988), 28.

p. 173: Native Americans have been in North America for at least fifteen
thousand years: Simon Worrall, "When, How Did the First Americans Arrive?
It's Complicated," *National Geographic*, June 9, 2018, https://www
.nationalgeographic.com/science/article/when-and-how-did-the-first
-americans-arrive--its-complicated-.

p. 174: In 2020, Donald Trump revoked reservation status . . . : Rory Taylor,
"Trump Administration Revokes Reservation Status for the Mashpee
Wampanoag Tribe amid Coronavirus Crisis," *Vox*, April 2, 2020, www.vox
.com/identities/2020/4/2/21204113/mashpee-wampanoag-tribe-trump
-reservation-native-land.

7: Black Squares Don't Save Lives

p. 182: policing in America began as an evolution of slave patrols: K. B. Turner,
David Giacopassi, and Margaret Vandiver, "Ignoring the Past: Coverage of
Slavery and Slave Patrols in Criminal Justice Texts," *Journal of Criminal Justice
Education* 17, no. 1 (2006): 181–195, doi:10.1080/10511250500335627.

p. 186: Nearly 80 percent of public-school teachers are white: "New Report Presents Data on the Race and Ethnicity of Public School Teachers," *Journal of Blacks in Higher Education*, September 28, 2020, www.jbhe.com/2020/09/new -report-presents-data-on-the-race-and-ethnicity-of-public-school-teachers.

p. 186: more than 50 percent of students in the United States are non-white: "Fast Facts: Back-to-School Statistics," National Center for Education Statistics, nces.ed.gov/fastfacts/display.asp?id=372.

p. 192: Black people and Native Americans have the highest rates of poverty in the United States: "Poverty Rate in the United States in 2020, by Ethnic Group," Statista, January 20, 2021, www.statista.com/statistics/200476/us -poverty-rate-by-ethnic-group.

p. 192: Many of the companies that sold these policies are still well known today . . . : "California Department of Insurance Slavery Era Insurance Registry Report to the California Legislature," California Department of Insurance, May 2002, www.insurance.ca.gov/01-consumers/150-other -prog/10-seir/upload/Slavery-Report.pdf.

p. 196: "Until the lions produce . . . only the hunter": Chinua Achebe, *Home and Exile* (Oxford: Oxford University Press, 2000), 73.

pp. 199–200: "If you stick a knife . . . admit the knife is there": quoted in Saladin Ambar, *Malcolm X at Oxford Union* (Oxford: Oxford University Press, 2014), 122.

8: The More You Know!

p. 201: today Black women are one of the most educated groups in America: Rachaelle Davis, "New Study Shows Black Women Are Among the Most Educated Group in the United States," *Essence*, October 27, 2020, www .essence.com/news/new-study-black-women-most-educated/.

p. 205: Some families pay up to $10,000 for courses . . . : James Wellemeyer, "Wealthy Parents Spend up to $10,000 on SAT Prep for Their Kids," *MarketWatch*, July 7, 2019, www.marketwatch.com/story/some

-wealthy-parents-are-dropping-up-to-10000-on-sat-test-prep-for-their
-kids-2019-06-21.

p. 207: Tanya McDowell, . . . charged with first-degree larceny for "stealing" an
education: Rick Green, "'Stealing' an Education for Her Son," *Hartford Courant*,
April 26, 2011, https://www.courant.com/news/connecticut/hc-xpm-2011
-04-26-hc-green-homeless-0426-20110425-story.html.

p. 207: Kelley Williams-Bolar . . . children in a better school district: Andrea
Canning and Leezel Tanglao, "Ohio Mom Kelley Williams-Bolar Jailed for
Sending Kids to Better School District," ABC News, January 25, 2011, https:
//abcnews.go.com/US/ohio-mom-jailed-sending-kids-school-district
/story?id=12763654.

p. 207: high-quality early education can be a huge factor in how individuals
perform in the workforce and on their economic prospects: Anthea Lipsett,
"Early Schooling Matters Most for Children," *Guardian*, November 27, 2008,
www.theguardian.com/education/2008/nov/27/primary-school-importance.

p. 207: Predominantly white school districts receive $23 billion more in
state and local funding . . . : Laura Meckler, "Report Finds $23 Billion Racial
Funding Gap for Schools," *Washington Post*, February 26, 2019, www
.washingtonpost.com/local/education/report-finds-23-billion-racial-funding
-gap-for-schools/2019/02/25/d562b704-3915-11e9-a06c-3ec8ed509d15
_story.html.

p. 207: Although less than 2 percent of the nation's students attend private
schools . . . : Scott Jaschik, "Do Top Colleges Favor Applicants Who Are
Extremely Wealthy?" *Inside Higher Ed*, March 22, 2021, www.insidehighered
.com/admissions/article/2021/03/22/do-top-colleges-favor-applicants-who
-are-extremely-wealthy.

p. 209: the average cost of tuition and fees . . . almost $23,000 per year: Farran
Powell, Emma Kerr, and Sarah Wood, "See the Average College Tuition in
2021–2022," *U.S. News and World Report*, September 13, 2021, www.usnews

.com/education/best-colleges/paying-for-college/articles/paying-for-college
-infographic.

p. 215: The United States has $1.5 trillion in federal student loan debt: Ben
Miller et al., "Addressing the $1.5 Trillion in Federal Student Loan Debt,"
Center for American Progress, June 12, 2019, https://www.americanprogress
.org/issues/education-postsecondary/reports/2019/06/12/470893
/addressing-1-5-trillion-federal-student-loan-debt/.

p. 215: women make almost 20 percent less than men: Shawn M. Carter, "The
Gender Pay Gap in the US Is Still 20 Percent—but Millennial Women Are
Closing In on Men," CNBC, August 7, 2017, https://www.cnbc.com
/2017/08/07/gender-pay-gap-is-still-20-percent-but-millennial-women
-are-closing-in.html.

p. 216: Black students have nearly *86 percent* more debt . . . : Richard Pallardy,
"Racial Disparities in Student Loan Debt," Saving for College, August 27,
2019, https://www.savingforcollege.com/article/racial-disparities-in-student
-loan-debt.

p. 216: almost half of all Black students defaulted on their student loans . . . :
Robert Kelchen, "New Data on Long-Term Student Loan Default Rates,"
Robert Kelchen (blog), October 6, 2017, robertkelchen.com/2017/10/06/new
-data-on-long-term-student-loan-default-rates.

p. 219: But what about the disproportionate ways that education is accessed . . . :
"High-Quality Preschool Can Support Healthy Development and Learning,"
Child Trends, April 30, 2018, www.childtrends.org/publications/high-quality
-preschool-can-support-healthy-development-and-learning.

9: The Heteronormative Agenda

p. 236: Modern science contradicts the notion that sexuality is in some way
a choice: A. Sanders et al., "Genome-wide Scan Demonstrates Significant
Linkage for Male Sexual Orientation," *Psychological Medicine* 45, no. 7 (May
2015): 1379–1388, doi:10.1017/S0033291714002451.

p. 236: Plenty of other animals practice homosexuality . . . : "1,500 Animal Species Practice Homosexuality," News-Medical.Net, October 23, 2006, www .news-medical.net/news/2006/10/23/1500-animal-species-practice -homosexuality.aspx.

p. 238: young people in the LGBTQ+ community are three and a half times more likely to attempt suicide: Ester di Giacomo, MD, et al., "Estimating the Risk of Attempted Suicide among Sexual Minority Youths: A Systematic Review and Meta-analysis," *JAMA Pediatrics* 172, no. 12 (2018): 1145–1152, jamanetwork.com/journals/jamapediatrics/article-abstract/2704490.

p. 238: 76 percent of LGBTQ+ youth felt that the political climate . . . sense of self: "National Survey on LGBTQ Youth Mental Health 2019," Trevor Project, www.thetrevorproject.org/wp-content/uploads/2019/06/The-Trevor-Project -National-Survey-Results-2019.pdf.

p. 246: only 30 of the 195 countries in the world have legalized same-sex marriage . . . : "Marriage Equality Around the World," Human Rights Campaign, www.hrc.org/resources/marriage-equality-around-the-world.

p. 247: seventy-one countries still have laws making same-sex relationships illegal: "71 Countries Where Homosexuality Is Illegal," Erasing 76 Crimes, updated March 2021, 76crimes.com/76-countries-where-homosexuality -is-illegal.

p. 247: in eleven of those countries, the death penalty may be imposed for same-sex acts: "Map of Countries That Criminalise LGBT People," Human Dignity Trust, www.humandignitytrust.org/lgbt-the-law/map-of-criminalisation.

10: The Price of Life

p. 250: Diabetes is fairly common in America . . . : "New CDC Report: More Than 100 Million Americans Have Diabetes or Prediabetes," Centers for Disease Control and Prevention, CDC Newsroom, July 18, 2017, www.cdc.gov /media/releases/2017/p0718-diabetes-report.html.

pp. 250–251: 28.9 million people in America lack health insurance: Jennifer Tolbert, Kendal Orgera, and Anthony Damico, "Key Facts about the Uninsured Population," Kaiser Family Foundation, November 6, 2020, www.kff.org /uninsured/issue-brief/key-facts-about-the-uninsured-population.

p. 251: 4.3 million of that number being children: Edward R. Berchick and Laryssa Mykyta, "Uninsured Rate for Children Up to 5.5 Percent in 2018," US Census Bureau, September 10, 2019, www.census.gov/library/stories /2019/09/uninsured-rate-for-children-in-2018.html.

p. 254: which can lead doctors to undertreat their Black patients for pain: Kelly M. Hoffman et al., "Racial Bias in Pain Assessment and Treatment Recommendations, and False Beliefs about Biological Differences between Blacks and Whites," *Proceedings of the National Academy of Sciences* 113, no. 16 (April 2016): 4296–4301, doi:10.1073/pnas.1516047113.

p. 254: non-white people and women receive inferior health care: Khiara M. Bridges, "Implicit Bias and Racial Disparities in Health Care," American Bar Association, *Human Rights* 43, no. 3 (August 1, 2018), www.americanbar.org /groups/crsj/publications/human_rights_magazine_home/the-state-of -healthcare-in-the-united-states/racial-disparities-in-health-care.

pp. 254–255: Black women are more than three times more likely to die while pregnant or giving birth than white women: Gianna Melillo, "Racial Disparities Persist in Maternal Morbidity, Mortality and Infant Health," *AJMC: American Journal for Managed Care*, June 13, 2020, www.ajmc.com/view/racial-disparities- persist-in-maternal-morbidity-mortality-and-infant-health.

p. 255: "racial and ethnic minorities receive . . . conditions are comparable": quoted in Khiara M. Bridges, "Implicit Bias and Racial Disparities in Health Care," American Bar Association, *Human Rights* 43, no. 3 (August 1, 2018), www .americanbar.org/groups/crsj/publications/human_rights_magazine_home /the-state-of-healthcare-in-the-united-states/racial-disparities-in-health-care.

p. 256: Those who participated in their employers' medical plans contributed, on average, nearly $7,000: "Average Employee Medical Premium $6,797 for Family Coverage in 2020," US Bureau of Labor Statistics, TED: The Economics Daily, October 2, 2020, www.bls.gov/opub/ted/2020/average-employee -medical-premium-6797-dollars-for-family-coverage-in-2020.htm.

p. 256: the median household income is less than $70,000: Jessica Semega et al., "Income and Poverty in the United States: 2019," US Census Bureau, September 15, 2020, www.census.gov/library/publications/2020/demo/p60 -270.html.

p. 258: More than twenty-six thousand people die each year in the United States because they don't have insurance . . . : Janice Hopkins Tanne, "More than 26,000 Americans Die Each Year Because of Lack of Health Insurance," *British Medical Journal* 336, no. 7649 (April 2008): 855, doi:10.1136 /bmj.39549.693981.db.

p. 258: the leading cause of bankruptcy: Kimberly Amadeo, "Do Medical Bills Really Bankrupt America's Families?" *The Balance*, April 30, 2021, www .thebalance.com/medical-bankruptcy-statistics-4154729.

p. 259: Other countries successfully provide health care to their citizens . . . : Nisha Kurani and Cynthia Cox, "What Drives Health Spending in the U.S. Compared to Other Countries," Peterson-KFF Health System Tracker, September 25, 2020, www.healthsystemtracker.org/brief/what-drives-health -spending-in-the-u-s-compared-to-other-countries.

p. 259: A CT scan . . . costs less than $100 in Canada but nearly $900 in the United States: Richard Knox, "Why Are U.S. Health Costs the World's Highest? Study Affirms 'It's the Prices, Stupid,'" WBUR News, March 13, 2018, www .wbur.org/news/2018/03/13/us-health-costs-high-jha.

p. 259: EpiPens . . . cost around $600, compared to $69 for the same medicine in the United Kingdom: Lydia Ramsey Pflanzer, "The EpiPen Costs 88% Less in the UK than in the US," *Business Insider*, September 29, 2016,

www.businessinsider.com/why-the-us-has-such-high-drug-prices-2016
-9?international=true&r=US&IR=T.

p. 259: the United States is consistently ranked low when it comes to
health outcomes: Roosa Tikkanen and Melinda K. Abrams, "U.S. Health
Care from a Global Perspective, 2019: Higher Spending, Worse Outcomes?"
Commonwealth Fund, January 30, 2020, www.commonwealthfund.org
/publications/issue-briefs/2020/jan/us-health-care-global-perspective-2019.

p. 260: New Zealand . . . has one of the highest life expectancy rates . . . : "Life
Expectancy at Birth, Total (Years) - New Zealand," World Bank, data
.worldbank.org/indicator/SP.DYN.LE00.IN?locations=NZ.

p. 261: a $1.1 trillion industry in the United States: "Health & Medical
Insurance in the US - Market Size 2005–2027," IBIS World, updated April 26,
2021, www.ibisworld.com/industry-statistics/market-size/health-medical
-insurance-united-states.

p. 261: the highest-paid health insurance CEO made $25 million . . . : Paige
Minemyer, "Centene CEO Neidorff Raked in Nearly $25M Last Year. Take a
Look What Other Insurance Execs Earned," Fierce Healthcare, May 3, 2021,
www.fiercehealthcare.com/payer/centene-ceo-michael-neidorff-raked-nearly
-25m-last-year-take-a-look-what-other-insurance.

p. 263: 70 percent of people living in the United States describe our current
health care system . . . : Justin McCarthy, "Seven in 10 Maintain Negative
View of U.S. Healthcare System," Gallup, January 14, 2019, news.gallup.com
/poll/245873/seven-maintain-negative-view-healthcare-system.aspx.

p. 264: which provides health insurance to about sixty-five thousand union
members and dependents: Elaine Low, "'Shocked, Hurt and Angry': SAG-AFTRA
Health Plan Overhaul Spotlights Broken U.S. System," *Variety*, August 20,
2020, variety.com/2020/tv/news/sag-aftra-health-plan-insurance
-changes-1234741151.

p. 266: the majority of Americans believe . . . health care coverage for all: Bradley Jones, "Increasing Share of Americans Favor a Single Government Program to Provide Health Care Coverage," Pew Research Center, September 29, 2020, www.pewresearch.org/fact-tank/2020/09/29/increasing-share -of-americans-favor-a-single-government-program-to-provide-health-care -coverage.

p. 271: Nearly one in five US adults experience mental illness each year: "Mental Health by the Numbers," National Alliance on Mental Illness, March 2021, www.nami.org/mhstats.

p. 271: more than 43 percent of adults are uninsured or underinsured . . . : "U.S. Health Insurance Coverage in 2020: A Looming Crisis in Affordability," Commonwealth Fund, August 19, 2020, www.commonwealthfund.org /publications/issue-briefs/2020/aug/looming-crisis-health-coverage-2020 -biennial.

11: You, Me, Us, Them

p. 292: In 2020, forty-four transgender or gender-nonconforming Americans were murdered . . . : "Fatal Violence against the Transgender and Gender Non-Conforming Community in 2021," Human Rights Campaign, accessed September 17, 2021, https://www.hrc.org/resources/fatal-violence-against -the-transgender-and-gender-non-conforming-community-in-2021.

p. 292: there were more than one hundred anti-trans bills introduced in state legislatures: Ivette Feliciano, "Pride: 2021 Has Set a Record in Anti-trans Bills in America," *PBS News Hour Weekend*, June 6, 2021, https://www.pbs.org /newshour/show/pride-2021-has-set-a-record-in-anti-trans-bills-in-america.

p. 296: "we have more trans people per capita in DC than anywhere else in the country": "LGBT Data and Demographics: District of Columbia," UCLA School of Law, Williams Institute, https://williamsinstitute.law.ucla.edu/visualization /lgbt-stats/?topic=LGBT&area=11#demographic.

12: Home Is Where the Rent Is (or Isn't)

p. 316: more than four million children and young adults experience houselessness each year: "Youth Homelessness Overview," National Conference of State Legislatures, www.ncsl.org/research/human-services /homeless-and-runaway-youth.aspx.

p. 316: one in every ten people age eighteen to twenty-five experience houselessness every year: M. H. Morton, A. Dworsky, and G. M. Samuels, *Missed Opportunities: Youth Homelessness in America: National Estimates* (Chicago: Chapin Hall at the University of Chicago, 2017), https://voicesofyouthcount .org/brief/national-estimates-of-youth-homelessness/.

p. 318: it costs less to house people than it does to police them . . . : Matthew Yglesias, "Giving Homes to the Homeless Is Cheaper Than Leaving Them on the Streets," *Vox*, February 20, 2019, www.vox.com/2014/5/30/5764096 /homeless-shelter-housing-help-solutions.

p. 318: policing nonviolent offenses of houseless people cost three times as much . . . : ibid.

p. 318: the Pacific Northwest experienced unprecedented heat waves that are estimated to have resulted in the deaths of eight hundred people: Kim Malcolm, John Ryan, and Paige Browning, "Nearly 800 People Believed to Have Died in Northwest Heat Wave," KUOW, July 12, 2021, https://www .kuow.org/stories/nearly-700-people-believed-to-have-died-in-northwest -heat-wave.

p. 318: many of whom were people without housing or with inadequate housing: Danny Peterson, "New Data Shows Scope of Heatwave-Related Homeless Deaths," KOIN, July 23, 2021, www.koin.com/news/special -reports/new-data-shows-scope-of-heatwave-related-homeless-deaths.

p. 319: Billionaires' cumulative wealth rose by nearly four trillion dollars during 2020: Aimee Picchi, "Billionaires Got 54% Richer during Pandemic, Sparking

Calls for 'Wealth Tax,'" CBS News, March 31, 2021,www.cbsnews.com/news /billionaire-wealth-covid-pandemic-12-trillion-jeff-bezos-wealth-tax.

p. 319: almost fifteen million Americans were behind on rent and facing eviction: Sam Gilman et al., "With Federal Moratorium Expiring, 15 Million People at Risk of Eviction," Aspen Institute, July 2021, www.aspeninstitute.org /wp-content/uploads/2021/07/AI-017-FSP-Report_Eviction-Report_r4.pdf.

p. 320: More than 3.5 million families with school-age children don't have reliable access to the internet: "More than 9 Million Children Lack Internet Access at Home for Online Learning," USA Facts, October 19, 2020, usafacts .org/articles/internet-access-students-at-home.

p. 321: Since the redevelopment was completed, the crime rate dropped by one-third . . . "positive outcomes": Jessica Williams, "Former Iberville Housing Complex Reimagined as New Community: 'It Changed for the Better,'" NOLA .com, November 14, 2019, www.nola.com/news/politics/article_23e7220a -057d-11ea-a319-5314db00d55d.html.

13: We Have Money for War but Won't Feed the Poor

p. 331: "In the councils of government . . . and will persist": "President Dwight D. Eisenhower's Farewell Address (1961)," Our Documents, www .ourdocuments.gov/doc.php?flash=false&doc=90.

p. 334: "Why should they ask me . . . been in jail for four hundred years": quoted in Mike Marqusee, *Redemption Song: Muhammad Ali and the Spirit of the Sixties*, 2nd ed. (New York: Verso, 2017), 214–215.

p. 335: fourteen of the top thirty highest-grossing films . . . : "Top Lifetime Grosses," Box Office Mojo, Internet Movie Database, October 7, 2021, www .boxofficemojo.com/chart/top_lifetime_gross/?area=XWW.

p. 335: There is a direct correlation to many people's thoughts . . . : Frédérick Gagnon, "'Invading Your Hearts and Minds': *Call of Duty* and the (Re) Writing of Militarism in U.S. Digital Games and Popular Culture," *European*

Journal of American Studies 5, no. 3 (Summer 2010), journals.openedition.org /ejas/8831#abstract.

p. 336: Junior Reserve Officers' Training Corps programs . . . : Charles A. Goldman, Jonathan Schweig, Maya Buenaventura, and Cameron Wright, "Geographic and Demographic Representativeness of the Junior Reserve Officers' Training Corps," RAND Corporation, 2017, https://www.rand.org /pubs/research_reports/RR1712.html.

p. 337: Many of the weapons that are no longer being used . . . : Paul McLeary and Lee Hudson, "U.S.-Made Weapons Seized by Taliban Could Lead to Regional Arms Bazaar," *Politico*, August 19, 2021, www.politico.com /news/2021/08/19/us-weapons-seized-taliban-506313.

p. 338: America spent more than $730 billion on the military . . . : "The Militarized Budget 2020," National Priorities Project, June 22, 2020, https: //www.nationalpriorities.org/analysis/2020/militarized-budget-2020/.

p. 338: the United States is not even ranked among the top twenty-five countries in education or health care: Stephen S. Lim et al., "Measuring Human Capital: A Systematic Analysis of 195 Countries and Territories, 1990–2016," *Lancet* 392, no. 10154 (October 2018): 1217–1234, doi:10.1016 /s0140-6736(18)31941-x.

p. 339: Hundreds of millions of dollars are spent annually by defense contractors: Alexander Cohen, "Top Defense Contractors Spend Millions to Get Billions," Center for Public Integrity, August 5, 2015, publicintegrity.org /national-security/top-defense-contractors-spend-millions-to-get-billions.

p. 340: "what was good for our country was good for General Motors, and vice versa": *Nominations: Hearings before the Committee on Armed Services, United States Senate, Part 2: Nomination of Charles E. Wilson to Be Secretary of Defense*, 83rd Cong. (1953), #250, 26, https://catalog.hathitrust.org/Record /010371216.

p. 340: a loan that GM has yet to fully repay: Paul Kiel and Dan Nguyen,

"Bailout Tracker: Bailout Recipients," *ProPublica*, updated August 30, 2021, projects.propublica.org/bailout/list.

14: America's Modern Slavery

p. 354: a process that might take a few months or even a few *years*: Tanzina Vega, "Court Delays in the Bronx Have Defendants Waiting Years, Suit Claims," CNN Money, May 10, 2016, money.cnn.com/2016/05/10/news /bronx-court-lawsuit/index.html.

p. 357: Black people . . . constitute nearly 40 percent of people in prison and jail: "Inmate Race," Federal Bureau of Prisons, March 26, 2022, https://www .bop.gov/about/statistics/statistics_inmate_race.jsp.

p. 357: Latinxs experience incarceration at 1.3 times the rate of whites: Ashley Nellis, "The Color of Justice: Racial and Ethnic Disparity in State Prisons," Sentencing Project, June 14, 2016, https://www.sentencingproject.org /publications/color-of-justice-racial-and-ethnic-disparity-in-state-prisons/.

p. 357: Native American men are four times more likely to go to prison than white men . . . : Jon Marcus, "Bringing Native American Stories to a National Audience," *Nieman Reports*, February 11, 2016, https://niemanreports.org /articles/bringing-native-american-stories-to-a-national-audience/.

p. 362: inmates working unreasonably long hours . . . : Ava DuVernay, dir., *13th*, Los Gatos, CA: Netflix, 2016, https://www.youtube.com/watch?v =krfcq5pF8u8.

p. 363: The Rockefeller Drug Laws weren't substantially reformed until 2009: "Criminal Justice Facts," Sentencing Project, www.sentencingproject.org /criminal-justice-facts.

p. 364: From the mid-1970s to the mid-1980s, incarceration in America doubled, and that number doubled *again* . . . : Ta-Nehisi Coates, "50 Years after the Moynihan Report, Examining the Black Family in the Age of Mass

Incarceration," *Atlantic*, October 2015, www.theatlantic.com/magazine
/archive/2015/10/the-black-family-in-the-age-of-mass-incarceration/403246.

p. 364: America has 5 percent of the world's population but *25 percent* of the
world's prisoners: "Mass Incarceration," American Civil Liberties Union, aclu
.org/issues/smart-justice/mass-incarceration.

p. 364: prison and jail populations would decline by almost *40 percent*:
"Criminal Justice Fact Sheet," NAACP, naacp.org/resources/criminal-justice
-fact-sheet.

p. 365: Black and Latinx students make up 70 percent of those involved in
school-related arrests or referrals to law enforcement: Sophia Kirby, "The Top
10 Most Startling Facts about People of Color and Criminal Justice in the
United States," Center for American Progress, March 13, 2012, www
.americanprogress.org/issues/race/news/2012/03/13/11351/the-top-10
-most-startling-facts-about-people-of-color-and-criminal-justice-in-the
-united-states.

p. 365: The probability that a Black man without a high-school diploma will be
imprisoned . . . : Melissa S. Kearney and Benjamin H. Harris, "Ten Economic
Facts about Crime and Incarceration in the United States," Brookings
Institution, May 1, 2014, www.brookings.edu/research/ten-economic-facts
-about-crime-and-incarceration-in-the-united-states.

p. 366: While some states are opting out of or modifying . . . : Darrel Thompson
and Ashley Burnside, "No More Double Punishments: Lifting the Ban on
SNAP and TANF for People with Prior Felony Drug Convictions," Center for
Law and Social Policy, August 24, 2021, www.clasp.org/publications/report
/brief/no-more-double-punishments.

p. 366: The incarceration rate of women has been growing at nearly double the
speed of men: "Incarcerated Women and Girls," Sentencing Project, November
24, 2020, www.sentencingproject.org/publications/incarcerated-women-and
-girls.

p. 366: The vast majority of these women experience poverty: "Words from Prison—Did You Know . . . ?" American Civil Liberties Union, aclu.org/other /words-prison-did-you-know.

p. 367: nearly 5.2 million Americans are restricted from voting due to conviction laws . . . : Chris Uggen, Ryan Larson, Sarah Shannon, and Arleth Pulido-Nava, "Locked Out 2020: Estimates of People Denied Voting Rights Due to a Felony Conviction," Sentencing Project, October 30, 2020, www .sentencingproject.org/publications/locked-out-2020-estimates-of-people -denied-voting-rights-due-to-a-felony-conviction.

p. 371: spending time in prison actually increases the likelihood that a person will reoffend: Francis T. Cullen, Cheryl Lero Jonson, and Daniel S. Nagin, "Prisons Do Not Reduce Recidivism," *Prison Journal* 91, no. 3 (September 2011): suppl 48S–65S, doi:10.1177/0032885511415224.

p. 371: some people are in such desperate situations that they intentionally go to jail: "Prison As Shelter in the U.S.A.," House the Homeless, January 2, 2018, housethehomeless.org/prison-as-shelter-in-the-u-s-a.

p. 372: Convict leasing, what you might think of when you hear the term "chain gang" . . . : Matthew J. Mancini, *One Dies, Get Another: Convict Leasing in the American South, 1866–1928* (Columbia: University of South Carolina Press, 1996).

p. 372: prisons *don't work*: Jarryd Bartle, "We Know That Prison Doesn't Work. So What Are the Alternatives?" *Guardian*, August 15, 2019, https://www .theguardian.com/commentisfree/2019/aug/16/we-know-that-prison-doesnt -work-so-what-are-the-alternatives.

p. 374: Portugal, Switzerland, the Czech Republic, and the Netherlands are just some of the countries that have decriminalized drug use: "Decriminalization Works, but Too Few Countries Are Taking the Bold Step," UNAIDS, March 3, 2020, https://www.unaids.org/en/resources/presscentre/featurestories/2020 /march/20200303_drugs.

p. 374: With one-fifth of incarcerated people in America serving time for drug offenses: Wendy Sawyer and Peter Wagner, "Mass Incarceration: The Whole Pie 2020," Prison Policy Initiative, March 24, 2020, www.prisonpolicy.org /reports/pie2020.html.

15: Is Everyone Really Welcome?

p. 378: Sixty-one million American adults live with a disability: "Disability Impacts All of Us," Centers for Disease Control and Prevention, last reviewed September 16, 2020, www.cdc.gov/ncbddd/disabilityandhealth/infographic -disability-impacts-all.html.

p. 378: 10 percent of Americans live with an invisible illness that could be considered a disability: "Invisible Disabilities: List and General Information," Disabled World, updated August 15, 2021, https://www.disabled-world.com /disability/types/invisible/.

p. 384: the employment rate for disabled people fell dramatically: Les Picker, "Consequences of the Americans with Disabilities Act," National Bureau of Economic Research *Digest*, December 1998, https://www.nber.org/digest /dec98/consequences-americans-disabilities-act.

p. 385: 12.6 percent of Americans who have a disability are unemployed: "Persons with a Disability: Labor Force Characteristics Summary," US Bureau of Labor Statistics, February 24, 2021, www.bls.gov/news.release/disabl.nr0.htm.

p. 385: only about 16 percent of disabled people over the age of twenty-five have a bachelor's degree or higher: "People with a Disability Less Likely to Have Completed a Bachelor's Degree," US Bureau of Labor Statistics, TED: The Economics Daily, July 20, 2015, www.bls.gov/opub/ted/2015/mobile/people -with-a-disability-less-likely-to-have-completed-a-bachelors-degree.htm.

p. 385: Only 5 percent of tables in new restaurants must have seating that is accessible: "Fixed Seating and Tables," *ADA Guide for Small Businesses*, US

Small Business Association/US Department of Justice, 1999, www.ada.gov/reachingout/servingcustomers.html.

p. 385: only 25 percent of the subway is accessible for people with disabilities: Clarisa Diaz, "Infographic: How Much of the NYC Subway Is Accessible?" *Gothamist*, March 5, 2020, gothamist.com/news/infographic-how-much-nyc-subway-accessible.

p. 385: less than 5 percent of homes are accessible for individuals with mobility difficulties, and less than 1 percent of housing is accessible for wheelchair users: "Assessing the Accessibility of America's Housing Stock for Physically Disabled Persons," *PD&R Edge*, US Department of Housing and Urban Development Office of Policy Development and Research, 2011, www.huduser.gov/portal/pdredge/pdr_edge_research_101315.html.

pp. 385–386: One billion people worldwide live with some form of disability: "Disability and Health," World Health Organization, December 1, 2020, https://www.who.int/news-room/fact-sheets/detail/disability-and-health.

16: No Human Is Illegal

p. 408: Bellingham, Washington . . . had a population of fewer than eighty thousand and was overwhelmingly white: "Bellingham, WA," Data USA, accessed January 3, 2022, datausa.io/profile/geo/bellingham-wa/#demographics.

p. 414: 97 percent of DACA recipients were employed or enrolled in school and that recipients' hourly wages had increased by 69 percent: Tom K. Wong et al., "DACA Recipients' Economic and Educational Gains Continue to Grow," Center for American Progress, August 28, 2017, www.americanprogress.org/issues/immigration/news/2017/08/28/437956/daca-recipients-economic-educational-gains-continue-grow.

p. 415: of the Nobel Prizes in science given to people affiliated with US universities, one-third are earned by immigrants: Suketu Mehta, "We Do Not

Come Empty-Handed: The Economic Case for Immigrants," *Time*, May 23, 2019, time.com/5594365/america-immigration-future-economic-growth.

p. 415: This issue has prompted many politicians to speak up to encourage Americans to have more children: Claire Cain Miller, "Would Americans Have More Babies If the Government Paid Them?" *New York Times*, February 17, 2021, www.nytimes.com/2021/02/17/upshot/americans-fertility-babies.html.

pp. 415–416: "In 2008, Bill Gates stated ... worldwide in 2016": Suketu Mehta, "We Do Not Come Empty-Handed: The Economic Case for Immigrants," *Time*, May 23, 2019, time.com/5594365/america-immigration-future-economic-growth.

p. 416: They start businesses at twice the rate of those born in the United States: Dan Kosten, "Immigrants as Economic Contributors: Immigrant Entrepreneurs," National Immigration Forum, July 11, 2018, immigrationforum.org/article/immigrants-as-economic-contributors -immigrant-entrepreneurs.

p. 426: Crimes related to immigration and/or immigration status . . . : Pete Williams, "Noncitizens Account for 64 Percent of All Federal Arrests, Justice Department Says," NBC News, August 22, 2019, www.nbcnews.com/politics /justice-department/non-citizens-account-64-percent-all-federal-arrests -justice-department-n1045286.

p. 426: "They're bringing drugs . . . I assume, are good people": quoted in Alexander Burns, "Choice Words from Donald Trump, Presidential Candidate," *New York Times*, June 16, 2015, https://www.nytimes.com/politics/first-draft /2015/06/16/choice-words-from-donald-trump-presidential-candidate/.

p. 426: undocumented immigrants are far less likely to commit crimes than US-born citizens . . . for property crimes: Michael T. Light, Jingying He, and Jason P. Robey, "Comparing Crime Rates between Undocumented Immigrants, Legal Immigrants, and Native-Born US Citizens in Texas," *Proceedings of the National Academy of Sciences* 117, no. 51 (December 2020): 32340–32347, www.pnas.org/content/117/51/32340.

p. 428: often there are not enough people to do all of the jobs in this country: Tim Henderson, "Help Wanted: Too Many Jobs and Not Enough Workers in Most States," *Stateline*, Pew Charitable Trusts, October 14, 2019, www .pewtrusts.org/en/research-and-analysis/blogs/stateline/2019/10/14/help -wanted-too-many-jobs-and-not-enough-workers-in-most-states.

p. 428: immigrants tend to compete for jobs with other immigrants: Adriana Kugler and Patrick Oakford, "Immigration Helps American Workers' Wages and Job Opportunities," Center for American Progress, August 29, 2013, www.americanprogress.org/issues/immigration/news/2013/08/29/73203 /immigration-helps-american-workers-wages-and-job-opportunities.

p. 428: "all these people from sh*thole countries": Julie Hirschfeld Davis, Sheryl Gay Stolberg, and Thomas Kaplan, "Trump Alarms Lawmakers with Disparaging Words for Haiti and Africa," *New York Times*, January 11, 2018, https://www.nytimes.com/2018/01/11/us/politics/trump-shithole-countries .html.

p. 431: whether we are a nation of immigrants or a nation of laws: Rosalyn Negrón, "A Nation of Immigrants or a Nation of Laws?" *Diggit*, September 30, 2019, www.diggitmagazine.com/column/nation-immigrants-or-nation-laws.

The Dictionary of Change

p. 462: immunity is granted overwhelmingly to white shooters of Black people: "Stand Your Ground Laws Increase Gun Violence and Perpetuate Racial Disparities," Coalition to Stop Gun Violence, March 2021, 10, https: //efsgv.org/wp-content/uploads/StandYourGround.pdf.

ACKNOWLEDGMENTS

From
Porsche Joseph

I would like to acknowledge and thank the experts who gave their valuable input and helped me learn more about these very substantial topics. Any errors or inaccuracies in the book are our fault and not theirs.

I want to thank all of the young people who pick up this book and are invested in making the world a better place. Although it is certainly not a job you asked for or deserve to inherit, you serve as a beacon of hope for a brighter future.

I would also like to extend a huge thanks to the special people featured in this book. Thank you so much for imparting your wisdom and sharing your valuable time.

To my mother, thank you for showing me what it means to be a lifelong learner. As I see you seek understanding and continue to grow on your journey to be more informed and show up for others, I am truly inspired.

To Kaylan Adair, the most fabulous editor in the industry: How lucky am I to have found such a great friend in you? Thank you for going on this adventure with me and helping me each step of the way. You are a visionary with a giant heart; I couldn't think of anyone more trustworthy to do this work.

I could not write this without acknowledging our dog, Stokely Joseph. Thank you for loving us unconditionally and dragging me outside, even during a pandemic, when it has been tempting to stay in for days on end. When you joined our family, you added the joy and vigor we so desperately needed in our household. I am aware you cannot read this, but I hope that you know you are the best good boy.

I saved the very best for last—my dearest Frederick. Your love and partnership are invaluable and I am so incredibly thankful for the person that you are. There are no words to describe my admiration for you. Thank you for your patience and guidance throughout this process. Thank you for challenging me to always try harder and encouraging me to leave everything we touch better than we found it.

From

Frederick Joseph

I'd like to extend my thanks to everyone who is featured in the work and everyone who had a hand in making it happen. It's truly an honor to share space with you as we attempt to water the seeds of change.

INDEX

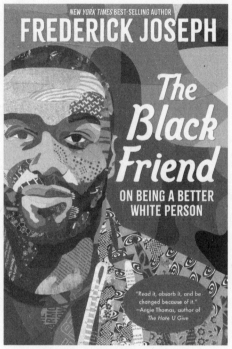

FREDERICK JOSEPH is the author of *The Black Friend: On Being a Better White Person*, which was an instant *New York Times* bestseller and received four starred reviews, as well as the memoir *Patriarchy Blues: Reflections on Manhood*. An award-winning activist, philanthropist, and marketing professional, he was named to the 2019 *Forbes* 30 Under 30 list, is a recipient of the Bob Clampett Humanitarian Award, and was selected for the 2018 Root 100, an annual list of the most influential African Americans. Frederick Joseph lives in New York City with his wife, Porsche, and their dog, Stokely.

PORSCHE JOSEPH is a writer and former educator who has worked for many years in philanthropy and the non-profit sector. *Better Than We Found It: Conversations to Help Save the World* is her debut book. She lives in New York City with her husband, Fred, and their dog, Stokely.